D1272801

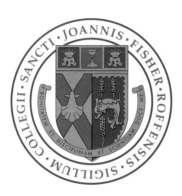

Lavery Library

St. John Fisher
College
Rochester, New York

THE CHIVALRIC ETHOS AND THE DEVELOPMENT OF MILITARY PROFESSIONALISM

HISTORY
OF WARFARE

General Editor

KELLY DEVRIES
Loyola College

Founding Editors

THERESA VANN
PAUL CHEVEDDEN

VOLUME 11

THE CHIVALRIC ETHOS
AND THE DEVELOPMENT OF
MILITARY PROFESSIONALISM

EDITED BY

D.J.B. TRIM

BRILL
LEIDEN · BOSTON
2003

This book is printed on acid-free paper.

Library of Congress Cataloging-in-Publication Data

The chivalric ethos and the development of military professionalism / edited by D.J.B. Trim.
    p.   cm. — (History of warfare , ISSN 1385-7827 ; v. 11)
    Includes bibliographical references and index.
    ISBN 9004120955
      1. Sociology, Military. 2. Standing army—History. 3. Chivalry. I.
    Trim, D.J.B. (David J. B.) II. Series

    U21.5 .C445 2003
    306.2'7—dc21   2002073527

Die Deutsche Bibliothek – CIP-Einheitsaufnahme

The chivalric ethos and the development of military professionalism / ed. by D.J.B. Trim. – Leiden ; Boston ; Köln : Brill, 2003
   (History of warfare ; Vol. 11)
   ISBN 90–04–12095–5

ISSN 1385–7827
ISBN 90 04 12095 5

PRINTED IN THE NETHERLANDS

CONTENTS

POSTSCRIPT: THE LAST GASP OF CHIVALRY?

ILLUSTRATIONS

1. Andrea da Cione ("Il Verrocchio"), "Bartolomeo Colleoni" (completed 1485), bronze statue (360 cm in height), Campo dei Santi Giovanni e Paolo, Venice.
2. Attributed to Jean Bourdichon (*c.* 1508), *parchemin* painting in Jean Marot, "Le voyage de Gênes", Bibliothèque Nationale, Paris: Manuscrit Français 5091.
3. Anon., "Blasius de Monluc Polemarchus", late sixteenth-century print, Musée d'Agen.
4. Heinrich Göding the Elder, "Ein Rennen getan mit Graf Hans Georgen zu Mansfeld . . . Anno 1556", oil on limewood (53 × 114 cm, with cartouche 87 × 183 cm), Rüstkammer, Dresden GG 16. (Photograph courtesy of Sächsische Landesbibliothek- Staats- und Universitätsbibliothek Dresden (SLUB), Abt. Deutsche Fotothek.)
5. Jacob de Gheyn, position for musketeers no. 25, from *Wapenhandelinghe van roers, musquetten ende spiessen*, (The Hague: 1607), engraving after Robert de Baudous (*c.* 1595).
6. Jacob de Gheyn, position for pikemen no. 25—also engraving after de Baudous (*c.* 1595).
7. Diego Velázquez, "La Rendición de Breda" (The Surrender of Breda), or "Las Lanzas" (1635), Museo Nacional del Prado, Madrid. (Reproduced by permission of the Ministerio de Educación, Cultura y Deporte, Spain.)
8. Anon., "King Charles I; Sir Edward Walker" (*c.* 1650?), oil on canvas (151 cm × 226 cm), National Portrait Gallery, London.
9. Robert Walker, "Oliver Cromwell" (*c.* 1649), oil on canvas (126 cm × 102 cm), National Portrait Gallery, London.

CONTRIBUTORS

DAVID J. B. TRIM is Lecturer in History, Department of Humanities, at Newbold College, and a Research Fellow in the Department of History at the University of Reading. He is an Associate Editor of *The New Dictionary of National Biography*, and has edited or co-edited four volumes of essays on medieval and early-modern military, political and religious history, including *Amphibious Warfare c. 1000–1700: Commerce, War and State Formation* (forthcoming).

MATTHEW BENNETT, Senior Lecturer at the Royal Military Academy Sandhurst, has published many articles and chapters on medieval military history. His books include *Agincourt* (1991) and *Campaigns of the Norman Conquest* (2001), and he co-edited *The Cambridge Illustrated Atlas of Warfare: The Middle Ages, 732–1487* (1996).

MICHAEL MALLETT, Emeritus Professor of History at the Centre for the Study of the Renaissance, University of Warwick, is a distinguished historian of fifteenth- and sixteenth-century Italy. His books include *Mercenaries and their Masters: Warfare in Renaissance Italy* (1974), *The Military Organisation of a Renaissance State: Venice c. 1400 to 1617* (1984) and, as co-editor, *War, Culture and Society in Renaissance Venice* (1993).

MALYN NEWITT is Charles Boxer Professor of History in the Department of Portuguese and Brazilian Studies at King's College London. He is the author or editor of many books on Portuguese colonial history, including *Portugal in Africa* (1981), *The First Portuguese Colonial Empire* (1985) and *A History of Mozambique* (1995). He is currently researching Portuguese military expansion in the Indian Ocean in the sixteenth century.

SIMON PEPPER is Professor, and Dean, of the University of Liverpool's School of Architecture and Building Engineering. His principal research field is the history of Renaissance military architecture, on which his best-known work is the seminal *Firearms and Fortifications* (1986) co-authored with Nicholas Adams; but he also publishes widely on twentieth-century social housing.

DAVID POTTER is Senior Lecturer in the Department of History at the University of Kent at Canterbury and has research interests in early modern French history. His books are *War and Government in the French Provinces: Picardy 1470–1560* (1993), *A History of France 1460–1560* (1995), *The French Wars of Religion: Selected Documents* (1998) and *Un homme de guerre a l'époque de la Renaissance: la vie et les lettres d'Oudart du Biez* (2001).

HELEN WATANABE-O'KELLY, Professor of German Literature at the University of Oxford, where she is a Fellow of Exeter College, researches on sixteenth- and seventeenth-century literature and culture. The author of *Triumphal Shews: Tournaments at German-speaking Courts in their European Context 1560–1730* (1992) and editor of *The Cambridge History of German Literature* (1997), her latest project is a book on *Court Culture in Dresden 1560–1733*.

LUKE MACMAHON works as a freelance editor for *The New Dictionary of National Biography*. He received his PhD thesis on the diplomatic administration of the early Tudors from the University of Kent in 2000. His chapter in this volume is based on earlier research on Henry VIII's final war with France in the mid-1540s.

FERNANDO GONZÁLEZ DE LEÓN, an Associate Professor of History at Springfield College, Massachusetts, is the author of several articles on the early modern Spanish army and the war in the Netherlands. His book on the high command of the Spanish Army of Flanders in the Eighty Years' War will be published in 2003.

MARTYN BENNETT is Reader in History in the Department of International Studies at Nottingham Trent University. An expert on both the military and social history of seventeenth-century England, he is the author of *The English Civil War* (1995), *The Civil Wars in Britain and Ireland, 1637–1651* (1997), and *The Civil Wars Experienced: Britain and Ireland, 1639–1661* (2000).

MARK A. WEITZ is Assistant Professor of Southern and Legal History at Auburn University, Montgomery, Alabama. He is the author of *A Higher Duty: Desertion among Georgia Troops during the Civil War* (2000), co-editor of *On to Atlanta: The Diary of John Hill Ferguson, 10th Illinois* (2002) and has also published on legal history.

ACKNOWLEDGEMENTS

I am grateful to Julian Deahl, commissioning editor at Brill, who showed great original enthusiasm for this project; and to Marcella Mulder, Assistant Editor, who greatly assisted in bringing the book to press and showed much patience with how long it took! I am infinitely indebted to all the contributors for producing such well-researched and thought-provoking essays, and especially to David Potter, Fernando González de León and Helen Watanabe-O'Kelly for providing superb illustrations. I am greatly beholden to Wendy Trim for thoughtful readings of various sections of the text and for many other things.

In addition, I am obliged to Lynda Baildam at the Newbold College Library who obtained books and articles on inter-library loan quickly and cheerfully. Further, work on this volume was greatly facilitated by access to the collections of the library of the University of Reading and to the various on-line aids to scholarship available through its Department of History—I am deeply grateful to the Department for making me a Visiting Research Fellow, which made that access possible. My own chapter, the Introduction and the lengthy process of editing were all completed during a sabbatical semester granted by the Staff Development Committee at Newbold College, which I gratefully acknowledge. I am also pleased to place on record how much I appreciate the support given to my on-going research by Newbold College's Vice-Principal, Michael Pearson and the Chair of the Department of Humanities, Penny Mahon. Jamie Zimchek showed great patience during a vital phase, which was much appreciated. Finally, thank you to colleagues at Newbold and in History at Reading for their encouragement, both for this book and more generally: especially to Frank Tallett and Ralph Houlbrooke at Reading, and to my fellow teachers in the Humanities at Newbold—above all, Peter Balderstone.

My contributors doubtless each have people to whom they would like to dedicate their own chapters but, exercising editorial prerogative, I dedicate the work as a whole to the memory of my grandfather, John Buckingham: born 11 December 1880; served as a volunteer in the Boer War (1899–1902) and the First World War

(1914–18); died 5 May 1959. Neither a professional soldier nor a chivalric warrior, he served his countries (Great Britain and New Zealand) steadfastly, and lived and died an English gentleman.

LIST OF ABBREVIATIONS

ARA	Algemeen Rijksarchief, Den Haag
Bib.	Bibliothèque
Bib. Nat.	Bibliothèque Nationale, Paris
BL	British Library, London
DNB	*Dictionary of National Biography; New DNB* (Oxford: forthcoming 2004)
EHR	*English Historical Review*
fo(s)	Folio(s)
HJ	*Historical Journal*
L&P Henry 6th	*Letters and Papers Illustrative of the Wars of the English in France during the Reign of Henry the Sixth, King of England*, vol. I, ed. Joseph Stevenson, Rolls Ser., 22 (London: 1861)
L&P Henry 8th	*Letters and Papers, Foreign and Domestic of the Reign of Henry VIII, 1509–1547*, ed. J. Brewer, J. Gairdiner and R. H. Brodie, 21 vols (London: 1862–1910)
MS(S)	Manuscript(s)
MS(S) Fr.	Bib. Nat., Manuscrits Français
n.d.	No date
n.p.	No place
OED	*Oxford English Dictionary* (2nd edn)
PRO, SP	Public Record Office, State Papers
RH	*Revue Historique*
ser.	Series
SP Henry 8th	*State Papers of Henry the Eighth*, 11 vols, Record Commission (London: 1830–1852)
TRHS	*Transactions of the Royal Historical Society*

1. Andrea da Cione ("Il Verrocchio"), "Bartolomeo Colleoni" (completed 1485), bronze
statue (360 cm in height), Campo dei Santi Giovanni e Paolo, Venice.

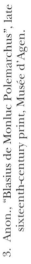

3. Anon., "Blasius de Monluc Polemarchus", late sixteenth-century print, Musée d'Agen.

2. Attributed to Jean Bourdichon (c.1508), *parchemin* painting in Jean Marot, "Le voyage de Gênes", Bibliothèque Nationale, Paris: Manuscrit Français 5091.

4. Heinrich Göding the Elder, "Ein Rennen getan mit Graf Hans Georgen zu Mansfeld ... Anno 1556", oil on limewood (53 x 114 cm, with cartouche 87 x 183 cm), Rüstkammer, Dresden GG 16. (Photograph courtesy of Sächsische Landesbibliothek-Staats- und Universitätsbibliothek Dresden (SLUB), Abt. Deutsche Fotothek.)

5. Jacob de Gheyn, position for musketeers no. 25, from *Wapenhandelinghe van roers, musquetten ende spiessen*, (The Hague: 1607), engraving after Robert de Baudous (*c.*1595).

6. Ibid., position for pikemen no. 25 – also engraving after de Baudous (*c.*1595).

7. Diego Velázquez, "La Rendición de Breda" (The Surrender of Breda), or "Las Lanzas" (1635), Museo Nacional del Prado, Madrid. (Reproduced by permission of the Ministerio de Educación, Cultura y Deporte, Spain.)

8. Anon., "King Charles I; Sir Edward Walker" (c. 1650?), oil on canvas (151 cm x 226 cm), National Portrait Gallery, London.

9. Robert Walker, "Oliver Cromwell" (*c.*1649), oil on canvas (126 cm x 102 cm), Nation Portrait Gallery, London.

CHAPTER ONE

INTRODUCTION

D. J. B. Trim

This volume examines the progress and effects of professionalisation on early-modern Western military society, which in this period means aristocratic society. The culture of aristocratic society in this period was chivalric; its dominant ideology was chivalry. This was itself a particular aristocratic sub-culture of Christianity, which was hegemonic in society more generally; however, chivalry was not only Christian, but also martial.[1] Chivalry is thus a factor that has to be taken into account when considering the development of professional militaries. Indeed, the two are often seen as incompatible. In light of this widespread perception, although a number of issues are dealt with by the following essays, the crucial, main problems are twofold. The first is that summarised by Michael Mallett in chapter 2: 'whether a decline of chivalry is a natural accompaniment to a growth of military professionalism'; indeed, whether it is a necessary precursor.[2] The obvious question that then arises is whether professionalism is naturally preceded or at least accompanied by a decline in aristocratic power. Probably the instinctive assumption of most non-specialists would be 'Yes!' to both questions and this has also traditionally been the answer given by scholars to the first. As these essays reveal, the reality (as so often in history) is more complicated than that.

In order to address these issues, however, it is necessary to explore a number of others. Thus, the following essays investigate the nature, importance and influence of chivalry in the late Middle Ages and early-modern era. They explore the actual practice of military operations and how war was waged during this period—often identified as witnessing a 'military revolution'. They consider the role of the nobility in war and assess the impact of chivalric and professional military values on noble culture, examining contemporary literary

---

[1] Keen (1984), 54–55. See also Trim (2002A), 68–69, 76–77.
[2] Below, pp. 67–68.

and artistic texts, as well as institutional and personal records. The nature of professionalism itself is also addressed—indirectly, in a number of essays; directly, later in this Introduction.

Furthermore, in examining the progress and effects of professionalisation on early-modern Western military society there is a need to look at origins, while it is often illuminating to look also at consequences of, or spin-offs from, a process. Thus, 'early-modern' is defined broadly. In addition, a prologue and epilogue consider, respectively, the development of the cult of chivalry in the earlier Middle Ages, and chivalry in the Confederate army in the American Civil War—perhaps the last war fought by a society that overtly considered itself chivalric (or at least chivalrous). The main body of the volume comprises nine essays focused on Europe from the late fourteenth century to the late seventeenth century. Of these, eight are case studies of particular nations at different points, while one is a study of a particular sub-profession in a range of European countries. It has proved impossible to cover all armies and societies of Europe at all points of the period *c.* 1400–1700. There are no studies of *reconquista* Spain, seventeenth-century Italy, or *grande siècle* France; Eastern Europe and Scandinavia are entirely overlooked, despite the military importance at various stages in this period of Denmark, Hungary, Poland-Lithuania and Sweden. In some of these cases, of course, there was no notable trend towards professionalism. However, in an ideal world, they would have been examined partly for comparative purposes to see why (and to what extent) they were *sui generis*. Space prevents such a thorough survey, so this volume is not a definitive history of the subject in late-medieval and early-modern Europe, but a collection of case studies. They cover, however, all the areas in which there was a significant development of military professionalism (except for Sweden), even though some countries are only covered for part of the period.

Virtually all the essays address practice rather than theory. Four (chapters 5, 9, 11 and 12) focus on the composition and attitudes of particular 'officer corps',[3] and most other chapters at least touch on this. However, operational, logistical and administrative expertise and efficiency are important defining criteria for military profes-

---

[3] Respectively: the sub-profession of architects-cum-engineers across Europe; and the armies of seventeenth-century Spain and England, and of the Confederate States of America.

sionalism, as we will see. Thus, the actual conduct of war is investigated in the majority of essays, since this is one of the best ways to test the development of military professionalism in a given army and/or aristocratic society.

What emerges is that 'chivalry' and 'military professionalism' are not necessarily dichotomous. A great deal can be meant by these terms (and their cognates) but in many respects they are not sharply distinctive concepts. The process of professionalisation, at least in the fifteenth through seventeenth centuries, was not a clear-cut struggle between the attitudes of modernity and a medieval world-view. Instead, the development of military professionalism was often an ambivalent process, founded in the texts of classical antiquity and frequently promoted by nobles who fully subscribed to the cult of chivalry and its values. The two ideologies overlapped in many armies and societies at many times in the past; attitudes deriving from the chivalric ideal still greatly influence the conduct and ethics of professional military personnel today. Even though the professionalisation process would, in the end, kill off chivalry (in the original sense), military professionalism nevertheless could and did develop in societies that adhered to the chivalric ethos.

The Nature of Military Professionalism

There are two parts to the equation in this volume's title: the chivalric ethos on the one hand and military professionalism on the other. This introductory chapter concentrates more on the second part than on the first: setting out ways of thinking about and categorising professionalism.[4] Chivalry has been analysed and its predominant characteristics explored by such distinguished historians as Maurice Keen, Richard Barber, Matthew Strickland and others, in a range of important works.[5] In contrast, the history of early-modern professionalism in general has not been as well served as it might be.[6] Military

---

[4] My analysis of professionalism has greatly benefited from discussions with and/or suggestions from Peter Balderstone, Matthew Bennett, Fernando González de León, Simon Pepper and Winifred Trim. I am grateful to each of them, though they are of course not responsible for the following analysis.

[5] E.g., Barber (1995)—the second edition of a seminal work first published in 1970; Keen (1984) and (1996)—the latter his collected essays; Strickland (1996). See also Vale (1981) and the essays edited by Anglo (1990).

[6] See Prest (1984); O'Day (1986).

professionalism in particular, especially in the medieval and early-modern periods, has generally been addressed by historians only briefly and in the context of other subjects, and it has been either ignored or misunderstood by social scientists.[7] Indeed, the subject has become regarded as a branch of military sociology, more than of history.[8]

Scholarly studies of chivalry and military professionalism have lacked both clear definitional framework and terminology. This has hindered attempts at comparative analysis. In one sense, medieval chivalrous military societies clearly cannot have been professional. When medieval or early-modern authors write of the 'profession of arms', what they really mean is the vocation of arms by current standards: thus, Shakespeare makes one of his soldiers observe in defence of his activities, ''tis no sin for a man to labour in his vocation'.[9] Medieval and early-modern nobles had a duty to fight on behalf of the rest of society: their social recognition or standing was intrinsic to them rather than reflecting membership of the professions (as with, say, doctors or lawyers today). 'Professionals' were originally those who fought, not because of a social obligation, or duty, to fight, but for money. Aristocratic warriors thus were inherently not professional in one sense of the word.

However, both 'chivalry' and 'professionalism' are capable of being understood in different ways. Chivalry is alternatively viewed as a code of conduct that was strictly observed and circumscribed the actions of military practitioners, and as an underlying socio-cultural ethos whose values informed but did not necessarily dictate the decisions of warriors subscribing to them. However, it has also been defined (albeit unconsciously) in opposition to the perceived values of the 'professional' military ethos that grew up in the era after chivalry faded away. In this sense, chivalry is taken to mean amateurish (though without ever being defined as such). Consequently, 'professional' has sometimes been taken to mean serious or competent.[10]

---

[7] Roy (1987) and Feld (1975A, B) explicitly consider soldiering as a profession in the early-modern period, but the former is an honourable exception, while, as I show in ch. 10, the latter's pioneering work cannot now be regarded as authoritative.

[8] See Grandstaff (2001) for a brief but useful survey of the literature on military professionalism.

[9] *Henry IV, Part I*, I, ii, 116–17. And see below, p. 23.

[10] E.g., the great early-modernist G. R. Elton, in the context of a discussion of

Matters are clouded because issues of organisation, permanence and pay are frequently conflated with those of social attitude and combat effectiveness.

The problem is thus that the chivalrousness or professionalism of medieval and early-modern soldiers can be (and has been) approached in quite different ways. Is efficiency the real issue at stake, or is it how knightly soldiers interacted with those around them, whether noble or non-noble, whether in armies or without? Professionalism can be regarded as being about the construction of vocational, occupational identities and structures; chivalry can be seen further as being about ethics—of the treatment of prisoners and non-combatants, in particular. In short, when discussing the chivalric ethos and military professionalism, scholars are very often using the same words but conducting different discourses.

Recognising this is the first step to achieving greater understanding. It is not necessary to reduce all discussions of 'chivalrousness' and professionalism to the same grounds: chivalry, after all, was a complex socio-cultural system and signs of chivalrousness can therefore be seen in different ways. Indeed, the essays in this volume conduct the debate on a variety of grounds; they thus bear witness to the richness (as well as perhaps to the confusion!) of previous scholarly approaches to this issue. It is necessary, however, to acknowledge that different discourses are being conducted and to recognise that there are different grounds of discussion.

I proceed on the assumption that identifying and categorising these different grounds is a necessary precondition for assessing the extent to which chivalry and professionalism influenced medieval and early-modern European armies. I first attempt to define terms, and propose a schema for thinking about professionalism. Based on this interpretative model, I then explore what the essays in this volume, together with the wider literature, indicate about the extent to which military professionalism developed in early-modern Europe, and its influence on aristocratic society and the state.

The first step is to deconstruct the term 'profession' and its cognates, 'professional', 'professionalism' and 'professionalisation'. The problem is that though these terms are in common use they always

---

greater military professionalism, wrote that warfare in sixteenth-century Europe 'grew in a sense more "serious"': Elton (1958), 13.

have been and still are remarkably ambiguous and mutable. It is
notable that there is no clear-cut agreement as to which occupations
are 'the professions' today.[11] What the *Oxford English Dictionary* terms
'the three learned professions' of Medicine, Law, and Divinity (i.e.,
clerical ministry—the priesthood) were the earliest occupations to be
accepted as professions and would still be universally accepted. Military
Service was historically accepted alongside them.[12] But in addition
today one might add the Civil Service, Teaching (which some would
split between schools and universities), Engineering, Science and
Architecture. It is a telling fact that the national laws of most European
states still do not 'generally contain any definition of the professions'.[13] Even lexicographers provide numerous definitions.[14] Some
historical studies of the developments of professions try to avoid this
problem of imprecise and indeterminate terminology by simply ignoring it and not proposing defining criteria.[15] An alternative approach,
adopted here, is to attempt a descriptive, rather than prescriptive
analysis, intended to identify and outline the salient and most generally acknowledged characteristics of a profession.[16]

What, then, are the distinctive qualities that mark what most scholars and practitioners today would term professions? Drawing on studies of military professionalism in other periods and on some studies
of the development of other professions in both early-modern and
modern Europe, I suggest that there are seven such markers:

1) a discrete occupational identity;
2) formal hierarchy;
3) permanence;
4) a formal pay system;
5) a distinctive expertise and means of education therein;

---

[11] O'Day (1986) 52, observes that 'the authors who write about' the professions
'don't seem to know' what they are.
[12] *OED, s.v.* 'profession': III.6.a.
[13] De Crayencour (1982), 17.
[14] *OED* lists 9 for 'profession' but as these are sub-divided it actually gives 12.
[15] E.g., Tropp (1957), 5, refers to 'the current senses of the term' (i.e., profession), without stating what these were; Sir George Clark, in his *History of the Royal
College of Physicians of London* (Oxford: 1964) 'devotes little or no attention to the
problematic nature of the concept of a profession in the early-modern period',
according to O'Day (1986), 53. Miller (1972) and Lake (1989) avowedly have as
their subject matter 'professional soldiers' and 'professional failure' respectively, but
make no attempt to define what these terms mean.
[16] De Crayencour (1982), 17.

6) efficiency in execution of expertise; and

7) a distinctive self-conceptualisation.

1. OCCUPATIONAL STRUCTURES AND IDENTITY. This is more than the 'similar interests, ambitions and life-style[s]' typical among members of a profession.[17] Such factors help to build what the military sociologist William B. Skelton characterises as 'corporateness':

> a feeling among group members that they constitute a subculture distinct from the rest of society; a high degree of self-government within that subculture sanctioned by the larger community; and institutions that uphold codes of group behaviour, educate aspiring practitioners, and add to the body of professional knowledge.[18]

Major steps in achieving this identity were, as military historians suggest, 'supplanting the community with the regiment' or other unit, and the introduction of uniform clothing. These in and of themselves did not achieve *occupational* identity, of course, but helped to create a feeling of separateness between soldiers and the rest of society.[19] This was in itself important since traditionally the knight and the soldier were one and the same.

Another study of military professionalism offers a model in 'which the recruitment, training, and assignment' of the members of an officer corps 'are carried out entirely in terms of internally formulated criteria'.[20] The link with the remaining 'markers' is implicit in this definition's language and, indeed, all these distinguishing markers are bound up together.

2. FORMAL HIERARCHY—recognised career paths. This is to some extent a sub-category of the first. A recognised career path is such an important occupational structure, however, that it is worth recognising separately. Rosemary O'Day, for example, stresses the importance of 'an accepted internal hierarchy' in her study of the early-modern English clergy, and this also emerges from the work of the pioneering historian of war and society, J. R. Hale.[21] M. D.

---

[17] O'Day (1979), 1.

[18] Skelton (1975), 444.

[19] Showalter (1993), 427–29 at 427; and see Keegan (1993), 342–43; Hale (1985), 150–51, also 127–28.

[20] Feld (1975A), 192.

[21] O'Day (1979), 1; it is implicit in Lake (1989) for whom 'professional failure' seems to be failure to follow an expected or hoped for career trajectory. Hale (1985), 130.

Feld, in two seminal articles on early-modern military professionalism, argues that 'the creation of objective standards for training and
commanding fighting men' and 'the emergence of objective criteria
for the management of the officer corps—education and experience
as opposed to birth and social position' were integral to and necessary for the emergence of professionalism in armies.[22] Hierarchy is
also connected to expertise and efficiency (the fifth and sixth markers) since the 'objective standards and criteria' used to determine
progression in the hierarchy related to mastery of a professional body
of knowledge and ability to put it into practice. The extent to which
members of a profession determine progression within their hierarchy has varied in different professions at different times, but a for-
mally constituted, reasonably transparent hierarchy is a *sine qua non*.

3. PERMANENCE. There is a clear relationship between the second
and third markers. Of course, 'permanent forces [can] settle into a
quasi-civilian state', as happened for example to the *compagnies d'ordonnance* in fifteenth-century France.[23] It is thus not automatically a
marker of a profession. However, distinctive occupational structures
and formal hierarchies virtually necessitate permanent existence. Ian
Roy argues that 'the continuance for a lengthy period of Englishmen
in arms [and] the emergence of permanent ranks' were crucial for-
mative steps 'in the development of the officer corps', at least in
England. Furthermore, all the defining characteristics of professionalism proposed in modern studies of military professionalisation pre-
suppose permanence. If a hallmark of the military profession from
the nineteenth century on is that it offers 'a career independent of
conventional social and political norms', this can only exist with a
permanent organisation.[24] Permanence is also bound up with the
next marker.

4. FORMAL PROCEDURES FOR PAY OR OTHER MEANS OF RECOMPENSE.
This marker is particularly characteristic of military professionalism:
'placing [an] army on a salaried basis . . . changed its social outlook',
while 'regularity of pay also systemized the concept of military duties.'[25]
Greater cohesion, which is associated with the creation of occupational structures and identity, is not a prerequisite, but troops with

---

[22] Feld (1975B), 419 and (1975A), 192.
[23] Hale (1985), 135.
[24] Roy (1987), 187; Feld (1975A), 205.
[25] Feld (1975B), 423, also 433.

cohesion are more likely to be successful in requests that such formal procedures be put in place.[26] Permanence is not a prerequisite for them, either, but it helps in creating them. In a short-term army, pay structures are more likely to be *ad hoc* and mutable, and a crucial step forward was when 'terms of service were no longer tied to the duration of a particular campaign but rather to the upkeep of a standing army'. This 'in itself would have been enough to change the nature of war' and is widely regarded as evidence of professionalisation.[27] The existence of formal procedures for pay is also connected with markers five and six because systematised payment (especially if determined within the discrete occupational structure) allows for specific reward for mastering a profession's distinctive expertise and demonstrating competence therein.

5. EXPERTISE AND EDUCATION: a distinctive body of knowledge that can or must be learned. One of the defining qualities of a profession is 'the development of an internalized and self-defined expertise', adherence to which 'is an essential characteristic of the professional'.[28] However, this is more than a distinct body of knowledge. It is a 'systematic body of specialized knowledge transmitted to [occupational] group members by a formal education process'. Such a formal education process, organised and governed at least partly by group members, who comprise organisations or institutions which assess competence, 'is the essence of any modern educated profession'.[29]

This formal process of training or education is also connected with identity, hierarchy and permanence. Not only can it help to create a common sense of identity since 'commit[ment] to the common enterprise' of mastering and then deploying distinctive skills and

---

[26] See Showalter (1993), 427–28.

[27] Feld (1975B), 422. See Corvisier (1976), 21; Weigley (1993), 11; Adams (1995), 34; Storrs & Scott (1996), 32.

[28] Harries-Jenkins (1975), 472; de Crayencour (1982), 19. Likewise, O'Day (1979), 1, sees the acceptance of 'internal . . . rules, regulations and codes of conduct' as a defining characteristic of professions in early-modern England.

[29] Skelton (1975), 443–44; Weigley (1993), 8. See ibid., xiii; Hale (1983), ch. 8; de Crayencour (1982), 18, 20–21. On the comparable importance of internal occupational training for defining and imparting expertise among lawyers, the clergy and teachers, see, e.g., Prest (1967); O'Day (1979), 28–29; Tropp (1957), 11–12. An example of an early-modern military organisation assessing competence was the *provveditori alle fortezze*, discussed by Pepper in ch. 5 (below, pp. 125, 141), but alternatively competence could be assessed by one's peers in a regiment—see, e.g., ch. 11 below, esp. pp. 293–94, 311.

knowledge creates a bond that can transcend ethnicity and language.[30] It also allows another hallmark of professionalisation—for men to achieve status within their distinct group (a necessary step for advancing in the hierarchy) by meeting 'the specifications of the corporate body of professional soldiers';[31] i.e., by demonstrating expertise, but as determined by their peers. A clearer hierarchical structure would thus be established, but one that was effectively at least partially controlled by the profession itself.

6. EFFICIENCY: the ability to put into practice the distinctive body of expertise in a reasonably competent and systematic fashion, at least in preparation if not always in combat. One study of the development of professionalism in the nineteenth-century British army highlights the importance of 'maintain[ing] an adequate level of effectiveness' as a defining characteristic of 'a professional military'.[32] However, efficiency is very much bound up with expertise—in the context of professionalism, it is not simply effectiveness in certain forms of combat, it is also a certain approach. Feld argues that 'the substitution of technical proficiency for personal prowess' was characteristic of 'the emergence of the modern armed force'. This was achieved by creating 'objective standards for training and commanding fighting men'.[33] Not only had 'specific standards of performance . . . to be articulated', but 'special skills developed for and applied to attaining them.'[34] Thus, to be efficient in this sense, it will be necessary to execute one's abilities in a certain way, not just execute them capably—indeed, capability becomes judged as much on the means as the ends.

7. DISTINCTIVE SELF-CONCEPTUALISATION; not expertise, but a *mentalité*. This is to some extent perhaps another sub-category of the first 'marker'; certainly a distinctive occupational identity can hardly exist without a peculiar self-conceptualisation and approach. Yet what we are talking about at this point is more than just an occupational identity: it is to some extent the mythology and culture of a particular social body and is also how its members view their activities characteristic to their profession. Consider doctors and nurses; foot-

---

[30] Showalter (1993), 429.
[31] Feld (1975A), 207.
[32] Harries-Jenkins (1975), 473.
[33] Feld (1975B), 419.
[34] Feld (1975A), 194.

ball referees and professional players; architects and construction workers; or, indeed, commissioned and non-commissioned officers. The members of each pairing have a different approach to their work (even though in each case both are essentially in the same business), different occupational structures, and a different set of vocational myths and distinctive cultural practices.[35] This 'professional culture' informs, and may determine, how members of a profession conduct themselves, especially in areas not dictated by professional expertise (or grey areas, which in practice will be many). This is why, when Feld argues for the creation of military professionalism in the army of the Dutch Republic, he writes about it in terms of a change in tradition *and* of an 'intellectual and social revolution'.[36] For professionalisation to have taken place there has to have been a change in *mentalité*, as well as in organisation.

This type of framework has been criticised by one leading historian of the professions as more sociological than historical and as teleological. She espouses an alternative, more overtly historical, approach: to examine 'the functions which professions performed in early modern society', seeking '*not* to trace the evolution of a modern phenomenon but to explore, for its own sake, a profession or its institutional form in the early-modern period'.[37] The problem with such an approach is that, given the unwillingness to define what constitutes a profession, it necessarily limits the scholar to taking an existing profession and examining its past practitioners and predecessors (whether or not they constituted a profession in the period being investigated). For how else can one say that one is studying a profession? Essentially, then, the historian would still be defining what profession means, but doing so, in effect, only in modern terms—this, surely, is deeply anachronistic.

The essays in this volume are by historians, not social scientists or military practitioners. They do take an historical approach. They do not trace the evolution of a modern phenomenon (for that is what military professionalism essentially is), but rather examine the military profession in a given timeframe, as a way of casting light on the particular vocation and occupation of the soldier in the late-

---

[35] Grandstaff (1997) characterises US Air Force NCOs as forming a subordinate profession.
[36] Feld (1975B), 422, 424–25, 428–29, at 424.
[37] O'Day (1986), 53.

medieval and early-modern epochs. However, an obvious issue to investigate is when soldiers, members of what would become a profession, acquired the hallmarks of a profession in the modern sense. This is not teleological; it is rather an important point in historical development and an obvious question to ask in a work that contributes to the history of professions. But it requires some kind of comparison and contrast. Furthermore, it is inevitable that the proficiency of medieval and early-modern militaries will be discussed in terms of their professionalism, since this is an obvious point of reference for modern readers (and practitioners). As we have seen, because of the terminological difficulties, without clear categorisation of what marks a profession, either kind of comparative analysis falls into confusion.

Thus, my intention has not been to imply 'that the historical dimension is important only as a way of describing the route to the present, as a means of indicating which groups achieved . . . *full* professionalisation first.'[38] Indeed, it is likely that in the period 1400–1700 full military professionalism was *never* reached. Rather, this framework has been intended as an aid to comparative analysis and, consequently, to better historical understanding.

Having suggested the putative distinctive traits of a profession, it is important to emphasise the difference between the noun, 'profession' and the adjective, 'professional' (though the latter word can also be a noun). As an adjective it can, after all, be applied to people or groups having some of the qualities of the noun. The *Oxford English Dictionary*'s definitions of 'profession' include: 'Any calling or occupation by which a person habitually earns his living' *and* 'The occupation which one professes to be skilled in and to follow'—the two are not the same.[39] It defines 'professional' as a noun thus: 'One who belongs to one of the learned or skilled professions'.[40] But it defines 'professional' as an adjective not only as meaning applicable to 'one who follows, by way of profession or business, an occupation', but also as meaning: 'Reaching a standard or having the quality expected of a professional person or his work; *competent in the manner of a professional*'.[41]

---

[38] Ibid., 52.
[39] *OED*, *s.v.* 'profession': 6.
[40] Ibid., *s.v.* 'professional': B.1.
[41] *Loc. cit.*, A.4.a, d (my italics).

It is potentially very helpful to use professional in this latter adjectival sense—as applicable to people who had some, or perhaps all, of the competencies of a professional (the noun) even though not satisfying all the criteria of the noun, perhaps through lacking certain structures or *mentalités*. After all, some of the seven markers suggested above could be present, at least to some degree, even where a profession in the modern sense did not exist.

For example, some medieval and early-modern armies had reasonably systematic methods of payment or recompense, and chivalry certainly had a distinctive self-conception and *mentalité*. To be sure, the question may then arise as to whether distinctive qualities must not just be present, but be present to a certain degree. It is also interesting to consider the extent to which chivalric warriors' *mentalité* differed from that of 'professionals' (if indeed it did differ significantly). For that matter, a recognised body of knowledge, necessary for practitioners to learn and be expert at, in order to be accepted as members of a fraternity, was certainly characteristic of medieval soldiers, as Matthew Bennett stresses in chapter 2. But how formalised was medieval expertise and the means by which it was imparted? Can medieval military society be regarded as fully or only quasi-professional? If the latter, when (and how) was it transformed sufficiently to become part of a process of professionalisation, as understood by Skelton, for example: that is, with 'professional standards and procedures . . . applied in fields formerly handled by intuitive or empirical means'?[42]

These are matters for debate, but also for more research. However, it is certainly the case that, in some ways, medieval and early-modern chivalric armies could be professional—showing signs of professionalism, even if not constituting a fully-fledged profession in the modern sense. The distinction between adjective and noun is a simple one, but it may be the easiest way to conceptualise some of the different grounds for debate. Different scholars (and this is true of contributors to this volume) have different emphases—noun and adjective—some considering whether soldiers comprised a profession, some considering which qualities of a profession they possessed and to what extent, if any. Recognising this can make comparative analysis more productive, by at least making it easier to conduct debate on similar grounds, rather than talking at cross-purposes.

---

[42] Skelton (1975), 444.

Military Professionalism in Early-Modern Europe

If the different meanings of terminology are borne in mind and the different markers of professions are sought in the early-modern period, it becomes evident that current scholarship on the development of military professionalism needs to be revised. Mainstream early-modern historiography generally locates the professionalisation of military society in Europe in the period between *c.* 1470 and *c.* 1620. Many scholars argue that European nobles in this long sixteenth century, due to a combination of military technological and wider socio-economic factors, lost their traditional interest in and enthusiasm for war and the cult of chivalry, in what some have termed the nobility's 'demilitarization', even their 'civilianization'.[43] This decline in the military role of the nobility is often said to have resulted in the opening of the soldier's career to men of all classes (or castes) and, in consequence, to the transformation of the aristocratic martial vocation into a military profession by the middle of the seventeenth century.

For example, M. S. Anderson recently asserted that 'War by the end of this period [1494–1618] was thus becoming more professionalized and "modern" than ever before.' This is probably true, but it needs to be thought of in the adjectival rather than an absolute sense—of war having more of the characteristics of modern military professionalism, rather than the implication which could easily be drawn—that it had become effectively modern and professional.[44] Other scholars are more categorical. I. A. A. Thompson argues that though the 1590s did not witness a military revolution, there was in that decade, in Europe as a whole, an 'increasing professionalism in war, a shift from prowess to proficiency, and from ascription to achievement in military status'; and M. D. Feld argues that around this period the Dutch actually achieved 'military professionalism'.[45] Others describe professionalisation as occurring earlier, however. Michael Hattaway writes of 'the change from an historical moment

---

[43] Storrs & Scott (1996), 3 (summarising a body of scholarship); Hale (1985), 91, and cf. ibid., 90–99, 135–41; Bitton (1969), 27–35; Billacois (1976); Howard (1976), 12–19, 23–24, 27–28, 39–42; Király (1982), 24, 35–39; Dop (1981), 23–31, 108–29, 154–55; Thompson (1992), 270–76; Keegan (1993), 13–14, 36–38; Corvisier (1995), 37, 254–55, 261. See also Trim (2002A), 69–70.

[44] Anderson (1998), 24.

[45] Thompson (1992), 262; Feld (1975A and B), but see ch. 10, below.

when fighting was a chivalric sport or form of group-specific behaviour to a moment when fighting was an occupation—from a moment when a fighter was regarded as a gentleman-amateur to one in which he was a professional'. He dates this change to (roughly) the 1570s and concludes that by 1608 the world of the 'knight . . . was long gone'.[46] To Simon Adams, 'the permanent forces of the [late sixteenth-century English] crown' were the 'products of a process of professionalisation that can be traced back the first half of the century'.[47] Gervase Phillips similarly regards the ability of the early Tudors 'to raise a trained and equipped army with speed and efficiency' as evidence of 'an embryonic professionalisation', while he also takes for granted that France in the same period already had developed 'a professional army'. Keen likewise perceives 'a more self-conscious professionalism' in Europe at large during the first half of the sixteenth century.[48]

Hale suggested that in the long sixteenth-century the literature of war became focused on 'the soldier as an effective campaigner rather than as a brother-in-arms, a loyal retainer, . . . loner [or] grail-searcher'.[49] Similarly, the important cultural historian Sydney Anglo asserts that the

> treatises on the art of war [that] poured from the presses of Europe throughout the sixteenth and seventeenth centuries . . . dealt with strategical and logistical problems from a technical standpoint which would have seemed alien to most knights and offered solutions which might have astonished them.'

Anglo concludes more generally that 'the knight', whose 'social place [was] . . . filled by the courtier', vanished 'as a distinctive religious-military type . . . during the Renaissance.'[50]

There is no question that changes in how the old martial values were perceived and understood were taking place (and accelerating) right across Christendom.[51] However, *plus ça change, plus c'est la même*

---

[46] Hattaway (1994), 84, 101. He refers to Foucault's the *homme de guerre* and the *militaire*, citing *The Foucault Reader*, ed. P. Rabinow (Harmondsworth: 1985), 186.

[47] Adams (1988), 9; cf. the assumptions inherent in Adams (1995), 34.

[48] Phillips (1997), 16, 15; Keen (1999), 291.

[49] Hale (1985), 129.

[50] Anglo (1990), xiv–xv; cf. Keen (1999), 290–91. For the inaccuracy of such views, see the reviews of contemporary French and Spanish military literature by Potter and González de León in chs 6 and 9.

[51] Storrs & Scott (1996), 4–13.

chose. Recent studies argue that, rather than triggering the decline or 'demilitarisation' of the noble classes, the changes (whether evolutionary or revolutionary) in the practice of war during the sixteenth and seventeenth centuries actually resulted in 'the increased "militarization" of noble life and culture'. In Europe generally, the conception of war as the natural occupation of nobles remained strong until the dawn of the nineteenth century.[52]

Remarkably, however, while scholars now generally accept that the nobility's military function in society endured, they are no less inclined to see a process of professionalisation at work. Thus, they argue that the élite became increasingly militarised because nobles sought to dominate the new military profession which was an integral part of the new fiscal-military state. The links 'between the nobility and military professionalism' were reinforced, with nobles eventually becoming 'the military professionals par excellence'; throughout Europe, 'the time-honoured beliefs that leadership in war was the peculiar preserve of the . . . aristocracy [and] that a nobleman never stood higher than when armed for battle at the head of his followers' continued to influence 'profoundly . . . [how] army and navy officers would view their profession, and the way the rest of society viewed them'.[53] Indeed, far from aristocrats having fewer opportunities for military service, they actually had more. Army sizes grew in the late-seventeenth and eighteenth centuries and nobles were ubiquitous in them, consigning all non-nobles to the ranks; if poorer nobles were similarly consigned to the lower grades of the officer corps, the second estate still dominated the professional military hierarchy. At the same time, aristocratic society continued to be dominated by the chivalric tradition. As a result, 'the gentlemanly traditions within the armed forces . . . continued to exert a pervasive influence, long after the passing from the scene of the chivalrous knight at arms and his replacement by modern methods of warfare'.[54] The alleged basis for the development of military professionalism has been turned upside down, but the consequences are perceived as the same.

---

[52] Ibid., 39 *et passim*; Rowlands (1997) and (1999); Honig & Herd (1996).

[53] Storrs & Scott (1996), 37, 35; Roy (1987), 184.

[54] Roy (1987), 215. See Howard (1976), 69–70, 94, 107; Rowlands (1997), 99–100 and (1999), *passim*; Storrs & Scott (1996), 14–17, 28–30, 39–40; Young (1987), 186–90.

At first sight, this seems to accord with contemporary evidence, yet as we will see, evidence that the vocation of arms had become a military profession by the mid-seventeenth century has been read out of context, or with an inadequate conceptual framework of the meaning of 'profession' and its cognate terms. Military professionalism has its roots in this period, but no more.

If by professionalise we mean 'To render or make professional', or 'To become professional; to proceed in a professional manner', then there is clear evidence that armies in this period were *beginning* to professionalise.[55] The Dutch army of the late-sixteenth and early-seventeenth centuries went through a series of reforms that certainly made it more professional (as discussed in chapter 10); it is often held up as the classic example of developing military professionalism.[56] For example, the Dutch 'impose[d] rationalized patterns of performance on their troops'.[57] They built up a specific corpus of knowledge for dealing with logistical problems, which was systematised from the late 1590s onwards. By the end of the seventeenth century it was very well advanced, with texts that formulated and perpetuated this knowledge dating back to the 1590s, albeit updated in light of later advances in practice.[58] This body of knowledge and its significance in the military society of the Netherlands is a sign of real professionalism[59]—at any rate among those entrusted with the army's supply—especially in comparison to armies of earlier generations, who may have had effective, but not systematic ways of dealing with logistics.

The sixteenth-century Spanish army, examined in chapter 9, lacked the systematised regulations governing organisation, logistics, tactics and military justice of its Dutch enemy. However, claims that 'Spanish veterans . . . were innocent of group training' are fallacious.[60] They were subject to 'disciplined patterns', capable of relatively sophisti-

---

[55] *OED*, *s.v.* 'professionalize': 1, 2.

[56] I discuss this in ch. 10, below.

[57] Feld (1975B), 421.

[58] ARA, Archief Raad van Staat 2287, 'Militaire Instructien'. John Stapleton examines Dutch logistics in the 1690s in his forthcoming Ohio State University PhD thesis on the Dutch army of William III.

[59] *OED*, *s.v.* 'professionalism': 1, 'Professional quality, character, method, or conduct'; 2, 'The position or practice of a professional as distinguished from an amateur; the class of professionals'. The cross-reference here is to 'professional' as defined under 4.a, for which see fn. 41 above.

[60] Brooks (2000), 75.

cated tactical manoeuvres and had available to them from the mid-sixteenth century tactical treatises on the conduct of military operations.[61] There are thus some of the markers of a profession present in the military societies of early-modern Spain and the Netherlands.

Contemporary literature seems to reflect these trends. Montaigne declared that 'the proper and only and essential place for the nobility in France is the military profession'.[62] The English lawyer and soldier Geoffrey Gates in 1579 published a treatise calling for better treatment of career soldiers and titled it *The defence of militarie profession*.[63] He not only refers to 'profession' repeatedly in this work, but also uses it in a strikingly modern way. Indeed, it is obvious that, like modern historians of the professions (such as Prest), Gates regarded lawyers and clergymen as the true professionals of the sixteenth century and his purpose is to elevate to this level the profession of arms in the eyes of the English gentry. He condemns (for example) those who 'despise the profession of Armes, as a vile, and damnable occupation'.[64] The problem was not with the status of the soldier in English society, which was high. It was rather that many among the élite viewed with suspicion those soldiers who fought for money rather than from an aristocratic vocation.[65]

In any event, Hale regards Montaigne's remarks as wry and cynical, rather than as genuine comment,[66] while Gates, in discussing law, divinity and arms as professions in the modern sense, is not typical of early-modern writers. The celebrated Elizabethan and Jacobean English general Sir Horace Vere (who, like Gates, served the Dutch and would thus be widely regarded as a professional soldier today), in 1610 referred to 'the profession' when writing to a friend. However, Vere was discussing service as a gentleman volunteer; far from being evidence for professionalism, the letter actually indicates the extent to which formal hierarchy of rank had yet to develop in Anglo-Dutch military circles.[67] The seventeenth-century

---

[61] Showalter (1993), 429; González de León (1996); and idem, ch. 9 below, p. 239, 250.

[62] Quoted in Bitton (1969), 27.

[63] Gates (1579). His use of profession is analysed in more detail in Trim (2003). On Gates, see *New DNB*.

[64] Prest (1987), 64, noting that, in the 16th-cent., medicine had not yet attained its later status; Gates (1579), 43.

[65] See Trim (2002B) ch. 2, esp. pp. 74–92.

[66] Hale (1985), 98.

[67] Vere to Adam Newton, 22 July 1611, Koninklijke Bibliotheek, *Handschriften*, 72.D.32.

English military and political theorist, Dudley Digges, reflecting on how gentlemen 'might be fitliest busied', discussed 'the warres' as well as 'Divinity', 'Lawe' and 'Physicke'—'the professions'—but then he also discusses courtiers and merchants.[68] If the latter might just about be regarded as a profession today, the former never would be; and Digges, unlike Gates, refers to none of these as *profession*: indeed, he terms medicine an art. Sir John Oglander, a contemporary of Vere and Digges, reflected on the need of a country gentleman, if he would be prosperous, to have 'some other vocation with his inheritance, as to be a courtier, lawyer, merchant or some other vocation'.[69] Here, again, the courtier is compared to the lawyer and merchant, but the occupations of the last two are not termed professions and the word chosen is suggestive—each is a 'vocation'.

The other terms, more frequently applied to war than profession, are also suggestive. Another of Digges's contemporaries, John Holles, called it 'an art or occupation'.[70] Earlier, the fifteenth-century Italian writer, Leon Battista Alberti, wrote of 'the *science and skill* of dealing with arms and horses and musical instruments', which he compared to 'the pursuit of letters and the fine arts'.[71] The early sixteenth-century Florentine politician Pier Filippo Pandolfini wrote of the discipline, rather than the profession, of arms, which he declared superior to all the other sciences and virtues.[72] This is not just a matter of contemporaries using different terms for what is effectively the same as the modern English word profession. Pandolfini and Alberti were effectively comparing the soldier to the artist and scholar, all of whom sought 'virtue and wisdom'; mastery of arms was compatible with the liberal arts (just as military architecture was practised by artists like Leonardo da Vinci and Michelangelo).[73] Holles meant

---

[68] Digges (1604), 77.

[69] Oglander diary, 25 Jun. 1632, in Stone (1965), 126.

[70] Seddon (1975), lvi.

[71] Alberti, *Autobiography* (after 1460?), extract in Wiesner, Ruff & Wheeler (2000), I, 241 (italics mine).

[72] Quoted in Hale (1983), 365: '. . . la virtù della disciplina militare la quale supera tutte le altre scienzie et virtù'.

[73] Peter Paul Vergerius, analysing ' "Liberal Studies" ' in 1392, defined them as 'those studies by which we attain and practice virtue and wisdom' and he gave 'the first place to history', as did Leonardo Bruni in 1405; Nicolò Machiavelli, in *The Prince* (1513), stated that the prince should 'have no other aim or thought, nor take up any other thing for his study, but war and its organisation and discipline', but recommended to this end that he first of all 'read history': Wiesner, Ruff & Wheeler (2000), I, 235–36, 240. Baldassare Castiglione's ideal courtier needed to be adept

that war could either be a vocation (for noble or gentlemen) or a paid livelihood (as for commoners).[74]

There is little evidence, then, that contemporaries, when conceptualising 'arms', thought of it as a profession in any of the senses identified earlier. Moreover, the military practice of the period also indicates that the martial vocation lacked the distinguishing characteristics of a profession. It was not permanent; it lacked a formal hierarchy as well as the associated systematic pay structures, and distinctive body of expertise and organisations to impart and assess it; and though it had a distinctive identity and self-conceptualisation, these derived from the aristocratic nature of most soldiers, not from their military occupation *per se*—indeed they arose from the chivalric ethos.

Up to the middle decades of the seventeenth century (and, in some countries, later), there was no 'officer corps' as such: the medieval 'knight' was in the process of being transformed into the 'officer'— but the process was not yet complete.[75] Governments still expected nobles to serve essentially for honour and from a sense of duty to his prince, and therefore to be content with ransoms and plunder: reimbursement of expenses and salary *per se* were considerably deferred, if paid at all. This was the case even in the army of the Dutch Republic, for all its reputation as regular and prompt payers of their troops.[76] Nobles could serve together, literally in the ranks, of a unit in which they predominated, or might command a unit made up of both other nobles and the non-noble, or units almost entirely drawn from peasants, yeomen, townsfolk, etc (and occasionally a commoner might be found in command of this last kind of unit). Exercising command might or might not be complicated by the social gradations which were older than the nascent rank structure operating alongside it.[77] In truth, there was no rank hierarchy in which one could 'rise' in the modern sense.[78] The company was the chief admin-

---

in literary arts, but mastering the martial arts was of equal or greater importance: Castiglione (1976), 57–58, 61, 88, 90–93. For the military interests of Leonardo and Michelangelo, see ch. 5 below, p. 119.

[74] See Trim (2002B), 205–6.

[75] Keen (1984), 240–43.

[76] See Trim (2002B), ch. 6; Feld (1975B), 422–23.

[77] Redlich (1964), 8–15, 46; Trim (2002B), chs 7–8; Boynton (1967), 103–4.

[78] Indeed, Hale (1985), 131, points out that there was 'no parallel ladder of command' to the hierarchy of the church, even in the legal or medical professions (such as they were).

istrative unit of the army and carried almost seigniorial prestige, duties and responsibilities. To be captain of a company was the main desire of a soldier. Generals and colonels had their own companies not least because it was often their rank as captain which gave them the right to higher command. Certainly there was little or no hierarchy between captain and general. Regiments were introduced only in the late sixteenth century and were still *ad hoc* structures in the seventeenth.[79] A captain could take command of a regiment, even of a small independent force, but then return simply to commanding his company.[80] Hale stresses the 'lack of a ladder of promotion within standing forces, and the absence of a correlation between such career structures as they did have and the appointments made to commands within a wartime army in the field.' An 'officer', in the contemporary sense of the word, was simply an office-holder—and this in an era when an office 'could also be a possession and . . . like a tenant's title to a piece of land, could be, with permission, leased or sold or passed on to an heir.' Until the mid-seventeenth century, it 'retained either this signification, which derived from medieval legal, fiscal or household appointments, or that of its alternative meaning, that of "functionary".'[81]

These facts tend to be forgotten by modern historians. One distinguished medievalist declares that Bayard 'was in an almost demonstrable way more of a loyal officer and less of a knight errant than had been, say, Jean de Boucicault . . . champion of the jousting field, crusader and veteran of a hundred years before him.'[82] Yet David Potter shows in chapter 6 that Bayard (who was probably as famous for his jousting as was Boucicault) very much subscribed to the chivalric ethos. If he was beginning to subordinate himself to his sovereign, this was not yet to the state. In any case, even if the statement is true, it is also true that Bayard is still almost demonstrably *less* a

---

[79] Oman (1937), 334–37, 376–79; Cruickshank (1966), 50–54; Redlich (1964), 108n.–9n.; Webb (1965), 57–58, 81–86, 123; Dop (1981), 130, 133; below, p. 187.

[80] This is neatly epitomised by the career of the sixteenth-century Welsh soldier, Roger Williams, on who see Miller (1972) for a good summary. Even in the mid-seventeenth century, of the 16 major-generals who famously acted as Cromwell's military governors in 1655–56, ten were appointed from regimental commands, but four were fortress governors who may or may not have been colonels; and two were appointed from the rank of major: Durston (2001): 42.

[81] Hale (1985), 130–31.

[82] Keen (1999), 291. For an alternative perspective on Bayard, see ch. 6, below, pp. 149, 159.

loyal officer and *more* a knight-errant than virtually all French officers of the late-seventeenth century and after.

To take another example, historians of Elizabethan England frequently describe many of the queen's English and Welsh soldiers as 'professionals'. This is accurate if the word is being used in the adjectival sense—they were experiencing a process of professionalisation. But they show few or none of the markers associated with a profession. Nor yet were they truly professional, as most readers would instinctively understand the word. The Dutch cultural historian, J. A. Dop, contrasts Sir John Norreys, commander of the initial Elizabethan expedition to the Netherlands in 1585, with the Earl of Leicester, who superseded Norreys in 1586. Norreys is portrayed as a professional, Leicester as an ignorant knight-errant, who eventually sent Norreys home because his professionalism showed up the earl's aristocratic amateurishness.[83] Francis Vere is described as 'that first-rate professional' by a best-selling biographer of Elizabeth I, a characterisation made more pointed because it is used implicitly to counterpoint Vere with the Earl of Essex, who is portrayed as amateurish, in his 'childish desire for vainglory'.[84] Yet Norreys and his brothers quarrelled bitterly with fellow senior officers over points of personal honour, and Vere's coterie physically attacked fellow officers who were critical of their patron.[85] The behaviour of these putative paragons of professionalism was like that of medieval chivalric warriors, more sensible of their honour than of the formal hierarchies characteristic of a profession. As the nineteenth-century historian J. L. Motley rightly observed, though the Norreys brothers had some qualities of the new, developing professionalism, they combined it with the spirit of 'knight-errantry'.[86] Sir John Wingfield and Sir Thomas Baskerville have been held up as examples of a new generation 'making soldiering their profession'.[87] However, Wingfield's conduct at the storm of Cadiz (1596), which cost him his life, was clearly inspired by the chivalric ethos and has been condemned by historians as quixotic. Baskerville privileged personal honour and

---

[83] Dop (1981), 153–55. See Adams (1988) 8 *et seq.*
[84] Plowden (2000), 90, 59.
[85] See *DNB, s.n.* 'John Norris' and 'Edward Norris'; Trim (2002B), 188.
[86] Motley (1879–80), I, 134.
[87] Plowden (2000), 57.

profit above all else and was a trusted client of the supposedly amateurish Essex.[88]

In sum, before the latter half of the seventeenth century even the
martially active members of the second estate were not members of
a profession. Until that time, there was no 'military profession' to
belong to. Not only had the nobility of Christendom not been 'civil-
ianized' by the mid-seventeenth century, it had not yet been 'professionalized' either.[89] Many European armies had professional aspects
and there were elements of professionalism in the conduct of many
European nobles. But actual military professions are only to be found
in the latter half of the seventeenth century and after.

Chivalry, Professionalism, the Nobility and the State

Where does this survey of the nature of professionalism and its standing in early-modern Europe leave us as regards the questions posed
at the beginning of the chapter? Few scholars would today subscribe
to the notion of a 'crisis' of the nobility that was fashionable amongst
a previous generation of early-modernists. Rather, there is a historiographical trend towards portraying the process of military professionalisation as part of a wider continuum of noble power and,
therefore, as relatively insignificant for historians of the European
élites, because it was not a dramatic change.[90]

The proficiency of many nobles in the martial arts is not in doubt.
K. B. McFarlane roundly declared that 'Henry VIII's army was no
less aristocratic than Edward III's and Henry V's. The belief that
in the later middle ages the noble soldier was being replaced by the
professional soldier of fortune lacks reality: the noble was still a
professional soldier.'[91] As Bennett, Mallett and Newitt indicate in
the next three chapters of this volume (and their conclusions agree
with those of a large body of medieval historiography), most chivalric warriors of the eleventh through fifteenth centuries had many

---

[88] Motley (1879–80), III, 386; *s.n.* Wingfield and Baskerville in *New DNB.*
[89] *Pace* Hale (1985), 91 *et seq.* and Storrs & Scott (1996), 4.
[90] See Storrs & Scott (1996), analysed in the subsequent paragraph; cf. Thornton
(1998), 58–59, an example of recent scepticism as to whether reforms in 'military
technology and organization . . . in the early modern period' resulted in 'dramatic
changes'.
[91] McFarlane (1973), 162.

professional characteristics. Put in those terms, continuity between these warriors with professional qualities and the military professionals of later centuries seems apparent. It is, indeed, to Christopher Storrs and H. M. Scott in their ground-breaking article: nobles, with their ethos of honour, comprised the military caste for a thousand years after the fall of the Roman Empire; then, even though the Reformation, the Scientific Revolution and the 'Enlightenment' all wrought great changes in society, they still monopolised the military profession; 'the noble "ethic" remained fundamentally a fighting one'. There is thus 'no inherent contradiction between nobility and military professionalism.'[92] If the eventual professionalisation of the nobility was not a dramatic step, then, is it of any wider significance whether it culminated in the mid seventeenth, eighteenth or nineteenth centuries?

The answer is 'yes'. Continuity in aristocratic society and culture between *c.* 1100–1800 does exist but it has been overstated. There were changes over the period, and the differences they produced, while not always radical, were rarely trivial.

Even though the rhetoric of honour (in its traditional forms) continued to inform noble self-conceptualisation well into the eighteenth century, simply because Enlightenment aristocratic culture drew on medieval and early-modern ideas of honour does not mean that eighteenth-century aristocrats understood them in the same way as their ancestors. The nobles of the sixteenth century were in a very different situation to those of the second half of the seventeenth century and after. Rather than serving the state, effectively as employees (as would their descendants), they served an individual (ultimately the sovereign, but often through the mediation of their 'lord' to whom their more immediate loyalty lay) as a friend or servant.[93] They might no longer be required to serve like feudal vassals, but the aristocratic martial vocation had yet to evolve into an aristocratically dominated

---

[92] Storrs & Scott (1996), 38–39.

[93] The process of subordination to the state had begun in the 16th century— Potter points out the importance of this trend in his study of early 16th-cent. France (ch. 6, see esp. pp. 160–61). But contemporaneously in other European countries, the nobility preserved their independence (e.g., in Portugal and Henrician England, as seen in chs 4 and 7), while in France during the Wars of Religion (1562–1598) the trend was decisively reversed, raising questions as to whether the process was either inevitable or unstoppable, at least in the short term.

military profession. By contrast, nobles of the middle of the seventeenth century and after *were* members of an officer corps. They were often required to go through relatively standardised, systematic training before they could take their place in a regulated, permanent hierarchical structure, which often incorporated non-nobles, if only as technical officers. It also had its own professional value system, which emphasised obedience.[94]

The professionalisation of military service was a major shift in European society in a number of ways. To understand it fully we have to understand the reality of what happened in the fifteenth to seventeenth centuries—not the completion, but certainly the development of military professionalism in many countries. We come back to the potential significance of adjective and noun—of 'professional' in the first case meaning 'having the qualities of' and in the second case meaning 'members of' a profession. Warner is sensitive to this distinction when he observes that for a knight to be 'chivalric did not mean that he was any the less practical since the two qualities were not mutually exclusive.'[95] What virtually all the scholars who argue for the professionalism of medieval and early-modern soldiers actually demonstrate is their proficiency. Reflecting the different terminological significance, chivalric warriors were, in sum, professional, in that they had some, often many, of the qualities of a professional. This is not just a point of interest for the long-term development of modern professions. It is also important for understanding early-modern Europe, because to ascribe military success or failure simply to professionalism or lack thereof, as have many military historians,[96] is misguided. The transformation of professional warriors into military professionals is clearly one of great consequence in the history of the professions.

Its importance is also considerable, however, for the wider history of political culture and society. As Jeremy Black points out, though it 'helped to ensure the continuation of ancestral political and social privilege', it also affected the performance of armies.[97] In any case,

---

[94] Hexter (1950), 19; Howard (1976), 54–55, 70; Storrs & Scott (1996), 13–15, 26–27, 34, 38– 39; Király (1982), 34–39, esp. 37–38; Zwitzer (1991), 130–33; Rowlands (1999), 304–5, 330.

[95] Warner (1998), 167.

[96] See Phillips (1997), 13–14, 16.

[97] Black (2000), 209.

the distinction Michael Howard draws between 'members of a warrior caste fighting from a concept of honour or feudal obligation'
and 'servants of the state . . . guaranteed regular employment, regular wages and career prospects and . . . dedicated . . . to the service
of their state' is it itself an important one.[98] If great nobles still exercised some sway over military administration, it was through influence
at court and patronage, rather than by 'prescriptive authority'[99]—
the continuity is worth noting, but the difference is still not a minor
one. The transformation of knights into officers changed the relationship between élites and the governments very much to the benefit
of the latter, and also enhanced the power of the state *vis-à-vis* the
rest of society.

This is not to say that military professionalism could develop only
in the service of the state. Arguably, as Professor Corvisier indicates,
the original military professionals were the *entrepreneurs de guerre*, or
military enterprisers. As an occupational group they had many of
the defining markers of a profession.[100] It was only later that professionalism was fully embraced by national or state military institutions. The emergence in the 1990s of 'private military companies'
with relatively high standards of professionalism indicates the possibility that military professionalism can exist independently of state-
based military institutions.[101] It is notable, however, that most so-called
PMCs recruit from national armies, whence comes their operatives'
professional ethos. In any case, the simple fact is that military professionalism developed hand in hand with the power of the state.
Entrepreneurs de guerre were 'professional' businessman as much as professional soldiers; nor is it a coincidence that many were nobles—
the values of chivalry meshed well with those of the military
enterpriser.[102] The change in the nobility's socio-military ethos (the
term of Matthew Bennett), subordinating nobles to the state, was a
vital part of a wider change in aristocratic *mentalité*. This undercut
the potential military entrepreneur, for his world-view no longer legit-
imated independent service at the *expense* of his state—it directed him
instead to loyal and obedient service to his own prince or com-

---

[98] Howard (1976), 54.
[99] Rowlands (1999), 305, 328–29 at 328.
[100] Corvisier (1995), 256. Redlich (1964) remains the standard work on military
enterprisers.
[101] See, e.g., O'Brien (2000).
[102] Redlich (1964), 411–14; Trim (2002B), *passim*, esp. chs 2, 8.

monwealth.[103] It is reasonable, then, to associate the development of military professionalism with the rise of the state: there may not have been a simple causal relationship, but the former undoubtedly advanced the latter.

This did not only have implications for European governments. The so-called 'rise of the West'—the expansion of Europe into the rest of the world—was carried out by states with powerful fiscal-military institutions. 'States that had a degree of coherence, continuity and bureaucratic development had several advantages in conflict with peoples with looser governmental structures.' Professional military structures and *mentalité* went hand in hand with that degree of coherence, continuity and bureaucratisation. They additionally provided an, if not the most, effective means of deploying the substantial, firepower-armed forces, that, probably more than simple technological change, gave European states an advantage in the rest of the world.[104] Malyn Newitt shows in chapter 4 how the Portuguese, the first Western power to break into trade of the Far East, relied on the enterprise of nobles, acting as much in their own regard as that of the state. The nobles' prioritisation of their own interests was a major factor in the decline of Portugal.[105] The nobility in the countries that rose at its expense—England, the Netherlands and France—albeit still independent-minded, were nevertheless bound to their respective states. Thus, the eventual evolution of European nobles 'into a service caste, acting as officers in the state's permanent forces, their main military virtue being obedience', was itself a significant metamorphosis.[106]

Finally, this transmutation also transformed the cult of chivalry—indeed ended it, at least in anything like its original sense. For those scholars who have posited that European armies and societies were professionalised between 1450 and 1650, it is a simple matter: the development of military professionalism made the chivalric ethos irrelevant. Anderson, for example, notes that 'side by side with' the modernisation and professionalisation of war in the long sixteenth century, 'there remained a substantial though diminishing legacy of attitudes rooted in the past and values derived from late-medieval

---

[103] Hexter (1950), 15, 19; Rowlands (1999), 304–5; Thornton (1998), 59.
[104] Black (2000), 76–78 at 77, 209–10; Keegan (1993), 343–47.
[105] Below, esp. pp. 103–5, 109, 111–14.
[106] Storrs & Scott (1996), 38–39. See Black (2000), 208–12.

chivalry.' But he concludes that by the beginning of the Thirty Years' War, the chivalric ethos was 'artificial, increasingly out of touch with reality' and that the myopic brutality of sixteenth-century warfare (owing something at least to the 'military revolution') served to 'expose the hollowness of chivalric ideals'.[107] However, this case is only partly persuasive. The particular point of the alleged hollowness of chivalry (raised by many scholars) is addressed by Matthew Bennett in chapter 2. As to the effects of the military revolution on military culture and ethics, Helen Watanabe-O'Kelly shows in chapter 8 how the chivalric Elector August of Saxony (d. 1586) fashioned himself both as master of the most up-to-date military technology 'and as latter-day knight';[108] while Fernando González de León demonstrates in chapter 9 and I argue in chapter 10 that adherence to the chivalric ethic flourished during the first half of the seventeenth century in the apparently professionalised Spanish and Dutch armies.

Indeed, medievalists reach a quite different conclusion: the noble cult of chivalry, with its aristocratic values, was completely compatible with professionalism. After all, as Mark Warner puts it, medieval warfare was characterised not by 'lightheaded chivalric folly', but rather 'by caution and an attention to the smallest detail.'[109] Mallett shows in chapter 3 that 'the apparent antithesis between the mercenary *condottiere* who dominated the Italian scene for much of the fourteenth and fifteenth centuries and the chivalrous traditions which exercised such a strong influence on northern and western European warfare . . . has been considerably exaggerated'.[110]

On the other hand, as we have seen, medievalists tend to demonstrate proficiency rather than professionalism. Moreover, although a simplistic cause-and-effect relationship of decline cannot be demonstrated, in the long run the chivalric ethos, with its emphasis on personal responsibility deriving from personal honour, was difficult, perhaps impossible to reconcile with professional structures. Certainly the concept of the 'knight' and the 'officer' did not sit comfortably together; the latter grew up after the former became militarily, as opposed to socially, defunct.

---

[107] Anderson (1998), 24–25.
[108] Below, at p. 213. Pepper in ch. 5, shows the compatibility of noble, chivalric values with the 'trade' of military engineer or architect.
[109] Warner (1998), 156.
[110] Below, p. 68.

The chivalric mindset is summed up in the *Yvain* of Chrétien de Troyes, in the declaration of a questing knight that he seeks:

> Avantures por esprover
> Ma proesce et mon hardement.[111]

It was by adventures, prowess, courage and endurance that a man proved himself honourable and hence worthy of his aristocratic status. In the fifteenth through seventeenth centuries, even though soldiers did not always behave honourably in 'textbook' (or conduct manual!) chivalric fashion, they were still largely motivated to go to war by the desire to acquire, or to demonstrate, honour. The Jacobean English soldier and writer George Chapman (whose translation of *The Iliad* was first published in folio in 1612–14), was translating Homer when he made Hector avow, in Book VI, that he was unable to put discretion before valour

> ... since the contempt of death
> Was settled in me, and my mind knew what a worthy was
> Whose office is to lead in fight, and give no danger pass
> Without improvement. In this fire must Hector's trial shine;
> Here must his country, father, friends, be, in him, made divine.[112]

Yet the popularity of Chapman's translation reveals the enduring power of the sentiments expressed by Chrétien de Troyes even in the seventeenth century. They also emphasise the individuality of honour—national, familial, social considerations were all subsumed within a personal trial. 'Chivalry could be (even ought to be) collegial, as the examples of the knightly orders of both fiction and history showed, [but] it could not be corporate.'[113]

An honourable reputation was prized so highly precisely because it was gained essentially by individual effort. The institutional structures associated with the distinctive characteristics of professions emphasised the group; occupational identity, hierarchy, expertise and efficiency all pointed towards, indeed helped achieve, subordination of the individual, not only to the state, but to the collective will of one's occupational peers. This was not immediate. Initially, as Guy

---

[111] Chrestien de Troyes, *Yvain* (*Le Chevalier au lion*), ed. T. Reid (Manchester: 1941), ll. 362–63, quoted by Brook (1988), 3: 'Adventures so as to prove/my prowess and my boldness'.
[112] Baker (1996), 33–34.
[113] Trim (2002A), 95, summarising relevant scholarship.

Rowlands points out, absolutist princes might 'sacrifice much "rational" and centralized efficiency' in order to satisfy their nobles' aspiration (with which they often sympathised) to prove their honour.[114] However: 'Institutionalised military education began to erode . . . the well-born individual's right to command on the basis of birth and a familiarity with horse and sword'.[115] And when progression became promotion, dependent on performance of patterns dictated partly by policy, rather than by prowess, the ethic of chivalry was undermined still further.

In sum, as François Billacois observes, in the late-sixteenth and seventeenth centuries, 'individual prowess and courage mattered less and less' in the art of war. They were being superseded in importance by the ability to calculate ballistics, logistics and tactics.[116] It is easy to cavil at this sweeping generalisation, inasmuch as personal skill at arms and what later generations of British soldiers would call 'dash' remained among the most highly prized qualities of officers in all European armies well into the twentieth century. Nevertheless, if overstated, this summary cuts to the essence of developments in this period. They partly reflected changes in military technology and the growing power of the state. But then, professionalised forces more effectively deployed new technology, and state power was partly expressed through newly-created professional institutions. The establishment of permanent hierarchies, with members reliant on their regular pay and emoluments, whose progression was linked to objective criteria relating to mastery of a formal body of knowledge (determined partly by the state), was not only integral to the development of a military professionalism that was truly professional. It also was bound eventually to undermine the individual skill and individualistic attitudes of the chivalric ethos.

---

[114] Rowlands (1997), 330.
[115] Hale (1983), 225.
[116] Billacois (1976), 269: 'La "furia", la prouesse, la vaillance individuelle ont de moins en moins: de place don cet art minutieux, fait de calcul, de balistique, de tactique l'infanterie . . .'.

Conclusion

What the studies of different nationalities and armies in early-modern Europe indicate is that, while the development of military professionalism did trigger a decline in chivalry, the latter is not a prerequisite to the former. Throughout Christendom, military professionalism began to evolve in traditional societies whose culture was essentially chivalric. This reflects the long-standing competence of medieval military men, whose subscription to the chivalric ethos did not prevent them taking their vocation seriously. Even those careers that might be assumed to have been the prerogative of the labouring classes, such as military engineer and gunner, were not, in this period, divorced from aristocratic society. Ironically, that would come after professionalism became fully fledged. So long as the life of the soldier was an aristocratic vocation, nobles would naturally seek mastery of a wide range of martial arts. Once it had become a formal profession, it was perhaps natural that, as in medieval guilds, different sub-divisions of what was essentially the same occupation would acquire their own *mentalité* and collective self-conception, becoming in effect separate professions. The socially subaltern would then be relegated to that branch of the military profession that seemed most analogous to 'trade', or to physical labour.

Again, then, it seems clear that although professionalisation helped to dissolve the mental ties holding European nobles to the chivalric ethos, this happened after, not before, the development of professionalism, which was initiated by noble society. Indeed, a widespread adherence to the chivalric ethos took a long time to be killed off by bourgeois, state-centred professionalism. This was partly because, from Sir Walter Scott on, authors of fiction, biography and the new genre of children's stories, successfully constructed and disseminating a sanitised version of the Middle Ages and chivalry. Although it was almost wholly unrealistic, their version of the chivalric ethos and the anachronistic incorporation into it of the contemporary military adventures of Europeans in Africa and Asia, proved extremely attractive to nineteenth-century British and American society. One may speculate that this idealisation of the past provided a welcome diversion from the socio-economic upheaval caused by industrialisation; while of course it helped to justify contemporary treatment of non-Anglo-Saxon races. The literary (and, from the 1920s, cinematic) fusion of the genres of chivalric romance with heroic adventure helped to make fashionable (not least with the middle class) a version of the cult of chivalry, which proved 'especially influential in constructing idealized conceptions of the contemporary officer'.[117] It is unsurprising that many even of the most professional of military men still yearn for at least some of the trappings of chivalry, as evinced by the perpetuation of chivalric rituals in the armies of virtually all Western states.

Some scholars denigrate this craving (albeit in an almost entirely Anglo-American context). Graham Dawson is ambivalent about the way that militant imperialism was air-brushed by the gloss of an (essentially invented) idealised 'chivalric ethos', expressed in 'phantasies' of masculine adventure. Alan Young is more categorical. His study of Tudor and Jacobean chivalric culture ends with a sweeping survey of the survival of its 'excesses' into the nineteenth and twentieth centuries. He asserts that

> Much of the rhetoric, the literature and propaganda associated with World War I demonstrates [that] the continuous diet of chivalric ideals so warmly received by so many upper- and middle-class Britains [*sic*] during previous decades provided a ready-made incentive and elicited a predictable response to the call to arms.[118]

And he concludes by taking for granted that 'the chivalric code in some way contributed to the English Civil War, the American Civil War, World War I, the rise of fascism in the 1930s, the Falklands War and the [then] current behaviour of South Africa's white minority'![119]

The chivalric ethos can only be regarded as having some responsibility for all these if chivalry is redefined in such a way that it loses its medieval and early-modern meaning. In the context of the American Civil War, as Mark A. Weitz shows in chapter 12, for all the pretensions of White southerners in the United States, their 'chivalry' was very different to that of its models 'and did not survive the rigours of modern war'.[120]

As for twentieth-century conflicts, chivalry was never a nationalist creed and the rise of nation-states arguably helps account for its

---

[117] Dawson (1994), 59, 72, 108–9 at 108, 112. See also Young (1987), 186–88; below, in ch. 12, p. 321; and Paris (1997), 33.

[118] Young (1987), 185–90 at 189.

[119] Ibid., 190. Cf. Dawson (1994), 188, 192 *et passim*.

[120] Below, p. 321.

waning.[121] The millions of ordinary civilians of British and Common-
wealth countries who served in the Great War were inspired to some
extent by quasi-chivalric notions of military and masculine heroism,
expressed in poems such as Rupert Brooke's '1914 Sonnet: I. Peace'
and Herbert Asquith's 'The Volunteer', as well as in the less well-
known but numerous adventure novels and serials that were a sta-
ple of popular culture. But another powerful motivation was the
defence of Britain and its Empire.[122] These were embodied in the
King-Emperor, but while fighting for a person is in keeping with
the chivalric ethos, the troops' loyalty was constructed far more in
terms of the modern nation state, which is not. The mass enlistment
of neighbours and work colleagues of all classes into battalions of
'pals', regardless of what military 'phantasies' animated them, demonstrates the extent to which the role of the soldier was no longer
identified with one social caste, or even with an occupation, but with
the citizen.

This point is even more apparent when one considers the armies
of the Continental republics such as France and Italy. The old nobility commanded, but they had become the members of a military
profession—they were no longer *the* martial class in society. The millions of citizens who fought in the First World War, including my
own grandfather, were not motivated by the values of military professionalism (though they were swiftly asked to accept them), but nor
were they actuated by the values of the aristocratic cult of chivalry.

Moreover, if the mass enlistments in Britain and its former colonies
in 1914–15 owed something to the chivalric ethos, so too did the
treatment of enemy wounded by medics of all European armies and
the extension of courtesies to captured officers. When the German
army, inspired by Fascism, abandoned these conventions on the
Eastern Front in World War II, it was a complete rejection of the
chivalric ethos. Equally, destruction or wholesale slaughter for its
own sake was contrary to chivalric values. Plunder of civilians was
an integral part of chivalric warfare and knights had always targeted
non-combatants, but such actions always had an *economic* purpose.

---

[121] Trim (2002A).
[122] Brooke, in Wiesner, Ruff & Wheeler (2000), II, 308 (Brooke); Asquith, in
Baker (1996), 163–64. See Paris (1997) 32 *et passim*. The willingness of Australians,
New Zealanders and Canadians to fight for the empire had, of course, already been
demonstrated in the Sudanese and Boer Wars.

Further, the laws of war adopted by chivalric societies reflected the ethics of chivalry, striving to protect churches and churchmen, and women—if they were often honoured in the breach rather than the observance, their very existence is telling and those who broke them frequently did face punishment.[123] The use of poison gas or the devastation of Dresden would surely not have been ordered by statesmen or commanders who adhered to the chivalric ethos in its true sense. And for all the superficial similarities between *bushido* and chivalry, the customary granting of 'honours of war' to garrisons by generals imbued with the ethic of chivalry, such as Spínola (to take but one example),[124] stands in sharp contrast to the fate of the garrisons of Singapore and Corregidor.

In short, it is true that the ethos of 'the age of chivalry . . . [was] alike its praise and condemnation"—that chivalry was always, in the words of Sean McGlynn, 'both a force for good . . . [and] a cover for military barbarity.'[125] However, the barbarity was no greater than that for which subsequent ideologies are responsible and the good should not be forgotten. Behind the polished façade of the chivalric ethos to which aristocratic society in medieval and early-modern Europe adhered was much brutality—but the atrocities of the nineteenth and, especially, twentieth centuries were the work of modern, 'enlightened', industrialised, nationalist society, which must bear the reproach for them. The nostalgic yearning within modern, professional armies for the chivalric ethos and its associated values, which at least ameliorated the worst of its excesses, is thus not to be regretted.

Yet, if it is perhaps healthy and humane it is also ultimately pointless. Chivalry was the code, or cult, of a particular culture and society. If the development of a distinct military profession had not eroded it, changes in the economy and society of Europe would still have killed it. The abandonment of quasi-chivalric values by Southerners during the American Civil War owed as much to the difference between the nature of war before and after the Industrial Revolution

---

[123] See, e.g., *L&P Henry 6th*, 17, 23–25, 494. The latter case concerns goods plundered from a bishop; the first two cases concern illegal plundering, including (the second case) a man pardoned because in his brigandage he had *not* forced women or committed acts of unnecessary violence. All indicate the limits of acceptable plundering.

[124] See below, p. 260 and plate 7.

[125] McGlynn (2001), 308, citing W. J. Ashley, *Edward III and His Wars 1327–1360* (London: 1887), n.p.

as to the professionalism of officers on both sides. But the differences between, for example, English military society during the reign of Henry VIII (considered by Luke MacMahon) and the English armies of a century later (examined by Martyn Bennett) are notable. The former had professional aspects, in the adjectival sense; the latter had aspects of a military profession. In conclusion, it seems clear that the development of military professionalism was not erected on an abandonment of the chivalric ethos, but that professionalisation did help to undermine it. In the long run, the values of military professionalism were solvent of those of chivalry.

Bibliography

Adams S. (1988) "A Puritan Crusade? The Composition of the Earl of Leicester's Expedition to the Netherlands, 1585–1586", in *The Dutch in Crisis, 1585–1588. People & Politics in Leicester's Time: Papers of the Annual Symposium of the Sir Thomas Brown Institute, 27 November 1987*, ed. P. Hoftijzer (Leiden: 1988).

——. (1995) "The Patronage of the Crown in Elizabethan Politics: the 1590s in Perspective", in *The Reign of Elizabeth I: Court and Culture in the Last Decade*, ed. J. Guy (Cambridge/Washington: 1995) 20–45.

Anderson, M. (1998) *The Origins of the European State System 1494–1618* (London & New York: 1998).

Anglo S. (1990) "Introduction", to *Chivalry in the Renaissance*, ed. S. Anglo (Woodbridge, Suffolk: 1990).

Baker K. (1996), ed., *The Faber Book of War Poetry* (London: 1996).

Barber R. (1995) *The Knight and Chivalry*, 2nd edn (Woodbridge, Suffolk: 1995).

Billacois, F. (1976) "La crise de la noblesse européene (1550–1650): une mise au point", *Revue d'Histoire Moderne et Contemporaine* 23 (19796) 258–77.

Bitton D. (1969) *The French Nobility in Crisis 1560–1640* (Stanford, Calif.: 1969).

Black J. (2000) *War and the World: Military Power and the Fate of Continents 1450–2000* (New Haven & London: 2000).

Boynton L. (1967) *The Elizabethan Militia, 1558–1638* (London/Toronto: 1967).

Brook L. (1988) "The Notion of Adventure in Guingamor", *Reading Medieval Studies* 14 (1988) 3–16.

Brooks R. (2000) "The Military Renaissance 1500–1650", in *The Times History of War*, ed. R. D. Brooks (London: 2000; St. Helens: 2000) 62–81.

Castiglione B. (1976), *The Book of the Courtier* [1528], trans. George Bull, revised edn (Harmondsworth: 1976).

Corvisier A. (1976) *Armées et sociétés en Europe de 1494 à 1789* (Paris: 1976).

——. (1995) *La Guerre: Essais historiques* (Paris: 1995).

de Crayencour J.-P. (1982) *The Professions in the European Community* (Brussels & Luxembourg: 1982).

Cruickshank, C. (1966) *Elizabeth's Army*, 2nd edn (Oxford: 1966).

Dawson G. (1994) *Soldier Heroes: British Adventure, Empire and the Imagining of Masculinities* (London & New York: 1994).

Digges D. and T. (1604) *Foure Paradoxes, or politique discourses* (London: 1604).

Dop J. (1981) *Eliza's Knights: Soldiers, Poets and Puritans in the Netherlands, 1572–1586* (University of Leiden: 1981).

Durston C. (2001) *Cromwell's Major-Generals: Godly Government during the English Revolution* (Manchester & New York: 2001).

Elton G. (1958) "Introduction", to *New Cambridge Modern History*, II, *The Reformation 1520–1559* (Cambridge: 1958) 1–22.

Feld M. (1975A) "Military Professionalism and the Mass Army", *Armed Forces and Society* 1 (1975), no. 1, 191–214.

——. (1975B) "Middle-Class Society and the Rise of Military Professionalism: The Dutch Army 1589–1609", *Armed Forces and Society* 1 (1975), no. 4, 419–42.

Gates G. (1579) *The Defence of Militarie profession. Wherein is eloquently shewed the due commendation of Martiall prowesse, and plainly prooved how necessary the exercise of Armes is for this our age* (London: 1579).

González de León F. (1996) "Doctors of the Military Discipline: Technical Expertise and the Paradigm of the Spanish Soldier in the Early Modern Period", *Sixteenth Century Journal* 27 (1996) 61–85.

Grandstaff M. (1997) *Foundation of the Force: Air Force Enlisted Personnel Policy, 1907–1956* (Washington, DC: 1997).

——. (2001) "Military Sociology", in *Reader's Guide to Military History*, ed. C. Messenger (London & Chicago: 2001) 363–64.

Hale J. (1983) *Renaissance War Studies* (London: 1983).

——. (1985) *War and Society in Renaissance Europe*, paperback edn (London: 1985).

Harries-Jenkins G. (1975) "The development of professionalism in the Victorian Army", *Armed Forces and Society* 1 (1975) 472–89.

Hattaway M. (1994) "Blood is Their Argument: Men of War and Soldiers in Shakespeare and Others", in *Religion, Culture and Society in Early Modern Britain: Essays in Honour of Patrick Collinson*, ed. A. Fletcher and P. Roberts (Cambridge: 1994) 84–101.

Hexter J. (1950) "The Education of the Aristocracy in the Renaissance", *Journal of Modern History* 22 (1950) 1–20.

Honig J. W. & Herd G. (1996) "A Consideration of a Reconsideration: Jeremy Black's View of 18th-Century Warfare" (unpublished paper).

Howard M. (1976) *War in European History* (Oxford: 1976).

Keegan J. (1993) *A History of Warfare* (London: 1993.)

Keen M. (1984) *Chivalry* (New Haven & London: 1984).

——. (1999) "The Changing Scene: Guns, Gunpowder and Permanent Armies", in *Medieval Warfare: A History*, ed. M. Keen (Oxford & New York: 1999) 273–91.

Király B. (1982) "Society and War From Mounted Knights to the Standing Armies of Absolute Kings: Hungary and the West", in *War and Society in Eastern Central Europe*, III, *From Hunyadi to Rákóczi: War and Society in Late Medieval and Early Modern Hungary*, ed. J. M. Bak and B. K. Király, Brooklyn College Studies on Society in Change, 12, Social Sciences Monographs/Eastern European Monographs 104 (New York: 1982) 23–55.

Lake P. (1989) "Richard Kilby: A Study in Personal and Professional Failure", *Studies in Church History* 26 (1989) 221–35.

McFarlane, K. B. (1973) *The Nobility of Later Medieval England: The Ford Lectures for 1953 and Related Studies*, ed. J. P. Cooper and J. Campbell (Oxford: 1973).

McGlynn S. (2001) "Land Warfare, 1000–1500", in *Reader's Guide to Military History*, ed. C. Messenger (London & Chicago: 2001) 306–9.

Miller A. (1972) "Sir Roger Williams: A Welsh Professional Soldier", *Transactions of the Honourable Society of Cymmrodorion* (1972 for 1971) 86–118.

Motley J. (1879–80) *History of the United Netherlands: From the Death of William the Silent to the Twelve Years Truce 1609*, 3 vols (New York: 1879–1880), vols I and III.

O'Brien K. (2000) "PMCs, Myths and Mercenaries: The Debate on Private Military Companies", *RUSI Journal* 145/1 (Feb. 2000) 59–64.

O'Day R. (1979) *The English Clergy: The Emergence and Consolidation of a Profession 1558–1642* (Leicester: 1979).

———. (1986) "The Professions in Early Modern England", *History Today* (June 1996) 52–55.

Oman C. (1937) *A History of the Art of War in the Sixteenth Century* (London: 1937).

Paris M. (1997) "A Different View of the Trenches: Juvenile Fiction and Popular Perceptions of the First World War, 1914–1939", *War Studies Journal* 3, no. 1 (Winter 1997) 32–46.

Phillips G. (1997) "The Army of Henry VIII: A Reassessment", *Journal of the Society for Army Historical Research* 75 (1997) 8–22.

Plowden A. (2000) *Elizabeth Regina: The Age of Triumph 1588–1603*, rev. edn (Stroud: 2000).

Prest W. (1967) "Legal Education of the Gentry at the Inns of Court, 1560–1640", *Past and Present*, no. 38 (1967) 20–39.

———. (1984) "Why the History of the Professions is Not Written", in *Law, Economy and Society: Essays in the History of English Law 1750–1914*, ed. G. R. Rubin and D. Sugarman (Abingdon: 1984) 300–20.

———. (1987) "Lawyers", in *The Professions in Early Modern England*, ed. W. Prest (London: 1987) 64–89.

Redlich F. (1964) *The German Military Enterpriser and His Work Force*, I (Wiesbaden: 1964).

Rowlands G. (1997) "The Ethos of Blood and Changing Values? Robe, Epee and the French Armies, 1661 to 1715", *Seventeenth Century French Studies* 19 (1997) 95–108.

———. (1999) "Louis XIV, Aristocratic Power and the Elite Units of the French Army", *French History* 13 (1999) 303–331.

Roy I. (1987) "The Profession of Arms", in *The Professions in Early Modern England*, ed. W. Prest (London: 1987) 181–219.

Seddon P. (1975), ed., *Letters of John Holles 1587–1637*, I, Thoroton Society Records Ser. 31 (Nottingham: 1975).

Showalter D. (1993) "Caste, Skill and Training: The Evolution of Cohesion in European Armies from the Middle Ages to the Sixteenth Century", *Journal of Military History* 57 (1993) 407–30.

Skelton W. (1975) "Professionalization in the U.S. Army Officer Corps during the Age of Jackson", *Armed Forces and Society* 1 (1975) 443–71.

Stone, L. (1965), ed., *Social Change and Revolution in England, 1540–1640* (London: 1965).

Storrs C. & Scott H. (1996) "Military Revolution and the European Nobility, c. 1600–1800", *War in History* 3 (1996) 1–41.

Strickland M. (1996) *War and Chivalry: The Conduct and Perception of War in England and Normandy 1066–1217* (Cambridge: 1996).

Thompson I. (1992) "The European Crisis of the 1590s: the Impact of War", in *The European Crisis of the 1590s: Essays in Comparative History*, ed. P. Clark (London: 1985) 261–84; reprinted in I. A. A. Thompson, *War and Society in Habsburg Spain* (Aldershot: 1992) same pagination, as ch. III.

Thornton T. (1998) " 'The Enemy or Stranger, That Shall Invade Their Countrey': Identity and Community in the English North", in *War: Identities in Conflict 1300–2000*, ed. B. Taithe and T. Thornton (Stroud: 1998) 57–70.

Trim D. (2002A) " 'Knights of Christ'? Chivalric Culture in England, c. 1400–c. 1550", in *Cross, Crown and Community: Religion, Government and Culture in Early Modern England, 1400–1800*, ed. P. J. Balderstone and D. J. B. Trim (Oxford, Bern, New York & Frankfurt-am-Main: 2002) 67–102.

———. (2002B) "Fighting 'Jacob's Warres'. The Employment of English and Welsh Mercenaries in the European Wars of Religion: France and the Netherlands 1562–1610", unpublished PhD thesis (University of London: 2002).

———. (2003) "Note: An Early View of Military Professionalism", *Journal of the Society for Army Historical Research* 81 (forthcoming 2003).

Tropp A. (1957) *The School Teachers: The Growth of the Teaching Profession in England and Wales from 1800 to the Present Day* (London: 1957).

Vale M. (1981) *War and Chivalry: Warfare and Aristocratic Culture in England, France and Burgundy at the End of the Middle Ages* (London: 1981).

Warner M. (1998) "Chivalry in Action: Thomas Montague and the War in France, 1417–1428", *Nottingham Medieval Studies* 43 (1998) 146–73.

Webb H. (1965) *Elizabethan Military Science: The Books and the Practice* (Madison, Wis.: 1965).

Weigley R. (1993) *The Age of Battles: The Quest for Decisive Warfare from Breitenfeld to Waterloo* (London: 1993).

Wiesner M., Ruff J. & Wheeler W. (2000) *Discovering the Western Past: A Look at the Evidence*, 4th edn, 2 vols (Boston & New York: 2000).

Young A. (1987) *Tudor and Jacobean Tournaments* (London: 1987; Dobbs Ferry, N.Y.: 1987).

Zwitzer H. (1991) *"De Militie van den Staat": Het leger van de Republiek der Verenigde Nederlanden* (Amsterdam: 1991).

PROLOGUE

WHY CHIVALRY? MILITARY 'PROFESSIONALISM' IN THE TWELFTH CENTURY: THE ORIGINS AND EXPRESSIONS OF A SOCIO-MILITARY ETHOS[1]

Matthew Bennett

In the spring of 1199, Richard I, king of England (also duke of Aquitaine) was energetically suppressing a rebellion amongst his Poitevin vassals. Whilst directing siege operations at the castle of Chalus-Chabrol he received his death-wound from a crossbowman defending the walls.[2] No-one, surely, could deny Coeur de Lion his chivalry, while his killer obviously was a professional soldier, a mere practitioner. This humiliating eclipse of a hero might seem to illustrate the dichotomy between the two ways of conducting war: chivalry—noble and elevating; and soldiering—a grubby trade. There were those amongst his contemporaries who said that Richard got his just desserts. The king had regularly employed crossbowmen, and was proud of his own skill with the weapon, despite its condemnation at the Second Lateran Council (1139).[3] The attempted ban was in keeping with the Church's attempts to restrain secular violence and to try and prevent Christians from killing one another, (although shooting unbelievers was quite acceptable). So this incident—this single shot—helps to show that historical reality is usually far more complicated that it is frequently represented. Chivalry has often been criticised by historians as a hollow code—an ideal not practised in

---

[1] Strickland (1996) must now be the starting point for any investigation in this area. An initial version of this essay was read to the 'Medieval and Early Modern Warfare' seminar at the Department of War Studies, King's College London, October 2000.

[2] Gillingham (1999) provides the best recent account, dismissing claims of Richard's impetuosity and greed in seeking out a hidden treasure, and giving differing accounts of the fate of his slayer pp. 323–31.

[3] The criticism, admittedly, comes from a hostile source: Guillaume le Breton, propagandist for the French king Philip II (1180–1223). See Gillingham (1999), 324; and Strickland (1996), 72, who points out that the clause condemns ordinary bows as well, something which historians have missed in their enthusiasm to consider the supposed novelty of the crossbow.

reality, indeed unrealistic—the idea of a professional military before the sixteenth century appearing almost a contradiction in terms. Yet what I hope to prove is that chivalry was essential to military professionalism at the time of its popularisation in the eleventh and twelfth centuries.[4] Indeed, to contemporaries, it is what the term meant: a legitimate, socially respectable code for warriors, allowing them to perfect their craft within a Christian context. After all, what is required in order for an activity to be considered a profession, and what are the markers which enable us to recognise professionalism today?[5]

First, perhaps, those entering a profession require a vocation. If this is expressed as a desire to kill others, especially within a Christian context, it might seem to be stretching the meaning of the word beyond real value; yet it is perfectly possible to speak of 'the profession of arms' in the modern world. Any profession has certain entry requirements: a combination of skills and ability to provide the wherewithal to carry out the job proficiently, recognised by ceremonial adoption. All professions have a code of behaviour which practitioners are expected to adhere to, and also by which they are judged should they be deemed to fall short in any way. Professionalism demands demonstrable competence, indeed excellence in a given field, enabling 'meritocratic' development. So a profession has a career structure, which might be in the form of an elaborate hierarchy, such as the Church or the Law, or can be a fairly 'flat' organisation like Academe. What matters most of all, though, and brings the real rewards, often financial in kind but also far less concrete in nature, is reputation. To build one is crucial in the estimation of fellow-practitioners and those outside the profession; to lose one is to destroy an individual's very right to be considered professional.

But is this all just playing with words? After all, the word 'professionalism' is a product of the mid-nineteenth century; 'professional' of the late eighteenth century; and 'profession', in its meaning as an occupation only dates to the late sixteenth century.[6] It is a young term, in an historical sense, so how can it be properly applied to

---

[4] I use the word 'popularisation' advisedly. Chivalric *mores* are identifiable in Carolingian high society two centuries earlier. See below.

[5] See the introduction, above, p. 6.

[6] See *OED*, *s.v.* 'profession'. The word does occur in the 13th century, but as a declaration, promise or vow made when entering a religious order. In the sense of 'The occupation which one professes to be skilled in and to follow' (and similar meanings) the earliest use cited is 1541, in referring to the medical profession. The

societies at the turn of the first millennium? Also, it is not without its ambiguities. A professional attitude might be praised; but if someone is simply professional in their approach, it can suggest a certain coldness or lack of humanity to others; while a 'professional foul', for example, is not seen as behaviour which adds lustre to a sportsman's reputation. In military-history terms, professionalism is usually viewed as a post-medieval development. It is associated with the recovery of classical military texts during the Renaissance, and essentially seen as a seventeenth century phenomenon (although with some earlier antecedents).[7] The creation of professional armies is not usually traced back beyond the last quarter of the seventeenth century. British Army regiments, for example, mostly have traditions dating back to the 1680s (although some claim earlier, mistier formations in the mid-century civil wars or the Restoration of 1660); and the army of Louis XIV—the terror of Europe—dates from the same period.

So how is it that I can claim that military professionalism is evident in the twelfth century, and how is it attached to chivalry? After all, most historians, when considering the period refer to mercenaries as professional troops. In one sense, this is fair enough; men who were paid wages are by one meaning of the word, professionals. But the danger is when 'professional' is used as a derogatory term for non-noble fighters and then used, openly or implicitly as a contrast with warriors who were serving by obligation, and so, it is assumed, had some form of higher motivation than those receiving filthy lucre. Medieval historians have understood for a very long time, however, at least dating back to a seminal article by John Prestwich (1981), that money was the sinews of war as much as in any other era of history.[8] In fact, I wish to argue that, by the standards of the age, mercenaries were often not professional—they were the very opposite—and it was when they failed to live up to professional attitudes

---

earliest use for 'Any calling or occupation by which a person habitually earns his living' is the 1570s.

[7] This comment is not intended to ignore the development of more permanent, 'standing armies' of fifteenth century France or Burgundy, nor the international military machine of Spain in the sixteenth century (e.g. the Spanish Road), rather to point out how the development of 'professional forces' are viewed today. Anyway, from a longer perspective, the former bodies resemble nothing more than 'household troops' assembled for centuries earlier, and the latter, the normal arrangements for any large land empire.

[8] Prestwich (1981), reprinted in Strickland (1992), 93–127.

that they drew opprobrium (as indeed did proper professionals when they also let themselves down).[9] And who were the mercenaries? In England, for example, it is fair to say that almost all troops who served on royal campaigns of more than a few weeks' duration received pay. The point of the 40 days' service owed by military tenants is that this was their obligation *at their own expense*. Any ruler or lesser lord who wished to conduct operations for longer expected to pay for the extended service. Not that pay was always forthcoming, of course, much depending upon the outcome of the fighting. A good example from the Conqueror's reign, which explores the complications of the relationship between the king and his troops, is the six-month campaign William conducted in 1069–70, including the scorched earth operations known as 'The Harrying of the North'. After holding his Christmas court at York, William led his men across the Pennines in mid-winter, to punish the 'many lawless acts of ... the Welsh and the men of Chester'.[10] According to his chaplain, the king faced a mutiny from his non-Norman followers, who complained about the bitter conditions and his relentless pursuit of his enemies. These men, described as coming from 'Anjou, Maine and Brittany', sought to be discharged from their obligations to serve. When the royal host eventually returned south in April 1070, William disbanded his forces at Salisbury.

> He distributed lavish rewards to the soldiers for all that they had endured, praised those who had shown prowess, and discharged them with warm thanks. But in his anger he kept back those who had wished to desert him for forty days after the departure of their comrades.[11]

Because these men are specifically described as coming from outside the duchy of Normandy, this suggests that their obligation to William was determined not by 'feudal obligation' but by cash payment. Yet the fit punishment was deemed to be the fulfilment of a vassal's obligation to serve at his own expense. While it is possible that these non-Norman troops had sworn an oath of fealty to William for the

---

[9] Conversely, when men described as serving for pay alone behaved well within the conventions of the age they were praised by contemporaries for their professional zeal. See Bennett (2000) 96–113.

[10] Orderic Vitalis (1969–80), IV, 234.

[11] Ibid., 236. King William's chaplain William of Poitiers wrote the *Gesta Guillelmi*, the last section of which is lost, but was used by Orderic in his description of the latter stages of the Conquest.

duration of the campaign, the story does show just how complex the situation was in regard of military service: there was no simple divide between the 'feudal host' and 'mercenary bands'.

There is also the issue of what kinds of soldiers are being described. In military-historical shorthand, medieval armies are often considered to be composed of 'knights'. That is to say men capable of providing themselves with a full set of equipment. In the eleventh and twelfth centuries this meant a long mail shirt or hauberk,[12] helmet and shield, lance and sword, together with at least one horse, but probably more to spare the charger (*destrier*) on the march and also provide mounts for an accompanying squire and servants.[13] These were then, the *equites*, distinguished from *pedites* or foot-sloggers that were probably in the majority in most forces.[14] Both horse and foot could be known by the generic name of *milites*, which in Classical Latin meant soldiers. Historians have made the term *miles* carry a great deal more significance, though. It has been consistently identified as meaning the same as French *chevalier*, so giving the word the connotation of a social rank. While this is not entirely wrong, it has led to much confusion. For in the narrative sources of the period *milites* is used to mean both knights and soldiers in general, depending upon context.

Historians have not always been sensitive to the distinction, and indeed sometimes it is invisible to us today. Clearly, social status is crucial in defining an élite and scholars of the last fifty years or so were certain that they had identified one. Building on the seminal work of Marc Bloch, French historians in particular have postulated the rise of the term *miles* from meaning simple soldier to that describing members of a military élite: the knight. The leader in this movement was Georges Duby, whose research into the charters of the Maconnais seemed to show that *c.* 1000–1030 the term took on a new significance in witness lists. This he ascribed to the breakdown of royal authority in France and the increasing need for lesser rulers:

---

[12] Hence the description *fief del haubert/feudum loricae* for estates held in return for military service.

[13] See Strickland (1996), 169; also Bennett (1989), 7–19 (repr. as appendix to Upton-Ward (1992), 175–88 and Bennett (1986), 1–11.

[14] Much depended upon the make-up of a force and what it was intended to do, of course. Mounted men were more valuable for raiding, infantry indispensable in sieges.

dukes, counts and castellans to surround themselves with military households. Duby (and others) ascribed this to a social and political crisis taking place around AD 1000: *'La mutation de l'an mille'* (also known in English as the 'Feudal Revolution'). His pupils produced regional studies from all over France, proving, more or less, (although with some variations) that this change had taken place everywhere and brought into being a new social class of *milites* = knights. This was then seen as an important factor in the creation of chivalry, which provided the knights with a justifying ideology.

Duby's methodology and analysis held sway for the half-a-century preceding the second millennium, but it was not without its detractors, and may have recently received its death-blow.[15] There was always the problem of England which, though a pretty well-documented place by the standards of the period in question, seemed to show different features of military obligation. This became tied in with the study of the 'Norman Conquest' by which English historians such as F. M. Stenton sought to show that 'feudalism' on the French model was introduced into England in 1066.[16] Other English historians, notably Eric John and latterly John Gillingham have been critical of this approach.[17] For Gillingham, the change was not so much in social structures, rather in manners. He can see little difference between the military obligations of pre-Conquest thegns and post-Conquest chevaliers. What he has identified, in series of articles over the last decade, is a change in military *mores*, what he calls the introduction of chivalry into England.[18] You could say, according to this analysis, that it was not the social status of the warriors that became more elevated, rather their ideals. There is a lot to like about this interpretation, and it finds parallels in the work of the French scholar, Dominique Bartélemy. He has criticised the whole idea of a social revolution around the millennium, leading to a militarisation of society and the rise of a new class. 'Strange revolution where the ruling elites hold onto power and bind to themselves a powerful subordinate class' (he quotes an English Marxist

---

[15] See Bloch (1962); Duby (1971). Barthélemy (1997) largely dismantles Duby's edifice—for a briefer and witty dissection, see Barthélemy (2001), 214–28.

[16] Stenton (1961).

[17] John, (1960), 145–48; Gillingham (1995), 129–53.

[18] Gillingham (1994), 31–55.

historian with approval).[19] While scholars of the Duby school had sought to stress that *miles* = *nobilis* (knight = noble) in the supposed rise of the warrior class, he points out that being military had always been an attribute of nobility. Yet in the words of my old tutor, R. Allen Brown: 'If all great men were knights this did not mean that all knights were great men.' Also, in just a few pages, Bartélemy calmly dismembers a generation of scholarship by showing that the charters of eleventh century France, region by region, show the same features as the supposedly pre-revolutionary materials.[20] He is dismissive of *l'ancien école*, 'the old school' as he calls it, and points how much it owes to the work of nineteenth century scholars who were keen to find nobility in family genealogies and to re-create sense of social hierarchy in genuinely post-revolutionary France. So the rise of the *miles* is no longer an acceptable thesis in the origins of chivalry. What does that leave us with?

In 1984, Maurice Keen's book, *Chivalry*, seemed to me then to say all that needed to be said.[21] He accepted the then orthodoxy of the rise of the *miles*; but his impressive book is not reduced by recent modifications in this view. One might indeed ask if the revision matters at all, since clearly a *chevalier* needed a horse and arms to be chivalric and these were costly items only available to the relatively wealthy. But it is worth bearing in mind that not all *milites* found in the sources are knights, and if their identification is uncertain, their behaviour should not be used to criticise chivalry itself. After all, they may not have signed up to the obligations of the code. And how did men join the chivalric élite? The ceremony of dubbing is well known, of course. In even its earliest form it involved the belting on a sword as a symbol of military manhood. And its earliest form long precedes period under discussion today. In the same year as Keen's book came out, Karl Leyser explored the Carolingian origins of knighthood. As far back as the first decades of the ninth century there are references to importance of the military belt so that 'the terms *miliciae cingulum, cingulum militare* stand for the sum total of the warrior's profession'.[22] The belt was given up on entering into a monastery (a common retirement home for the military

---

[19] Barthélemy (1997), 224, citing Chris Wickham, without direct reference.
[20] Ibid., 287–96.
[21] Keen (1984).
[22] Leyser (1994), 549–66 (quotation at 555).

aristocracy) or could taken away for criminal or dishonourable acts
(under the direction of Canon Law). Interestingly, though, the word
dubbing comes from the secular, vernacular world. French *adouber /
adoubement* means simply to equip someone, so, as Jean Flori has
pointed out, not every reference to dubbing means ceremonial initiation into knighthood.[23] But it did mean that also, and it is in the
Anglo-Saxon Chronicle that the first use of the word appears when
William the Conqueror dubbed his youngest son in 1086 (*dubbade . . .
to riddare*).[24] The ceremony seems very like those of the Carolingian
period where princes were accepted into the adult military community, as William himself had been nearly fifty years earlier, allegedly
at the hands of the king of France. The role of the Church is not
very evident, just a decade before the First Crusade, although there
were moves afoot to remedy that. Certainly, by the beginning of the
thirteenth century Christian imagery dominated the literary texts concerned with knighthood, although the majority of knightings were
still in a secular setting. But this brings us on to another area of
investigation into the professionalism of chivalry. Perhaps the most
important factor for any profession must be widespread recognition
of its legitimacy; because violence is generally regarded as illegitimate in a Christian community, something had to happen to change
that view.

It was Georges Duby (again) who, in his book *The Three Orders:
Feudal Society Imagined*, developed the idea of the rise of the *milites* in
social respectability.[25] The idea was not new in the eleventh century, but Duby pointed to several commentators who he believed
were important in this development. These churchmen identified *ora-
tores* the monks and priests as the most important, standing above
the orders of the warriors (*bellatores*) and peasants (*laboratores*). In the
late tenth century, bishops in southern France were organising public oath-swearings to try and limit violence. This produced a social
formula known as the Truce or Peace of God, which sought to
reduce the damage done widespread warfare and brigandry.
Ecclesiastical in inspiration, it was soon taken up and promulgated

---

[23] Flori (1976), 915–40. Flori has written so copiously on chivalric matters, with
five books and four-score articles published by 1998, that citation is difficult: Flori
(1998) contains his full bibliography.
[24] *Anglo-Saxon Chronicle* version 'E', cited in Gillingham (1994).
[25] Duby (1980).

by secular authorities. In the 1020s, most of the 'princes' of France were calling assemblies to announce the instigation of controls over violence. The Truce of God was intended to limit warlike activity to certain days of the week (essentially only Tuesday through Thursday was permissible) while the Peace of God sought to protect the vulnerable members of the community from harassment by *milites*. These groups included the religious and clerical population, but also women and children (especially those without male protectors), the humble peasantry upon whose industry everyone else depended, and the merchants who needed to travel the roads unmolested if trade was to flourish.[26] The problem was that these injunctions cut across customary rights to what can be called 'private violence': in other words, the tendency for those who possessed the tools of violence to utilise them in disputes over inheritance, land, property, rights or dynastic alliances. This tendency has been identified as 'feud' (and more tendentiously, as 'blood feud').[27] Whatever the technicalities of this debate, it is certain that the reforming Church of the mid-eleventh century onwards was intent upon bringing the violent elements of the Christian community (as the popes conceived it) under some form of control.

More than that, pontiffs from Leo IX (1049–54) onwards sought to provide the *bellatores* with some kind of direction. Leo's successor gave that great land-grabber, Robert d'Hauteville 'Guiscard', a papal banner in recognition of the Norman's protection (in the racket sense) of papal rights in central Italy (1059). Just a few years later Alexander II provided another banner to legitimise William the Bastard's invasion of England. In 1073, Cardinal Hildebrand, the greatest engine of the papal reform movement, became pope as Gregory VII. He envisaged a *militia sancti Petri* which would serve the papacy's interest and provide a sword arm to the pope's spiritual authority. Of course, the individual who was supposed to do this was the Western Emperor, who for over a century now had been the king of Germany, and took on his responsibility whenever he could manage to bring his court and attendant military support south of the Alps to receive coronation in Rome. The tragedy of Gregory VII's pontificate was that he found himself in conflict with his secular other-half and died in exile a dozen years later; but the civil war which the dispute

---

[26] Head & Landes (1992).
[27] See Bennett, (1996), 126–40.

engendered in Germany flared up on-and-off for half a century. It was the pontificate of Urban II which saw a great leap forward in ecclesiastical direction of warfare and indeed in the Christianising of violence. Urban's background was French and aristocratic. He had been a monk at Cluny, the richest and most influential monastery In Latin Christendom at the time, and he well understood the motivation of the Frankish *bellatores*, whom the Church wished to direct. In an open-air sermon at Clermont in November 1095, possibly by design, but more likely by accident, he initiated the trans-continental military pilgrimage for the recovery of the Holy City of Jerusalem, which became known as the First Crusade.

The theoretical justification for the use of war in a spiritual cause took well into the thirteenth century to work out, but what Christian warriors of the turn of the twelfth century understood was that their previously derogated 'profession of arms' was now as sure a path to Heaven as that of the non-violent religious as long as it was employed in a suitable cause. St Anselm of Lucca provided the theological justification for this move and it was widely celebrated, most famously in the remark of Guibert de Nogent: 'In our own time God has instituted a Holy War, so that the order of knights . . . may find a new way of gaining salvation . . . in their normal costume, and in the discharge of their own office, and no longer need to be drawn to seek salvation by utterly renouncing the world in the profession of the monk.'[28] In his essay '*Equestris Ordo*: chivalry as a vocation in the twelfth century', Colin Morris has pointed out that other turn of the twelfth century texts chose the word 'ordained' for knights entering into their profession. Furthermore, the eminent social commentator John of Salisbury considered courtesy next to godliness![29] Good manners and virtuous behaviour were what was expected of professional warriors. Not all could live up to these standards, of course. St Bernard of Clairvaux famously punned that the warriors of his day were not *militia* (warriors) but *malitia* (a social evil): so he pushed the idea further—the armed monks of the Military Orders.

In the most perceptive recent account of the motivation of crusaders, Marcus Bull describes the importance of a group which he names 'arms bearers', in the success of the First Crusade.[30] I intro-

---

[28] Quoted by Keen (1984), 48–49.
[29] Morris (1978), 87–96.
[30] Bull (1993).

duce the term at this point because it is particularly relevant. It both reduces the terminological confusion surrounding the word knight and suggests another development—that of heraldry. For it was in the early twelfth century that this system of individual differentiation emerged. Despite the plethora of decorations on the shields of the warriors shown in the Bayeux Tapestry (*c.* 1077) these are not heraldic. The Citeaux Bible of the first decade of the twelfth century shows the beginning of some sort of recognisable system. By the 1130s an illustration in the 'Chronicle of John of Worcester' has shields bearing chevrons and bars. Two aristocratic seals display arms which became hereditary: Waleran, earl of Worcester's *checky* (*c.* 1139) and Richard, earl of Hertford's *chevronny* (*c.* 1146). The enamel funerary plaque of Geoffrey le Bel, which may date to his death in 1152, shows *azure six lions rampant or*, and (something which does not seem to have been much noticed) his cloak is lined *vair* suggesting that heraldic rules were being applied by this period.[31]

The crucial decade for the adoption of heraldry seems to have been the 1130s, and this not by accident. Despite all the problems of not being recognised in warfare, and especially on the battlefield (epitomised by William needing to raise his helmet to shows his soldiers that he was unharmed during the fighting at Hastings), even rulers did not possess personal arms before then.[32] The stimulus was probably new form of entertainment known as the tournament. I choose the word entertainment advisedly, because there had always been some kind of military games practised by warriors, and Nithard describes such manoeuvres taking place in front of the Carolingian emperor, Louis the Pious; but twelfth-century tournaments seem to have been different. Although the first references to tournaments date to the 1060s, the real tourneying fever does not seem to have taken off until the 1120s. Jousting is described as taking place between the young knights of opposing forces during siege operations at Wurzburg, in 1127, outside Lincoln and Winchester in 1141, and many other places.[33] Of course, there was nothing new in that kind of skirmishing, but the 1130s did see the creation of an ideal of courtly

---

[31] Ailes (1982). Geoffrey's son Henry II Plantagenet probably used two or three lions similarly coloured, while Richard I may have been the first king to use what became the royal coat of arms: *gules three lions regardant passant or*.

[32] Wilson (1985), plate 68, and many other representations.

[33] Barber & Barker (1989).

tourneying expressed, for example, in Geoffrey of Monmouth's historical fantasy about King Arthur's Camelot. William of Malmesbury ascribes the flight of Stephen's right wing at the battle of Lincoln (1141) which led to the king's capture, to his men being prepared for the joust only to find their opponent, lords made bitter by loss of their lands ('The Disinherited') out for blood.[34]

I suspect that the monk of Malmesbury enjoyed the discomfiture of the royalists (especially as he supported the other side), which may have led him to misrepresent the value of jousting as a military skill. For, twelfth-century tournaments were far from restrained occasions, in which singleton combatants jousted across a barrier. Rather they were like real warfare. Around 1200, Roger of Hoveden wrote: 'He who has seen his blood flowing, who has felt his teeth cracking under an opponent's blow, who has lain on the ground with his enemy over him, and still not lost his courage; he who has been thrown to the ground time after time, only the more staunchly to stand up again—he may go into battle with high hopes.'[35] In 'a society organised for war', as more than one commentator has described it, political leaders played a real role in war, putting themselves at risk in both the front line of battle.[36] Clearly, they had to be able to manage horse and arms competently. Indeed, if they excelled in these warrior arts then they could win the hearts of their followers and achieve political goals through military display. A paragon of chivalry (in the true meaning of the word) like Richard the Lionheart, was justly famous for his personal exploits. Where were these skills learned?

It hardly needs repeating that anyone with expectations of a military career learnt to ride early: 'You may make a horseman of a boy before the age of seven; after that never'. Yet all who could afford to rode. In addition, the warrior had to learn to handle horse and arms—no mean feat. The need to carry the shield in the left hand and the lance or sword in the right meant that the reins had be held long, which must have reduced their influence on the horse's head. Indeed, contemporary epic poetry describes the reins being let

---

[34] William of Malmesbury (1998), 84–85.

[35] Roger of Hoveden (1867B), II, 207. The occasion is the knighting of Geoffrey, younger brother of Richard the Lionheart, who, ironically, was killed in a tournament at Paris aged only 28.

[36] This is not to be seduced by chivalric myth into forgetting that more fighting took place in disease-ridden siege lines than in open battle.

go all together. The medieval style of riding long (with a straight leg) further reduced the rider's ability to steer his mount with the normal riding 'aids'. (This may explain the severe bits and sharp spurs favoured by knights.) So any mounted warrior already possessed consummate skill.

Current orthodoxy is that the Franks developed a new lance technique in the mid-eleventh century. Holding the lance rigid under the arm, rather than using it two-handed or above the head, effectively made the mounted warrior into a projectile, carried forward by his horse. There is a well-known quote from Anna Komnene, a Byzantine princess writing in the 1140s, to effect that a 'mounted Frank would bore his way through the walls of Babylon'. Certainly her father feared the Frankish charge and instructed his Turkish horse-archers to shoot down their horses: 'for a Frank on foot . . . becomes nature's plaything' adds Anna.[37] It was not quite as simple as that, and some historians believe that the 'couched lance' was not introduced until a century later.[38] But I am happy to stick with D. J. A. Ross's interpretation of the introduction of the new technique c. 1060, represented visually in the Bayeux Tapestry and verbally in the phrase '*pleine sa hanste*'.[39] This is found in the *Chanson de Roland* and other *chansons de geste* (these 'songs of deeds' were very military-orientated epic poems). The phrase means a thrust that hurls the opponent out of his saddle and back over the tail of his horse a full lance's length away. The phrase is both evocative and an accurate description of the blow, as I shall show later. It may not coincidental that the first reference to a tournament—in 1062 and 1066—occur at just the moment which Ross identifies.

How important was the couched lance in war? In their book on the tournament, Richard Barber and Juliet Barker say that it was 'largely responsible for the Frankish conquests in the Mediterranean and Crusades . . .'.[40] This may be to overstate the case (as I shall explain later) although the emphasis is perfectly understandable in the context of their work. Obviously how the lance was handled was

---

[37] Anna Komnene (1969), 415–16. It is worth noting that the Byzantines had a long tradition of describing the impetuosity of 'the fair-haired races', as they called the westerners.
[38] See Cirlot (1985).
[39] Ross (1951), 1–10.
[40] Barber & Barker (1989), 14.

only of significance in actual combat, although I do not underesti-
mate the fear of the lance as a factor in determining both the strategy and tactics of opponents who lacked the technique. There seems
little doubt that it was adopted by Islamic warriors, who engaged in
lance attacks (that is if they had not thought of it in the first place!)
by the 1140s.[41] For it is in the *Memoirs* of Usahmah ibn Munkhid,
from Shaizar in northern Syria that we find the best description of
how the lance should be held: 'This is my opinion: it is indispensable for anyone who wants to give a blow with a lance to press his
hand and his fore-arm against his side on the lance, and let his
horse guide itself as best it can at the moment which he strikes. For
if a man moves his hand or his lance, or bends his hand to guide
his lance, the blow leaves no trace and does no damage.'[42] Usahmah's
tales are full of great lance blows and their effects. In his very first
encounter: 'At the head of the Franks appeared a knight who had
thrown down his coat of mail, unburdening himself in order to be
able to overtake us. I hurled myself on him and struck him full in
the chest. His body fell a good way from his saddle.'[43] Later he
jousts with heavily armoured-knight: 'I hurled myself on the knight,
struck him, and my lance pierced his body, coming in front almost
a cubit in length. The lightness of my body, the violence of the blow
and the speed of my horse tumbled me out of my saddle. I got into
it again, flourished my lance, quite convinced that I had killed the
Frank, and collected my comrades.'[44] Usahmah exemplifies the dramatic nature of lance wounds from the case of one of his own men
who had been attacked by a Frank: 'He had three great gashes on
either side, not to mention his elbow which had been struck and
lopped-off by the cut of the blade, as the butcher joints his meat.
The man died at once.'[45]

Usahmah's stories help to support some of the seemingly exaggerated scenes found in the *chansons de geste* and other western vernacular works describing knights fighting. From the *Roland* comes an
epic blow by Oliver: 'He smashes his shield and tears his hauberk,
plunges the streamers of his banner into his chest and hurls him

---

[41] Nicolle (1996), II, 158, 251.
[42] Ousama (1929), 54.
[43] Ibid., 52.
[44] Ibid., 52–53.
[45] Ibid., 63.

dead from the saddle a lance's length.'[46] Lest this be thought poetic exaggeration, it can be matched by Fulcher of Chartres' eyewitness description of King Baldwin I of Jerusalem in battle at Ramla in 1101: 'Brandishing his lance, from which flew the white banner . . . he ran through an Arab opposite him. The flag remained in the Arab's belly when he was knocked to the ground from his horse. But Baldwin pulled out his lance as I, standing near, witnessed, and he at once carried it ready to slay others.'[47]

It is worth mentioning a special technique at this point known as the *tor Franceis*—the French turn. This meant that a rider could swing his horse around after delivering a charge in order to return to the banner which waved above his unit, either to rally or to deliver another attack. Clearly this could have been practised while jousting across a barrier; but it must have been even more important in the open field, whether tourneying or in war. Curiously, the best reference I have to this technique is from a humorous setting. The hero Rainouart, who figures in the Guillaume d'Orange cycle, begins his career as a kitchen boy, because he is a captured Saracen. Only later does his noble ancestry emerge. He is a burlesque character, gigantic in stature, and, because he is a menial, he is at first unused to knightly weapons. His main fighting tool is a *tinel*, a huge club with which he brains his opponents. His use of the *tor Franceis* allows him to charge at a knightly opponent, avoiding his lance and then swing around behind him, catching him on the back of his head with his club, so knocking him to the ground.[48] So, clearly, to a military audience the technical skills of the lance attack did matter.

Apparently the chivalrous sons of Henry II were: 'all of the same mind, that is, to be superior to others in the use of weapons, and they knew that one would not have the essential skills when they were needed unless they were practised in advance.'[49] And indeed: 'The famous King Richard, observing that extra training and instruction of the French made them correspondingly fiercer in war, wished that the knights of his kingdom should train in their own lands, so

---

[46] 'Song of Roland' (1978), ll. 1227–29 (my translation). See also 'Song of Roland' (1990).

[47] Fulcher of Chartres (1969), 158.

[48] *Chanson de Guillaume* (1949–50), I, ll. 3268–72. See also *Girart de Vienne* (1930), ll. 2352 and 2383 for a less explicit use of the turn by the knightly Renier.

[49] Roger of Hoveden (1867A), II, 166–67.

that they could learn from tourneying the art and custom of war and so that the French could not insult the English knights for being crude and less skilled.'[50] For on his return from crusade in 1194, Richard the Lionheart established five tourneying areas around England.[51] This had the additional purpose of raising money for the Exchequer since knights who wished to tourney there were required to purchase a license—on a sliding scale from two marks to a landless knights up to twenty marks for an earl. (Men who had failed to acquire these licenses could also be fined later.) All participants had to be already knighted, although some young men might be dubbed only on the eve of a tournament. This seems to have been what happened at the celebrations for the wedding between Geoffrey of Anjou and the Empress Mathilda in 1127, when Count Fulk of Anjou requested that Henry I knight his son in order that he could take part. One of the most influential modern military historians of the medieval period, J. F. Verbruggen, cites the introduction of tournaments into England by Richard I as producing victories over the French at Fréteval in 1194 and Gisors in 1198. The English who had formerly felt themselves to be inferior in arms now did not hesitate to attack '40 French knights with only 30 of their own'.[52]

But in concentrating on the English experience I have got ahead of myself rather. For the sons of Henry II were only learning from the French tradition, as the last quotation indicates. A common term for tournament in the twelfth century was *conflictus Gallicus*, and it was in northern France in the 1170s and 1180s when the sport really took off. Certainly it had been popular at feasts and special occasions from the 1130s onwards, as Geoffrey of Monmouth's fantasy of the court of King Arthur bears witness; but in the last quarter of the twelfth century, we see the emergence of a kind of tournament circuit such as Richard I was imitating in England. Our best source for this is *L'Histoire de Guillaume le Maréchal*, a long poem about the life and deeds of William Marshal (1147–1219) composed in the late 1220s from the reminiscences of his squire, John de Early.[53]

---

[50] Barber & Barker (1989), 25.
[51] Ibid. The locations were established between: Salisbury and Wilton, Wiltshire; Warwick and Kenilworth, Warwickshire; Stamford and Warinford, Suffolk; Brackley and Mixbury, Northamptonshire; and Blyth and Tickhill, Nottinghamshire, providing a fair spread across England.
[52] Verbruggen (1997), 30–36. Also Verbruggen (1947), 161–80.
[53] *Guillaume le Maréchal* (1891–1901). An English translation of this valuable text

It is generally accepted that *Guillaume le Maréchal* provides the best insights into what tournaments were like at the end of the twelfth century and what lessons knights were meant to take away from them. Although, as Larry D. Benson has pointed out, the poem owes much to the works of Chrétien de Troyes—the Marshal's deeds are viewed through the glass of romance—it still describes a kind of war-fare.[54] Remember that the tournaments were fought *between* two places. The English sites were some three to five miles apart, as seem to be the villages in the *Guillaume le Maréchal*. The significance of this distance is that it allowed the participating troops of knights to manoeuvre across the terrain and use it to advantage for cover or ambush. The *mêlées* were very different from the formalised jousts of the later Middle Ages; they were effectively fought just like war. Even the weapons do not seem to have been blunted. Also, foot-men accompanied the knights, armed with spears and bows. It may be that their role was mainly to defend the inviolate bases (*reçets*) and to pick up the prisoners, for their weapons would have been deadly to the knights' horses and spoilt the main aim of the game. Yet, Philip of Flanders apparently encouraged his footmen to hook knights of their horses with their polearms. At a tournament in 1170, Baldwin of Hainault's knights got drawn into a bloody encounter with Geoffrey of Louvain's men; and fearing treachery in 1175, Baldwin took 200 knights and 1,200 footmen to the tournament of Lagni-sur-Marne. This is matched in Chrétien's *La Conte du Graal* where Count Thiebaut only accepts a challenge to a tournament only after being assured that he has enough archers and knights to protect his town.[55]

Despite these real dangers, the main aim was still the capture of opponents who were then ransomed for the cost of their horse and arms. We know how profitable this was from William Marshal's experience. He teamed-up with a companion, Roger de Gaugi, in the late 1170s. At the height of the season in autumn there were fortnightly tournaments. No wonder that in two years the pair took over one hundred knights' horses and equipment.[56] *Guillaume le Maréchal*

---

has long been in preparation; but has yet to appear. See Crouch (1990), for the best biography of the Marshal.

[54] Benson (1980), 1–24.
[55] Ibid., 5, 13.
[56] Ibid., 12.

is full of funny stories about how William collected his spoils. These
were told around the fire, with much drinking, in the evenings after
the games. As an insight into male military culture the source can
hardly be bettered.

But *Guillaume le Maréchal* goes further than describing the deeds of
the jousters; it also tells us about the tactical use of knightly cavalry.
J. F. Verbruggen has explained how knights were used to acting in
concert in small groups, in tens, twenties and thirties. These troops
were known as *conrois* (rather confusingly also the term for the main
battleline, on occasion).[57] They were made up of the household, local
and kin groupings, presumably people who knew one another well.
At tournaments, troops followed great men, such as Henry the Young
King or Philip, count of Flanders, and these leaders competed against
one another. Knights drew up behind their regional banners: England,
Normandy, Flanders, Artois, Champagne, Anjou and so on. The
essential divide in the late twelfth century was between the Angevins
and the Capetians, with their respective supporters.

Guillaume le Maréchal provides us with the best information as to
how the units manoeuvred. Maintaining good order and close formation are identified as essential for success in tournaments. The
first one described in the source, which took place between Gournai
and Ressons (in eastern Normandy) contrasts the good order which
the Young King's troop kept with the vainglorious disorder of their
opponents. Given that the knights worked in teams to unhorse and
capture individuals, this was clearly facilitated by keeping together.

> The [Young King's] line which rode out
> Kept serried ranks in battle formation,
> Against opponents who fell into disorder
> Through their pride, because of their numbers.
> Of the many who rode out in front of their lists,
> None jousted lightly,
> None began without the intention,
> Of capturing another if he could.
> But too many rode in great disorder,
> Upon the troops of the Young King (Henry);
> [Who] received them manfully,
> Intending to turn them in flight.
> There one could see men heartily brained
> By the blows of maces and swords

---

[57] Verbruggen (1997), 35–36.

Among the heads and arms [waving],
But those who had come on so vainly;
Turned about discouraged;
Unable to keep themselves together
They all ran away from the weapons
Flying in so disorganised a manner
That none was able to support another
In no part of [the field] wherever they went.[58]

The tournament gathered together
Many men of good appearance
Who knew well how to handle arms
And the best techniques to use.
The French came on in great disorder
Violently they sought the encounter.
And when the [Young] King's men saw them
They loosed their reins before moving off,
Then charged, and in their assault,
Met them so fiercely,
That they pierced and broke [through their opponents],
So that none of them could keep together.
When the [Young] King's units advanced
[The French] were already turned in flight;
As many pursued as fled;
Then they rallied in many places:
Those that fled as well as those that pursued,
So great was the defeat.[59]

The same was true in war. At the battle of Brémule in 1119, the impetuous charge of the French under their king, Louis VI, led to his defeat by his rival king Henry I of England. Similarly, the rebel Waleran of Meulan charged recklessly in a skirmish at Bourgthéroulde in 1124. (Admittedly these defeats were against dismounted opposition.) On both occasions, though, the disorder was put down to the pride of the attackers, proverbial for the French, and due to snobbery on the part of Waleran, who thought too little of the garrison troops who opposed him.[60]

Guillaume le Maréchal also cites the cunning ploy of Philip, count of Flanders, who withheld his knights from the mêlée and only committed them after he saw that all the other troops were in total disorder. By so doing he cleaned-up and gained many ransoms.

---

[58] *Guillaume le Maréchal* (1891–1901), 92, ll. 2497–2518 (my translation).
[59] Ibid., 102–3, ll. 2797–2815 (my translation).
[60] See Bradbury (1985), 46–50 for an analysis of these battles.

> The count of Flanders held back
> Not joining the tournament
> Until everyone was exhausted
> Disordered in the mêlée.
> When he saw the opportunity,
> Being an experienced warrior
> He launched a flank attack.
> Then was many a saddle emptied,
> And many a knight overthrown,
> All injured and cast down.
> Many were captured and many ransomed,
> By whoever got there first,
> Those leading the squadrons' charge.
> It is madness to allow men to fall into total disorder.[61]

It should be remembered that it was axiomatic in cavalry encounters, and would later be enshrined in the drill manuals of the seventeenth century and onwards, that whoever committed the last squadron had the best chance of victory. It also is noticeable that Philip's tactics included a flanking manoeuvre. This had provided victory at Tinchebrai over his brother Robert, for Henry I of England in 1106, and many other occasions.[62] Yet this could only be achieved by a disciplined force, following the banner of its leader (just like a later cavalry regiment).

The only detailed evidence we have for how mounted knights were deployed in war comes from the Old French *Rule of the Temple*. According to this each 'Commander of Ten' carried a banner, as did the Marshal when leading a charge. It was the Templars' duty to keep close to their banners and to rally on them after a charge, whether in defeat or victory. In the secular world, the banneret, leading some 50 to 100 men, presumably had the same role. One thing absent from the Templar Rule, which is otherwise so explicit about military activity, is any mention of training manoeuvres for the Knights Brothers when moving *en eschielles* (in squadrons). Indeed, they were forbidden even to engage in the *béhourd* without the Master's special permission.[63] This was a much safer form of joust, with light lances and padded jackets, and often became little more than a shoving match on horseback. Despite one famous casualty outside Dover

---

[61] *Guillaume le Maréchal* (1891–1901), 100, ll. 2723–36 (my translation).
[62] Verbruggen (1997), 103–07
[63] Ibid., 77–80, 89, 97–102. See also Bennett (1989).

in 1216 (Geoffrey de Mandeville),[64] *béhourd* must have been presumed pretty tame, frequently being restricted to the squires. If tourneying was forbidden to the Templars, then this could obviously be because of the moral danger in which the Church believed the activity placed participants. But the issue remains of the how even experienced men such as the Brothers of the Military Orders could actually manoeuvre on the battlefield.

For medieval armies were aggregates of much smaller groups, who were used to hunting and fighting together, but were unused to operating in a larger force. It was rare, even on Crusade, for there to be more than one or two thousand knights, but even these small numbers proved very difficult to handle by the commanders of the day. In battle, co-ordination is everything, yet a medieval general had what was largely a one-shot weapon at his disposal. The only division of the army was into van, centre and rear battles and it is difficult to perceive any further subdivisions within these 'battles' apart from the different arms which composed them. Nowhere was this more difficult to manage than on crusade, and so I shall end with crusading examples. The crusaders marching from Jerusalem to Ascalon in August 1099 seem to have been split into nine bodies of mixed horse and foot in a box formation of three-by-three, capable of facing attack in any direction. In fact, in the actual encounter with the Fatimid Egyptian forces they reverted to the 'three-battle' formation, although a reserve troop was available to counter a flank attack by Bedouin light cavalry.[65] It should not be forgotten that this was a veteran force, used to fighting together after three years of campaigning. Such experience produces tactical expertise.

That close order was the key to victory was proverbial. The poet Ambroise says of the crusader formation on the march from Acre to Jaffa in 1191, that it would have been impossible to 'throw an apple or a plum' amongst the knights without it falling on a lance or helmet. This obviously exaggerated formula comes straight from the repertoire of the *chansons de geste*.[66] Yet in this situation it was

---

[64] Barber & Barker (1989), 29.

[65] Verbruggen (1997), 104–5, 208–9, 220–21. See also Bennett (2001), 1–18, citing Raymond d'Aguilers (1968), 133. Smail (1956/1996) provides the classic account. France (1994) updates Smail's conclusions generally, and, at 357–65, presents a new analysis of the battle of Ascalon (12 Aug. 1099).

[66] Verbruggen (1997), 16, 65, 73, 232–39 (battle of Arsuf); Ambroise (1897)—a complete verse translation of this valuable source can be found in Ambroise (1941).

true. Richard the Lionheart demanded tight control over the twelve bodies of knights, protected behind a sleeve of footsoldiers down either flank, while the experienced and disciplined Templars and Hospitallers took it turn to take the van and rearguard. On the 6 September, approaching Arsuf, Saladin risked a battle with this formation. The western version of events has the Hospitallers, who were losing too many horses in the rearguard, charging before Richard had given orders to do so. But Saladin's secretary, Beha ad-Din, describes 'the Frankish cavalry mustering in the middle of their infantry and taking their lances'. His picture is one of a concerted and well-ordered attack. The infantry closed up to leave gaps in the line. The cavalry shouted 'like one man', and charged the three Muslim divisions separately. 'They then charged twice more driving the Muslims back to the ridge.'[67] I like to think that the crusaders— Bretons and Angevins, Poitevins, English and Normans, Champagnois and many other unspecified French knights who made up the dozen mounted contingents of Richard's force—had learnt something at the tournaments of northern France. These gatherings were clearly a prime means for passing on the core body of military skills associated with chivalry. For, as both a social code and a practical guide to warfare, chivalry helped to create military professionalism in age when it is usually assumed to have been absent.

Bibliography

Primary Sources

Ambroise (1897) *Ambroise, L'estoire de la guerre sainte*, ed. G. Paris (Paris, 1897).
——. (1941) *The Crusade of Richard the Lionheart*, trans. M. J. Hubert, with notes by John L. La Monte (New York, 1941).
Anna Komnene (1969) *The Alexiad of Anna Comnena*, trans. E. R. A. Sewter (London, 1969).
Fulcher of Chartres (1969) *A History of the Expedition to Jerusalem 1095–1127*, trans. F. R. Ryan and ed. H. S. Fink (Knoxville, 1969).
Girart de Vienne (1930) ed. F. Yeandle (New York, 1930).
La Chanson de Guillaume (1949–50) ed. D. MacMillan, 2 vols (Paris, 1949–50).
Guillaume le Maréchal (1891–1901) *L'Histoire de Guillaume le Maréchal*, ed. P. Meyer, Société de l'Histoire de France (Paris, 1891–1901).
Orderic Vitalis (1969–80) *Ecclesiastical History*, ed. M. Chibnall, 6 vols (Oxford, 1969–80).

---

[67] Cited by Lyons & Jackson (1982), 337–38.

Ousama (1929) *The Autobiography of Ousama*, trans. G. Potter (London, 1929).
Raymond d'Aguilers (1968) *Historia Francorum qui ceperunt Iherusalem*, trans. J. H. and L. L. Hill (Philadelphia, 1968).
Roger of Hoveden (1867A) *Chronica*, ed. W. Stubbs, Rolls Series, 4 vols (London, 1867).
——— (1867B) *Gesta Henrici Secundi*, ed. W. Stubbs, Rolls Series, 2 vols (London, 1867).
"Song of Roland" (1978) *La Chanson de Roland*, ed. F. Whitehead (Oxford, 1978).
——— (1990) *The Song of Roland*, trans. D. D. R. Owen (Woodbridge, Suffolk: 1990).
Upton-Ward, J. M. (1992), ed., *The Rule of the Templars* (Woodbridge, Suffolk: 1992)
William of Malmesbury (1998) *Historia Novella*, ed. E. J. King, trans. K. R. Potter (Oxford, 1998).
William of Poitiers (1999) *Gesta Guillelmi*, ed. M. Chibnall and R. H. C. Davis (Oxford, 1999).

Secondary Sources

Ailes, A. (1982) *The Origins of the Royal Arms of England: Their Development to 1199*, Reading Medieval Studies, Monograph no. 2 (Reading, 1982).
Barber, R. and Barker, J. (1989) *Tournaments: Jousts, Chivalry and Pageants in the Middle Ages* (Woodbridge, Suffolk: 1989).
Barthélemy, D. (1997) *La mutation de l'an mille a-t-elle eu lieu? Servage et chevalerie dans la France des Xe et X^{ie} siècles* (Paris, 1997).
———. (2001) "Modern Mythologies of Medieval Chivalry", in *The Medieval World*, ed. Peter Linehan and Janet L. Nelson (London, 2001) 214–28.
Bennett, M. (1986) "The Status of the Squire: The Northern Evidence", *Proceedings of the 1st and 2nd St Mary's Knights Conference*, ed. C. Harper-Bill (Woodbridge, Suffolk: 1986) 1–11.
———. (1989) "*La Règle du Temple* as a Military Manual or How to Deliver a Cavalry Charge", in *Studies in medieval history for R. Allen Brown*, ed. C. Harper-Bill, C. J. Holdsworth and J. L. Nelson (Woodbridge, Suffolk: 1989) 7–19.
———. (1996) "Violence in Eleventh Century Normandy: Feud, Warfare and Politics", in *Private, Public and Ritual: Studies in Late Antiquity and Early Medieval Violence and Society*, ed. G. Halsall (Woodbridge, Suffolk: 1996) 126–40.
———. (2000) "The Impact of 'Foreign' Troops in the Civil Wars of King Stephen's Reign", in *War and Society in Medieval and Early Modern Britain*, ed. Diana Dunn (Liverpool: 2000) 96–113.
———. (2001) "The Crusaders' 'Fighting March' Revisited", *War in History* 8 (2001) 1–18.
Benson, L. (1980) "The tournament in the romances of Chrétien de Troyes and *L'Histoire de Guillaume le Maréchal*", in *Chivalric Literature: Essays on Relations between Literature and Life—The Later Middle Ages*, ed. Larry D. Benson and John Leyerle, Studies in Medieval Culture 14 (Kalamazoo, 1980) 1–24.
Bloch, M. (1962) *Feudal Society*, trans. L. A. Manyon (2nd edn, 1962).
Bradbury, J. (1985) *The Medieval Archer* (Woodbridge, Suffolk: 1985).
Bull, M. (1993) *Knightly Piety and the Lay response to the First Crusade: the Limousin and Gascony, c. 970–c. 1130* (Oxford, 1993).
Cirlot, V. (1985) "Techniques guerrières en Catalogne féodal. Le maniement de la lance", *Cahiers de Civilisation Médiévale*, 28 (1985) 35–43 and 8 plates.
Crouch, D. (1990) *William Marshal: Court, Career and Chivalry in the Angevin Empire 1147–1219* (London, 1990).
Duby, G. (1971) *La Société aux X^{ie} et XIIe siècle dans la région mâconnaise* (2nd edn, 1971; repr. École des Hautes Études, 1982).
———. (1980) *The Three Orders: Feudal Society Imagined*, trans. A. Goldhammer (Chicago, 1980).

Flori, J. (1976) "Sémantique et société médiévale: le verbe *adouber* et son évolution au 12e siécle", *Annales E.S.C.* (1976) 915–40.

——. (1998) *Croisade et chevalerie XIᵉ–XIIᵉ siécles*, Bibliothèque du Moyen Age, XII (Paris, 1998).

France, J. (1994) *Victory in the East: a military history of the First Crusade*, (Cambridge, 1994).

Gillingham, J. (1994) "1066 and the Introduction of Chivalry into England", in *Law and Government in Medieval England and Normandy: Essays in Honour of Sir James Holt*, ed. G. Garnett and J. Hudson (Cambridge, 1994) 31–55.

——. (1995) 'Thegns and Knights in eleventh-century England: Who was then the Gentleman?', *TRHS*, 6th ser., 5 (1995) 129–53.

——. (1999) *Richard I* (Yale, 1999).

Head T. & Landes R. (1992), eds. *The Peace of God. Social Violence and Religious Response in France Around the Year 1000* (London, 1992).

John, E. (1960) *Land Tenure in Early England* (Leicester, 1960).

Keen, M. (1984) *Chivalry* (New Haven & London, 1984).

Leyser, K. (1994) "Early Medieval Canon Law and the Beginnings of Knighthood" [an essay orig. published in 1984], in Leyser, *Communications and Power in Medieval Europe: The Carolingian and Ottonian Centuries*, ed. Timothy Reuter (London, 1994) 549–66.

Lyons, M. C. and Jackson, D. E. P. (1982) *Saladin: The Politics of Holy War* (Cambridge, 1982).

Morris, C. (1978) "*Equestris Ordo*: Chivalry as a Vocation in the Twelfth Century", in *Studies in Church History* 15 (1978) 87–96.

Nicolle, D. (1996) *Medieval Warfare Source Book*, 2 vols. (London, 1996)

Prestwich, J. (1981) "The Military Household of the Norman Kings", *EHR* 96 (1981), reprinted in Strickland (1992), cit. above, 93–127.

Ross, D. J. A. (1951) "Pleine sa hanste", *Medium Aevum* 20 (1951).

Smail, R. C. (1956/1996) *Crusader Warfare 1099–1192* (Cambridge, 1956; new edn, with intro. by C. Marshall, 1996).

Stenton, F. M. (1961) *The First Century of English Feudalism* (2nd edn, Oxford, 1961).

Strickland, M. (1992), ed., *Anglo-Norman Warfare* (Woodbridge, 1992).

——. (1996) *War and Chivalry: The Conduct and Perception of War in England and Normandy, 1066–1217* (Cambridge, 1996).

Verbruggen, J. F. (1947) "La tactique militaire des armées de chevaliers", *Revue du Nord* 29 (1947) 161–80.

——. (1997) *The Art of Warfare in Western Europe during the Middle Ages from the Eighth century to 1340*; orig. published as *De krijgskunst in West-Europa in de Middeleeuwen, Ixe tot begin XIVᵉ eeuw* (Koninklijke Akademic voor Wetenschappen, Letteren en Schone Kunsten van Belgïe: 1954), trans. Sumner Willard and S. C. M. Southern; 1st edn (Amsterdam, Oxford & New York: 1976); 2nd rev. and expanded edn (Woodbridge, Suffolk: 1997).

Wilson, D. M. (1985) *The Bayeux Tapestry* (London, 1985).

STUDIES IN CHIVALRY AND PROFESSIONALISM IN
LATE-MEDIEVAL AND EARLY MODERN EUROPE

CHAPTER THREE

CONDOTTIERI AND CAPTAINS IN RENAISSANCE ITALY

Michael Mallett

There has been little discussion in Italian historical literature of either the 'golden age' of chivalry or the chivalric revival of the fifteenth century, encouraged by princes and emerging national and patriotic sentiments. Apart from the Normans of southern Italy, Italians were little involved in the crusading armies or the religious military orders, except as their carriers and suppliers; the dark days of the foreign mercenary companies in the fourteenth century provided few echoes of Lull or Froissart; and the emerging territorial states of the fifteenth century are better known for their pursuit of classical and urban values than for nostalgia for a medieval past or concern for leadership and unity. Thirteenth-century jurists, like Bartolo da Sassoferrato, insisted that the chivalric traditions of northern Europe were a debasement of true chivalry which was of Roman and not barbarian origin.[1] Furthermore, the idea of Italy as essentially backward in its military institutions and practices, and out of touch with contemporary European developments, has long been a part of an historiographical tradition.[2]

However, it is now increasingly recognised that in terms of emerging military professionalism Italy was a precocious breeding ground, and it could even be argued that it was the absence of a strong chivalric tradition that encouraged the growth of 'modern' military institutions in the Italian states. Nevertheless, before we pursue that argument too far it will be necessary to consider more critically the idea of the Italian peninsula being somewhat isolated from the mainstream of European chivalric tradition, and to confront the problem of whether a decline of chivalry is a natural accompaniment to a

---

[1] Bayley (1961), 207–8. For general discussion of Italian chivalry, see Cardini (1981), Fasoli (1958), Gasparri (1992) and Keen (1984), 38–41.

[2] See n. 4 below for reference to humanist criticism of the condottieri and n. 48 for later views of Italian warfare.

growth of military professionalism. Gina Fasoli in a discussion of the
origins of chivalry in Italy remarked that the early knights were 'guer-
rieri di professione', although she goes on to admit that with the
advance of feudalism and the growth of courts, this became a more
difficult correlation to maintain.[3] Here, we are primarily concerned
with the late Middle Ages and Renaissance period when the spread
of universities, of literacy, and of the influence of urban societies,
was demanding a rather more complex definition of professionalism.
In Italy, in particular, the quest for professional status spread far
beyond the military world.

Late Medieval Italian Warfare

An obvious starting point for this discussion must be the apparent
antithesis between the mercenary condottiere who dominated the
Italian scene for much of the fourteenth and fifteenth centuries, and
the chivalrous traditions which exercised such a strong influence on
northern and western European warfare, and indeed were under-
going a notable revival in the early fifteenth century.[4] That this contrast has been considerably exaggerated will be one of the main
themes of this essay. The point is often made in recent writing on
chivalry that the medieval practice of warfare often differed substantially from the chivalric ideals of 'good war'. However, for the
moment let us consider what made the Italian military scene rather
different to that prevailing in north-western Europe.

In the first place, most of Italy was far less heavily feudalised than
France, England or even Germany. With the exception of the old
Norman kingdom of Sicily, which included Naples and southern
Italy, a rural society based on fiefs, mutual obligations between lords
and vassals, and peasant serfdom had not been either systematically
introduced or coherently maintained. Chivalrous society and its traditions were essentially linked to the feudal world, and their accept-

---

[3] Fasoli (1958), 84.
[4] For general accounts of the nature of Italian warfare, and particularly of the
role of the condottieri, see Ricotti (1844–5); Pieri (1952), 205–319; Mallett (1974);
Lenzi (1988); Mallett (1991); and Covini (2000). The humanist views on the condottieri are discussed in Bayley (1961), 178–95. For an overall view of European
chivalry, see Keen (1984) and Vale (1981).

ance in Italy depended more on imitation of northern example than on natural growth. Italy was relatively little affected by the great outpouring of chivalric literature in the twelfth and thirteenth centuries.[5] A major explanation for this contrast in social structure and literary interests was the advanced nature of the Italian economy and of Italian urbanism. It was the cities of northern Italy which successfully opposed the effective imposition of Imperial rule in the twelfth and thirteenth centuries, and it was the cities that became the foci of political development and wealth. Initially the cities provided the manpower for armies and by the fourteenth century were extending their control over the countryside and the rural populations. In the conflicts which developed among the emerging city-states in the late thirteenth and fourteenth centuries there was some attempt by urban governments to impose obligations for their defence on the local rural nobility, but with liquid wealth available it was easier and safer to rely on temporary contracts with foreign mercenaries for this purpose.[6] The mercenaries in the warfare of this period came from all over Europe and from a variety of military traditions; Bretons, Burgundians, Provencals and Gascons rubbed shoulders with Catalans, Germans, Hungarians and English. Many were also from Italy, but rarely from the territory dominated by the city which was employing them. Most of the leaders of these mercenary companies were nobles, but the situation in which they found themselves, employed by a faceless urban regime, defending an alien and often hostile population, left little room for chivalrous niceties or long-term commitment. The ready availability of such mercenaries, often seeking employment during truces in northern wars, encouraged the city-states to dispense with their services as soon as possible at the end of the campaigning season and to give little thought to the problems of longer-term defence. In these circumstances, the chivalrous traditions of loyalty, defence of the poor and weak, gallantry and steadfastness in war and respect for the enemy were scarcely encouraged. The native rural aristocracy, which had been touched by these chivalrous ideas, was initially treated with suspicion by the

[5] Ruggieri (1963), chaps. 1–4; Barber (1974), 77–8, 141–3; Dorigatti (1996), 105–9. But see also Larner (1988) for a more optimistic view of the flowering of chivalric culture in Italy in the late 13th century.
[6] Thirteenth-century warfare is discussed in Waley (1988), 53–4, 97–101; Settia (1993), 91–198; Mallett (1974), 6–24; and Jones (1997), 382–90.

emerging urban elites; those who moved to the towns tended to be excluded from any role in communal government.[7]

However, despite these reservations about the role of chivalric ideals and traditions in fourteenth-century Italy, one can be too dismissive of their impact. It is true that, apart from Naples where the Angevin rulers made at least two attempts to create lay orders of knighthood, there seemed to be little interest in this characteristic late medieval aspect of chivalric revival. The Kingdom of Naples was the one monarchical state in the peninsula and one of the primary motives behind the setting up of the new orders there was to draw the military class into a greater loyalty to the crown. However, the prime mover behind the initiative of Luigi da Taranto, consort of the Angevin queen Joanna I, to establish the Company of the Knot (1352) was the influential Florentine banker, Nicola Acciaiuoli, who was a leading councillor of the Angevin house for many years.[8] Acciaiuoli was almost more Neapolitan than Florentine with his numerous fiefs and a knighthood conferred by the king, but he represented that merging of the aristocratic and urban patrician worlds that was characteristic of late medieval Italy. The rural aristocracy may have been suspect but their life style and ideals began to be imitated by increasingly self-conscious urban elites. The practice in Florence of conferring knighthoods, not only on defenders of the city but also on middle class burghers who had no military ambitions or qualifications, while derided by many contemporaries, was an indication of the continued social significance of knighthood.[9] In the Lombard cities the distribution of knighthoods continued to be largely confined to soldier members of the leading families.[10] Thus, in an informal way not only the signorial city-states with their courts and their military cultures, but also the surviving republics, linked themselves to the chivalric world. Tournaments became part of urban festivities as well as continuing to be the centrepieces of military

---

[7] For detailed accounts of the warfare of the 14th century, see: Ricotti (1844–5), vol. I; Mallett (1974), 25–50; Lenzi (1988), 79–104.

[8] Boulton (1987), 213–16.

[9] Salvemini (1896); Bayley (1961), 206–8. Bayley points out that in Florence the Parte Guelfa was a sort of umbrella organisation for the urban knights; in Venice the Cavalieri di San Marco had a similar function, although with a clearly military orientation.

[10] Hyde (1967), 92–102.

training;[11] the philosophical debate about the relative values of nobility of birth and nobility of deeds, which arose in the thirteenth century and contributed to the chivalric revival of the late Middle Ages, became also an obvious talking point for the urban elites. The court of Gian Galeazzo Visconti in late fourteenth-century Milan was a meeting place for the long serving condottieri of the Duke, and the councillors and merchants of the Milanese elite.[12]

Military Professionalism and Permanence

Mention of the Visconti court and the late fourteenth century brings us firmly back to the question of professionalism, and continuity of employment as a key factor in the growth of military professionalism. The marauding condottieri of the central years of the fourteenth century were, in a sense, professionals; they made a living from war, and the booty and extortions of war; their companies were reasonably well organised and were composed of skilled men-at-arms. But they acknowledged no loyalties, even to their temporary employers, and discipline and control were extremely difficult to impose given the ever-changing composition of the companies. By the later fourteenth century the possibilities of imposing a degree of control were improving; the flow of men and companies from the north began to dry up as the Hundred Years' War entered a period of prolonged stasis, and Italian captains began to take their place, often defeating the foreign companies in the process.

The archetypal figure of John Hawkwood, rapacious English mercenary condottiere and eventually long-serving Florentine captain-general, passed away in 1394. His career represented a sort of watershed; his military successes and expertise were such as to tempt Florence to abandon the old policies of giving short-term contracts to any available captains, and to try seriously to retain the loyalty of the outstanding captain of the day. It has to be said that it was the threat of destruction by the increasingly stable cadre of Visconti captains that pushed the Florentines into this position, and the relationship with Hawkwood was to be unique in their history.[13] However,

---

[11] Barber (1974), 159–92; Barber & Barker (1989), 77–90; Larner (1988), 122 et seq.
[12] Mesquita (1941), 174–86.
[13] For a recent review of Hawkwood's career, see Fowler (1988).

the emergence of larger regional states as a result of the assimila-
tion of the smaller satellite cities and rural areas, gave greater self-
confidence and above all greater resources to those states, and
eventually greater stability to the political system in northern and
central Italy.

The prolonged wars generated by the expansionist policies of Gian
Galeazzo Visconti in the late fourteenth and early fifteenth centuries,
and the more sustained rivalry between the three major states, Milan,
Venice and Florence, in the 1425–54 period, were the background
to substantial changes in the nature of Italian warfare. War took on
a new seriousness and became an ever-present threat which required
the maintenance of substantial standing forces in peacetime.[14] Military
contracts were extended from three or six months to one year to
cover the winter following a campaigning season, and then eventually to two and three years. The condottieri were called upon to
commit themselves to more extended periods of service which in
time drew the employing states into creating mechanisms for closer
supervision and more detailed organisation. Arrangements had to be
made for billeting the companies, for creating a *modus vivendi* between
them and the rural population, for raising and paying out the funds
necessary, and subjecting the troops to frequent inspections to ensure
the maintenance of appropriate levels of equipment and skill. Most
of the condottieri seemed gradually to accept the process; pay was
usually erratic, and the watchfulness and supervision of civilian com-
missaries and officials irksome, and by no means effective in elimi-
nating all the traditional devices for exploiting their employers. But
it gradually reduced the need for a hand-to-mouth existence for
many of the companies and prepared the way for a more settled
way of life and even a degree of concerted action on the battlefield.
Milan and Venice led the way in these directions, both of them
maintaining armies of 20–25,000 men through the almost continuous wars fought for control of central Lombardy between 1425 and
1454. Florence, although subject to the same pressures and allied to
Venice for much of the period, lagged significantly behind in its
development of military institutions and its willingness to create long-
term relationships with condottieri.[15]

---

[14] Extensive discussion of the trends towards permanence and long service in the
Venetian and Milanese armies is to be found in Mallett & Hale (1984), part I, and
Covini (1998) and (2000).
[15] Mallett (1979).

Changing attitudes towards the condottieri themselves were a significant part of the new atmosphere. The Visconti dukes of Milan and the Venetian political leaders, many of whom had experience of naval warfare, recognised the importance of attracting good military leaders and retaining their loyalty. For Milan this process meant a greater willingness to offer employment to, and to encourage the military careers of, the Lombard rural aristocracy;[16] Venice moved somewhat more slowly in this direction as the Terraferma state had only been recently acquired and the nobility of Padua and Verona, and other recently subjected cities, were still regarded with some suspicion. However, both states began a policy of offering estates to their military captains to provide them with rural power bases and with quarters for their companies. Enfeudation was revived as the normal mechanism for this purpose, although the fiefs given to condottieri did not carry a commitment to military service, only an oath of loyalty and obedience.[17] The service of the captains continued to be controlled by contracts (*condotte*) although the annual or biennial renewal of the contracts was tending to become a formality. Alongside the offer of fiefs and estates went various other rewards, including cash bonuses, military contracts or bureaucratic posts for sons and relatives, pensions for the disabled or retired, and lavish welcoming ceremonies when the condottieri made formal visits to Milan or Venice.[18] The development of formal arrangements for the long-term employment of condottieri and their companies is clear in the Venetian state from the moment of the occupation of Verona and Padua in 1404–5. The Milanese documentation for the first half of the fifteenth century remains to be explored, but signs of greater permanence were clearly there during the period of Gian Galeazzo Visconti (1385–1402), and by the middle of the fifteenth century the organisation of companies in permanent employment was fully in place.[19] For Florence the evidence suggests relatively little concern for the maintenance of significant military organisation in time of peace, in the first half of the fifteenth century.

The move towards greater permanence in the institutions and practices of war, apparent in northern and parts of central Italy in

---

[16] Covini (1998), 91–3.

[17] The question of the new feudalism is discussed at length in the work of Giorgio Chittolini. See, particularly, Chittolini (1979) and (1981). For a recent summary, see Covini (1998), 94–100.

[18] Mallett & Hale (1984), 186–97.

[19] Covini (1998), 3–14.

the first half of the fifteenth century, had an impact also on the life style of the companies and the men in them. Condottieri, who traditionally tended to come from the lesser rural nobility, had always relied heavily on their areas of origin and their estates for recruitment. This in itself provided a certain continuity in the composition of the companies and this was enhanced with the provision of a *nido* (nest) in the territory of the employing state. More significantly, the development of year-round contracts, and hence prospects of reasonably long-term employment, enabled the larger companies to build up their internal organisation and develop hierarchies within their ranks.[20] The development of two famous 'schools' of warfare in the early fifteenth century, the Sforzeschi and the Bracceschi, was linked to this growing stability within the companies. Muzio Attendolo Sforza became noted for the discipline and control of his troops in battle, and those who served under him, many of them relatives from the Romagna, carried forward the tradition over the next two or three generations. The rival tradition was that established by Braccio Fortebracci da Montone, an Umbrian whose methods depended more on surprise and speed of manoeuvre. Most of the condottieri of the 1420s and 1430s had served under one or other of these captains, and their apprenticeship was an important part of their formation and their reputations.[21] Thus we see emerging in the greater continuity and permanence of military organisation, in the emphasis on discipline and fidelity to the state, in the development of hierarchical structures within long-serving companies, and in the implications for training and the improvement of skills, a substantial move towards professionalism. The broader cultural implications of this will be discussed later in this essay.

The reputation of the condottiere undoubtedly improved in this period. This was not just because of the increasingly effective mechanisms for retaining loyalty and for ensuring good service, but because popular attitudes towards the soldiery were changing. Even in Florence where fear of a military take-over and suspicion of condottieri remained deeply imbedded in the communal psyche, the early years of the fifteenth century saw signs of a thawing of these attitudes. Expansion

---

[20] Del Treppo (1973).
[21] Mallett (1974), 67–75. Covini (1998), 169–70, has questioned the long-term influence of these two traditions. For recent discussion of the role of Braccio, see Waley (1993).

of the state and particularly the long-desired conquest of Pisa in 1406, contributed to this as much as the ultimately successful confrontation with Gian Galeazzo Visconti.[22] Renewed interest of the humanists in the Roman origins of chivalry and in Roman military literature generally, accompanied, and in certain respects clashed with, a growing enthusiasm for chivalric romances spreading from northern Europe. Successful condottieri were likened to classical military heroes and fresco portraits of Hawkwood and Niccolò da Tolentino, Florence's military leader in the war with Lucca in the 1430s, were commissioned for the walls of the cathedral. A tradition of humanist military writing, starting with Leonardo Bruni's *De Militia*, continued through the century to the essentially professional treatises of the first half of the sixteenth century.[23] Martial exercises and the handling of arms became an essential feature of humanist education programmes, and tournaments, both as public spectacles and as opportunities for serious practice and training, continued to grow in popularity. The revived interest in chivalry and in the military aspects of classical history and literature can in part be explained as a symptom of the aristocratisation of the upper levels of urban society, but it was also associated with the political and military needs of the Italian states, and with the complex mechanisms of military permanence with which they surrounded themselves. Such interests were certainly not peculiar to soldiers, and while there are many instances of condottieri possessing libraries which included both classical and contemporary military texts, it would be misleading to see in this a tendency towards professional specialisation. The cultural life of the northern Italian princely courts was particularly affected; numerous fresco cycles, such as Pisanello's jousting scenes in the Gonzaga palace in Mantua (*c.* 1447) and those with chivalric themes decorating the Trinci palace in Foligno and Bartolomeo Colleoni's country seat at Malpaga, bear witness to the closeness of Italian court culture to that of northern Europe. The sons of Italian princes were often sent to the courts of France and Burgundy for a part of their education, and election to the knightly orders of the Garter, the Golden Fleece and St. Michel was much prized by Italian princes and captains.[24]

---

[22] Brucker (1978), 300–1.
[23] Bayley (1961), 219–315.
[24] Clough (1990), 35–47; Mallett (1974), 207–30; Settia (1985).

The chivalric revival of the fifteenth century has often been derided as no more than anachronistic play-acting; the dominance of the knights and the heavy cavalry had been fatally undermined, it is supposed, at Crecy, Poitiers and Agincourt by the English archers, and at Sempach and Morgarten by the Swiss pikes and halberds.[25] But one only has to look at the military institutions of the fifteenth century, the growing insistence of states on maintaining the heavy cavalry in a state of constant readiness, and indeed at the structure and composition of the European armies in the late fifteenth century, to realise that for the time being at least the training and efficiency of that arm and the traditions associated with it remained very live issues.

This was certainly the case in Italy as the companies returned to their billets in the spring of 1454 following the negotiation of the peace of Lodi, which was to be the beginning of a somewhat calmer period of Italian politics. This was four years after Francesco Sforza, the main heir to the Sforzesco school of condottieri, had succeeded in taking over the Duchy of Milan, having married the natural daughter of the last Visconti duke, Filippo Maria. Sforza's success was only in part a military one; it also owed much to a factional struggle within the duchy and to a diplomatic realignment of Florence with Milan. It signalled the achievement of the highest ambition for a condottiere, to secure a position of independent political lordship and establish a dynasty. But Francesco Sforza's career was not just an example of what could be achieved by a determined and ambitious military captain; it also indicated that audacity and military strength had to be linked to political acumen and diplomatic skill. For twenty years Sforza had manoeuvred from a power base within the Papal State in the Marches, shifting his allegiances discreetly, building up his military strength and reputation, avoiding the slur of infidelity, while apparently making his services indispensable. In his sixteen years as Duke of Milan he brought the interminable Lombard wars to an end, discreetly shelving the Milanese obsession with recovering the lands lost to Venice; he presided also over the efforts of the Italian states to preserve an uneasy equilibrium in the aftermath of the wars, and moved firmly against efforts by the Angevin

---

[25] The continued relevance and popularity of chivalric ideals and practices in the 15th century has been successfully defended by Keen (1984), 200–37; and Vale (1981), 147–74.

house to interfere in Italian affairs and recover control of Naples. In other words he showed statesman-like qualities which provided a different role model to his contemporaries among Italian condottieri to that inherited from the fourteenth century.[26] The emphasis on long service, fidelity, discipline and well-honed military skills which had come to pervade the Italian military scene by the middle years of the fifteenth century justified the increasing use of the term 'captain' to describe the military leaders.

Condottieri and Captains, 1454–94

The 40 years which followed the peace of Lodi in 1454 have often been seen as years of peace in which the companies were demobilised and the condottieri, with one or two notable exceptions, turned away from the arts of war and took up new roles as landowners and cultural patrons. It was at this point, we are often told, that Italian warfare lost its edge and became out of touch with broader European developments. The achievements of the Swiss infantry in the 1470s and the gradual build-up of the French artillery train are said to have made little impression in Italy, and hence the débacle in 1494 when Charles VIII's army, led by these new arms, marched unopposed through Italy.[27]

However, there were many reasons for Charles' temporary success in 1494; they were on the whole political and social rather than military. The years after Lodi can only in a very relative sense be described as peaceful; they intervened between two periods of intensive warfare, but were filled with spasmodic wars and constant threats of war. Active and intensely suspicious diplomacy and diplomatic reporting filled the gaps between the wars and ensured that Italian governments were very fully informed, both about the military strengths and intentions of their Italian neighbours, and those of the ultramontane powers. Italian troops and captains campaigned in France in the War of the Common Weal, and joined in large numbers the army of Charles the Bold of Burgundy. The Swiss and the Austrians

---

[26] The role of Francesco Sforza as soldier and military leader has been extensively explored by Covini (1998), chaps. 1–5.

[27] Pillinini (1970), particularly 7–15, outlines well many of the fallacies inherent in earlier writing about the 1454–94 period.

were confronted on the Alpine frontier, and the Turks countered in
Friuli in the 1470s and driven out of Otranto in 1481. What we
see, therefore, in this period, is a bedding down of the military institutions, which had been largely created under the pressure of war,
in an atmosphere of constant preparedness. With contracts becoming a formality and the reputation of military leaders depending on
loyalty, on the quality of their troops, and on a new, broader, role
in society, the condottieri were being transformed into professional
captains, closer in a sense to the select captains of the ordinance
companies in France.[28]

Once again it is in Milan and Venice that we can see these developments most clearly.[29] Francesco Sforza, at the moment of his accession to the dukedom in 1450, incorporated his own long-serving and
highly organised company into the Milanese army. Many of his
squadron leaders were given fiefs in accordance with established
Visconti custom, and maintained their position as close advisers of
the new ruler. In 1454, following the peace and its consolidation by
the setting up of the Italian League in the following year, both Milan
and Venice had sufficient confidence in the loyalty of their condottieri, and their willingness to accept government edict, to enable
them to enforce a more extensive demobilisation than had been customary during the brief truces of the war period. This demobilisation was achieved by reducing the size of the companies in accordance
with the terms of the contracts, which by this time stipulated the
reduced levels of employment expected in peacetime. Very few condottieri were actually dismissed and therefore the traditional problem of demobilised companies holding the countryside to ransom did
not arise. As part of the reorganisation a clear distinction began to
emerge between the condottiere companies scattered in billets across
the state on half pay, and select troops maintained at a greater level
of preparedness either on the frontiers or close to the capital. Such
companies, exemplified in Milan by the *famiglia ducale* and the *lanze
spezzate*, and in Venice again by the increasingly numerous *lanze spezzate* and the strategically based companies of leading captains like

---

[28] The best source for information on Italian politics and warfare for much of
the second half of the fifteenth century, is now the edition of Lorenzo de' Medici's
letters, the coverage of which has reached 1486; see *Lettere* (1977–2000). Pillinini
(1970) remains a very useful summary of the period.
[29] Mallett & Hale (1984), 43–5, 65–71; Covini (1998), part I; this covers the
period 1450–80.

Colleoni at Malpaga, were commanded by captains selected by the state.[30] Theoretically the men in these companies were paid individually by state paymasters, to avoid the money passing through the hands of the captain and strengthening the distinction that these men were employed directly by the state. This was a practice which tended to lapse in the more widely dispersed condottiere companies. Francesco Sforza, in his self-appointed role as arbiter in Italian disputes and local crises, dispatched elements of his permanent troops to various parts of Italy in the years after Lodi. By this time the Papal State and the Kingdom of Naples had been drawn into a more coherent pattern of peninsular politics following the final victory of the Aragonese dynasty over the Angevins in the south, and the re-emergence of a more self-confident papacy following the end of the Schism and the collapse of the Conciliar Movement. This meant that the institutions of military permanence established in northern Italy were taken up by the Aragonese kings and the popes from the 1450s onwards.

In Naples Alfonso V and his successor, Ferrante, relied heavily on recruits from the extensive royal estates to provide the permanent element of the Neapolitan army, while the great feudatories had obligations to serve when called upon and maintained companies in a partial state of readiness.[31] For the popes in the second half of the fifteenth century, the problem was one of restoring order in Rome and throughout the Papal State after a long period of weak control. This meant, on the whole, that each pope had to take sides with one or other of the baronial factions and use their military strength to discipline their rivals. It was in this atmosphere that Orsini and Colonna captains gained their experience, but also learnt that loyalty to one pope would rarely be recognised by the next. This led some of them to seek service with, and rewards from the Aragonese dynasty in Naples.[32]

Thus, by the second half of the fifteenth century, the development of military institutions in Italy had taken on a peninsula-wide rather

---

[30] For discussion of the *famiglia* and the *lanze spezzate*, see Covini (1988), 45–6, and Mallett & Hale (1984), 65–9.

[31] An excellent paper by Francesco Storti, "Il principe condottiero: le compagnie militari di Alfonso duca di Calabria", read at the conference held in Lucca in May 1998 on *Condottieri ed uomini d'arme nell' Italia del Rinascimento*, will be published shortly.

[32] Mallett (1974), 119–20.

than a regional basis. Neapolitan and papal troops began to appear
fighting alongside those from the northern states, and institutional
practices spread from army to army. Pope Paul II (1464–71) used
Venetian military officials, like Chierighino Chiericati, to reform and
strengthen the organisation of the papal army,[33] and the extensive
role of Milanese contingents in fighting off the attempted Angevin
reconquest of Naples in 1460–2, gave opportunities for Aragonese
officials to copy the new institutions. Throughout Italy there was a
tendency to move towards uniform company strengths, based on full
companies of 100 men-at-arms, divided into squadrons of 25. The
practice of putting companies together for fighting purposes into
colonelli commanded by colonels was widely accepted. There was a
developing tradition of senior military command being confined to
noble families, whether of long aristocratic lineage, or more recent
signorial or military background. The leading Italian captains of the
late fifteenth century were members of the Este, Gonzaga, Bentivoglio,
Trivulzio, Sanseverino, Montefeltro, Orsini and Colonna families,
together with the ennobled descendants of Sforza and Braccio da
Montone. In this sense there was, at this stage, no replacement of
the nobility in military leadership by non-noble professional soldiers,
as is sometimes postulated for northern Europe; in Italy that phenomenon was more characteristic of the late fourteenth and early
fifteenth centuries. Ideas about the nobility of birth were returning
to the humanist agenda.[34]

The creation of garrison and billeting areas for troops on a long-
term basis led not only to an increasing reliance on local officials to
supervise the day-to-day administration of the companies, but also
to the emergence of high profile centrally-controlled administrators
to direct the complex operation. In Venice an attempt to involve
members of the Venetian nobility in these tasks in the years after
Lodi was abandoned in favour of a return to the use of professional
administrators (*collaterali*) in permanent employment, which had developed during the wars.[35] In Milan the Sforza dukes favoured even
tighter personal control through the use of temporary commissions
given to trusted court bureaucrats (*famigliari cavalcanti*) to deal with
particular problems and circumstances.[36] In Rome the Camera

---

[33] Zorzi (1915).
[34] Babil (1991), 17–18.
[35] Mallett & Hale (1984), 103–13.
[36] Covini (1998), 133–44; Covini points out that these confidential emissaries of

Apostolica became the focus for much of military administration, and in Florence a special permanent committee established in 1480, the Otto di Pratica, replaced the Dieci di Balia, which had only been appointed in time of war, as the focus of decision-making in the fields of foreign affairs and defence.[37]

The objectives of these burgeoning administrative structures was not just the maintenance of forces of heavy cavalry. While the Sforza maintained substantial bodies of trained infantry in permanent service, most of the other states preferred to rely on professional infantry constables, retained on a permanent basis with small followings, who were expected to recruit and train infantry quickly in emergencies. A restraint on all these practices was finance; the shift from armies raised temporarily for war to a greater permanence was vastly expensive in the long term even if, in the short term, pay rates could be reduced. Many expedients were available for controlling these expenses: limitations on the number of infantry retained in permanent service was one of them, as they could be recruited and trained more quickly than cavalry; delayed and incomplete payments to the cavalry companies was another; neglect of munitions supplies, and particularly artillery was a third. The extent to which such economies seriously compromised Italian arms is very difficult to assess. It is certainly true that Italian infantry, although frequently trained in the use of the pike, was no match for the Swiss in the early years of the Italian Wars. It is also true that protracted arrears of pay seriously affected discipline, and as often as not captains would be forced either to use their own funds, or borrow from bankers, in order to pay and retain control of their troops. This had the effect of making the captains substantial creditors of the state and therefore reluctant to abandon its service. As for equipment stocks, for every company that was adjudged poorly equipped there were others which attracted admiration for their turnout and expertise. Gaspare Vimercati, one of Francesco Sforza's captains transferred to Milanese service in 1450 ran a model company which was responsible for the successful subjection of Genoa in 1464.[38] Artillery, on the whole, remained the direct responsibility of the state, although some large condottiere companies had a small artillery train. Both Milan and Venice established

the duke often had military functions, as well as the diplomatic ones described by Leverotti (1992).

[37] Mallett (1988).

[38] Covini (1998), 69–73.

artillery schools in the second half of the fifteenth century and were reasonably well equipped with guns. They were aware of the advances in technology being made in France and were seeking to imitate them. However, in this area the potential costs were enormous and there was little chance that even Venice could match the sums that the French kings were prepared to invest.

Mention of artillery brings us back to the question of the relationship between chivalric values and military professionalism. The long established belief that it was gunpowder weapons which shattered the ideals of feudal warfare, and that it was the gunners who were the first true professionals, was seriously undermined by a famous essay published by John Hale in 1965.[39] Hale pointed out that the chorus of complaint and cries of foul play which accompanied the increasingly lethal impact of guns in the fifteenth century, came largely in the literature of chivalric revival and was itself an indication of the significance of that revival. In the military world the practical effectiveness of the new weapons was noted and exploited; there was little evidence there of Machiavelli's well known scepticism about their value.[40] Francesco Sforza was reported, by Bartolomeo Gadio who was responsible for munitions in Milan for 25 years, to have commented that crossbows had clearly been superseded by firearms.[41] The guns of Bartolomeo Colleoni and Federico da Montefeltro were pitted against each other at the battle of Molinella (1467), and those of Alfonso, Duke of Calabria, threatened to open the road to Florence to the Neapolitan army as Colle Val d'Elsa and Poggio Imperiale were stormed in 1479.[42]

Captains like Colleoni and Federico di Montefeltro made a great deal of money out of war and preparation for war. They spent it lavishly on their estates and palaces, libraries and art collections, as well as on their companies and the broader entourages with which they surrounded themselves. Federico, as count and later duke of Urbino, took care to link himself to each of the major states in turn, except for Venice which he served only once, in his youth. This was

---

[39] Hale (1965) & (1985), 94–5.
[40] N. Machiavelli, *Discorsi*, II, 17.
[41] Covini (1998), 165 n. 20; for the importance of Gadio, see ibid., 147–8.
[42] For a recent discussion of the battle of Molinella-Riccardina, see Covini (1998), 199–202; on Colleoni's use of artillery, see *Bergomum* (2000), 48–9; on the 1479 campaign in Tuscany, see *Lettere* (1977–2000), IV, 224, 234, 238–9, & 243–8.

always done by negotiation and often with a stipulation that he need not fight against his most recent employer. He had the reputation of having never been defeated in war, and his advice on military matters was constantly sought.[43] Colleoni, on the other hand, apart from two brief periods in Milanese service, was linked to Venice for most of his career and was captain general of the Republic for the last 20 years of his life. His visit to Venice in 1458, to take part in the celebrations for the election of Doge Pasquale Malipiero, was one of the great events in the social calendar of the city and the occasion for a tournament in Piazza San Marco in which 70 men-at-arms fought on each side.[44]

Baldassare Castiglione was brought up in this courtly world of the late fifteenth century when the military captains were an integral part of an increasingly aristocratic society. He wrote in *Il Cortegiano* that 'the first and true profession of the courtier must be that of arms', but drew an interesting distinction between the courtier-soldier who must excel in arms and the military commander who needed to have 'professional knowledge of such things and other appropriate qualities'.[45] For Castiglione the gifted amateur was superior to the tedious professional, but he accepted that the soldier-scholar deserved the highest praise. Castiglione himself was a poor and somewhat reluctant soldier and this helps to explain the ambiguity in his approach to the role of late fifteenth-century Italian captains. Sydney Anglo commented recently that his courtier was 'just barely recognisable as a knight',[46] and this perhaps has some truth for the quiet backwater of a court which Urbino had become by the early years of the sixteenth century. But the court of Duke Federico or of the Sforza, or indeed of King Ferrante of Naples, a generation earlier, would have appeared somewhat different. In these ambiences war, the organisation of war and the training for war dominated the daily business and the discussions. The literature which emerged from and circulated within these courts was the literature of war, whether it was the late chivalric writings of Luigi Pulci and

---

[43] For Federico's interest in chivalry, see Clough (1990), 33–4; his political and military significance has been most recently discussed in Baiardi *et al.* (1986), particularly in the essays of Isaacs, Chittolini and Puddu.

[44] *Bergomum* (2000) has the most recent collection of material on Bartolomeo Colleoni.

[45] Castiglione (1967), 57–8.

[46] Anglo (1990), xi.

Matteo Boiardo, patronised respectively by Roberto da Sanseverino
and Ercole d'Este, the humanist panegyrics of Antonio da Cornazzano,
Giovanni Simonetta, or Roberto Valturio, or the serious military treatises of professional soldiers like Diomede Carafa and Orso Orsini.[47]
The themes of the soldiers' treatises were order, discipline and good
management of armies those of the humanists were gallantry and.
honour. They seem to be two worlds talking to us, but in fact they
were one.

The Italian Wars: An Epilogue

1494 has often been seen as a turning point in Italian history; the
beginning of centuries of foreign domination, the end, for the time
being, of any hope for a more unified Italy. The invasions, the years
of conflict between French and Spanish, the victimisation of the
Italian states, appeared to represent a return to the worst days of
the fourteenth century. Disloyalty and infidelity seemed once more
to pervade the military scene; all the brave talk was silenced and
the military institutions withered. The 'crisis of Italy' depicted by
Guicciardini and Machiavelli was presented as a combination of the
overwhelming superiority of French and. Spanish arms, and the inherent defects of the Italian mercenary system. Modernity and professionalism characterised the invading armies, while the Italian states
had not even the cloak of chivalry to hide their military nakedness.[48]
    Machiavelli's solution to the problem of Florence's military weak-
ness was neither chivalric nor professional. It was a part-trained,
largely rural, militia, a solution which had been much discussed by
the humanists in the fifteenth century, and tested, with very limited
success, by a number of Italian states and by France.[49] However,
what is important to remember is that the crisis, in so far as it was
a military one, was largely Florentine; the other Italian states had
created reasonably effective military organisations to counter the

---

[47] Murrin (1994), 21–2; Covini (1998), 166–71; Zancani (1990), 20–4; Settia
(1985).
    [48] The literature of 'crisis', going back to the contemporary writings of Guicciardini,
Machiavelli and Giovio, is extensive, and Piero Pieri (1952), in his conclusions
(595–615), has led the way towards a vindication, of at least Italian arms. The volume recently edited by David Abulafia (1995) provides a number of insights into
the problems.
    [49] Mallett (1990).

ambitions of their neighbours and the occasional forays of the out-side powers. What they were not able to cope with, or to combine successfully against, was a determined assault aimed at occupation and exploitation by monarchical powers which, by the end of the fifteenth century, had considerable advantage in manpower and wealth. These powers could indeed exploit the jealousies between Italian states, the factionalism and the widening gaps in society between ruling elites and the rest; but in the last resort it was the ability of France and Spain to pour reinforcements of men and money into Italy that enabled them to overwhelm the Italian states and maintain their confrontation with each other. What is interest-ing is that it was France, noted for the precocious development of its military institutions, and at the same time for the strength of its chivalric traditions, that lost out to the new and untested union of Castile and Aragon. The Spanish and, later, the Imperial armies were quicker to adapt to the large scale use of infantry and the logis-tical problems raised by campaigning in and occupying foreign soil.[50]

What is also interesting is the role that continued to be played by Italian captains and Italian troops, whether as new subjects of the invaders in the case of Milanese and Neapolitans, or as their allies or opponents. Gian Giacomo Trivulzio and Francesco Gonzaga led French armies, and Prospero Colonna and the Marquis of Pescara those of Spain. The artillery which won the battle of Ravenna for the French was Ferrarese, and many of the arquebusiers who won Bicocca and Pavia for the Emperor were Italians.

In 1497, shortly before the second French invasion and the demise of the regime of Ludovico Sforza in Milan, a great tournament was held in Brescia to celebrate the visit of Caterina Cornaro, the Queen of Cyprus, to her brother Giorgio who was currently the Venetian podestà of the city.[51] Among those who participated in the mock battle which formed the centrepiece of the festivities were several of the sons of Roberto da Sanseverino and their companies, which were part of the Milanese standing forces, the company of Nicola Orsini, count of Pitigliano, who was shortly to become Venetian captain general and whose base was at nearby Ghedi, and finally the

---

[50] The Italian Wars, and military and diplomatic transformations associated with the period, have become live issues following the protracted historical debate about 'Military Revolution'. I am currently completing a book on the Wars and their impact on military institutions and Italian societies.

[51] Mallett & Hale (1984), 199–200.

companies of members of the Brescian nobility, whose services had become increasingly welcome in the Venetian army in the second half of the fifteenth century. Elements of that Venetian army had only recently returned from the south where they had been assisting the Great Captain, Gonsalvo de Cordoba, and his Spanish expeditionary force, to evict the French army of occupation left after the retreat of Charles VIII in 1495.[52] The celebrations in Brescia, and the military expertise and experience on display, fit oddly with the idea of an extensive military crisis in Italy. They also illustrate the fusion of chivalric ideals and practices with the development of many of the criteria of military professionalism.

Professionalism did not destroy the chivalric world any more than guns did; it was always a part of medieval warfare. The growth of a 'more self-conscious professionalism', as Maurice Keen recently called it, helped to stimulate and maintain an enthusiasm for chivalric culture.[53] Greater permanence, and the institutional implications of permanence, were the keys to the new professionalism. Permanence increased skills and fostered loyalty, loyalty to the state as well as to the captains; it enabled commanders to gain expertise in organising troops, in maintaining discipline and morale, and above all in planning ahead; it fostered comradeship and collective courage, as opposed to the gallantry of the knight errant. Growing permanence was a significant feature of fifteenth-century European warfare, and nowhere more so than in Italy. Saying this is not an attempt to shift the so-called 'military revolution' back to the fifteenth century; the growth of permanence cannot be revolutionary, it is a gradual and oscillating process, dependent on the broader orientation of foreign relations, on available resources, and on changing states of mind. Once again the Renaissance appears as a transition rather than a turning point!

Bibliography

Abulafia D. (1995) *The French Descent into Renaissance Italy, 1494–5* (Aldershot, 1995).
Anglo S. (1990), ed. *Chivalry in the Renaissance* (Woodbridge, Suffolk: 1990).
Babil A. (1991) *Knowledge, Goodness and Power; the Debate over Nobility among Quattrocento Italian Humanists* (Binghamton, 1991).

---

[52] Mallett & Hale (1984), 57–8. Now see also the essay of Carol Kidwell on this campaign in Abulafia (1995), 295–308.
[53] Keen ed. (1999), 290–1.

Baiardi G. C., *et al.*, eds. (1986) *Federico da Montefeltro: lo stato, le arti, la cultura*, I, Lo Stato (Rome, 1986).

Barber R. (1974) *The Knight and Chivalry* (London, 1974).

——. and Barker J. (1989) *Tournaments: Jousts, Chivalry and Pageants in the Middle Ages* (Woodbridge, Suffolk, 1989).

Bayley C. C. (1961) *War and Society in Renaissance Florence: The 'De Militia' of Leonardo Bruni* (Toronto, 1961).

Bergomum (2000) *La figura e l'opera di Bartolomeo Colleoni*. Convegno di studi, aprile 1999. Numero monografico di *Bergomum* XCV, 1–2 (2000).

Boulton D. J. D. (1987) *The Knights of the Crown* (Woodbridge, Suffolk: 1987).

Brucker G. A. (1978) *The Civic World of early Renaissance Florence* (Princeton, 1978).

Cardini F. (1976) "La tradizione cavalleresco nell'Occidente medievale", *Quaderni medioevali* 2 (1976) 124–42.

——. (1981) *Alle radici della cavalleria medioevale* (Florence, 1981).

——. (1992) *Guerre di primavera* (Florence, 1992).

Castiglione B. (1967) *The Book of the Courtier*, trans. and ed. G. Bull (London, 1967).

Ceccopieri M. V. B., ed. (1993) *Braccio da Montone. Le compagnie di ventura nell'Italia del XV secolo* (Narni, 1993).

Chickering H. and Seiler T. (1988), eds. *The Study of Chivalry: Resources and Approaches* (Kalamazoo, 1988).

Chittolini G. (1979) "Infeudazioni e politica feudale nel ducato visconteo-sforzesco", in idem, *La formazione dello stato regionale e le istituzioni del contado* (Turin, 1979) 36–100.

——. (1981) "Signorie rurali e feudi alla fine del Medioevo", in *Comuni e signorie: istituzioni, società e lotte per l'egemonia* (*Storia d'Italia*), diretta da G. Galasso, IV, Turin, 1981) 597–676.

Clough C. H. (1990) "Chivalry and Magnificence in the Golden Age of the Italian Renaissance", in Anglo (1990), cit. above, 25–48.

Contamine P. (2000), ed., *War and Competition between States* (Oxford, 2000).

Covini M. N. (1985) "Condottieri ed eserciti permanenti negli stati italiani del XV secolo in alcuni studi recenti", *Nuova rivista storica* 69 (1985) 329–52.

——. (1998) *L'Esercito del Duca. Organizzazione militare e istituzioni al tempo degli Sforza (1450–1480)* (Rome, 1998).

——. (2000) "Political and Military Bonds in the Italian State System, 13th to 16th centuries", in Contamine (2000), cit. above, 9–36.

Del Treppo M. (1973) "Gli aspetti organizzativi economici e sociali di una compagnia di ventura italiana", *Rivista storica italiana* 85 (1973) 253–75.

Dorigatti M. (1996) "Reinventing Roland: Orlando in Italian Literature", in Pratt K. ed., *Roland and Charlemagne in Europe: Essays in the Reception and Transformation of a Legend*, King's College London Medieval Studies 12 (1996) 105–21.

Duby G. (1977) *The Chivalrous Society* (London, 1977).

Fasoli G. (1958) "Lineamenti di una storia della cavalleria", in *Studi di storia medioevale e moderna in onore di Ettore Rota*, ed. F. Vaccari and P. F. Palumbo (Rome, 1958) 83–93.

Fowler, K. (1998) "Sir John Hawkwood and the English condottieri in Trecento Italy", *Renaissance Studies* 12 (1998) 131–48.

Fubini R. (1994) *Italia Quattrocentesca; politica e diplomazia nell' età di Lorenzo il Magnifico* (Milan, 1994).

Gasparri S. (1992) *I'milites'cittadini: studi sulla cavalleria in Italia* (Rome, 1992).

Hale J. R. (1965) "Gunpowder and the Renaissance: An essay in the history of ideas", in *From the Renaissance to the Counter Reformation*, ed. C. Carter (New York, 1965) and reprinted in Hale J. R. *Renaissance War Studies* (London, 1983) 389–420.

——. (1985) *War and Society in Renaissance Europe, 1450–1620* (London, 1985).

Hanlon G. (1998) *The Twilight of a Military Tradition: Italian Aristocrats and European conflicts, 1560–1800* (London, 1998).

Hyde J. K. (1966) *Padua in the Age of Dante* (Manchester, 1966).

Jones P. J. (1997) *The Italian City-States, 1100–133* (Oxford, 1997).

Kaeuper R. (1999) *Chivalry and Violence in Medieval Europe* (Oxford, 1999).

Keen M. (1984) *Chivalry* (New Haven, Conn., 1984).

——. (1999) *Medieval Warfare: A history* (Oxford, 1999).

Larner J. (1988) "Chivalric Culture in the Age of Dante" *Renaissance Studies* 2 (1988) 117–30.

Lenzi M. L. (1988) *La pace strega; guerra e società in Italia dal XIII al XVI secolo* (Montepulciano, 1988).

Lettere di Lorenzo de' Medici, vols. I–VIII, ed. N. Rubinstein *et al.* (Florence, 1977–2000).

Leverotti F. (1992) *Diplomazia e governo dello stato. I 'famigli cavalcanti' di Francesco Sforza (1450–1466)* (Pisa, 1992).

Mallett M. E. (1974) *Mercenaries and their Masters: Warfare in Renaissance Italy* (London, 1974).

——. (1979) "Preparation for war in Florence and Venice in the second half of the 15th century", in *Florence and Venice: Comparisons and Relations*, ed. S. Bertelli *et al.* (Florence, 1979), I, 149–64.

——. (1988) "The Florentine *Otto di Pratica* and the beginning of the War of Ferrara", in *Florence and Italy. Renaissance Studies in honour of Nicolai Rubinstein*, ed. P. Denley and C. Elam (London, 1988) 3–12.

——. (1990) "The Theory and Practice of Warfare in Machiavelli's Republic", in *Machiavelli and Republicanism*, ed. G. Bock *et al.* (Cambridge, 1990) 173–80.

——. & Hale J. R. (1984) *The Military Organisation of a Renaissance State: Venice c. 1400–1617* (Cambridge, 1984).

Mesquita, Bueno De, D. M. (1941) *Giangaleazzo Visconti, Duke of Milan, 1351–1402* (Cambridge, 1941).

Mozzarelli C. ed. (1978) *Patriziati e aristocrazie nobiliari: ceti dominanti e organizzazione del potere nell' Italia centro-settentrionale* (Trent, 1978).

Murrin M. (1994) *History and Warfare in Renaissance Epic* (Chicago and London, 1994).

Pieri P. (1952) *Il Rinascimento e la crisi militare italiana* (Turin, 1952).

Pillinini G. (1970) *Il sistema degli stati italiani, 1454–1494* (Venice, 1970).

Puddu R. (1982) *Il soldato gentiluomo* (Bologna, 1982).

Ricotti E. (1844–5) *Storia delle compagnie di ventura in Italia* (Turin, 1844–5), 2 vols.

Ruggieri R. (1963) *L'umanesimo cavalleresco italiano da Dante al Pulci* (Rome, 1963).

Salvemini G. (1896) *La dignità cavalleresca nel comune di Firenze* (Florence, 1896).

Settia A. (1985) "'*De re militari*': cultura bellica nelle corti emiliane prima di Leonardo e di Machiavelli", in *Le sedi della cultura nell' Emilia Romagna* (Milan 1985) pp. 65–90.

——. (1993) *Comuni in guerra. Armi ed eserciti nell' Italia delle città* (Bologna, 1993).

Vale M. (1981) *War and Chivalry: Warfare and Aristocratic Culture in England, France and Burgundy at the end of the Middle Ages* (London, 1981).

Waley D. (1988) *The Italian City-Republics* (London, 1988, 3rd ed.).

——. (1993) "I mercenari e la guerra nell'età di Braccio da Montone", in Ceccopieri (1993), cit. above, 111–28.

Zancani D. (1990) "Antonio Cornazzano's *De integrità della militare arte*", in Anglo (1990), cit. above, 13–24.

Zorzi G. (1915) "Un vicentino alla corte di Paolo II: Chierighino Chiericati e il suo *Trattatello della Milizia*", *Nuovo archivio veneto*, new ser., 30 (1915) 369–434.

Addendum

The paper of Francesco Stovti referred to in n. 31 has now been published in *Condottieri e nomini d'arme nell' Italia del Rinascimento* ed. Mario Del Treppo (Liguore editore: Naples 2001) pp. 327–46. The volume contains a number of other interesting contributions to the themes discussed here.

CHAPTER FOUR

THE PORTUGUESE NOBILITY AND THE RISE AND DECLINE OF PORTUGUESE MILITARY POWER 1400–1650

Malyn Newitt

The emergence of Portugal as a major military and naval power and its subsequent decline illustrates many of the themes in the history of war during the transitional period between the feudal and the modern army which is often referred to as the "military revolution". This essay argues that Portuguese military success was achieved by the successful use of an amphibious military strategy and by the development of fortified strongholds defended by artillery and supplied from the sea. Although the Portuguese built up considerable expertise in engineering and in handling artillery, the recruitment, training and command of its armed forces and the design of its warships did not keep pace with changes taking place elsewhere in Europe. The failure to modernise was to undermine and virtually destroy the empire Portugal had built up in the East and came near to destroying its Atlantic empire as well.

In 1415 the Portuguese undertook one of the most spectacular amphibious assaults of the age when they seized the Moroccan port of Ceuta. Holding onto the conquest caused Portugal to devote an ever-growing part of the resources of the Crown and the church to Moroccan warfare. Ceuta was defended against some fierce sieges and in 1437 a Portuguese counterattack on Tangier was repulsed. However, in 1458 began a sixty-year period of continuous warfare and conquest which saw Portugal occupy every port of any significance in western Morocco between Ceuta and Agadir, and establish hegemony over extensive areas of the Moroccan interior. In October 1514 a Portuguese raiding force reached the very walls of Marrakech—the capital of western Morocco—and although the force was not strong enough to carry out an assault on the city, the Portuguese knights, in a gesture of contempt for their enemies, chalked their names on its walls before departing.[1]

The Moroccan campaigns had, at least in part, been designed to establish a monopoly over the valuable trade of the region and, in particular, over the gold trade with the states of the western Sahel. In pursuit of this objective the Portuguese competed with the Castilians for control of the Canary Islands, a key base for control of the Atlantic coast of Africa, and fought a vicious war at sea which culminated in Castile securing the islands in exchange for recognising Portugal's control of the trade of Guinea. To complete their control over this area of the coast the Portuguese also fortified a base at Arguim (*c.* 1445) and later built the castle of El Mina (1482), on the coast of modern Ghana, to siphon off the gold trade towards the Gulf of Guinea.

In the 1490s, while Castile conquered Granada and the Canary Islands and began its own invasion of Morocco, Portugal was poised to undertake another spectacular military conquest. Vasco da Gama's discovery of the sea route to India (1497–9) was quickly followed by the seizure of the key African and Asian ports of Sofala, Kilwa, Ormuz, Goa and Malacca, and by the beginning of a cycle of Asiatic and African warfare which was to lead by the mid-1500s to Portuguese control of most of the ports of western India, the Gulf and eastern Africa.

The high water mark of Portuguese military power was probably the three decades of 1540–1570. During this time, while the Turks extended their conquests in the eastern Mediterranean, the Portuguese confronted Turkish forces in the Indian Ocean alone and decisively defeated them, extending their territory along the coasts of northern India, establishing a dominant military presence in the Moluccas, and founding the trading cities of Macao and Nagasaki. During this time Portuguese military architecture also reached its peak of sophistication and provided fortified bases that were virtually impregnable to Asiatic armies and fleets. This was also a period when freelance Portuguese military forces intervened effectively in the wars in Ethiopia, Burma, Arakan and Ayuthia.

However during this period there were already signs of relative decline in Portuguese military power. In Morocco the fall of Santa

---

[1] For a general description of the warfare in Morocco and for this incident in particular see Cook (1994), 148.

Cruz (Agadir) to Moroccan assault in 1541 led to the abandonment of four other coastal *fortalezas* and a decisive breach in Portugal's commercial stranglehold.[2] Meanwhile Portugal's ability to maintain military and naval superiority in Malabar and in the seas off Malacca was being effectively challenged by Calicut and Aceh. However, it was only after 1570 that Portugal began to suffer major military reverses. Most spectacular was the defeat of Al Kasr el Kebir in Morocco in 1578—notable not only for the death of the Portuguese king and the subsequent union of the kingdom with that of Castile, but also for its revelation of the lack of manpower and archaic tactics of the Portuguese. In 1575, after six years of attempted conquest, the Portuguese had to admit defeat in their attempt to conquer the mines of Monomotapa in central Africa and in 1576 they were expelled from Ternate in the Moluccas. In Angola the determined attempt at military conquest, begun in 1575, had by 1589 ended in stalemate. Although Portugal was still able to make significant conquests—in Ceylon after 1593 and in east Africa from 1595—these were achieved by the extensive use of locally recruited troops who fought in a manner traditional in local wars. At best these victories disguised the decline in Portugal's military strength which was brutally exposed with the outbreak of war with the Dutch and the English in the late 1590s.

In the early seventeenth century Portugal began to experience military defeat on an unprecedented scale. Ships were routinely lost in conflict with the Dutch and the English, and the islands and even the coasts of Portugal were raided with impunity. Although for a time the Portuguese were safe within the walls of their massive forts, these were put under increasing pressure as the Dutch and English built local alliances and maintained naval blockades. The loss of Ormuz in 1622 saw the beginning of a military collapse—Bahia in 1624, and the rest of Northern Brazil in 1630, El Mina in 1637, Luanda and São Tomé in 1640, Malacca in 1641, Muscat in 1650, Colombo in 1656 and Cochin in 1663.

This military decline of Portugal took place over a long period of time and it is perhaps remarkable that Portugal was able to sustain its empire for so long. Moreover, Portugal's losses, as Sanjay Subrahmanyam has pointed out, were caused more by determined Asiatic and African resistance to Portugal than by defeats inflicted by the

---

[2] Cook (1994), 194–7.

Dutch and English.[3] The loss of Japan and Ethiopia in the 1630s, for example, were due almost exclusively to local efforts to expel intrusive foreign influences. Reverses in southern India and Ceylon were also more the result of local resistance than Dutch or English intervention. However, as Boxer has pointed out, by the seventeenth century Portugal had fallen behind its rivals in almost every aspect of military and naval equipment and organisation. It could no longer compete in ship design or in financial or manpower resources. Above all it had fallen behind in the building of a professional army—the recruitment, organisation and training of its armed forces, and in the deployment of these forces in war.[4]

Portuguese Armed Forces in the Fifteenth Century

The Portuguese armed forces which faced the Castilians at Aljubarrota in 1385, and which captured Ceuta in 1415, were still what might be described as a feudal army. The core of this army was the feudal "host" which consisted of the major princes and nobles with their armed followers. The great nobles had traditionally received *contias* from the Crown, grants of lands or revenues, made to them at birth, which committed them to military service as *vassallos del rey* and obliged them to provide a specified number of "lances".[5] These "lances" were drawn from the large noble households in which the sons of the minor gentry (*fidalgos*) sought preferment and employment, although they were sometimes raised from the towns (*concelhos*) over which the nobles had jurisdiction. The followings of the great nobles, in effect, constituted private armies which could operate independently of the Crown—the classic example being the exploits of the forces under the command of the Constable, Nun' Alvarez Pereira, during the war against Castile in 1383–5 and his threat to leave Portugal if the king interfered with his command. As well as serving under their master in the king's army, the military followers of the great nobles might also be sent on raids or piratical cruises. In return they could expect to be paid and maintained,

---

[3] Subrahmanyam (1993).
[4] Boxer (1969), ch. 5 "The Global Struggle with the Dutch".
[5] Monteiro (1998), 34.

to be provided with their arms and to be offered material rewards and continuous employment.

As well as receiving *contias*, the nobles who were numbered among the *vassallos del rey* were paid a daily sum (*soldo*) while they were on campaign and were obliged to return this, or pay some other penalty, if they quit the campaign or otherwise avoided service. In theory this system restricted the major obligation for military service to the higher nobility but, during the wars which brought João of Avis to the throne in 1385, much of the nobility sided with Castile and João was forced to raise troops as and where he could, rewarding men of lower birth who joined his service.

Of particular importance was the part played by the knights of the four Military Orders (Santiago, Avis, Cristo and Hospital) and during the fifteenth century the Orders were brought under royal control by the systematic appointment of members of the ruling dynasty to the Masterships of the Orders. The Orders not only controlled frontier and coastal fortresses with their arsenals but were also expected to provide "lances" for any army that was assembled.[6] The knights of the Orders, particularly the Orders of Christ and Santiago, provided an invaluable reserve of manpower which the Crown was able to utilise in the organisation of overseas expansion. Leaders of exploratory expeditions, donatory captains of the islands and commanders of the overseas fortresses were routinely selected from among the members of the Orders.[7]

In addition to the *vassallos del rey* and their "lances" were the soldiers supplied by the chartered towns (*concelhos*). The most significant of these were the crossbowmen (*besteiros*), a semi-professional corps which had been established during the fourteenth century. These men were specially selected from the artisan class and were granted considerable fiscal privileges to maintain themselves ready, trained and equipped, for war. They were spread throughout the kingdom and formed the core of any force that had to be raised for internal police duties or for the defence of the kingdom which, in the fifteenth century, came to include the defence of the African fortresses. On paper this corps, which elected its own leaders, numbered about 5,000 men.[8] There were also the so-called *aquantiados* (taxpayers).

---

[6] Monteiro (1998), 79–84.
[7] For the role of the Orders in overseas expansion see Subrahmanyam (1997), ch. 2.
[8] Monteiro (1998), 61.

According to the level at which they were assessed, these men had to maintain either a horse or foot soldier and his arms, or just the horse or equipment, a commitment which might range from supporting a fully armoured horseman to providing the spear and shield for a humble foot soldier.

This military obligation was very unpopular and its abuse was the subject of endless complaint. For example, Fernão Lopes records that when the Earl of Cambridge arrived in Portugal with his army in 1381, the king took the horses of the *aquantiados* to mount the English force without any compensation being paid to their owners.[9] However, the idea that there was an obligation on ordinary citizens to undertake military service was rooted in the communal autonomy claimed by the *concelhos*. Time and again Portuguese monarchs had to turn to these provincial levies to provide them with some kind of an army, and in one form or another this popular military force remained the core around which Portuguese armies were built until the time of Napoleon.[10]

The public ideology of these feudal armies was still that of chivalry and crusade. *Fidalgos* sought the formal honour of knighthood and Azurara, whose writings are modelled on the chronicles of chivalry, maintained in the *Crónica da Tomada de Ceuta*, written in the 1450s, that the main reason for the expedition against Ceuta in 1415 had been the desire of the Infantes (the sons of the king) to be knighted on the field of battle rather than at a tournament.[11] In his *Crónica dos Feitos de Guiné*, he tells stories of the armed men in the service of the Infante Dom Henrique (Henry the Navigator) receiving the accolade on the beaches of West Africa after a successful slave raid.[12] Crusade against the Moors was also prominent in the ideology of soldiers who often sought the justification for what they were doing in the traditional language of crusading—none more so than Dom Henrique himself.[13] However, a knighthood was not just a military honour. It could carry with it membership of one of the Military Orders of knights with their vast corporate wealth. Military success

---

[9] Lomax & Oakley (1988), 69. This book consists of extracts from the chronicles of Fernão Lopes.
[10] Monteiro (1998), 44–58.
[11] See Bethencourt & Chaudhuri (1998), I, 120.
[12] Beazley & Prestage (1896) I, 48.
[13] Thomaz (1994), ch. 1.

might be rewarded with the grant of lordships, towns or castles in the control of the knights. Well into the sixteenth century this class showed a predisposition to continue with traditional forms of mounted warfare, even though the wars of the fifteenth century largely consisted of amphibious raids and sieges along the Moroccan coast where the rapid development of firearms was making the mounted knight increasingly obsolete.[14] It is significant that the king himself felt the need to be protected not only by a guard of knights but also by a special corps of crossbowmen.

Behind the language of chivalry and honour was the reality of what military activity meant in practice. War was expected to pay for itself and to provide the major pathway to a prosperous career. Lack of resources at the disposal of the Crown had always meant that *contias* and *soldos* were paid from the proceeds of confiscations, ransoms or plunder. Nobles for their part had to reward their followers, and plunder, ransoms, and slave raiding became so important that they often determined the shape of campaigns and the whole direction of strategy. The voyages "of discovery" down the coasts of Africa, organised after 1430 by the Infante Henrique and other noblemen, were openly and explicitly a series of raids designed to obtain slaves for sale or important "Moors" who might be ransomed.

The forces raised by the nobles and the *concelhos* were supplemented by the king's personal guards, by individual soldiers of fortune who were attracted by the prospect of war, and by mercenaries or "allies". Examples of such mercenary forces were the archers and knights in the service of John of Gaunt and the Earl of Cambridge who helped win the battle of Aljubarrota in 1385 or Muslim fighters from Granada and soldiers recruited in one of the Spanish kingdoms who were experts in the use of firearms or in engineering. As these men were often extremely experienced and skilled, they formed a highly important part of any Portuguese army of the period.

During the wars of the late fourteenth and early fifteenth centuries Portuguese armies seldom numbered as many as 10,000 men. The army which won the famous victory over the Castilians at Aljubarrota apparently numbered only 6,500 men, 700–800 of whom were English mercenaries. After his recognition as king, João of Avis was usually able to muster 4,000 mounted men for his campaigns

---

[14] For the royal guard see Monteiro (1998), 28–30 and Serrão (1977–), III, 247.

against Castile, a number which suggests an overall army size of
about 10,000 men. Nevertheless much larger armies were apparently
assembled for the African campaigns in the first part of the fifteenth
century. For the attack on Ceuta in 1415, João is alleged to have
had an army of over 30,000 and, although that figure is probably
exaggerated, it seems likely that as many as 14,000 men were assembled for the attack on Tangier in 1437, while the army used for the
capture of Arzila in 1472 is supposed to have numbered 25,000
men.[15]

As recorded by the chroniclers the core of these armies was made
up of the mounted men, and maintaining such an army involved
not only problems of recruitment and manpower but also the logistical problems of keeping such large forces shod, fed and paid. In
the fourteenth and fifteenth centuries a royal arsenal had been established in Lisbon where military equipment was stored, while the
knights of the Military Orders were expected to maintain weapons
and stores in their fortresses. With the development of the African
voyages and the conquests in Morocco, the *Casa de Ceuta* (later the
Casa de Guiné) was created to co-ordinate the fitting out of ships and
expeditions. These arrangements proved effective in enabling the
Crown to organise the annual trading voyages, and even larger expeditions such as those of Cão, Dias and da Gama, but they were
stretched to the limit when a major military campaign had to be
mounted.

The almost continuous state of war in Morocco put added pressure on this type of traditional army and each expeditionary force
had to be improvised with difficulty from whatever manpower was
available. Jorge von Ehingen has described one such expedition,
undertaken probably in 1457, for the relief of Ceuta. His account
deliberately conjures up images chivalrous warfare in which knights
set out for any theatre of war where adventure and honour might
be found. The army had been assembled in Lisbon and, as a visiting knight, he had been invited to join the expedition. He was fitted
out by the king and on arrival at Ceuta was given the command of
a sector of the town manned with troops, presumably mercenaries,
from the Low Countries. Having beaten off attacks on the walls, the
Portuguese garrison, consisting of 400 horse and 1,000 foot soldiers,

---

[15] For a discussion of the size of Portuguese armies see Monteiro (1998), 92–98.

had sallied out and occupied some of the high ground overlooking the town. It was there, on a plain between the two armies, that von Ehingen fought and killed a Moorish champion in single combat in a deliberate enactment of the ideals of chivalrous warfare of the Reconquista.[16]

If feudal armies could be assembled for individual campaigns, such armies could not be retained permanently for garrison duty. The Crown's resources were only able to pay small numbers of permanent soldiers, and the defence of the Moroccan fortresses came more and more to depend on artillery—technology being developed to supply a shortage in costly manpower. The Moroccan towns were fortified, refortified and crammed with artillery. Experiments were made in construction, and in providing gun emplacements and bastions to replace old-fashioned curtain walls—though the Moroccan fortresses always retained high towers used for lookout purposes.

However the real foundation of Portuguese military and naval power rested upon the use of artillery in conjunction with seapower. During the fifteenth century Portugal's most successful military operations were seaborne attacks on coastal towns in Morocco or on villages and settlements within striking distance of the sea. At first Portuguese attacks were not very sophisticated with ships landing troops who then fought ashore in the conventional manner, but by the middle of the century Portuguese ships were not only carrying artillery but were using this to support landings and to attack targets on land. For their longer voyages down the African coast and to the islands, the Portuguese developed the traditional Mediterranean caravel and incorporated one or more pieces of artillery which were used to overawe local populations or to defend the ship itself from attack. Small guns were even mounted on the long boats which were used to go ashore. Mounting artillery on ships overcame the problem of moving heavy guns, which was faced by armies operating on land. The massive iron cannon of the fifteenth century could only be moved slowly and with difficulty, and were nearly useless in any military action except long drawn-out sieges. A ship, however, could become a floating battery, easily manoeuvrable, relatively secure from sorties or counterattacks and able to mount the largest guns of the day.[17]

---

[16] Letts (1929), 32–37.
[17] See discussion in Cipolla (1965).

It has been suggested that in the fifteenth century the Iberians were leaders in developing the use of artillery. Fernando's army assembled to fight Castile in 1381 had bombards, and although older forms of siege engine continued to be used for another fifty years, it was artillery which enabled the Portuguese to seize Al Kasr in 1458, Arzila and Tangier in 1472 and thereafter to occupy one Moroccan coastal town after another. It was also guns which enabled the Castilians to win the final struggle against the Granada kingdom in 1492.[18] As with other European armies, the expansion of the use of firearms in Iberia helped to make the old feudal armies obsolete. Guns needed expert handling and maintenance, they had to be supplied with munitions and mounted with expertise on board ship or in specially constructed gun emplacements in fortresses. Moreover the guns had to be manned the year round as the Moroccan fortresses were subject to surprise attacks. All this increased the need for professional and permanent forces.

Finally there was the issue of command. As has already been shown, the followings of the leading *vassallos del rey* or the Military Orders could constitute private armies. Many of the castles in Portugal itself were controlled by the Military Orders or by noble families who had the right to appoint the *alcaide-mor*, or commander. In addition the *aquantiados* and *besteiros* had their own elected commanders. Welding these disparate forces together into a single army was not easy. In times of war the kings would often appoint a *fronteiro-mor*, who might be a royal prince,[19] to take overall command in some region of the country, but the issue of who would command the armed forces flared up again in a dangerous manner in the early days of the Estado da Índia. It was only partly resolved by the nomination of a viceroy or governor, and fleet commanders were still able to claim that they had independent authority. For example, in 1511 Diogo Mendes tried to exercise a command independent of Afonso de Albuquerque and was arrested by the latter and deported to Portugal. It is significant that even such a prestigious commander as Albuquerque was so unsure that he would be obeyed that he not only regularly held a council of his captains before making major

---

[18] Cook (1994).
[19] Monteiro (1998), 139.

military decisions but also considered it necessary to consult all the "*fidalgos* and noble persons of the fleet".[20]

Moroccan Warfare in the Early Sixteenth Century

After 1458 Morocco remained one of the major theatres of war for the Portuguese, but it was war which had its own particular characteristics and which encouraged the persistence of certain archaic forms of military organisation. As far as the Portuguese had a strategy in Morocco it was to control all the main ports and to impose their dominance over the commerce of the country. This policy was continued down the Atlantic coast to Guinea where Portuguese-controlled *feitorias* monopolised seaborne trade as far as the equator and the mouth of the Zaire. To achieve this the Portuguese tried to work with local rulers and to extend their protection to the communities in the hinterland of their factories. This policy offered a reasonable prospect of success while the major states in the Moroccan interior were engaged in seemingly endless civil war. By the second decade of the sixteenth century considerable areas of the Moroccan coastal region had become in effect Portuguese protectorates.

However, this policy was increasingly undermined by the very commanders appointed by the king of Portugal to govern the Moroccan *praças*. These commanders were drawn from the military nobility and they were responsible for recruiting their own officers and soldiers who had to be rewarded in the manner traditional in this kind of warfare—through plunder, ransoms and slaves. The captains were increasingly left to fend for themselves and there was even a case of a captain using his own money (in fact the dowry of his wife) to build his own castle, at Santa Cruz de Guer, which he subsequently sold to the Crown.[21] Not surprisingly this "privatisation" of warfare resulted in a policy of plunder and extortion, with the fortress commanders raiding the Moroccan hinterland, sometimes with spectacular success. A raid carried out by the captain of Safi, Nuno de Ataíde, in 1511 resulted in 567 prisoners, 1000 head of cattle, 300 camels and horses and 5,000 smaller livestock.[22]

---

[20] Birch (1880), III, 48–9, 100.
[21] Details in Peres (1931), III, 454–55.
[22] Lopes (n.d.), 47.

Raids of this kind helped perpetuate old-fashioned forms of mounted warfare. The garrisons of the North African *praças* were made up of units of horse and foot soldiers. The mounted soldiers—the *cavaleiros*—saw themselves as men of rank and, according to David Lopes, "in the wars with the Moors a good cavaleiro could only fight with other mounted men". Patrols of horsemen were sent out daily to scour the country round the Portuguese towns and, when the alarm was sounded from the lookout posts, a troop of armed horsemen would be available at once to meet the emergency. When the Castilian viceroy of Granada visited Arzila in 1517, a demonstration was given of Portuguese preparedness and 250 armed horsemen assembled as soon as the alarm was sounded.[23]

However, warfare in Morocco encouraged another development, which was increasingly resorted to in a Portugal suffering from severe shortages of manpower. This was to employ locally recruited auxiliary troops who naturally fought in a manner traditional to Morocco, whose activities were rooted in local tribal, family and clan loyalties and whose objectives were often not those of Portugal. In this way the main fortresses, Arzila, Mazagan and Santa Cruz (Agadir) became independent of Lisbon and pursued their own locally focused policies.

When these fortresses were faced, as they frequently were, with massive Moroccan reprisals, Lisbon would be called on to send relief fleets. In the early part of the century these were usually able to keep the fortresses supplied with men, munitions and materiel, their guns driving attackers away from the beaches and covering troop landings and the provisioning of the towns. However, the reliance of Portugal on ships and hastily assembled relief expeditions disguised a growing military weakness and, as a strategy, failed completely when the ships were not able to get near enough to help, as at Graciosa in 1489, or when the Moroccans mounted effective batteries to command the sea approaches as at Mamura in 1515.

Throughout the fifteenth and much of the sixteenth centuries the Moroccan fortresses were the training ground for the Portuguese military. Service in these fortresses was popular with the nobility, partly because they were near to Portugal and partly because the regular

---

[23] Ibid., 41, 48. For a description of the military organisation of the Moroccan fortresses see 41–49.

raiding parties that set out from the forts into the interior of Morocco provided ideal opportunities for learning the profession of arms, for excelling in individual enterprise and for gaining wealth in the form of plunder and ransoms. Time and again, when the king of Portugal had to raise a force of experienced men, it was to the North African garrisons that he turned. For example, the men who accompanied Francisco Barreto to East Africa in 1569 were described as veterans from North Africa, while the expedition's second in command, Vasco Fernandes Homem, had made his name at the siege of Mazagan in 1562.[24] However, it seems likely that warfare in North Africa helped to entrench attitudes and ideologies which were obstacles to modernisation in military matters. Warfare in Morocco perpetuated the religious ideology of crusade and with it an undue emphasis on individual prowess achieved in small scale mounted raids, although the experience of siege warfare countered this to some extent by emphasising the need for technical competence and the implementation of the latest ideas in military technology and architecture.[25]

The Estado da Índia and Portuguese Warfare in the East in the Sixteenth Century

The founding of the Estado da Índia in 1505 led to a significant increase in Portugal's military commitments. There were new fortresses being built in the East and large fleets of war ships to be manned, projects on which the success of the Estado da Índia depended. It was in this context that the court brought forward a proposal to establish a standing army under its own direct control. The project was hotly contested by the leading nobles who feared the loss of patronage and power that would result from the ending of the practice of military service by the nobility.

In the event the armies and fleets sent to the east formed a kind of hybrid. Captains of the ships and fortresses continued to be selected from among the service nobility. In the late fifteenth century, and

---

[24] Martyn (1994), 121.
[25] Subrahmanyam (1997), 54–58 argues that the objective of winning control of Jerusalem was a dominant influence on king Manuel in the early sixteenth century and that messianist influences at court remained powerful until the defeat and death of Sebastião in 1578.

particularly during the reign of João II (1481–95), the Crown had attracted increasing numbers of the lesser gentry to attend court and to seek patronage from the Crown rather than from the great nobles. *Fidalgos* entering Crown service in this way were rewarded with retaining fees and pensions (*moradias*). They came to form a service nobility from which the king drew the manpower for his administration and for military operations. For example, seventy-seven of these service nobles, called *moradores da casa del rey* (pensioners of the royal household), accompanied Francisco de Almeida to India in 1505, categorised as either *cavaleiro, escudeiro, moço fidalgo*, or *moço da câmara*— among them was Fernão de Magalhães (Magellan).[26]

In this way there grew up a system of mutual expectations, obligations and rewards which was to characterise Portuguese military service at least until the eighteenth century. *Fidalgos* would be expected to serve the Crown but would, in their turn, look to be rewarded for this service with patronage. Patronage might take the form of promotion in the royal service, a lucrative command of a ship or fortress, or a grant of lands, revenues, titles and pensions of one kind or another. In the fourteenth and early fifteenth centuries the Crown's ability to reward service had been limited and had resulted either in the depletion of the royal patrimony or in a ruthless policy of confiscations from political enemies. However, by the sixteenth century the Crown's sources of patronage had immeasurably increased. In 1500 the Crown controlled two of the four Military Orders of knights and had acquired extensive church patronage through the *padroado real*. At the same time expansion overseas in Morocco and West Africa provided additional wealth and expanded the number of offices and commands at the Crown's disposal. The proliferation in the number of fortresses involved a huge growth of military office holding. Fortresses required officers and technicians of all kinds for their maintenance and these came to form a new military hierarchy with appointments and promotion largely controlled, at least at first, by the Crown.[27]

Occasionally a member of the higher nobility would take a command—as in the case of Francisco de Almeida, who was appointed

---

[26] "Livro do Assentamento de 1505 da Casa da India", in Baxter & Silva Rego (1962), 76–85. Sometimes a nobleman would call himself *fidalgo da casa del rey* or *fidalgo escudeiro da casa del rey*.

[27] Bethencourt and Chaudhuri (1998), vol. 1.

first viceroy of the Estado da Índia in 1505 or the Duke of Braganza who commanded an expedition to Morocco in 1514—but most of the commanders were lesser nobles who progressively built their careers in Crown service. A striking feature of this officer corps was the network of family relationships that grew up. Commanders of fleets tried to recruit relatives and members of connected families, presumably to provide some guarantee of loyalty within their commands. This again was to be a factor that militated against the emergence of a wholly professional army.

The manpower that accompanied the expeditions—the soldiers and sailors, gunners, artisans, clerks and support personnel were all enlisted in the service of the king and their names were enrolled in the Casa da Índia. Ordinary soldiers were known as *homens d'armas* (men at arms). Gunners (*bombardeiros*) commanded by a constable (*condestabre*), musketeers (*espingardeiros*) and crossbowmen (*besteiros*) were singled out for higher pay and for a greater share of any booty, and they were probably recruited, as they had been in the fifteenth century, from the privileged corps of crossbowmen maintained in the Portuguese provinces.[28] They received a wage, were provided with arms and were subject to the *regimentos*—the orders issued by the Crown to regulate the conduct of the fortresses and ships.

Because the men enlisted for long periods (inevitably involving years of service), nominally received pay from the Crown and were subject to the *regimentos*, the Portuguese forces in the East came to acquire something of the character of a standing army supported by an increasingly complex royal bureaucracy. However, in practice, elements of the old feudal army survived and reasserted themselves. This was most clearly seen in the way the forces were raised. Some of the men were volunteers, including many non-Portuguese, in particular Germans, Flemish, Italians and Castilians, who were attracted to service in India, and there were also a number of condemned criminals (*degredados*) who were enlisted in remission of their punishment and who were sometimes detailed to undertake specially dangerous missions.[29] But to a large extent the recruitment of the men

---

[28] "Regimento do Capitão-mor D.Francisco de Almeida", Baxter & Silva Rego (1962), 157–265, especialy 249–251.

[29] For *degredados* see Monteiro (1998), 88–90. Some women convicts were also sent to the East. See "Rol do Pagamento do Mantimento de Fevreiro de 1506 na Fortaleza de Sofala", Baxter & Silva Rego (1962), 425–447, especially 435.

still depended on the captains. Men would enlist in the retinue of a particular captain and, in spite of their official pay in Crown service, would look to their captain not only to command them but also to provide for them and to reward them appropriately. In this way it was common for a well-known and successful captain to be able to recruit more successfully than an unknown man or one with a bad reputation.

In the fifteenth century the Portuguese had mounted some major military operations—large even by the standards of the rest of Europe. Major expeditions continued to be organised in the sixteenth century as well. Large amphibious expeditions would be assembled for the wars against the Turks in the Indian Ocean or occasionally for operations in Morocco but for the most part the sixteenth century saw a smaller scale of military operation. The Estado da Índia consisted of the viceregal capital and a string of fortified towns and ports around the rim of the western Indian Ocean. Although there was a large Portuguese population in Goa, the other posts had small, and often very small, numbers of Portuguese. A fortress might have fifty or a hundred soldiers, seldom more, while the ships assigned to each station would again have only a score or so of Portuguese on board. Military operations usually took the form either of raids on enemy ports and shipping, invariably carried out by seaborne assault, or of the defence of the fortresses against enemy attacks.

The typical raid would be mounted from small boats, often propelled by oars (*fustas*). These might carry one or more small pieces of artillery and a score or so men. They depended for their success on speed, manoeuvrability and surprise. They could sail up river estuaries in the dark and mount attacks at dawn or burn enemy shipping seeking refuge up river. In such raids the Portuguese would carry hand guns (*espingardas*) but for the most part depended on more traditional weapons, like crossbows, swords and pikes which were less at risk from water.

Success in this type of warfare wholly depended on the close relation of the captain and his men. The men looked to the captain for sustenance and reward and he had to provide them with their share of any plunder. In the course of the sixteenth century the fortress captains came to acquire control of the Crown's commercial monopolies, so that their appointment to command a fortress became less a commission in royal service and more a permission to exercise a private commercial monopoly for three years. In these circumstances the captains depended entirely on the collaboration of their men and the quasi-feudal bonds were reinforced. Captains appointed their own retainers to accompany them and the fortress garrisons became a form of private army. When the captain left at the end of his commission, the men would depart with him to his next command or return to Goa, sometimes leaving the fortress entirely unmanned. The Portuguese armed forces therefore were bound together by a cement of personal loyalty to individual captains who rewarded their followers through distributing loot, facilitating their private trade and appointing them to posts under their command.

Portuguese Warfare in the Later Sixteenth Century

As the sixteenth century progressed there was an increasing tendency for "Portuguese" armed forces to be made up of locally recruited soldiers. One factor contributing to this was the shortage of European Portuguese but another was the need for the Portuguese to fight in circumstances where their equipment, training and weaponry were not always appropriate. To remedy these problems they recruited soldiers from the regions where they were fighting. Indian, Sinhalese *lascarins* and African soldiers formed the bulk of the armies, while Asian crews or African slaves manned the ships. The locally recruited soldiers were usually armed and organised in their own manner and expected to be rewarded in ways familiar to their society. Tonga warriors recruited by the Portuguese in eastern Africa, for example, expected to be rewarded with female captives after a successful campaign. In Ceylon *lascarins* were called out under their traditional leaders (*mudaliyars*) and the desertion of large numbers of these during the campaign of 1603 was attributed by contemporaries to the failure to grant adequate rewards to the soldiers.[30]

The struggle against the Turks in the Indian Ocean had mostly been fought at sea or by using the amphibious techniques with which the Portuguese were familiar. However, in the second half of the century Portugal became increasingly committed to campaigns on land which it had always previously avoided. The policy of conquering and occupying territory appears to have been stimulated by

---

[30] Abeyasinghe (1966), 49.

the desire to emulate the Spaniards and discover and exploit gold
and silver mines in Africa. But it was also prompted by the need of
the Estado da Índia for greater resources of manpower, finance and
materiel, and by the desire of the Jesuits for a more forward con-
version policy. Between 1570 and the end of the century major campaigns were launched in eastern Africa, in Congo and Angola and
in Ceylon. At the same time the revival of interest in Morocco,
which was encouraged and led by the unstable young king Sebastião,
culminated in the dispatch of a large and ill-fated army in 1578.

During the same period Portugal's Atlantic Islands and mainland
Portugal itself came under increasing attack from English, French
and Moroccan privateers while, after the union of the Crown with
that of Castile in 1580, attacks by the Dutch rebels also became
more frequent. Portugal had to reorganise and reconstruct its coastal
defences and was soon involved in a naval war that stretched from
the coast of Portugal to China.

To meet these challenges Portugal was able to deploy military
resources which had not been significantly modernised since the
beginning of the sixteenth century. Each ship in the annual fleets
which were dispatched from Lisbon to the East carried a thousand
or more soldiers and crew. The soldiers were all entered on muster
rolls and were obliged to serve the Crown for seven years. However,
they were not assigned to any kind of regiment or company and there
were neither barracks, nor adequate maintenance for them once they
reached the East. The soldiers found their own lodgings and waited
for the summons to join an expedition. When an expedition was organised, the individual captains raised their men from among the soldiers available in Goa or the other Indian towns. Many captains in
fact ensured their complement of soldiers by unofficially paying their
maintenance or allowing them to eat in their houses during the
period between campaigns.[31] The armies that were mustered in this
way were very small by European standards. Pero Lopes de Sousa
is said to have mustered 1,200 Portuguese for the invasion of Kandy
in 1594 and Jerónimo de Azevedo had 800 in 1603 for a similar
enterprise, but these were the largest armies ever assembled and during most of the wars of the early seventeenth century in Ceylon the
captain-generals seldom had more than 400 Portuguese in total.[32]

---

[31] Burnell (1885), I, 188–192 and Gray (1887–1890), II, 122.
[32] Abeyasinghe (1966), 15, 43.

Even so, for much of the year the soldiers were effectively unemployed and many of them were reduced to a state of penury. According to contemporary accounts these soldiers formed a lawless element in the population and many of them deserted to find well rewarded employment in the armies of Asiatic rulers.

After seven years of service, a soldier could either apply for a passport to return to Portugal where he would present certificates of service to the king, or he could acquire the status of a *casado*—literally a married man. *Casados* were no longer included on the muster rolls as soldiers and assumed civilian status. They could expect to take part in local affairs, embark on commercial activities, own property and, of course, found families. *Casados* were still liable for military service in defence of their local *fortaleza* or town but they were not expected to enlist for offensive operations.[33] In areas where Portugal controlled a lot of territory, as in the *Provincias do Norte*, Bardes and Salsette, Ceylon or East Africa, land was often granted to individual Portuguese with a condition, reminiscent of Portugal itself in the middle ages, that they supply one or more mounted men for local defensive purposes, or, in the case of East Africa, that they recruit local forces drawn from the peasants who inhabited their *prazos*.

In addition to what might be described as purely "Portuguese" armed forces, there existed other formations. In most of the towns and *fortalezas* in the East the local Christian population, including many people of mixed race, were also liable for military service. François Pyrard describes the muster of Indian Christians who paraded monthly before the viceroy and he comments significantly that the Portuguese did not take part in these musters so that no one should know their numbers.

In Portugal itself little had been done to modernise the armed forces. In 1562 the fortress of Mazagan in Morocco was attacked by a large army equipped with heavy artillery. Portugal's effort to relieve the fortress, successful as it proved, nevertheless showed a serious state of unpreparedness. The Regent, queen Catherine, made three attempts to assemble a relief force. At first forty-six court nobles volunteered and one of them, a member of the queen's council, raised a company and paid for a ship out of his own pocket. When further relief was required two more noblemen raised companies,

---

[33] Gray (1887–90), II, 125.

500 soldiers were recruited in Andalucia and the garrison of Tangiers was ordered to provide 400 men. A third relief expedition was then mustered. This time seven captains were appointed to raise companies of 200 men while captains were sent to the towns of the Algarve—Silves, Lagos, Tavira, Faro and Loulé—to raise companies there. The Duke of Braganza, the most important nobleman in Portugal, was also ordered to raise 2,000 men. In the end the expedition sailed under the command of Francisco Barreto, a former viceroy of India, with 3,000 men. In each expedition, we are told, some young noblemen enlisted without royal permission.[34]

In 1569, soon after reaching his majority at the age of fourteen, king Sebastião, who had great military ambitions, revised the tangle of regulations governing the obligation for military service. This now became a general obligation falling on all able bodied males, and the local forces were placed under a *capitão-mor* for muster and training. The *capitaes-mores* were local nobles, *alcaides* of towns or officers elected by town councils. The term *Ordenança* was used for the first time to describe these local forces which had to turn out to defend their districts or to protect the coasts against pirate attacks.[35] The *Ordenança* were supposed to form a reserve of men trained in the use of arms from whom troops could be raised for military campaigns in time of need.

These changes, in fact, did little to equip Portugal with modernised, professional armed forces and the army that was raised for the expedition to Morocco in 1578 had little unity of organisation and was pieced together from a wide variety of sources just as the relief expeditions to Mazagan had been sixteen years earlier. The 20,000 fighting men with whom Sebastão invaded Morocco were made up of soldiers hired from Spain and from the Pope, Lutheran mercenaries from Germany and Flanders and five *tercios* of Portuguese, one of them made up of volunteer *fidalgos* and the other four traditional Portuguese levies from the regions. Moreover the army was not properly equipped with artillery or with horses.[36] None of the Portuguese, not even their officers, could be described as professional soldiers and only a contingent from the garrison of Tangier had any

---

[34] Martyn (1994), 107, 111, 118.
[35] "Exército" in *Dicionário ilustrado da História de Portugal*.
[36] Cook (1994), 247; Brooks (1964), 12–20.

real training in warfare. The result was a catastrophic defeat and the death of the Portuguese king.

An intriguing theory has been advanced to explain why no one who took part in the battle admitted to having seen the king die—a theory which, if true, would illustrate the excessive extent to which chivalrous ideals still survived at the Portuguese court. As the historian José Saraiva puts it, "according to the ethos of chivalry, to confess to having seen the king die, without having given one's life for him would be infamous"—therefore no one could be found to testify to the king's death and the legend that he had somehow survived the battle began to gain credibility.[37]

Portuguese armed forces were still hampered by the two concepts that had dominated their armies in the Middle Ages. First was the notion of a service nobility—men of a certain social standing who recognised an obligation to serve the Crown but who expected to be rewarded for their service. Distinctions were made between different levels of service noble (*fidalgos da casa del Rey, moços fidalgos, cavaleiros fidalgos, moços da câmara, escudeiros fidalgos* etc.) but *cavaleiros* were still expected to provide their own horses and accoutrements. Soldiers served in the East with the hope of being made knights—even though this was an honour now devalued because "very cooks boys and others as mean as they, are made knights".[38] In the fifteenth century these men had raised their own companies of "lances" and the expectation that captains would recruit their own men continued. Linschoten, writing about Goa in the 1580s, says that each captain "of their own purses give them something beside their pay, for that every captain seeketh to have the best soldiers".[39] By the end of the sixteenth century, in many of the commands, there was no longer even the pretence that the soldiers were serving the king. Captains were expected not only to recruit but also to pay their soldiers from the profits of the commercial monopolies they held. For example, the captain of Mozambique paid for the garrison of fort São Sebastião, was responsible for the upkeep and maintenance of the fortifications and, in addition, had responsibility for the forts of Sofala, Sena and Tete and for half a dozen or more earth stockades and forts in the

[37] Saraiva (1978), 175.
[38] Burnell (1885), I, 189.
[39] Ibid., 190.

interior. To these he appointed and paid captains and provided the
garrisons with arms and munitions.[40]

Fortresses

During the sixteenth century the Portuguese seldom had occasion to
assemble, drill and deploy large armies in sustained military campaigns. Their warfare techniques became increasingly specialised to
meet the needs of their empire and to carry out the smallscale operations required to sustain the authority of the fortress captains in
their own localities. However, they did have plenty of experience of
defending fortresses against attack by large armies and in the field
of defensive warfare they became particularly effective.[41]

Portugal's Moroccan fortresses, captured by amphibious assault,
were frequently attacked by large land based armies. Initially the
Moroccans sought to storm the fortresses by sheer weight of numbers and, if this failed, they resorted to blockade. To defend these
fortresses the Portuguese compensated for their lack of manpower
by the use of artillery. Large guns were mounted on specially built
bastions which were added to the high crenellated curtain walls which
had been developed as protection against archers and assault by scal-
ing ladders. The fortresses were also designed to be supplied by sea
so that a protected maritime access was a key to their design.

As the Moroccans gradually acquired their own artillery the
Portuguese adapted their designs, lowering and thickening the walls,
constructing glacis and angled walls which not only allowed enfiladed
fire from the garrison but deflected incoming cannon shot. The
fortresses built in the east incorporated these designs, the Portuguese
often employing the latest Italian designs and even Italian architects,
as the *trace italienne* technique of fortification was developed and elab-
orated in Europe.[42] They also became expert in countermining—the
firing of countermines being one of the principal reasons for the successful defence of Mazagan. As a result the Portuguese fortresses
were extremely difficult to capture and, as was shown at Diu in 1536
and 1548, at Mazagan in 1562 and at Mozambique in 1607 and

---

[40] Newitt (1995), ch. 5.
[41] Moreira (1989).
[42] For example see Boxer and Azevedo (1960).

1608, could be defended by comparatively small numbers of men and even by civilians.[43]

Portuguese Armed Forces During the Dutch Wars

During the long drawn out struggle with the Dutch which lasted from the 1590s to 1663, the Portuguese armed forces have been represented both by contemporaries and by subsequent historians, as hopelessly weak and outclassed. As early as the first decade of the seventeenth century, the French traveller François Pyrard commented on the way the Portuguese drafted criminals and children to make up the numbers on their ships and how these were unwilling to face the Dutch and frequently surrendered without a fight. The Italian Francisco Carletti, returning to Europe on board a Portuguese ship early in the seventeenth century, commented on the incapacity of the gunners and explained how the office of chief gunner was frequently given to someone of no experience.[44] Pyrard made the same judgement, observing that "their men are not capable of great fatigue, and their officers ... are rarely expert in their several offices".[45]

Moreover the lack of discipline among Portuguese soldiers and sailors was almost universally commented upon. Linschoten describes how on his voyage out to India in 1583 fighting broke out among the company during ceremonies to celebrate the crossing of the Line,

> which proceeded so far, that the tables were thrown down and lay on the ground, and at the least a hundred rapiers drawn, without respecting the Captain or any other, for he lay under foot, and they trod upon him, and had killed each other, and thereby had cast the ship away, if the Archbishop had not come out of his chamber among them, willing them to cease....[46]

He says that when on campaign the captains and the soldiers sit together at the same table, explaining such egalitarianism by saying that otherwise the soldiers "would not esteem him or obey him".[47] The same year mutineers seized fourteen ships in a Portuguese armed

---

[43] For the sieges of Mozambique see Axelson (1960), ch. 2.
[44] Carletti (1965), 233.
[45] Gray (1887–1890), II, 209.
[46] Burnell (1885), I, 17.
[47] Ibid., 190.

flotilla because the soldiers had been refused prize money.[48] Boxer quotes the Bishop of Cochin writing about Portuguese soldiery in 1621, "they consider it an honour rather to fly than to fight; punishments are not enforced and military discipline is brought to nought".[49] Indiscipline was not only a problem among ordinary soldiers for it was common for a *fidalgo* to refuse to take orders from someone he considered to be of lesser social rank.[50]

C. R. Boxer, in his account of the Portuguese-Dutch wars, comments on the physical weakness of the Portuguese compared with the robust Dutch and German mercenaries fighting for the VOC [Dutch East India Company], on their poor equipment and on tactics which amounted to little more than a shout of "Santiago" and an undisciplined charge.[51] Apparently the Portuguese made much use of a weapon called a *bacamarte*—a kind of blunderbuss "much used all over India, having a barrel 3 spans in length, a flint-gunlock, and firing bullets of 2 or 3 ounces, 50 of them being rammed down in a single charge; so that one shot from it wreaks as much havoc amongst a crowd of people in a street as would a swivel-gun". Such a weapon, if it did not kill the soldier firing it, could only be used once in a combat otherwise decided by swords or pikes.[52]

The inability of the Portuguese ships to fight their English or Dutch counterparts on equal terms is legendary. During the wars in the Gulf in the 1620s and 1630s, the Portuguese made use of galleons and smaller naval vessels to good effect but the Portuguese Indiamen were unseaworthy at the best of times, and, when confronted with the smaller but more heavily armed ships of the Dutch or English, were often helpless targets and were smashed to pieces without being able to make any effective reply. The problem lay partly in ship design but more in the lack of experienced soldiers and gunners on board.

Portugal's military difficulties were compounded by shortage of manpower and financial resources and by a lack of professional military competence. Although the populations of Portugal and the Netherlands were approximately the same size, the Dutch were able

---

[48] Pearson (1987), 97.
[49] Quoted in Boxer (1930), xlviii.
[50] This issue is discussed in Boxer (1980), 31 and elsewhere.
[51] Boxer (1969), ch. 5.
[52] Boxer (1930), 62.

to make up shortages of manpower by hiring mercenaries. Moreover their experiences during the Thirty Years War in defence of their southern frontier against the Spanish ensured that their forces were trained in the latest military techniques. The Portuguese sought to make good their manpower shortages by the recruitment of troops locally among the African and Asian populations. But these troops, although experienced enough in local conditions, were not able to compete with the Dutch in modern branches of warfare.

Perhaps the greatest disparity was in the qualities of the "officer corps". There were some extremely able Portuguese military commanders during this period, men such as Ruy Freyre de Andrada, Nuno Alvares Botelho or Francisco de Seixas Cabreira, but Portugal continued to appoint noblemen or *fidalgos* to commands, often in reward for past service, and these expected to make a fortune from trade rather than to undertake military duties. This system caused increasing resentment among the Portuguese resident in India who were experienced in local affairs, but time and again saw important posts given to incompetent *fidalgos* from Portugal who sometimes never even came to the East in person to take up their commands.[53] The Portuguese system confused purely military functions with the complex social relations of the *fidalgos* and their families and clients and the system of leasing out the Crown's trade monopolies. As François Pyrard wrote

> most of them, nay all, captains, masters, master's mates, keepers, even the mariners and gunners, and others get their offices by favour, or for money, or in recompense for their services or past losses; also that these offices are given to the widows or children of such as have died on voyages or elsewhere in the service of the king; then do these sell them to whom they will, without judging his capacity or merit.[54]

For most of these commanders, the first priority was to get a return on their investment in purchasing the trade monopoly which went with their commands or to provide dowries for daughters and patronage for their family and clients. This leasing out of the monopolies on short, three year contracts, met the needs and demands of the aristocracy but was hardly an adequate answer to the mobilisation of resources through the VOC which supplied the Dutch war machine.

---

[53] Boxer (1980), 11–12.
[54] Gray (1887–1890), II, 209.

Conclusion

The Portuguese feudal army of the late middle ages absorbed an ideology rooted in crusade and religious conflict in Morocco. This ideology was taken with them to the East and was used to legitimise their attempts to impose commercial monopolies by force of arms, and their practice of taking and distributing booty from their enemies. The armed forces depended on the service nobility who raised and commanded the units and who maintained companies of soldiers loyal to themselves. The scale of warfare in the East and the need to adapt to local conditions, together with chronic shortages of manpower, led the Portuguese to become increasingly reliant on Asiatic troops and on the strength of their fortresses. They were unable or unwilling to modernise their forces along the lines being pioneered in Europe, and faced the Dutch and English in the seventeenth century with archaic ships, armaments and command structures. Their forces lacked the professional skills, organisation and back up which underpinned the European armies of the day. Above all, their officers and commanders continued to be drawn from a nobility which for the most part saw the holding of commands as a way to make a fortune rather than as a military responsibility.

Bibliography

Abeyasinghe T. (1966) *Portuguese Rule in Ceylon 1594–1610* (Colombo, 1966).
Axelson E. (1960), *Portuguese in South-East Africa 1600–1700*, Johannesburg, 1960).
Baxter T. W. and Silva Rego A. da (1962), eds., *Documents on the Portuguese in Mozambique and Central Africa* (Lisbon, 1962).
Beazley C. R. and Prestage E. (1896), eds., *The Chronicle of the Discovery and Conquest of Guinea*, 2 vols, (London, 1896).
Bethencourt F. and Chaudhuri K. (1998), eds., *História da Expansão Portuguesa*, 5 vols, (Lisbon, 1998).
Birch W. de G. (1880), ed., *The Commentaries of the Great Afonso Dalboquerque*, 4 vols, (London, 1880).
Boxer C. R. and Azevedo Carlos de (1960), *Fort Jesus and the Portuguese in Mombasa*, (London, 1960).
———. (1930) ed., *The Commentaries of Ruy Freyre de Andrada* (London, 1930).
———. (1969) *The Portuguese Seaborne Empire* (London, 1969).
———. (1980) *Portuguese India in the Mid-Seventeenth Century* (Delhi, 1980).
Brooks M. E. (1964) *A King for Portugal* (Madison, 1964).
Burnell A. C. (1885) ed., *The Voyage of John Huyghen van Linschoten to the East Indies*, 2 vols (London, 1885).
Carletti F. (1965) *My Voyage around the World*, trans H. Weinstock (London, 1965).

Cipolla C. (1965) *Guns and Sails in the Early Phase of European Expansion, 1400–1700* (London, 1965).

Cook W. F. (1994) *The Hundred Years War for Morocco* (Boulder, 1994).

Dicionário ilustrado da História de Portugal (Lisbon, 1985).

Gray A. (1887–1890) ed., *The Voyage of François Pyrard*, 2 vols (London, 1887–1890).

Letts M. (1929) ed. and trans., *The Diary of Jorg von Ehingen* (London, 1929).

Lomax D. and Oakley R. J. (1988) eds. *The English in Portugal 1367–87* (Warminster, 1988).

Lopes D. (n.d.) *A Expansão em Marrocos* (Lisbon, n.d.).

Martyn J. R. C. (1994) *The Siege of Mazagão* (New York, 1994).

Monteiro, J. G. (1998) *A Guerra em Portugal nos Finais da Idade Média* (Lisbon, 1998).

Moreira R. (1989), *História das fortificações portugueses no mundo* (Lisbon, 1989).

Newitt M. D. D. (1995), *A History of Mozambique* (London, 1995).

Pearson M. N. (1987) *The Portuguese in India*, New Cambridge History of India, vol. I (Cambridge, 1987).

Peres D. *et al.* (1931) *História de Portugal* (Barcelos, 1931).

Saraiva J. H. (1978) *História concisa de Portugal* Lisbon (1978).

Serrão J. V. (1977–) *História de Portugal*, 14 vols to date (Lisbon, 1977).

Subrahmanyam S. (1993) *The Portuguese Empire in Asia* (London, 1993).

——. (1997) *The Career and Legend of Vasco da Gama* (Cambridge, 1997).

Thomaz, L. F. (1994) *De Ceuta a Timor* (Linda-a-Velha, 1994).

CHAPTER FIVE

ARTISANS, ARCHITECTS AND ARISTOCRATS: PROFESSIONALISM AND RENAISSANCE MILITARY ENGINEERING

Simon Pepper

The artillery-makers and gunners of Renaissance Europe, and the military architects and other construction specialists who devised and built the early artillery fortifications represented the genesis of what were to become important but separate branches of Early Modern armies. In the transitional phases covered by this chapter, artillerists and fortification engineers were—as we shall see—often one and the same. However, the geography of progress in these closely related fields was interestingly different. Northern and central Europe is credited with early leadership in the manufacture of guns, while fifteenth-century France and Burgundy were amongst the first emerging powers to incorporate artillery into their military establishments in ways which significantly enhanced its exploitation.[1] It was from southern Europe, in the late-fifteenth and early-sixteenth centuries, that the key architectural response emerged in the form of bastions.[2] Projecting forward from lowered and widened gun platforms to bring defensive artillery closer to the besiegers, sunk in deep ditches to present a smaller target, and with all of the perimeter swept by flanking fire from concealed batteries, the open bastion—particularly in its fully developed triangular or arrow-head form—represented a fundamentally different approach to defensive architecture from the tall, circular, or semi-circular gun-towers of the late Middle Ages. Although some elements of what was to become known to contemporaries as the *trace Italienne* can be identified in early modern fortifications in other countries, the key developments were seen to be primarily Italian in origin, and the spread of bastioned fortification from

---

[1] Dubled, 1976; Contamine, 1972, pp. 230, 238–9, 311–17, 534; Vale, 1975, pp. 57–72 and Vale, 1981, pp. 129–146.
[2] Hale, 1965.

southern into northern Europe provides a very suitable case study into the means whereby technical innovations were transmitted, and of the specialists who acted as the agents of diffusion.

This process of diffusion and the professionalisation of military engineering that made it possible are the focus of the following paper, which concentrates on the part played by the new specialists in the spread of bastioned fortifications. It needs to be added, of course, that the conditions of Balkan frontier warfare, the *petit guerre* of the Wars of Religion, and the particular needs of coastal fortification often justified the use of different architectural solutions.[3] There was also a well-developed central-European tradition which employed enormously enlarged round or semi-circular gun-towers, earth ramparts and a variety of elaborate ditch defences well into the sixteenth century, and in some cases even later.[4] It would be a mistake to assume that these alternative forms were ineffective, and I have argued elsewhere that such an assumption can seriously distort our view of Early Modern fortification. But in what might be called "mainstream" Western European siege warfare of the sixteenth century, the *trace Italienne* proved its effectiveness time and again, and the extent to which fortress designers were able to understand and handle the bastioned system quickly became a touchstone for their standing as experts. For the specific purposes of this paper, the competent application of Italian bastioned design is taken as the primary indicator of progress and of the diffusion of expertise in the new military architecture.

How these ideas were disseminated, what kind of men or institutions contributed to the process, how they were trained and selected for what has always been seen to be a specialism demanding a variety of practical, administrative and theoretical skills are all topics that will be explored. By focussing initially on the relatively well-studied Italian origins of the new military architecture and the different groups that made up the "profession" in that country, I hope to establish a template against which the less thoroughly researched professional context of fortress design in northern Europe can be evaluated.

---

[3] Pepper & Adams, 1986, pp. 17–27; Pepper, 1999, pp. 338 and 346–7.

[4] The Germanic alternative tradition is best-known from the treatise of Albrecht Dürer (1527), but is ignored or at best sidelined in most accounts of early modern fortification. But see Neumann, 1988 and Bogdanowski, 1996.

* * *

Although Italians were given credit for the early development of the bastion, it is no easy matter to classify the men who constituted the Italian military architectural "profession." One modern attempt to do so by Horst De La Croix yielded a distinction between the all-rounder civilian professionals active in fortress design during the fifteenth century and first half of the sixteenth, and the more explicitly military figures who dominated the action and the treatise literature published in the second half of the sixteenth century. De La Croix, an art historian, looked first to architects and engineers—the two Renaissance titles being for all practical purposes synonymous in Italy.[5] Many of the well-known architects associated with the early development of Renaissance fortifications were polymaths who from time to time engaged in military designs and in some cases became actively involved in war. Leonardo da Vinci, Fra Giocondo, Bramante, and Michelangelo were all men of this kind, as was Francesco di Giorgio Martini who stands out from the others on account of the very large number of fortresses which he built or modernised for the Dukes of Urbino, and the Kings of Naples, and for his front line service. At the second siege of Naples in 1495 he may well have excavated and exploded the gunpowder mine which brought the long French defence of the Castelnuovo to an abrupt end.[6] Francesco di Giorgio was also part of a lengthy tradition of all-rounders who at particular stages of their careers became practically full-time military architects.[7]

Individuals not immediately identified either as architects or engineers also made important early contributions. The scientist, Mariano Taccola (*De Machinis*, MS originating in the 1430s), illustrated guns

---

[5] De la Croix, 1960.

[6] For the mine see Bury, 1982, pp. 23–30 and most recently Pepper, 1995, pp. 284–5. The best recent survey of Francesco di Giorgio is Adams, 1993.

[7] It was a tradition of mixed activity that lasted into the eighteenth and even the nineteenth centuries. Balthassar Neumann (1687–1753) came into the service of Wurzburg through the Prince-Bishop's cannon-foundry and artillery, and continued to build fortifications long after he was recognised as Germany's leading Baroque church and palace architect. Viollet-le-Duc (1814–79) is best known for his conservation architecture, in which the reconstruction of medieval castles and town walls were prominent features, but served as deputy chief military engineer for the defence of Paris in 1871 and became an effective advocate for the radical transformation of France's fortifications after the Franco-Prussian war. Pepper & Hughes, 1983, pp. iii–xvii.

in his treatise on machines and what appears to be a gunpowder mine, although the first use of this last device was much later. Vannoccio Birringucci (1480–1539) and Niccolo Tartaglia (1506–59) were both also primarily scientists, with a scientist's knowledge of explosives and a reputation as artillerists—or at least as theorists of artillery technology. Tartaglia's *Nova scientia* (1537) and his later *Quesiti e inventioni diverse* (1546) and Birringucci's *De la Pirotechnia* (1540) were amongst the earliest printed books to treat of contemporary fortification design and siege methods, albeit at a very simple level. Some early gunners—not surprisingly—also applied their talents to fortress design. By the turn of the fifteenth and sixteenth centuries, Basilio della Scola, who had made his reputation as a gunner in France, was clearly accepted in Italy as a reliable authority on both artillery and fortification, and has been credited with the design of works in his native Vicenza and Verona, as well as Rhodes.[8] Basilio had served in France for many years and commanded of one of Charles VIII's famously-effective artillery trains for the invasion of Italy in 1494–1495—a fact noted in Venetian documents as a kind of qualification, which of course it was. He returned to Venetian service in 1495 and was charged with the manufacture and proving of new artillery on the Republic's testing range on the Lido as part of the rearmament programme initiated by the French campaign.[9] In 1501 Basilio displayed in Venice a wooden model of a fortress with the aim of showing "what is being done in France, Italy . . . Germany and elsewhere."[10] Models, of which more will be said later, were critically important in the explanation of complex architectural forms at a time when formal drawing techniques were not yet standardised—to say nothing of the difficulty frequently experienced by non-architects in understanding technical drawings. Basilio famously deserted Venice for the French during the Battle of Agnadello,[11] but it is his activity rather than his ethics which is of interest here, together with this fragment of evidence for some kind of public debate—or perhaps it was a programme of public instruction—about changing patterns of fortification, which evidently took place in Venice, with the help of models as visual aids.

---

[8] Zorzi, 1958–59.
[9] Pepper, 1995, p. 290, n. 112.
[10] Buisseret (ed.), 1998, p. 125, quoting Sanuto.
[11] Mallett & Hale 1984, p. 87

Many professional soldiers of course involved themselves in both artillery and engineering, but any generalisation about career patterns in the technical arms is particularly hazardous without detailed knowledge of their social background, education and initial military experience. A few examples, however, will serve to illustrate the range of participants and to highlight some of the areas of uncertainty surrounding the roles actually performed by individuals from very different walks of military or building life.

Gian Giacomo dell'Acaya (d.1570), Baron of Segine, fortified the important city of Lecce (from 1539) for the Spanish crown, expanded his own fief of Acaya into one of southern Italy's first planned fortress towns (1521–35) and built or modernised fortresses in literally dozens of southern sites. Acaya was one of a surprisingly small number of magnates to graduate from a purely proprietorial interest in military architecture to become accepted as a leading specialist.[12] Francesco Maria della Rovere (1490–1538), Duke of Urbino, was another member of the senior nobility whose mastery of the new technology was such that he enjoyed the status of expert and is credited with the design of schemes in Urbino, the Church States, and in the mainland as well as the overseas territories of Venice for whom he served as captain general from 1523.[13] Indeed, the Duke of Urbino made no secret of his belief that few captains and—with three exceptions, one of them dead—no military architects understood the threats and opportunities of defensive sites.[14] Alessandro Farnese, Duke of Parma and Imperial Governor of the Low Countries, also enjoyed high standing in technical affairs and at times acted as what today would be called a design consultant. In 1589 he gave detailed advice on the fortification of Lucca whilst serving in Flanders, and the word used in the documents—"ideata" or conceived—suggests an active design contribution, rather than comment on someone else's work. Drawings certainly went to and fro between Lucca and Flanders,

[12] Monte, 1996, pp. 15–32.

[13] Legnago (1525–33), Pesaro, Verona and Vicenza (1530), Senigallia (1536), Zara (1533–35) and Corfu (1537) as well as variety of regional defensive studies are credited to the Duke of Urbino by Concina, 1983, pp. 24–31.

[14] Adams, 1999, pp. 55–62. The *Discorsi Militari* were published in 1583, long after the Captain General's death, as a series of speeches, comments of military affairs, and anecdotes which may well have been told in camp, surrounded by friends and fellow soldiers. Not strictly a treatise, it was nevertheless highly valued and often quoted for the insights of one of the period's finest soldiers.

but whether Farnese's drawing was in his own hand, or that of
another, is unknown.[15] Farnese could evidently read architectural
drawings, in itself a small skill, but one that significantly opened up
the potential for his own active involvement. But these are fragments
of evidence. That senior nobility planned strategy, and discussed and
approved fortification layouts is clear enough; but the precise nature
of their involvement in detailed design, or construction, generally
much less so.

The active engagement of the "nobility of the sword" in different
aspects of siege warfare is altogether easier to establish. But the career
which saw Gabriele Tadini da Martinengo of Bergamo (1480–1543)
progress from an artillery specialist in Venetian service at the sieges
of Padua (1509), Brescia (1512) and Bergamo (1516) to a position
in Crete as engineer-general with the rank of Captain of Infantry
was to be characterised by an unusually close involvement in the
less aristocratic parts of the job. Martinengo left Crete to join the
Knights of St John in their defence of Rhodes (1522–23) where he
distinguished himself in the countermining operations. There he was
credited with the invention of an underground listening device, the
pebble on a drum, which was subsequently known as Martinengo's
tamburo. In 1525 he was made a knight of the order and appointed
Prior of Barletta, by which name he appears in many later treatises.
Service for the Emperor followed in Spain, North Africa, Sicily and
Vienna, and as general of artillery at Pavia (1525) and Genoa (1527).
Ancient family connections were essential to knighthood in the order
of St John, but it was first in the artillery and later in the dirty,
dangerous and invisible underground warfare of mining and coun-

---

[15] Besides being one of the greatest soldiers of his age, Alessandro (1545–92) was
the grandchild of Charles V, through his mother Margaret, the illegitimate daughter of the Emperor, who had later married Ottavio Farnese (thus strenghtening the
Gonzaga position in Italy). Alessandro was consulted over various details of the
design of Lucca's fortifications, and energetically pursued his own construction programme in Parma and Piacenza, and in the Low Countries during the early stages
of the Eighty Years War. Martinelli & Puccinelli, 1983, p. 26 describe the reception of a plan sent from the Low Countries by Alessandro Farnese. "Il 5 aprile
1589 la pianta ideata da Alessandro Farnese era gia arrivata a Lucca e venica
mostrate al Consiglio Generale riunito. [Footnote] Due giorni dopo, il 7 aprile
1589, l'offizio convocava l'ingegnere Vincenzo Civitali e, dopo avergli fatto vedere
il disegno mandato dalle Fiandre, gli ordinava di fare una *copia di quella parte di
ponente tenendo il resto sotto secretezza*." Civitali was later instructed to correct various
small errors, chiefly the lack of dimensions in Farnese's drawing.

termining—so often the preserve of commercial artisan miners drafted in for the purpose—that Martinengo established his reputation.

The nobility was of course the traditional feeder for the profession of arms. Architecture was much less obviously so. Although birth opened many doors in civil life, military architecture offered the "civilian" architect a route into the emerging officer corps when competence as a designer and builder was combined with a personal readiness to fight. Giovanni Battista Belluzzi (1506–54) was born a gentleman of San Marino and after some years in the wool trade in Bologna and the Roman court of the Colonna, married into the family of the Urbino architect, Girolamo Genga, who gave him an architectural training. After a diplomatic mission to Florence in 1543, Cosimo de' Medici engaged him as a military architect working on numerous Florentine fortress construction projects and in 1548 he initiated the fortifications of the Duke's new city of Cosmopolis (present day Portoferraio) on the island of Elba. In 1551 Belluzzi saw active service at Mirandola in Lombardy, and in 1553 he accompanied the Imperial army in the early stages of the Emperor's war against Siena, being wounded at the siege of Montalcino. He recovered in time to enter Siena in disguise in July 1553 to spy out the underground network of water supply conduits (a possible route into the city) and by the end of the year was in action again in Corsica.[16] In February 1554 he was granted the rank of Captain of Infantry and given command of a company of 300 foot at the siege of Siena. Almost certainly Cosimo intended the captaincy as a reward for his conduct in the field rather than as an active command, for on 2 March 1554 he was given his patent as *ingegnere del campo*. The Duke of Florence was furious when he received word that his chief engineer had been gravely wounded on 6 March leading his company in the assault on a relatively unimportant Sienese fortress, and saddened when news reached him of Belluzzi's death at the end of the month.[17]

Belluzzi had prepared a draft treatise on earthwork fortification— a technique he had employed for the refortification of Pistoia in the 1540s—and when this treatise appeared in print many years later in a somewhat corrupted form, it articulated very strongly what De

---

[16] For Belluzzi's underground spying see Adams, Lamberini and Pepper, 1988.
[17] Pepper & Adams,1986, p. 177 drawing on biographical information in Daniela Lamberini's edition of Belluzzi (1980).

La Croix identified as the soldier's attitude to military architecture.[18] Architects, together with other civilian *dottori*, it argued, were to keep out of a subject of which they knew nothing and could learn nothing from their classical libraries because "books don't fight."[19] No single individual, whether soldier or civilian, could master all of the skills needed for modern fortification. Only an experienced soldier would be capable of appreciating the defensive and offensive potential of a site, and anticipating the tactical situations likely to arise during a siege. The soldier needed to be supported by *un buon Capitano maestro di muratori*, by which he probably meant a builder combining the functions of a master mason and foreman, or clerk of works. The builder was explicitly not required to have all of the architect's skills. It would be sufficient to have a knowledge of mathematics and the qualities of materials, as well as the ability to draw plans and to estimate costs. If these ideas were truly those of Bellucci, he perhaps gave too little weight to his own social origins, education and architectural training in favour of his new-found taste for action. But it is likely that these attitudes were shared by a growing number of fortification professionals who by the second half of the sixteenth century saw themselves primarily as soldiers. These men valued combat experience above theory and—particularly the untitled amongst them—were punctilious about their use of military ranks.

By this time fortification practice had expanded far beyond the design and construction of permanent city walls or citadels. State of the art design was increasingly carried out in the inherently flexible reinforced earth and turf construction favoured by Belluzzi.[20] Alessandro Farnese, with his knowledge of campaigning in the Low Countries, had argued strongly that the Lucchesi should employ these techniques for their own city walls, but this advice was more often followed in Northern Europe. Everywhere, however, earthworks were employed in fieldworks, siege lines, frontier defence systems and the massive entrenched camps used by armies in the field. Here, it is reasonable to suppose that many officers with experience of work

---

[18] Belluzzi, 1598.

[19] Quoted by De la Croix, 1960, pp. 273–5.

[20] Earthwork in the field was sometimes simply a cut-and-fill process, whereby soil from a ditch was piled into a self-retaining bank. More often it was reinforced by fascines (bundles of twigs) and hurdles (as in modern woven fencing sections). For semi-permanent or permanent works a much more elaborate internal structure of timber was required, for which see Pepper & Adams, 1986, pp. 70–78.

with pioneers could make a fair fist of surveys, layout and the super-vision of field construction. Permanent masonry fortifications, how-ever, continued to be built throughout the sixteenth century, and here the increasing complexity and size of the projects demanded traditional architectural and building construction skills. In Italy the field became dominated by a relatively small number of what might be called dynastic practices, which sometimes enjoyed the logistical and administrative support of state offices. Both circumstances char-acterised the work of the most prolific Italian fortress builders of the mid-sixteenth century, Michele Sanmichele of Verona (1484–1559) and Antonio da Sangallo the Younger of Florence (1485–1546), who it is believed were the only two living architects regarded as com-petent by the demanding standards of Francesco Maria della Rovere.[21]

Sanmichele fortified his native city with some of the more influential early bastions as well as his famous classically-inspired gates. He worked extensively for the Republic of Venice at the *terrafirma* fortresses of Legnago, Peschiera, Orzinuovi, Brescia, Bergamo and Padua; over-seas in Crete, Greece and Dalmatia; and finally on the seaward approaches to Venice itself where his military masterpiece, the sea-fort of Sant'Andrea, still stands. From 1542 the administration of Venetian fortresses on the *terrafirma* and overseas was made the respon-sibility of a new magistracy, the *Provveditori alle fortezze* which, within the limitations of sixteenth century bureaucracy, greatly facilitated policy formation, surveys, the administration of revenue and the sys-tematic employment of a growing cadre of specialists.[22] Michele Sanmichele was by then already established as Venice's leading fortification expert and, not surprisingly, his name recurs with the greatest frequency. His son Zuan Hieronimo, his brother-in-law Luigi Brugnoli and nephews Alvise and Bernardino Brugnoli began as his assistants, but succeeded in their own right to numerous commis-sions. Vasari tells us that before Zuan Hieronimo died of a fever in Cyprus he handed over to Luigi Brugnoli—then engaged on forti-fying Famagusta—all of his designs and descriptions to be taken to the *Signoria*.[23] The incident illustrates two important features of the professionalisation of military architecture—the way that key indi-viduals such as Michele Sanmichele were often supported by close

---

[21] See above, Adams, 1999, p. 56.
[22] Hale, 1971, pp. 182 ff.
[23] Vasari/Gaunt, 1963, III, p. 280.

relatives as well as by state offices, and the care that was taken to conserve the drawings that recorded progress in a rapidly developing field.

The activity of the Sanmichele-Brugnoli circle was mirrored closely by that of the other leading dynasty in Italian military architecture, the Sangalli. The family spanned three generations. Antonio da Sangallo the Younger was a Florentine by birth, and learnt much of his military architecture from his uncles, Antonio the Elder (1455–1534) and Giuliano (1445–1516), who were both active in the pioneering days of modern fortification. His own working life was based largely in Rome, where early fortification commissions for Pope Julius II (1503–13) at Civita Castellana and the Vatican gave him the experience to construct the new bastions and ramparts of Civitavecchia (1512–20), the main papal west coast naval base, and possibly the first Italian city of any size to be completely encircled with new bastions and ramparts.[24] In 1526 Antonio joined Michele Sanmichele in a survey of papal fortresses on the northern frontiers then threatened with invasion by the Imperial army which was to sack Rome in 1527. Antonio served with the Papal-Imperial army besieging Florence in 1529–30, which was his only personal experience of active service. The fall of the last Florentine Republic in 1530 marked a watershed in Italian politics. As the new regimes of Spanish-dominated Italy and the aggressive papacy of Paul III consolidated themselves behind strong walls, work flowed in to the group best able to handle fortification projects on a vast scale. For the Medici Dukes of Florence Antonio and his team built the Fortezza da Basso (1534–35). For the Farnese Pope they fortified Ancona— the main Adriatic naval base—and the Rocca Paolina in Perugia. For the Farnese family they worked at Parma, and Piacenza, and built the new city of Castro. Shortly before his death Sangallo began the refortification of Rome's Aurelian walls, a vast project which if had been completed would have involved some 14 kilometres of new fortifications. Behind Antonio lay the resources of the *Fabrica* of St Peters, the Papal office of works to which his title of "architetto di tutte le fabriche pontificie" gave him access. But designers and trusted supervising architects were still needed for works on sites scattered

---

[24] The new fortress town of Acaya is a close rival for this distinction, of course, but the southern town was very much smaller than Civitavecchia.

throughout central and northern Italy. Not entirely kindly Vasari called the team which made this volume of work possible the *Setta Sangallesca*, "the Sangallo Seven".

Besides Antonio the Younger himself it included his brothers Francesco (c.1490–after 1552) and Giovanni Battista called "il Gobbo" (1496–1548), his cousins Bastiano called "Aristotele" (1481–1551) and Giovan Francesco (1484–1530, who died before the busiest period), and Nardo dei Rossi (a builder who married the daughter of Antonio's sister Lucrezia). The seventh member was at various times Antonio the Elder (who died in 1534), and Antonio's son, Orazio (*c.* 1528–68). It was Orazio's son, Antonio (b. 1550), who collected many of the dynasty's drawings and presented them to the Grand Duke of Tuscany to form the nucleus of what became the Uffizi drawings collection.[25]

Drawings in the days before simple reprographics or readily available illustrated books represented a resource of enormous value, containing surveys of distant sites, preliminary proposals, and working up sketches, as well as a relatively small number of final presentation sheets. The Seven's drawings collection was also its library, containing *inter alia* faithful copies of illustrations from earlier manuscript treatises and designers' notebooks. Gustina Scaglia has analysed the copyists and sources for the drawings of machines in Sangallo's corpus, identifying sketches originating in Mariano Taccola's treatise, Francesco di Giorgio's different codices, the collection of the so-called Anonymous Sienese Engineer, Ghiberti's *Zibaldone* and Leonardo's notebooks which contained sketches of many of Brunelleschi's hoists and cranes, to say nothing of Giuliano da Sangallo's *Taccuino senese* (so-called for the city library where the notebook can be found). Scaglia was chiefly interested in the various machines, hoists, cranes, mill wheels and pumps that attracted the attention of the Sangallo circle for their potential usefulness on building sites. Her study indicates very clearly the extent of copying which, together with the dynastic approach to the training of specialists, ensured the transmission of ideas within the nascent profession before the printed treatises began to be published.[26]

Papal and other princely courts with their libraries, museums and drawings collections provided a somewhat different kind of training

---

[25] Adams & Pepper, 1994.
[26] Scaglia, 1994. See also Reti, 1963, pp. 287–97.

for educated patrons. Paul III (1534–49) himself presided over controversial debates prompted by the different proposals for the
refortification of Rome, debates which brought together high church
officials, senior military officers and a variety of specialist and non-
specialist military architects amidst charges of incompetence and pla-
giarism from individuals who believed themselves slighted or robbed
of credit for innovations.[27] The pope himself intervened from time
to time in matters of fortification: and in one notable comment in a
letter to Antonio da Sangallo rejected the design for the city-facing
front of Perugia's Rocca Paolina which he regarded as too civic for
its repressive function: "I want you to make a fortress here."[28]

If Alessandro Farnese by the 1580s used plans (and possibly even
drew them himself), how widely did such skills extend amongst the
uppermost tier of rulers in the first half of the sixteenth century
when the bastioned system was disseminated? The evidence, such as
it is, suggests that—as in Basilio della Scola's time—presentations
would still more often than not have been by means of models,
although some mid-sixteenth century treatise authors were just starting to propose the use of perspectives or three-dimensional drawings
of fortifications to save on the extraordinarily high cost of models.[29]
Pope Clement VII, evidently studied Tribolo's large cork model of
Florence, its surroundings and defences during the Papal-Imperial
siege of the Last Republic in 1529–30. This had been built under
clandestine circumstances and smuggled out of the besieged city at
considerable risk to its makers, who would no doubt have been very
glad to have used a plan if this had been acceptable to their masters.[30] In the middle of the century the Emperor Charles V personally inspected a model of the fortress he proposed building in

---

[27] De La Croix, 1960, saw these arguments as the starting point for the late
Renaissance concept of intellectual property, and its theft.

[28] Frommel & Adams, 1994, I, p. 103.

[29] Cataneo, 1554, fol. 1.

[30] Vasari/Gaunt, III, p. 165 in the Life of Niccolo, called il Tribolo, Sculptor
and Architect (1500–1550), gives the following: "In 1529, during the siege of Florence,
when Pope Clement wished to see where best he could dispose his army, he had
arranged that a plan of the city should be taken and the country round at a radius
of a mile, with the hills, rivers, houses, churches, piazzas, streets, bastions and other
defences. The charge of this was given to Benvenuto di Lorenzo by Valpaia, a master watchmaker and excellent astrologer, who especially excelled in making plans.
He wished for the help of Tribolo, who was very good at such work and in esti-
mating the height of mountains and the depressions. It was done at no small risk,
as they stayed out all night to measure the roads, the heights of campaniles and

Siena to curb the excesses of that turbulent city, and Cosimo de'
Medici, Duke of Florence, is depicted by Vasari inspecting a model
of Siena and its fortifications whilst planning the rebellious city's
reconquest.[31] These rulers evidently believed themselves qualified to
judge such matters, and although Vasari's scene is fictional, Cosimo
intervened so frequently at a tactical level during the war of Siena
that the picture is entirely credible. During the sixteenth century
Venice began a collection of fortress models for cities in the Republic's
terrafirma and overseas empires, presumably to assist informed government decisions.[32] In 1597–98 a certain Filippo Pigafetta—traveller, geographer and courtier—attempted to persuade the Grand
Duke Ferdinand I of Tuscany to fit out one of the rooms in the newly
completed Uffizi gallery as a museum of fortress models by claiming, falsely, that such a museum already existed in the Escorial.[33]
The tradition was eventually transmitted to France in the late seventeenth century, giving rise to the magnificent collection of *plans
relief* which began its life in the grand gallery of the Tuileries. There
official visitors could fully appreciate the "gloire" projected by an
impressive array of French border fortresses—possibly more impressive as models than as incomplete projects—and recent developments
or proposals could be explained directly to the monarch at a regular

---

towers, using the compass and taking the cupola as a centre. This task occupied
many months, when the plan was made of cork for the sake of lightness, the whole
being compressed in a space of four braccia. It was then packed secretly in some
bales of wool consigned to Perugia, with orders to be sent to the Pope, who made
constant use of it during the siege, keeping it in his room and following the operations with great interest according to his advices, as to the state of the camp, the
locality of the skirmishes, in short for all the incidents and discussions and disputes
that took place during the siege." The size of the model: ". . . *in a space of four braccia*" could mean 4 braccia × 4 braccia (say, 8 feet square), or 4 square braccia (2
braccia × 2 braccia, or 4 feet square). The latter could be concealed in a bale of
wool, the former would have had to be made in sections (as were the larger French
plans en relief).

[31] Pepper & Adams, 1986, p. 60 and Forster, 1971.

[32] Concina, 1983, pp. 184–5 published the Venetian "Ordine ai Rettori sulle
fortezze" of December 1550 which required all new projects or modifications to
fortifications to be approved by the Rectors either on site, or by means of models,
and required the models to be stored in the roofspace of the new palazzo (i.e. the
post-fire offices) under lock and key, and a register to be kept recording each occasion a model was consulted, as well as the official who had access. Clearly the
Venetian collection enjoyed high security, as opposed to the public exhibition of
the later French models. For the collection of models of overseas fortresses now
held in the Naval Museum in Venice, see Gerola, 1930–31, pp. 217–21.

[33] Frinz, 1988.

weekly briefing.[34] As we shall see in connection with England, however, royal patronage did not always ensure state of the art design, particularly when the king was misleadingly convinced of his own expertise in all matters military.

* * *

France almost certainly deserves recognition for a more important role in the early stages of the fortress revolution than it has so far received. Relatively little research has been published on the French response to modern artillery in their own military architecture, but it is fair to say that some elements which characterised the early Italian experiments in bastioned fortification can also be found in late-fifteenth century French fortresses.[35] French engineers certainly worked in Italy in the pioneering era of the new military architecture. A Frenchman, Enrico Laufer, was effectively chief engineer in Venetian service during the 1470s whilst Italians, such as Basilio della Scola, evidently found useful experience in fortification as well as artillery in French service only a few years later.[36] In short, it is not easy to disentangle French from Italian innovations because French involvement in Italy's politics, wars and culture at all levels—particularly following 1494–95 when numerous Italian artists, architects and engineers went back with Charles VIII's army to France—made mutual absorption of military technology practically inevitable. The southern theatre of French operations which embraced chiefly Lombardy and Savoy-Piedmont, and in the 1530s and 1540s extended to include much of modern southern France, was a truly integrated Franco-Italian milieu. On the Italian side of the mountains "French" fortresses defended Turin (captured in 1535) at Vercelli, Fossano, Moncalieri, Carignano and Savigliano; while Pinerolo and Susa secured the road through the Alps. In Provence, the key cities of Marseilles, Avignon, Tarascon and Arles were all defended after 1535 against Imperial counter-invasions by modern fortifications that were generally constructed in earthwork. John Hale's analysis of the

---

[34] Faucherre, 1989, p. 25. For the Naples models, Colletta, 1981 and for Sweden, Englund, 1967.
[35] DeVries, 1992, p. 267. See also Fino, 1970; Jones, 1981.
[36] Mallett & Hale, 1984, pp. 95, 85–7, and Zorzi, 1958–59.

post-1535 French fortification programme suggests that it was this which established the new bastioned earthwork fortification technology firmly in the consciousness of France's ruling class.

The French defensive strategy after 1535 was evidently devised by Anne de Montmorency, the commander in chief, working from maps which he studied so closely that—in Martin du Bellay's words—"he convinced himself that he already possessed the land in the same way that he owned the map."[37] At Avignon, the new works were laid out by Montmorency himself, advised by two senior Italian officers—the Prince of Melfi and Stefano Colonna—who were both experienced soldiers, but not engineers. Any engineering specialists—and it is difficult to believe that there were none—remain unknown. However, the presence of senior Italian officers in French councils of war is likely to have exercised as much influence—probably more—than the persuasive powers of all but the most highly-regarded engineers, whether Italian or French. At Pinerolo, local responsibility for the fortifications was exercised by the Modenese garrison commander, Guido Rangone, a soldier who had already overseen the modernisation of Piacenza's fortifications and could draw on the specialised services of Baldassare Azzale, a surveyor of Ferrara, and the Bolognese military engineer, Girolamo Marini (c. 1500–53).

Marini was to prove an important figure in the dissemination of fully-formed Italian ideas when in 1545 he accompanied the chronicler Martin du Bellay—who was by then serving as Francis I's Lieutenant in the Champagne—on a tour of inspection of France's northern frontier. By this time Marini had already assisted in the construction of "French" fortresses at Pinerolo and Moncalieri, had served Francis I at the siege of Perpignan in 1542, at the sieges of Landrecy and Luxembourg in 1543 (where he remained to rebuild the captured works), and at St Dizier in 1544, where he was reported to have designed the fortifications and again remained to assist in their defence against the Emperor. His personal standing with King Francis is indicated by the award of the Order of Saint Michael following his distinguished service at the siege of Landrecies.[38] Founded

[37] Du Bellay/Buchon, 1836, p. 582 quoted by Hale, 1982, p. 385. Martin du Bellay was close to the centre of power, for shortly afterward in 1543 he served as Francis I's Lieutenant in Champagne.
[38] Promis, 1863, pp. 614–27. Marini was killed in action at Therouanne. Blaise de Monluc wrote that "he was judged to be the best man in Italy in siegecraft"

in 1469 by Louis XI, the Order of Saint Michael the Archangel was until the creation of the Order of the Holy Spirit in 1578 France's only monarchical order, with statutes "copied almost verbatim from those of the Order of the Golden Fleece" and a membership restricted (in theory, at any rate) to thirty-six "gentilshommes de nom et d'armes sous la grande maîtrise du Roi . . ." Membership was increased to fifty in 1565, in response to numerous breaches of the previous limit. Although not as exclusive as the Collar of Savoy (15 knightly members), or the Garter (24 knights), the Order of Saint Michael was clearly a signal distinction for a foreign-born military architect.[39]

Marini's northern frontier survey of 1545 yielded a commission to design two new frontier towns and their bastioned fortifications: Vitry-le-Francois, which dominated an important crossing of the Marne between St Dizier and Chalons; and Villefranche-sur-Meuse, located between Dun-sur-Meuse and Stenay, both until recently in Imperial hands. The street plan of Vitry was a square grid. The street plan of Villefranche, however, was the first radial design to be built "on the ground" following numerous Renaissance essays on paper, notably those of Filarete and Francesco di Giorgio.[40] In the radial designs a series of streets radiated outwards from a central *place d'armes* to the bastions, looking rather like the spokes of a wheel. The external trace of the ramparts and bastions (although rectangular in both of Marini's schemes) were increasingly to be laid out using regular polygonal geometry (the pentagon, hexagon, and octagon being the most common for all but the very largest undertakings). Antonio da Sangallo the Younger had evidently been attracted by the same thought for his drawings contain a sketch for one wedge-shaped segment of what looks like a radial entrenched camp.[41] The radial idea was to be explored obsessively in many of the military treatises printed in the second half of the sixteenth century, and was eventually adopted for the first time on a large scale in Italy at Palmanova, the fortress-city founded by Venice in 1593 on the Republic's eastern *terrafirma* border. Since Marini was author of both

---

but upon checking his trenches found "he was doing nothing that would of any use"—a typically dismissive remark which may or may not have been justified. Quoted by Hale, 1982, p. 387 citing the *Commentaires*, I, pp. 129–30. De la Croix, 1960, p. 277 cited only the first half of the quote.

[39] Boulton, 1999, pp. 85–136. See also Boulton, 1987.

[40] De la Croix, 1960, *passim*.

[41] Frommel & Adams, 1994, I, p. xxx (Uffizi A 1245).

of the French new town plans in 1545—square grid and radial—it was as if he had seized this early chance to demonstrate his command of the two classic approaches advocated for new military foundations—show-pieces for the *trace Italienne* in its most thoroughgoing form.

The radial idea was quickly copied on the Imperial side of the border; but it would be wrong to conclude that Marini's contribution was critical to the arrival of bastioned developments in the north. He was clearly a major player in the Franco-Italian sphere of influence; but even before the new French foundations of 1545, fortification design in northern Europe had taken a major step forward as the result of a project of altogether greater magnitude, the construction by the Emperor Charles V of a complete bastioned enceinte around the important city of Antwerp in 1542.

* * *

Until the Imperial refortification of Antwerp in 1542–43 to a bastioned design by Donato Boni Pellezuoli of Bergamo, the Low Countries were no more advanced than other parts of the North. Antwerp's scheme, however, was much the most modern large-scale urban fortification scheme in the region, and it attracted widespread attention. Antwerp, after all, was one of the great cities of Europe.[42] None of the largest—and very few medium sized—Italian cities at that time boasted *complete* up-to-date bastioned systems of defence. The ambitious Roman refortification project of Paul III was only executed in fragments.[43] Milan was to embark upon complete refortification a few years later, at enormous cost and no little conflict with propertied interests, all of which was to cause great unrest in the city and contribute eventually to the dismissal of Ferrante Gonzaga, the Spanish Governor, for abuse of power.[44] Imperial power in the

---

[42] Torfs & Casterman, 1871, pp. 69 ff.

[43] Pepper 1976, pp. 162–9.

[44] No traces now remain of the controversial Milanese fortification project of 1548/49 to provide a new bastioned front some 500 to 700 metres outside the medieval circuit, with a circumference of 11,000 metres. The scheme was the work of many architects, but chiefly Olgiati (1541–57). It also contributed to the removal from office of Ferrante Gonzaga, the Imperial governor. Ferrante Gonzaga, to be sure, was also accused of sale of offices, the distribution of public property to associates,

Netherlands, however, even if not always wisely employed, was strong enough to force through the Antwerp refortification scheme and, in 1567, to impose a five-bastioned star-shaped pentagonal citadel to dominate the same city. The new citadel was designed by Francesco Paciotto of Urbino, and was closely modelled on his own widely admired pentagonal citadel design for Turin which had been built in 1564–66. It was to have been the prototype for a further six identical citadels planned by the Spanish authorities to secure the Low Countries. Although this ambitious programme of repressive military architecture was to be overtaken by the very events it sought to forestall, the bastioned enceinte of Antwerp brought modern fortifications to one of the most important northern European cities just before the French had begun to fortify the much smaller towns on their frontier with the Spanish Low Countries.[45]

What we have observed is the rapid diffusion of an essentially new technique in fortification which, originating in both theory and practice in central Italy, was firmly established in key parts of north-west Europe well before the middle of the sixteenth century. The spread of the *trace Italienne* clearly pre-dated the treatise publications which are sometimes credited with this process. Although manuscript treatises were circulating privately during the first half of the sixteenth century and illustrations from them were finding their way into drawings collections, the printed and illustrated specialist fortification treatises only began to appear in significant numbers during the 1550s. Thereafter the printed technical literature was clearly an important new factor in the process of diffusion—at least amongst the book-owning and reading classes.[46] Before the 1550s, however, the printed literature was very limited. Battista della Valle's *Vallo: Libro continente*

and excessive taxation. Critically, as an Italian, his power was much envied and resented by hard-line Castilians. But it was the criticism of his fortification policy which he defended to the Emperor, see Beltrami, 1897; also Scotti, 1977, pp. 97–103; Scotti 1988, p. 207 where Gonzaga is cited: "... è assai miglio consiglio sarebbe il fortificar et el castello et le città." For general background, Leydi, 1985; and for Olgiati, De Moro, 1988.

[45] The Italian military architects already established in the Spanish Low Countries in 1542 are discussed in Van den Heuvel, 1988).

[46] De la Croix, 1963. The increasingly treatise-based profession of the seventeenth century, was obviously much better informed in an academic sense; but whether this actually led to freer thinking or (as Christopher Duffy has suggested) into a more hidebound rule-dominated approach is a topic that would bear further examination.

appartentie ad capitanij: retenere et fortificare una cita con bastioni: artificij de fuoco: polvere: e de expugnare una cita . . . oépera molto utile con la experentia de larte militare (Venice, 1524) treated in very general terms of the defence of places and, although very simple, was widely circulated (running through eleven editions in 37 years, which made it the genre's best seller by a wide margin). Albrecht Dürer's German treatise appeared in 1527 and, despite its excellent illustrations and specialist content, did not evidently exercise great influence outside of the German-speaking world.[47] The "international edition" was published in Latin in 1537, but this was unlikely to have been any more widely read by the military community. In any event, Dürer's treatise promoted an approach to fortification that fell outside the mainstream of the Italian bastioned system. The key period of diffusion—from the 1520s to the 1540s—was one that saw a diaspora of Italian architects such as Marini, and, perhaps just as important if less well recorded in this context, the participation in Northern campaigns of French and Imperial officers of all nationalities with first hand experience of the Italian theatre of operations.[48]

* * *

The delayed English absorption of the new technology sheds further light on the dynamics of this process. The English experienced the power of French artillery at the end of the Hundred Years War, and proceeded to incorporate gun loops in many fortifications at about the same time.[49] Thereafter progress in England was slow, and major fortification campaigns only began again in the sixteenth century when Henry VIII's ambitions for adventure took his army once more to the continent. Henry VIII's campaign against Therouanne

---

[47] *Etliche Underricht, zur Befestigung der Stett, Schloss und Flecken* (Nuremberg, 1527). Dürer's ideas were certainly known in Italy, witness the use of the artist's famous illustration of a city under siege which is used as a background for Stradano's fresco (part of Vasari's programme in the Palazzo Vecchio, Sala di Clemente VII, Florence) depicting Cardinal Ippolito de' Medici's visit to Hungary in 1532. Fara, 1999, pp. 67–8 points out that the late-sixteenth century italian treatises (those of Busca and Theti) borrow ideas, drawings and geometrical diagrams from Dürer's treatise, a copy of which (he suggests) may have been owned by Antonio da Sangallo the Elder.

[48] Viganò, 1994.

[49] Saunders, 1989, pp. 34–52, particularly p. 45.

and Tournai in 1513, and his subsequent refortification of Tournai (1513–17)[50] with massive circular guntowers, may well have served as an obstacle to subsequent progress in England because it taught the king a kind of fortification which was already on the eve of obsolescence. Thus when Henry VIII fortified the south coast of England against the Imperial invasion which was expected to follow his first divorce, his builders drew their ideas partly from the Germanic tradition imported by some of the foreign experts on the English payroll, and partly from what Henry himself, his courtiers and gentry—who are credited with leading roles in the realisation of this project—remembered from Tournai. The "Device" programme of 1539–40—although enormously expensive, and not without interest in the specialised field of coastal defence—was by this date out of step with the most advanced contemporary continental developments. The English south coast defences were in fact built just a few years before Henry and his court had yet another opportunity to learn from the French, who were by then employing some of the best Italian architects on the market.

In 1544 Henry VIII formed an offensive alliance with Charles V against Henry II of France. Charles quickly took Luxemburg but St Dizier was stoutly held for two months, a defence which blunted the Emperor's enthusiasm for the war and moved him to conclude a separate peace on 18 September, without informing his English ally. Henry took Boulogne on 14 September after a 6-week siege but never succeeded in breaking the French defence of Montreuil. To salvage something from the campaign, Henry VIII then embarked on the extensive refortification of Boulogne and its approaches. The English also fortified the anchorage at Ambleteuse (between Calais and Boulogne), and began a new fort—Fort Blackness—near Cape Griz Nez. Boulogne was held until 1550 when it was returned to France for the sum of 400,000 gold crowns. English defences in the Pale were by then restricted to Guines and Calais itself, which fell to the surprise attack by the Duke of Guise on 7 January 1558.[51] Guines fell two weeks later.[52]

As with the coastal "Device" programme, the King took an active personal interest in the design of the new works. Henry VIII had

---

[50] Cruickshank, 1969, pp. 169–75.
[51] Potter, 1983. See also van Dyke, 1911 and Lennel, Vol. II, pp. 263–82.
[52] Tomkinson, 1998, pp. 121–41.

been present at the siege of Boulogne, and after its capture acquainted himself with its details, leaving very precise instructions for John Rogers, the surveyor chiefly responsible for works under the wider authority of William Lord Grey, the Governor. Shelby's biography of the surveyor shows how Rogers—despite conflict with Lord Grey and other officers, but with the increased confidence and backing of the king—assumed progressively more authority as the programme progressed. The outcome was a complex of fortifications reinforcing Boulogne's medieval walls and the detached forts commanding the approaches to the port, all of which conformed to the basic dictates of the *trace Italienne*. A number of the outer forts were disgracefully abandoned without proper resistance when the French began to press their siege aggressively, but Boulogne itself held out until the settlement of 1550.

Rogers emerges as an interesting figure, who rose to a position of considerable authority from humble origins. First recorded as a journeyman mason at Hampton Court palace in 1533, his next appearance was as Master Mason at Guines castle in 1541. At Guines he worked under Richard Lee, beginning a decade of activity which saw these two names linked on many of the more important English military construction sites. From Guines, Rogers moved to Kingston-upon-Hull as Surveyor of the Works building new fortifications against the Scots and their French allies, and (indicating a much broader competence in matters of building) making drawings for the remodelling of the royal manor at Hull. Postings to Carlisle and Wark on the Scottish border followed in 1543, together with a reconnaissance mission to Tantallon Castle, the Douglas stronghold in East Lothian, where he was instructed "to viewe the castle secretely and to bring his majeste a true plat and perfaict description of every parte of the same."[53] In February 1544 Rogers was made Clerk of the Ordnance at 8d per diem, a salary which he continued to draw after his appointment in the Autumn of 1544 as Surveyor of the Works at Boulogne, where he remained throughout the French siege and—with only minor absences—until the end of the English occupation in 1550. After Henry VIII's death in 1547 Rogers's career lost much of its impetus, but he was employed in Ireland, Portsmouth, and Berwick before becoming Surveyor of Calais in 1556 at a salary of £20 a

---

[53] Shelby, 1967, p. 49.

year, plus a life annuity of £10 and the use of a house in the town. Here he was unable to complete the major refortification needed if this exposed English possession was to be held against the French. Rogers was amongst those made prisoner when Guise took Calais in January 1558. Probably he died in captivity later in the same year.

For a man with obscure origins in the building trade, Rogers had done exceptionally well out of military architecture to be able to leave in his will a London house, the lease of a manor in Somerset (spoils from the Monastery of Glastonbury), and the lease on the former priory at Folkestone, in addition to property in Calais. His widow was granted a royal annuity of 20 marks (£13.6s.8d.) in recognition of Rogers's many services to the crown.

Rogers's colleague, Sir Richard Lee (1513?–1575), did better. Lee ended his days as a knight (sometimes described as the first English engineer to be so honoured) and the recipient of numerous pensions and properties, including the priory of Newent in Gloucestershire and most of the former monastery of St Albans. Lee's active career as an engineer included major works at Berwick (where he served as Surveyor of Works), campaigns in Scotland, in the Netherlands, and at Dieppe and Le Havre (which he fortified for the Protestants in the early years of the French Wars of Religion).

Shelby suggests that John Rogers too might have been knighted had Henry VIII lived longer, for Rogers does seem to have enjoyed a special relationship of trust with the king which protected him from those whose feathers had been ruffled by a low-born building tradesman evidently not afraid to speak his mind when crossed on matters of construction. But this is to overlook the niceties of sixteenth century society. Richard Lee was a soldier, who moved into military engineering from active service and a family background in the gentry. An early position at court as page of the king's cups brought Lee the grant of an annuity of £6 in 1528, at the age of 15 or 16, when the much older John Rogers may well have still been serving his apprenticeship as a mason. Lee's social and military background was much closer to that of Italian contemporaries such as Belluzzi (from a gentle Urbino family and with his Florentine captaincy), or Marini (with his French knighthood in the Order of Saint Michael), and it is no surprise to find him elevated above even such a capable and well-paid builder as Rogers. When the decisive moves toward the international adoption of the *trace italienne* took place, the social standing of those involved on the design side clearly had a bearing on their authority, on the trust placed in them by rulers, and—most important in large scale construction campaigns— on the ease with which gentlemen could deal with other leaders in military and civil society.[54] The social divide between John Rogers— master mason, surveyor, and part-time spy—and Sir Richard Lee— international soldier, courtier, and fortification expert—encapsulates a number of distinctions which were probably even more important in military circles than in civil and ecclesiastical architecture. These factors—which *in some parts* of Italy probably helped to advance progress because of expertise or at least understanding on the part of military society's leading figures—may well have contributed to the relative backwardness of England's military engineering.

*   *   *

The words "in some parts of Italy" are important. Technical progress in fortification and access to expert professional guidance was not evenly distributed throughout Italy, the original home of the triangular bastion. Although Sir John Hale convincingly demonstrated the development of early triangular fortifications in Tuscany and the Marche in the late fifteenth century, and his colleague Michael Mallett identified different but earlier responses to artillery in Lombardy and the Veneto, it was not until the 1530s and 1540s that fully-formed triangular bastions could properly be described as the standard Italian solution. Even then, there were many places where progress was slower. The bastioned circuit of Lucca—probably the most complete Italian surviving example of a major urban defensive system from the sixteenth and early seventeenth centuries—was only started in 1543 when the republic, lacking experts of their own, sought the

---

[54] The authority and trustworthiness of men working for government in the sixteenth century is explored by Eric Ash in connection with the Elizabethan engineering works to Dover harbour between 1579 and 1583. Thomas Digges, who eventually emerged as the expert in charge of the project, brought to the task a Cambridge education (mathematics), military experience, politics and status as a Kentish landowner with the necessary local connections to ensure the success of the project: Ash, 2000, pp. 239–68. The same qualities secured the advancement of another leading Elizabethan soldier and expert in siege warfare, Sir William Pelham, who came from a family of landed gentry (his father was also a knight from Laughton in Sussex), but who acquired considerable property himself after a military career based in the Office of Ordnance: Ambler, 1998, pp. 163–82.

advice of foreigners. Some fifteen non-Lucchesi architects (not count-
ing their distinguished consultant, Alessandro Farnese) headed the
republic's construction programme before the famous circuit was
completed in 1650.[55] Between 1516 and 1525 Lucca defended itself
against the threat of gunpowder artillery with one of the last major
urban systems of round guntowers, or *torrioni*. Nor were the Lucchesi
alone in this policy. Verona—soon itself to become something of a
sixteenth century showpiece for modern fortification—invested in *torrioni* at much the same time as the Lucchesi, and of course the
English who were then fortifying Tournai. Venice and Naples employed
circular bastions for the first twenty years of the sixteenth century
in many of their major projects. It is often easier for historians to
spot trends than for those responsible at the time for major expenditure, and who faced the hard choices that needed to be made
between well-tried techniques and the often unproven cutting edge
of progress.

If the international movement of experienced personnel was the
most important factor in dispersing bastioned fortification before the
great era of treatise publication, what were the key factors which
drove creative progress forward in bastioned fortification design and
generated the personal expertise and quality of built work which
merits the term, professional?

The existence of the dynastic architectural practices certainly played
an important part by concentrating expertise, providing training, and
the opportunity to discuss problems and alternative solutions. This
was the basis of the *bottega* or workshop in which Renaissance artists
and architects were normally trained, but more than one generation
of the Sangalli in Florence and Rome, and the Sanmichele family
in the Veneto, concentrated an enormous body of expertise. The
expatriate Pasqualini in Jülich provided much the same training envi-
ronment, and there were also soldier dynasties—the Savorgnani and
Martinengi are good examples—in which technical know-how was
transmitted between generations from a very early age. When these
dynastic circles were also associated with offices of state, the administrative support provided by the civil servants, and the close links
which those offices established with senior government officials, a
potent instrument for development was forged. Thus Antonio da

---

[55] Martinelli & Puccinelli (1983), *passim*; Pepper, 2000A, pp. 15–16.

Sangallo the Younger's leading position in the Papal *Fabrica*, and the support available to Michele Sanmichele from the *Provveditori delle fortezze* greatly increased the capacity of these men to handle major jobs on widely separated sites. The short-lived English Office of Works in Henry VIII's time, and the Office of Ordnance under Elizabeth, no doubt had similar qualities, if generally less talent upon which to draw. Connections of this kind do not always secure quality work, it has to be said, but some states were clearly aware of this problem.

The Venetians seem to have led the way in the development of a semi-permanent cadre of fortification experts whose qualifications were properly tested. Mallett identifies the beginnings of a central military engineer's office in the second half of the fifteenth century.[56] By 1542 it was formalised by the institution of a new magistracy, the *Provveditori delle fortezze*. Hale's valuable study of the *Provveditori* was critical of the short-sighted economies which placed an understaffed secretariat at the centre of a system which employed too few part-time site engineers (necessitating constant switching of personnel from one site to another, and lengthy absences) who themselves often lacked the authority and prestige to deal on anything like "professional" terms with the high-ranking *capi di guerra* "like the duke of Urbino or Marcantonio Martinengo, for whom the planning of fortifications was one of the talents expected of the well-educated, all-round soldier." But a number of full-time permanent engineers were also employed. These were high quality professionals, appointed under a selection system that demanded testimonials from senior officers in mainland cities or overseas colonies where candidates had worked, and formal interviews to which candidates were expected to bring models and drawings. Practical tests were sometimes set. "In one case an applicant was told to draw the Lido forts." The Venetian appointment system for engineers described by Hale sounds very similar to that used to establish the seafaring qualifications of those who were licensed to command the Republic's galleys.[57] Hale

---

[56] Mallett & Hale, 1984, p. 95.

[57] Lane, 1973. See also the interesting discussion of the *Curriculum Vitae* presented to Pope Sixtus V *c.* 1583 by a certain Jacomo Fontana, describing himself as Architect and Gunner, in an attempt to retrieve his post at Ancona from which he had been fired. Much can be extracted from this early CV about the working life of a minor specialist figure, and, although the circumstances are not quite the same as that of

quotes the report from the panel which in 1581 interviewed the Florentine, Bonaiuto Lorini: "We summoned him before us and he showed us drawings and other designs in his own hand from which, and from his accompanying remarks, we could see clearly that he is professionally competent, quick to apprehend, of solid and mature judgement in his replies and suggestions, and, lastly, full of excellent and useful new ideas."[58] Lorini joined Giovan Battista Bonhomo, Francesco Malacreda and Zenese Bresciano as the fourth full-time military engineer then employed by the Republic.[59]

War itself was the great selector, of course; and wartime emergencies also continued to discover talent in hitherto unsuspected places. Siena had produced Francesco di Giorgio Martini and Baldassare Peruzzi, in their different ways both notable in military architecture. By the 1550s when the last republic defended its territories against the Emperor and the Florentines in one of most bitterly-contested final campaigns of the Italian Wars, the fortifications were built by a scratch team of artists, architects, surveyors and mathematicians who in many cases were probably no more qualified than their contemporary English counterparts.

Giovanbattista Peloro, aged sixty-nine when re-engaged in 1552, was the most experienced local military architect and—despite his advanced age—was heavily employed in and around Siena throughout the bitter campaigns of 1553–55. Pietro Cataneo, a skilled mathematician and author of one of the earliest printed treatises, *I quattro primi libri di architettura* (1554), worked for the Republic in 1552–53 but then left the city, possibly to supervise publication of his treatise in Venice. In his case, the rush to publish a treatise which contained a number of chapters on fortification, outweighed any advantages that might have been gained from further personal experience of active service. The most surprising discovery amongst Siena's emergency fortification designers was Maestro Giorgio di Giovanni, a

---

a normal job application, the format of his manuscript (and the attached drawings) may well give us pointers: Adams, 1996, pp. 7–12.

[58] Hale, 1971, p. 182.

[59] Lorini was recognised as a leading authority, author of an influential treatise on military architecture, and one of the key designers of Palmanova (Venice's most ambitious project, constructed mainly in the 1590s). His personal qualities were not appreciated by Giulio Savorgnano, successor to della Rovere as Captain General, who praises his skill as a draughtsman, but complains of his volatility (which made him too impatient to record dimensions accurately), dishonesty and homosexuality in a document cited by Adams, 1999, p. 57, note 7.

painter trained by Beccafumi who in peacetime worked as a fresco artist and occasional architect. Maestro Giorgio took over, remodelled and completed the Imperial citadel in Siena which had provoked the city's rebellion. Work at half a dozen provincial sites took him all over Siena's southern territory, often in perilous conditions. When his horse was shot from under him by a Spanish patrol, the architect penned a request for compensation and permission to return home to wife and family. Maestro Giorgio's finest hour came at Montalcino, a key position some twenty miles south of Siena, where he supervised the fortifications which resisted an eighty-day siege in 1553 and remained throughout the fighting to complete the works, and to carry out repairs, as well as the construction of underground countermines. Although reported by the Sienese civilian commissioner in Montalcino to be "utterly exhausted by danger and fatigue" he remained at his post, proving to have just those qualities which marked out the real military engineer, the ability to work under fire.[60] When a peacetime artist could respond in this way to the conditions and requirements of actual siege warfare, apparently with great success, it forces us to re-examine many of our assumptions about the qualities and background needed for success in the increasingly militarised nascent profession, as well as the sharper distinctions sometimes drawn by the treatise authors between soldiers and civilians.

If the new profession embraced aristocrats, architects and artisans, what of chivalry *qua* chivalry? Suffice it to say that in the period covered by this paper, there is abundant evidence that attitudes to siege warfare were profoundly influenced by the traditional rules governing the attack and defence of fortified places, and there are sufficient examples of siege themes in tournaments and other court events to suggest serious attempts to assimilate the most advanced form of modern warfare.[61]

Professionalism, as that term has been used in this paper, concerns what today would be called competence, and was not merely advertised in the growth of a specialist literature, but tested in the interview and appointment systems of states like Venice. As we have

---

[60] Pepper & Adams, 1986, pp. 185–9.
[61] A recently published paper of mine explores aspects of traditional siege law, siege ritual, and the symbolism of city walls in Renaissance Europe. See Pepper, 2000B.

seen, men from very different stations in society were seen to have such qualities. Architects and builders with the necessary skills and courage still served in the front line alongside siege warfare specialists with military origins in the artillery, or the increasingly important engineering skills of underground mining. Although soldiers were beginning by the middle of the sixteenth century to assert themselves aggressively in print and to suggest that the day of the civilian architect was past, distinguished civilian architects (the Sangallo and Sanmichele circles, Buontalenti, Paccioto, even the elderly Michelangelo, and academic figures such as Pietro Cataneo) still exercised an important role in fortification design. Members of the traditional military nobility could also be found in the new technical specialisms (Martinengo is a classic early example), while senior nobility (the Dukes of Urbino and of Parma) were evidently esteemed for their expertise in the broader, strategic aspects of fortification, and consulted—sometimes at very long range—on major civic or regional programmes. Anne de Montmorency, the French commander in chief, was evidently heavily involved in field and urban fortification. Henry VIII was an enthusiastic amateur. Although a number of the rising stars in the field (Belluzzi and Marini have both been considered in some detail, and others such as Castriotto perhaps merit such treatment) came from the minor nobility or gentry, there was clearly also room for artisans (such as Maestro Giorgio di Giovanni in Siena, or John Rogers in English service) to achieve positions of considerable responsibility and trust in a field where any technical shortcomings would be harshly exposed in the crucible of war. By the middle years of the sixteenth century, the "profession" was a very broad church.

Bibliography

Primary Sources

Belluzzi G. B. (1598) *Nuova inventione di fabricar fortezze, di varie forme . . .* (Venice, 1598).
Cataneo, P. (1554) *I Quattro primi libri de architettura* (Venice, 1554).
Du Bellay, M. (1836) *Memoirs*, ed. J. A. Buchon (Paris, 1836).
Dürer, A. (1527) *Etliche Underricht, zur Befestigung der Stett, Schloss und Flecken* (Nuremberg, 1527).
Monluc, B. de (1911) *Commentaires*, ed. P. Courtault, 2 vols (Paris, 1911)
Sanuto, M. (1879–1903) *I diarii*, ed. N. Barozzi, G. Berchet, R. Fulin and F. Stefani (58 volumes, Venice, 1879–1903).
Vasari, G. (1963), *Lives of the Painters, Sculptors and Architects*, trans. A.B. Hinds and ed. William Gaunt (4 vols, 1963).

Secondary Sources

Adams, N. Lamberini, D. and Pepper, S. (1988) "Un disegno di spionaggio cinque-centesco. Giovanni Battista Belluzzi e il rilievo delle difese di Siena al tempo dell'assedio," *Mitteilungen des Kunsthistorischen Institutes in Florenz* 32 (1988), pp. 558–79.

Adams, N. (1993) "l'architettura militare di Francesco di Giorgio," in Francesco Paolo Fiore and Manfredo Tafuri (eds), *Francesco di Giorgio architetto* (Siena, 1993), pp. 126–62.

Adams, N. & Pepper, S. (1994) "The Fortification Drawings" in Christoph L. Frommel and Nicholas Adams (eds.), *The Architectural Drawings of Antonio da Sangallo and his Circle* (Cambridge, Mass., 1994).

Adams, N. (1996) "The *Curriculum Vitae* of Jacomo Fontana, Architect and Chief Gunner," in Cecil L. Striker (ed.), *Architectural Studies in Memory of Richard Krautheimer* (Mainz am Rhein, 1996), pp. 7–12.

———. (1999) "Censored anecdotes from Francesco Maria I della Rovere's *Discorsi Militari*," *Renaissance Studies* 13 (1999), pp. 55–62.

Ambler, R. W. (1998) "Wise and Experimented": Sir William Pelham, Elizabethan Soldier and Landlord, *c.* 1560–87," in Andrew Ayton and J. L. Price (eds), *The Medieval Military Revolution: State, Society and Military Change in Medieval and Early Modern Europe* (London & New York, 1998), pp. 163–82.

Ash, E. H. (2000) "A perfect and absolute work": Expertise, Authority, and the Rebuilding of Dover Harbour, 1579–1583," *Technology and Culture* 41 (2000), pp. 239–68.

Beltrami, L. (a cura di) (1897) *Relazione di Don Ferrante Gonzaga, Governatore do Milano, inviato all'Imperatore Carlo V nel 1552 in difesa della progettata cinta di bastioni* (Milano, 1897).

Bogdanowski, J. (1996) *Architektura Obronna w Krajobrazie Polski* (Krakow, 1996).

Boulton, D. J. D. (1999) "The Monarchical (and Curial) Orders of Knighthood before the Reformation: A Reassessment in the Light of Recent Research," in F. Paillart (ed), *Les Ordres de Chevalerie* (Paris, 1999), pp. 85–136.

———. (1987) *The Knights of the Crown: The Monarchical Orders of Knighthood in Later Medieval Europe 1325–1520* (Woodbridge, Suffolk, 1987).

Buisseret, B. (ed.) (1998) *Envisioning the City: Six Studies in Urban Cartography* (Chicago, 1998).

Bury, J. (1982) "The Early History of the Explosive Mine," *Fort* 10 (1982), pp. 23–30.

Colletta, T. (1981) *Piazzeforti di Napoli e Sicilia, le 'Carte Montemar' e il sistema difensivo meridionale al principio del Settecento* (Naples, 1981).

Concina, E. (1983) *La macchina territoriale: la progettazione della difesa nel Cinquecento Veneto* (Bari, 1983).

Contamine, P. (1972) *Guerre, État et Société à la fin du Moyen Âge: Études sur les armées des rois de France, 1337–1494* (Paris, 1972).

De la Croix, H. (1960) "Military Architecture and the Radial Plan in Sixteenth Century Italy," *Art Bulletin* 42 (1960), pp. 263–90.

———. (1963) "The Literature of Fortification in Renaissance Italy," *Technology and Culture* 6 (1963), pp. 30–50.

De Moro, G. (1988) "Giovanni Maria Olgiati (1495–1557): contributo all riscoperta di un inzegnero," in Carlo Cresti, Amelio Fara and Daniela Lamberini (a cura di), *Architettura militare nell'Europa delo XVI secolo (Atti del Convegno di Studi, Firenze, 25–27 novembre 1986)* (Siena, 1988), pp. 253–70.

Cruickshank, C. G. (1969) *Army Royal. An Account of Henry VIII's Invasion of France 1513* (Oxford, 1969).

DeVries, K. (1992) *Medieval Military Technology* (Orchard Park, NY, 1992).

Dubled, H. (1976) "L'artillerie royale Francaise à l'epoque de Charles VII et au debut du regne de Louis XI (1437–1469): Les freres Bureau," *Memorial de l'artillerie Francaise* 50 (1976), pp. 555–637.

Englund, B. (1967) "Fästningsmodeller Fran Erik Dahlberghs Tid: En preliminär undersökning," *Meddelanden fran Armemuseum* 28 (1967), pp. 11–52.

Fara, G. M. (1999) *Albrecht Dürer teorico dell'architettura: una storia italiana* (Florence, 1999).

Faucherre, N. (1989) "La Construction de la Frontière: De l'Usage Stratégique des Plans en Relief," in Antoine de Roux, Nicolas Faucherre and Guillaume Monsaingeon, *Les Plans en Relief des Places du Roy* (Paris, 1989), pp. 11–54.

Fino, J.-F. (1970) *Forteresses de la France Médiévale* (Paris, 1970).

Frinz, W. (1988) "Dal modello al dipinto: macchine da guerra di Archimede alla fine del Cinquecento," in Carlo Cresti, Amelio Fara and Daniela Lamberini (a cura di), *Architettura militare nell'Europa delo XVI secolo (Atti del Convegno di Studi, Firenze, 25–27 novembre 1986)* (Siena, 1988), pp. 409–16.

Frommel & Adams, N. eds, (1994) *The Architectural Drawings of Antonio da Sangallo and his Circle* (Cambridge, Mass., 1994).

Forster, K. (1971) "Metaphors of Rule: Political Ideology and History in the Portraits of Cosimo I de'Medici," *Mitteilungen des Kunsthistorischen Institutes in Florenz* 15 (1971), pp. 65–104.

Hale, J.R. (1965) "The Early Development of the Bastion: An Italian Chronology *c.* 1450–*c.* 1534," in J. R. Hale, L. Highfield and B. Smalley (eds), *Europe in the Late Middle Ages* (London, 1965), pp. 466–94.

——. (1971) "The First Fifty Years of a Venetian Magistracy: The *Provveditori alle fortezze,*" in Anthony Molho and John A. Tedeschi (eds), *Renaissance Studies in Honor of Hans Baron* (DeKalb, Illinois, 1971), pp. 501–29.

——. 1982 "The Defence of the Realm, 1485–1558," in H. M. Colvin *et al*, *The History of the King's Works* (London, 1982), IV, *1485–1660* (pt. II), pp. 367–401.

Gerola, G. (1930–31) "I plastici delle fortezze venete al Museo storico navale di Venezia," *Atti dell'istituto veneto di scienze, lettere ed arti,* 90/2 (1930–31), pp. 217–21.

Jones, M. (1981) "The Defence of Medieval Brittany: A Survey of the Establishment of Fortified Towns, Castles and Frontiers from the Gallo-Roman Period to the End of the Middle Ages," *Archaeological Journal* 138 (1981), 149–204.

Lamberini, D. ed (1980) "Giovanni Battista Belluzzi: il trattato delle fortificazioni di terra" in *Documenti inediti di cultura toscana,* 4, pp. 375–517 (Florence).

Lane, F. (1973) "Naval Actions and Fleet Organisation, 1499–1502," in J. R. Hale (ed.), *Renaissance Venice* (London, 1973).

Lennel, F. (1908–10) *Histoire de Calais* (2 vols, 1908–10), II, pp. 263–82.

Leydi, S. (1985) *La linea esterna di fortificazioni di Milano 1323–1550,* in *Storia urbana,* 31 (1985), pp. 3–29.

Mallett, M. E. & Hale, J. R. (1984) *The Military Organisation of a Renaissance State: Venice c. 1400–1617* (Cambridge, 1984).

Martinelli, R. & Puccinelli, G. (1983) *Lucca: Le mura del Cinquecento; vicende costruttive dal 1500 al 1650* (Lucca, 1983)

Monte, A. (1996) *Acaya: Una città-fortezza del Rinascimento meridionale* (Lecce, 1996).

Neumann, H. (1988) *Festungbaukunst und Festungbautechnik* (Koblenz, 1988).

Pepper, S. (1976) "Planning versus Fortification: Antonio da Sangallo's Project for the Defence of Rome," *Architectural Review,* 159 (March 1976), pp. 162–9.

——. (1995) "Castles and Cannon in the Naples Campaign of 1494–95," in David Abulafia (ed.), *The French Descent into Renaissance Italy, 1494–95: Antecedents and Effects* (Aldershot, 1995), pp. 263–94.

——. (1999) "Military Architecture in Baroque Europe," in Henry A. Millon (ed), *The Triumph of the Baroque: Architecture in Europe 1600–1750* (Milan, 1999), pp. 332–47, see pp. 338 and 346–7.

——. (2000A) "Sword and Spade: Military Construction in Renaissance Italy," *Construction History* 16 (2000), pp. 13–32.

——. (2000B) "Siege Law, Siege Ritual, and the Symbolism of City Walls in Renaissance Europe," in James D. Tracy (ed.), *City Walls: The Urban Enceinte in Global Perspective* (Cambridge, 2000), pp. 573–604.

Pepper, S. & Hughes, Q. (1983) "Introduction" to E. E. Viollet-le-Duc, *Annals of a Fortress* (1874/1983), pp. iii–xvii.

Pepper, S. & Adams, N. (1986) *Firearms and Fortifications: Military Architecture and Siege Warfare in Sixteenth-Century Siena* (Chicago, 1986).

Potter, D. (1983) "The duc de Guise and the Fall of Calais," *EHR* 97 (1983), pp. 481–512.

Promis, C. (1863) "Gl'ingegneri e gli scrittori militari bolognesi del XVᶜ XVI secoli," *Miscellanea di storia italiana*, ser. 1, IV (Torino, 1863): 614–27.

Reti, L. (1963) "Francesco di Giorgio Martini's Treatise on Architecture and its Plagiarists," *Technology and Culture*, 4 (1963), pp. 287–97.

Saunders, A. (1989) *Fortress Britain: Artillery Fortification in the British Isles and Ireland* (Liphook, 1989).

Scaglia, G. (1984) "Drawings of Machines, Instruments and Tools" in Frommel & Adams, eds, *The Architectural Drawings of Antonio da Sangallo and His Circle* (Cambridge, Mass, 1994), I, pp. 81–97.

Scotti, A. (1977) "Per un profilo dell'architettura milanese (1535–1565)", in *Omaggio a Tiziano: la cultura artistica milanese nell'età di Carlo V (Catalogo della mostra al Palazzo Reale, Milano, 27 aprile–20 luglio 1977)*, Milan, 1977, pp. 97–103.

Scotti, A. (1988) "Cittadelle Lombarde di fine Cinquecento: il castello di Milano nella prima età spagnuola," in Carlo Cresti, Amelio Fara e Daniela Lamberini (a cura di), *Architettura militare nell'Europa del XVI secolo (Atti del Convegno di Studi, Firenze, 25–28 novembre 1986)* (Siena, 1988), pp. 207–17.

Shelby, L. R. (1967) *John Rogers: Tudor Military Engineer* (Oxford 1967).

Tomkinson, J. (1998) "The Henrician Bastions at Guines Castle," *Fort*, 26 (1998), pp. 121–41.

Torfs, L. & Casterman, M. A. (1871) "Les agrandissements et les fortifications d'Anvers," *Annales de l'acadèmie d'archèologie de Belgique*, 2nd ser., VII (1871), pp. 69 ff.

Vale, M. (1975) "New Techniques and Old Ideas: The Impact of Artillery on War and Chivalry at the end of the Hundred Years War," in C. T. Allmand (ed.), *War, Literature and Politics in the Late Middle Ages: Essays in Honour of G. W. Coopland* (Liverpool, 1975), pp. 57–72.

——. (1981) *War and Chivalry: Warfare and Aristocratic Culture in England, France and Burgundy at the end of the Middle Ages* (London, 1981)

Van den Heuvel, C. (1988) "Un'escussione di testimoni ad Anversa (1542): l'introduzione dell'urbanistica e dell'architettura militare italiana nei paesi bassi," in Cresti *et al*, *Architettura militare* (1988), pp. 253–70.

Van Dyke, P. (1911) "Francois de Guise and the Taking of Calais," *American Historical Association Annual Report* (1911), I, pp. 99–103.

Viganò, M. (a cura di) (1994) *Architetti e ingegneri militari italiani all'estero dal XV al XVIII secolo* (Istituto Italiano dei Castelli, Livorno, 1994).

Zorzi, G. (1958–59) "Alcune notizie di Basilio della Scola, architetto militare vicentino, e delle sue fortificazioni a Vicenza e Verona," *Atti dell'Istituto Veneto delle Scienze, Lettere ed Arti*, 117 (1958–59), pp. 53–77.

CHAPTER SIX

CHIVALRY AND PROFESSIONALISM IN THE FRENCH ARMIES OF THE RENAISSANCE

David Potter

On the evening of 14 September 1515, flushed with his fortunate victory at Marignano, Francis I asked Pierre Terrail, seigneur de Bayard to dub him a knight. Bayard refused at first, saying that an anointed king was already the first chevalier of his realm, but at length acceded to the king's request.[1] Francis perhaps aimed, by this calculated act, to signal his regard for the military nobility of his kingdom in a period when chivalric propaganda and tournaments were increasingly convoked into the service of royal power. The act struck contemporaries as notable, setting on course Bayard's eventual emergence as the quintessential chivalric figure in the imagination of his time, and took place at the end of a battle which was, wrongly, seen as a great victory for the traditional arm of French military might, the heavy cavalry. In the next great military crisis of his reign, Francis was to continue to act out the role of the chivalrous knight facing overwhelming odds in declaring after the battle of Pavia 'de toutes choses ne m'est demeuré que l'honneur et la vie qui est saulve.'[2]

Despite this evident attention to chivalric conduct, it is the 'professionalisation' of French armies in the early modern period that has become an historical commonplace, though the definition of that process is often vague and military change in most cases is incremental rather than sudden.[3] There has never been much clarity

---

[1] See Champier (1991), 195–6 (bk. III, ch. III). It was sometimes believed that members of the house of France were chevaliers from their baptism. It was certainly the case that since Charles VI all French kings had been dubbed at their coronations and there were dubbings for knighthood at Francis I's coronation in January 1515.

[2] Champollion-Figeac (1847), 129.

[3] Corvisier (1976), 16–30. As will be seen below, the terms 'profession' and 'vocation/vacation' were used differently, the former sometimes signifying a 'calling' the

about the period in which it was actually taking place. The formation of the so-called 'standing army' in 1445 has often been regarded
as a crucial turning-point, yet the broad lines of development were
apparent from the later fourteenth century, though the *ordonnances* of
that year did confirm the centrality of the aristocratic cavalry in
French military thought.[4] The aim here is to assess how far the un-
doubted survival of chivalric values shaped the thinking of the French
military class in the period of military change from the mid-fifteenth
to the late sixteenth century. The structures of the French army of
the Renaissance emerged from the experience of reconquest from
the English in the years from 1420 to 1460, years of remarkable
successes against apparently great odds, shaped by adaptation to new
tactics and disciplines.[5] If in the 1460s the crown's forces were still
relatively small, the victories over the English in Guyenne and Normandy crowned a generation of rebuilding. The wars with Burgundy
and Brittany accelerated change and the involvement in Italy from
1494 speeded this up as part of the general military change that was
overhauling all major European armies and created the basic patterns of French military organisation of the *Ancien Regime*: the affirmation
of royal control of armies, military bureaucracy and heavy state
expenditure on dynastic war.[6] Thereafter, much of the energy and
organisational capacity of the French state of the Renaissance was
channelled into the wielding of armed force and its deployment at
home and abroad. By the closing decades of the fifteenth century,
the French royal army was the most formidable in western Europe
for its size and renown.[7] Gaston Zeller thought that military innovation in France was so rapid between the 1520s and the 1550s that
Henri II's army had more in common with that of Henri IV than
that of Charles VIII. There is, though, a great deal of continuity in
formations like the *gendarmerie* and crucial developments in the admin-

---

latter a full-time occupation (see below, notes 17, 152 p. 177). 'Professionel' in the
sense of 'trained' is not used. Contamine (1972), conclusion. This is still the *locus
classicus* and point of departure for any study of the French army in this period.

[4] Space precludes a systematic discussion here of the structures of the French
army in the late 15th and early 16th century. The present writer hopes to publish
a study entitled "A Military Revolution? Tradition and Innovation in the French
Royal Army of the Renaissance."

[5] The most recent overview of the subject is Contamine (1992), I, 209–301.

[6] On this period see Dickinson (1954), introduction; Lot (1962); Zeller (1943),
51–86; and, most recently, Wood (1996).

[7] This point is emphasised particularly for the cavalry by Contamine (1972), 290.

istrative supply system and artillery were well under way before the end of the fifteenth century.[8]

The wars fought by France from the late fifteenth to the mid-sixteenth centuries, especially in Italy, would have been defined as 'guerres de magnificence' rather than 'guerre commune'.[9] The latter embraces what earlier theorists had sometimes called 'guerre mortelle' (waged by non-nobles) in which no ransoms were taken, and 'guerre à feu et à sang', usually envisaged as a non-chivalric form of warfare.[10] The conventions of chivalric war—personal bravery, consideration for enemies under a code of rules, loyalty, generosity, gratitude for favours done, courtesy to women, above all the pursuit of honour through the path of 'virtue'[11]—had to be stretched in order to accommodate many of these conflicts which, after all, often embodied vast geo-political and strategic objectives as well as dynastic interests. As in earlier periods, the line between 'guerre à feu et à sang' and chivalric war was repeatedly blurred. At Mézières in October 1521, jousts were held between 'champions' on horseback and on foot between the French garrison and the besieging force under Nassau. Yet within weeks, both sides were carrying out 'guerre à feu et à sang' along the borders of the Ardennes which du Bellay thought were the origin of 'les grandes cruautez qui ont esté faictes aux guerres trente ans après.' Similarly, serious skirmishing at Thérouanne in 1543 was accompanied by an invitation from Sir John Wallop to the sieur de Villebon that 'if he had any gentlemen under his charge that wold breke any staves for theire ladis sake' he would appoint champions.[12]

Pressures for change and adaptation on the part of governments and commanders, faced with ever more stark and demanding challenges, coexisted with profoundly traditional social ideas. Most

---

[8] Zeller (1943), 51; Contamine (1992), I, 231–56; Contamine (1984), 249–80.

[9] Pannier & Meyer (1877), 12.

[10] See Keen (1965), 104–6. Looting and burning were, though, permitted under the laws of war (ibid., 97–100). In the 16th century this was especially typical on the borders with the Low Countries, see Potter (1993), 200–32.

[11] Vale (1981), 14–16.

[12] Du Bellay (1908–19), 1:148–9, 152; Florange (1924), II, 22. We could also note the mutual cruelties between the French and the garrison of Novara in 1522, the latter accused of eating hearts, disembowelling and feeding their horses from the entrails (du Bellay, ibid., I, 221). Wallop to the Council, 31 July 1543, *SP Henry 8th*, IX, 459 (*L&P Henry 8th*, XVIII, i, 979); BL, Harl. MS 288, fo. 3 (*L&P Henry 8th*, XVIII, ii, 13).

writers in the sixteenth century assumed that the nobility's calling was war; for Guillaume du Bellay, war was 'la coustume et ordinaire vacation de la noblesse de France'. Monluc in his *Commentaires* was categorical: 'Songés, vous qui estes nés gentilhommes, que Dieu vous a faicts naistre pour pourter les armes, pour servir vostre prince et non pour courre le lièvre ou fere l'amour.' Montaigne was more measured but made same point: 'La forme propre, et seule, et essentielle, de noblesse en France, c'est la vacation militaire.'[13] Indeed, the view expressed in *Le Jouvencel* that 'ceulx qui ne sont nobles de lignée, le sont par exercice et mestier d'armes' was now far less common.[14] However, during the first half of the sixteenth century the heavily-armoured aristocratic cavalry lost their monopoly of mounted warfare with the advent of the light horse, *chevau-légers* and *reiters*, German mounted pistoliers. By the end of the sixteenth century the system was on the verge of complete change.[15]

Philippe Contamine, in his study of the mediaeval French army, concluded that service in the heavy cavalry had become 'une qualité, une profession, un "état"'.[16] The great military exempla of the fifteenth and early sixteenth centuries—from *Le Jouvencel* through the various lives of Bayard to the Memoirists—were figures who conveyed simultaneously the living values of chivalry and the consciousness of warfare as a *métier*, a 'profession des armes'[17] requiring training and with strict conventions. The literary evidence for military thought in this period may be conveniently divided into three: firstly the literature of chivalry proper and edifying biography, secondly the increasingly important format of the military commander's memoir and finally the systematic military manual or meditation on war.[18] It has been all too common to regard the chivalric literature of this period as the last gasp of the dying middle ages or the perpetuation

---

[13] Du Bellay (1908–19), IV, 343 (prologue to the Ogdoades); Monluc (1864–72), I, 431; Montaigne (1925) II, 99, 'Des recompenses d'honneur.'

[14] The text goes on: 'le harnoys est de telle noblesse que, depuis que ung homme d'armes a le bacinet en la teste, il est noble et souffisant de combatre ung roy.' See *Jouvencel* (1887), I, 80–81.

[15] Love (1991), 511–33.

[16] Contamine (1972), 545.

[17] The term used by Du Bellay (1908–19), I, 138 when he criticises a fortress commander who treats for surrender in person 'chose non usitée parmy les hommes qui font profession des armes.'

[18] For a useful bibliography of the literature of chivalry published in the period, see Cooper (1990), 195–238.

of some kind of false consciousness.[19] Huizinga, though he sought to emphasise the importance of chivalric ideals in the late middle ages, characterised them as increasingly at odds with reason of state and concerns for wealth and power.[20] Jean Jacquart saw in the figure of Bayard a 'témoin dépassé d'un monde révolu' or 'le signe d'un monde qui se meurt', faced by the disappearance of the nobility's monopoly of armed force and increasingly challenged position socially.[21] A common cause of difficulty has been the confusion of the code of chivalric conduct with an imagined 'system' within which feudal warriors regarded themselves as independent of royal power, by 1500 long defunct in its pristine form. In addition, two attitudes are often confused: the first, we may call the idea of war as primarily a 'courteous' action governed by he strictest rules of 'honour', the second the idea of all forms of war as enriching and exalting in themselves.[22] As Philippe Contamine has shown, the fifteenth century saw the formation of a 'société militaire'[23] which, while retaining the ideals of chivalry, gradually moved away from the individualistic concepts of chivalric warfare embodied in Geoffroy de Charny's *Le Livre de la Chevalerie* (c. 1350–52), in which the 'gens d'armes' have the right to wage war 'en leur chief'.[24] Yet, in France the train of life of the *petite noblesse* retained enough in common with that of the chevaliers for them to be at least comparable with these men of higher rank and an able captain could at least aspire to a following analogous to those of great lords.[25] Thus the ideals of chivalry remained in being because they remained relevant to the warrior class of the age and the libraries of nobles were well equipped with manuscripts and

---

[19] E.g., Kilgour (1937), 27. P.F. Barrière (1961), 44: 'la chevalerie militaire s'affaiblit, et la vogue même des romans de chevalerie ... témoigne de sa transformation en un système plus décoratif que puissant.' See also Hauser (1963), 39.

[20] Huizinga (1960), reworked in chs 2–9 of Huizinga (1924). For a useful appreciation of his ideas, see Morgan (1990), 96–7 and Keen (1977).

[21] Jacquart (1987), 11–12, 366–67.

[22] Jouanna (1981), I, 347–8.

[23] Contamine (1972), 545–51.

[24] De Charny (1996), 62–3, 86. See Contamine (1972), 184–7. In Jouvencel (1889), II, pp. 155–6, to a remark in the Council: 'Véez-cy tant de vaillans gens qui ont tant traveillié pour la chose publicque de ce royaulme et y ont tant de foys exposé leur vie', the Chancellor replies: 'La maniere de bien les pourveoir, c'est de leur donner excercice, par quoy ilz n'oublient point les armes et qu'ilz puissent avoir leur vie honnestement et honnorablement.'

[25] Contamine (1972), 442 *et seq.*

printed books which mingled history and chivalry in the honour of
their houses.[26]

The changes which had overtaken the idea of 'chevalerie' in the
late mediaeval period are illustrated by the fact that, as at Marignano,
the dubbing of knights usually took place at the end of and not
before a battle[27] and have been seen as a visible sign that 'chivalry'
was being transformed from a rite of initiation for youth into one
of recognition and reward for the distinguished.[28] The number of
knights had seen a precipitous decline in France, as in England, during the later middle ages, for a number of reasons but principally
because knighthood had come to viewed as a social distinction and
not a function of war. Antoine de la Sale in the middle of the
fifteenth century argued that the écuyer 'quant il a bien voyagé et
a esté en plusieurs fais d'armes dont il en est sailly à honneur et
qu'il a bien de quoy maintenir l'estat de chevalerie' is ready for such
promotion, 'car aultrement ne lui est honneur, et lui vault mieulx
estre bon escuier que ung povre chevallier.'[29] The Italian wars, unsur-
prisingly, visibly embodied an attempt to anchor international conflict
in this world of the 'estat de chevalerie' but the renaissance of chivalric ideas took place at a time when that 'estat' had already become
a rare and prized commodity.

This Renaissance of chivalric values in the Italian Wars, saw their
perpetuation through a rage for works such as the mediaeval Spanish
chivalric romance, *Amadis de Gaule*, published in French from 1540

---

[26] Keen (1984), 219; Jones (1988), 381.

[27] For Florange's reception of knighthood from Francis I after Marignano, see
Florange (1913), I, p. 198. At Ceresole, Blaise de Monluc received knighthood after
the battle from the duc d'Enghien: Monluc (1864–72), I, 117. As late as Fornovo
and Novara, dubbings had taken place before the battle. Needless to say these
battlefield dubbings had little in common with the full ritual (largely defunct in
France since the 14th century) of the bath, veillée, remise du cingulum, remise
d'éperons etc.: see Contamine (1976B), 282. For the possible continuation of dubbing before a battle, see Du Bellay (1908–19), I, 226 on Bicocca (fought in 1522).

[28] Contamine (1976B), esp. 272–83. In 1513 Louis XII declared that he had created the lieutenant in the *sénéchaussée* of Quercy a chevalier 'qu'il soit en couraige
de perseverer' in his service (BN, MS Fr. 5085, fo. 46).

[29] La Sale (1935), 234, 'Comment ung escuier se doit faire chevallier.' See Lannoy
(1878) 414: 'Ne devroit chevalier estre fait se il n'avoit corps, lignage, meurs et conditions dessus declairées, et que de leur vertu, hardement et vaillance durant le
temps qu'ilz sont escuiers, en apparust aux princes' and p. 411: 'chevalier à droit
esleu doit estre de très noble et france condition.' See also *Rosier de guerres* (1925),
ch. IV: 'des chevaliers' (unpaginated); and Contamine (1976B), 269.

onwards.[30] This had a special resonance in France where the heroic figures it deployed, cloaked in an assumed aura of historicity, prefigured in some sense the warrior kings of the Renaissance. Its greatest vogue was in the middle decades of the sixteenth century when it seems effectively to have pushed the Arthurian cycle out of fashion.[31] The dedicatory poem introducing book 8 (1548) made the point clearly. By Perion and Amadis:

> Le puissant Roy de France est entendu,
> Et tout le sang royal d'eux descendu . . .

Its translator dedicated the book to the Constable de Montmorency as 'le Cheualier à la grante Espée', a direct echo of the book's main character.[32]

If the Amadis cycle was a literary craze, other works sought to blend history and edification. *Le Jouvencel* (which went through five printed editions from 1493 to 1529), Symphorien Champier's 1510 translation of Llull's *Libro de la Orden de Caballeria* (in some ways the most influential work on chivalry throughout the middle ages),[33] his 1525 biography of Bayard[34] and that of 1527 by the Loyal serviteur[35] as well as Jean Bouchet's life of La Trémoille[36] all added considerably to the genre. The latter portrays battle very much in the tones of the *Amadis*: siege warfare is 'contre la nature des François et Gaules'

---

[30] The *Amadis* was assembled from earlier texts and published by Garcia Ordoñez de Montalvo at Salamanca in 1510. It was translated into French from 1540 by Nicolas Herberay sr des Essarts and knew its greatest success in the reign of Henri II. 17 similar works appeared between 1544 and 1579. See Baret (1853).

[31] Bourciez (1886), 63, in which he describes the book as the 'bréviaire' of that court. La Noue (1967), 162 points out that 'sous le règne du Roy Henri second, ils ont eu leur principale vogue.' See Cooper (1990), 177–84. For the snapping up of vol. 6 on its appearance in 1545, see Broussillon (1895–1903), no. 2587 (I owe this reference to Mr. Malcolm Walsby).

[32] Cooper (1990), 183.

[33] Llull (1972). Llull's work had been written around 1276. It was already known in French—see Minervini's introduction to ibid; and Keen (1984), 11.

[34] Champier (1992). Crouzet, introduction to ibid. 7–13, argues that the Bayard story should be read in terms of its influence on following generations. Champier, a physician by training, married Bayard's cousin Marguerite de Terrail and entered the service of duke Antoine of Lorraine, Bayard's chief and was present at the battle of Agnadello and actually knighted by the duke after Marignano (ibid., 194).

[35] "Serviteur" (1878).

[36] Bouchet (1839). On the historical content of this work, see Hamon (1901), 179–84 and Britnell (1986), 115–21, 138–39.

lesquels, s'ils ne donnent en colère et fureur, perdent leur force et
hardiesse au dissimuller... les François devroient avoir l'oeil et ne
altérer ne changer leurs anciennes meurs... le dissimuler est bon à
gens qui n'ont esté nourrys en leurs aises et qui sont coustumiers de
supporter longuement le froit, le chault, la fain, le soif... mais ceulx
qui ont leurs aises suyvies, comme le François, ne les peuvent pas
longtemps supporter sans maladie... [les Francoys] sont plus fors en
la première pointe.[37]

There seems almost to have been a competition to find the contemporary equivalent of an Arthurian hero fighting in the Italian
wars. Denis Crouzet has seen in this regeneration of chivalry, conceived by Champier (following Llull) as an order instituted by God
after the fall to defend justice. In this view, chevaliers are to be seen
first and foremost as warriors of the faith defending the Catholic
religion.[38]

On a more mundane level, we can observe a continuing attention to the courteous aspect of warfare, an ability to switch from
furious combat to 'esbatement' with an enemy as though the whole
thing were a game,[39] the generous and friendly treatment of enemies after combat,[40] the restitution of an enemy commander's per-

---

[37] Bouchet (1839), 801, 803. 'Il disoit la principalle force des François estre en
emotion et fureur, et que le Roy ne les devoit arrester à aucun siège. Ce qui ne
fut trouvé bon' passage from *Annales d'Aquitaine*, quoted in Britnell (1986) 139. For
similar terms, see du Bellay (1908–19), I, 144, where the gendarmerie française 'ne
se laisse comparer à autre nation' in terms of its 'furie'.
[38] Crouzet, Introduction to Champier (1992), 44, 52. With characteristic hyper-
bole he suggests that the death of Bayard took on the quality of Christ-like suffering;
cf. also Crouzet (1993).
[39] E.g. "Serviteur" (1878), 316–7 at the battle of Ravenna, near the close of the
battle, when Bayard invites Nemours: 'allons nous esbatre ung peu', they meet some
Spanish arquebusiers and Bayard invites them: 'Messeigneurs, vous vous esbatez
comme nous, en attendant que le beau jour commence' inviting them to share a
mutual ceasefire. They were answered with all courtesy.
[40] See the courteous treatment of Bayard after the battle of the Spurs in 1513,
as recorded by the "Serviteur" (1878), 358–62 (though Bouchet gives a rather
different account). When Monluc issued forth from Siena in 1555 he was given a
metaphorical round of applause by the marchese di Marignano and his Spanish
troops: 'et là nous embrassasmes, et me mirent au milieu d'eux, et allasmes, tousjours parlant du siège, jusques à ce que nous feusmes ung mil au delà de Sainct
Lazare': Monluc (1864–72), II, 104. This is confirmed in contemporary sources, see
Courteault (1908), 294. See Monluc's letter to Pope Pius IV, Marignano's brother,
1562: Marignano had said to him after the siege 'che egli et io correvamo une
medesima fortuna essendo noi poveri gentilhuomini, che per le nostre virtù avan-
vamo i gran signori.' (ibid., 294, n. 2)

sonal effects.[41] There is also the snobbery of a Bayard refusing in 1509 to fight on foot alongside German landsknechts 'qui n'ont leur honneur en si grande recommandation que gentilzhommes.'[42] The rituals of chivalry, in the form of the tournament, involved stylised and sometimes insensate violence; most notably they were the apotheosis of the individual.[43] Brantôme relates, for instance, that Bayard was never willing to take high command since he found it more in his nature to act as an individual captain 'que d'estre contrainct par une si grande charge et gesné de sa liberté à ne combattre et mener les mains quand il voulait.'[44] Clearly, Bayard's life was thought to express an ideal which ignored the notion of professionalism as career structure, though it should also be remembered that, in the French army at least, it was not until the 1540s that larger commands in the form of colonelcies of foot emerged.

Though these [hero-figures] are often portrayed as 'joyeux' and larger than life,[45] they are also modest when appropriate.[46] A quality all of them have in common is their loyalty to their king and 'maistre.' La Trémoille's biography is, in its earlier passages, a fictionalised account plainly based on an amalgam of classical myth and chivalric romance,[47] yet the core constitutes an argument for loyalty to the king: his title of 'chevalier sans reproche' is attributed to 'sa grant loyaulté et fidélité qu'il eut tousjours aux roys et à la maison de France, et parce qu'il fut pur et nect de toute tyrannie.'[48]

---

[41] Brissac in 1558, see Villars (1850), 299: 'L'acte fut trouvé si courtois par le duc de Sesse, qu'avec mil et mil remerciements qu'il en fist il envoya donner au maréchal un beau cheval d'Espagne. Nos guerriers d'aujourd'huy ... n'auroient garde d'embrasser ces courtoisies.'

[42] "Serviteur" (1878), 182: 'Pense l'Empereur que ce soit chose raisonnable de mettre tant de noblesse en péril et hazart avecques des piétons dont l'ung est cordoannier, l'autre maréchal, l'autre boulengier et gens mécanicques qui...'

[43] The 1493 tournament of Sandricourt, like that at St Inglevert a century before, was thought prodigious at the time. Nothing could be nearer 'des faits desdits chevaliers de la Table Ronde' though 'tant de durs horions se donnerent que à tous coups sortoit le feu des espées et du harnoys.' See Vayssière (1874), 66, 34. See also Contamine (1986). Florange (1913), I, 62–3, recounts how in the Italian campaign of 1510, the grand maître de Chaumont was fatally wounded in an impromptu snowball fight on the march which involved 400 men.

[44] Brantôme (1864–96), II, 388.

[45] Louis XII was 'fort joyeulx et de bon couraige'; Chaumont 'homme joyeulx et le meilleur compaignon du monde': see Florange (1913), I, 29–30, 62.

[46] E.g. Bouchet (1839), ch. 30, p. 798; Monluc (1864–72), II, 257–8.

[47] Jouvencel (1887), I, 39–46 shares with the La Trémoille biography a long discussion on the undesirability of attending court for the young knight.

[48] Bouchet (1839), ch. 32, p. 807, col. 2.

All this is despite that king's rejection of the hero's sound advice.[49]

How did these chivalric values shape the qualities expected of perfect warrior, the "homme de bien"?[50] There is no doubt that there was a powerful and vibrant literary tradition on the waging of war (if not the 'art' of war) in late mediaeval and Renaissance France, much of it influenced by Vegetius.[51] *Le Jouvencel*, in many ways a key text in this respect, is best described as part romance, part biographical compilation (the latter increasingly common in the sixteenth century) and may be read in a way which illustrates precisely these tensions between chivalry and professionalism. The topos of the life of the unknown squire who through prowess makes his mark on the wider stage would have a long life in front of it. *Le Jouvencel* was probably influenced by Geoffroy de Charny and has been seen as the conduit through which the practical side of chivalric ideals of the French tradition were transmitted to the military men of the Renaissance.[52] We can see in it a certain intermingling of the qualities of honour and chivalry, war as the principal form of expression for the nobleman, and a conception of the role of the *homme d'armes* as a defender of his country. For the compiler of this work, in some of the most well-worn words of the military literature, the Jouvencel, after a feast and good cheer following an expedition exclaims:

> c'est joyeuse chose que la guerre; on y oït, on y voit beaucoup de bonnes choses, et y apprent moult de bien. Quant elle est en bonne querelle, c'est justice, c'est deffendre droicture. Et croy que Dieu ayme bien ceulx qui exposent leur corps à vouloir faire la guerre et faire la raison aux ingratz ... Et, quant la guerre prent en cest entendement, c'est ung plaisant mestier et bon à jeunes gens. Car ilz sont amez de Dieu et du monde. On s'entr'ayme tant à la guerre. On pense en soymeismes: Laisseray-je ad ce tirant oster par sa cruauté le bien d'autruy, ou il n'a riens. Quand on voit sa querelle bonne et son sang bien combatre, la larme en vient à l'ueil. Il vient une doulceur au coeur de loyaulté et de pitié de veoir son amy, qui si vaillament expose son

---

[49] Ibid., 775, col. 1, 800, col. 2, 803, col. 1.

[50] The definition of the "homme de bien" in military terms is to be found in Montaigne (1925), 98: 'ce n'est à dire aultre chose qu'un vaillant homme.' There were other approved characteristics: Teligny 'gentil chevalier et homme fort experimenté' (du Bellay (1908–19), I, 211), Bussy d'Amboise 'honneste et gentil compaignon' (Florange (1913), I, 54).

[51] Blanchard (1989).

[52] Charny (1996), introduction, 29–64; Vale (1981), 31.

corps pour faire accomplir le commandement de nostre createur. Et puis on se dispose d'aller mourir ou vivre avec luy, et pour l'amour ne l'abandonner point.

It is important to note that the 'querelle' must be just.[53] In this vein, it was natural to regard insouciance as essential: 'Quant ils eurent souppé a grant joye et grant liesse, comme la guerre le requiert, car elle hait gens tristes et paoureux.'[54] However, the chivalric attitude thus expressed is not simple. As has been seen, the compiler notes that in his time 'les nouvelletez' have changed the face of war and that in every age military thinking has to be renewed.[55] He goes on to insist that success stems from careful training and preparation, not least observation and spying on enemy positions.[56] Professor Allmand has suggested that, in view of the emphasis on training, strategy, tactics and ruses in the conduct of war and the preparation of soldiers, we have in *Le Jouvencel* a form of professionalism *avant la lettre*, but which continues to be expressed in chivalric terms.[57] In turn, even Bayard was in later life to learn to command infantry and use artillery and, of all ironies, was to be shot by an arquebus.[58] Eight books of *Amadis de Gaule* were to be translated into French

---

[53] *Jouvencel* (1887), II, 20–21. Compare with Montaigne, often so contemptuous of war, (1925), IV, 261: 'De l'expérience': 'Il n'est occupation plaisante comme la militaire; occupation et noble en execution (car la plus forte, genereuse et superbe de toutes les vertus est la vaillance) et noble en sa cause ... cette courageuse harmonie de la musique guerrière.' See the words of La Trémoille on his son's death at Marignan: 'en acte de vertu pour le bien public et en juste querelle': Bouchet (1839), 792 col. 1.

[54] Passage quoted in Contamine (1972), 527; Jouvencel (1889), II, 118: 'ne pensa que à faire bonne chière et entreprendre sur ses ennemis.'

[55] *Jouvencel* (1887), I, 17, the author also specifically dismisses the argument that all that can be said on war has been by the point 'qui ne cesseroit jamais de renouveller les sciences, si trouveroit-on tousjours quelque chose de nouveau.' For the real Jean du Beuil's perplexity when faced by larger armies—'comment gouverner tant de gens', often taken as the voice of chivalry faced by military innovation— see the document printed by Favre in the Introduction to ibid., I, cclxxx–xxxi, based, however, on an uncertain source.

[56] *Jouvencel* (1887), I, 33–4, discussion of 'subtillitez de guerre'; ibid., I, 92: 'c'est l'un des grans pointz de la guerre que de sçavoir la convine de ses ennemis'. For an extended discussion of military tactics leaning heavily in Vegetius, see ibid., II, 31–84. In the 1380s Honoré Bovet in *L'arbre des batailles* had of course accepted the use of stratagems to knights (see the trans. by Coopland, Bovet (1949), 154–5).

[57] Allmand (1999), 463–81.

[58] Jacquart (1987), 156–7 (on infantry command), 270–71 (on ruses), 366–7. At Marignano, Champier (1992), 194, describes Bayard directing artillery against the Swiss. It is of course possible to overdo the symbolism of the fact of Bayard's death

between 1540 and 1548 by the sieur des Essarts, a *commissaire ordinaire de l'artillerie* in Picardy under the *grand maître* de Brissac.[59]

In addition, the author of *Le Jouvencel*, unlike Charny, stresses the public role of the homme d'armes who will be pitied by all if, having 'bien servi le Roy et le royaume', he falls on hard times: 'Au moins meurt-il en grant et hault honneur'. The soldier now has a primary duty to defend the community and the cause must be 'méritoire.'[60] Maitre Nicole in *Le Jouvencel* propounds an analogy between the 'estat de chevalerie' and the arms and hands of the body defending the head 'lequel est ordonné en cestui corps mistique pour deffendre et conserver en paix et union encontre les ennemis l'estat, de l'Eglise, et les autres membres inferiores.'[61] This principle is much the same as that expressed by Bovet in *L'arbre des batailles* when he emphasises the 'commune utilité de tout le royaume' in the service of the king in war above all others. For him professionalism meant the discipline and obedience of the well-trained knight which, he argued, must be accepted as 'l'ordonnance de deue chevalerie'. For Olivier de La Marche, the lesson drawn from Bovet was that 'nulle chose n'est faicte contre le commandement du chief ne de ses lieutenans.'[62] The profound tension between chivalric society—at its height in the fourteenth century—and kings who saw themselves as both its supreme advocates and its masters resulted by the fifteenth century in an ideology of chivalric royal service in the public good.[63] Royal *ordonnances* had long striven to regulate the evils of uncontrolled military activity. The Edict of 1354 imposed the *Quarantaine le Roy* on private war and that of 1431 insisted that the true role of the nobility was 'en nostre service contre noz ennemis et adver-

---

at the hands of an anonymous arquebusier. The battlefields of Crécy and Agincourt need simply be mentioned.

[59] Nicolas de Herberay, sieur des Essarts, is so qualified on the title page of book 8 (Paris: 1548).

[60] *Jouvencel* (1889), II, p. 100; I, p. 56; I, p. 118: praise for 'tout homme qui expose son corps à soustenir la bonne querelle et à secourir son souverain seigneur' II, pp. 154–7.

[61] Caron (1994), 281. See also Stanesco (1988).

[62] La Marche (1883–88), II, 320; Bovet (1883), 105–7, Bovet (1949), 129, 131, 137, on primacy of royal service); see Contamine (1972), 202–4; Wright (1976), esp. 28.

[63] On this tension, see Kaeuper (1988), 192–9. The idea underlies the approach of the *Rosier des guerres*: 'aussi on est tenu combatre pour son pays ... la propriété des roys et des princes et de leurs chevaliers considerans que leur estat et vocacion est pour le bien commun deffendre' (presentation copy, Bib. Nat., MS Fr. 442, fos 58[r], 59[r]). The point is also made by Allmand (1999), 463–81.

saires'.[64] Earlier conduct books addressed to young noblemen such as Chartier's *Breviaire des nobles*, argued that loyalty meant 'servir leur roy et leurs subgés défendre'.[65] *Le Jouvencel*, then, suffused by the experience of war in the generation from 1420 to 1460, expresses his chivalric values in a world which he is aware has been transformed by military change. Seyssel in *La Grant Monarchie de France* conceives of a nobility 'prête à le servir en tous affaires et exposer les biens et les corps pour la défense du royaume et pour le service du roi.'[66] Champier in his life of Bayard, puts its summation at the point of death into the mouth of Bourbon: 'c'est une chose piteable veoir se bon chevalier ainsi mourir, qui si noblement et loyaulment a servy tousjours ses princes, roys de france, sans aulcune reprehention.'[67] Similarly in 1568 the author of the *Advertissement envoyée à la noblesse* could speak of a nobility bound to serve the King who,

> ou il a esté question de combattre pour le pays & pour l'extension des limittes, ou pour empescher que le moindre de noz villages ne fust couru & fourragé par les estrangers, ils n'ont iamais faict refus d'y hazarder et prodigueur & leurs personnes, & la substance de leurs maisons.[68]

Chivalry and professionalism (in the sense of expertise) were, then, for the French aristocracy, two sides of the same coin. Though not quartered in barracks, as in the armies of the later seventeenth century, ordinary soldiers still lived in a world apart from the civilian population; such at least is the conclusion from the criminal cases in which they were involved.[69] Jean Molinet expressed this when speaking of the rigours of the military life: 'Vous, rices bourgeois et aultres honguars . . ., vous ne vouldriez avoir VI lieues de tel chemin pour tout l'avoir de vostre coffres.'[70] The theme of the 'pains' of military life was a common one. In the late fifteenth century, a writer on government (Robert de Balsac?) insisted on the king's need to pay his gens d'armes regularly 'car ilz gaignent leurs gaiges a grant poine et a grant travailh de leurs personnes . . . et sont povres conme

---

[64] Cazelles (1960); Thomas (1889), 72–75; Charny (1996), "Introduction", p. 62.
[65] Chartier (1988); Caron (1994), 281. See also Kaeuper (1988), 244.
[66] Seyssel (1961), 121–3.
[67] Champier (1992), 209.
[68] Anon. (1576), sig. B (often wrongly attributed to Jean du Tillet).
[69] Potter (1997), 288–89.
[70] Molinet (1935), I, 68–69.

Job.' In the early sixteenth century Pierre Gringore could write of
the 'peines et ennuitz' endured by soldiers, including hunger, thirst
heat, cold, dust, rain, snow, and harsh discipline; similar terms were
used by Jacques de Silly-Rochefort in his famous speech in the Estates-
General of 1560.[71] Many nobles still thought their military activities
set them apart. *Le Jouvencel* was clear that 'il doit avoir gens pour la
justice et hommes pour la guerre, et ne doit estre une meme chose',
echoed by the *Rosier des guerres* which declared that 'si la doctrine
des armes est mise en oubly, il ne y a nulle différence entre paisans
et Chevaliers.'[72]

One of the most striking and in some ways distinctive features of
military history in Renaissance France is the increasing evidence of
the desire, on the part of old soldiers, to write exemplary memoirs
for the edification of the young or as records of their times. The
genre is hardly new, of course, but received a decided boost during
the Renaissance.[73] They are expressed in an often ironic language
in which 'hommes de bien' engage in 'affaires' or 'passetemps' (battles), in sieges 'vont voir' their enemies, who are sometimes 'eston-
nez' at their attacks and suffer 'inconveniens' (portmanteau word for
any gross adversity), in battle are sometimes involved in a 'desordre'
(a rout). The typical format is set by the *Mémoires* of Robert III de
La Marck, seigneur de Florange (1491–1536), later marshal of France,
written in captivity in 1525–6 and describing the campaigns in Italy
and in the Low Countries which he knew about directly or through
his father.[74] Two points about him stand out: firstly his self-image
as 'l'Adventureux' (he claimed to have come to the court of Louis
XII to offer his services at the age of eight and to have left for the
Italian wars as soon as possible, much as Jean Bouchet portrays La
Trémoille as eager to go to Louis XI's court to serve while still very

---

[71] Contamine (1983–4), 163; Gaguin (1903), II, 454–56; Anon. (1561). See also
Brantôme (1864–96) VII, 236 on the 'maux, misères et tourmens' that are the lot
of the soldier.
[72] Jouvencel (1889), II, 98; *Rosier des guerres* (1925) unpaginated, ch. VI under
heading 'Des regles de batailles'
[73] See Knecht (1989).
[74] 'Pour monstrer et donner à congnoistre aux jeunes gens du temps advenir en
le lisant y prouffiter sans entrer en paresse': Florange (1913), I, 2. The *Mémoires*
were not published until 1731, from a highly defective text, which broke off in
1521 though Florange was writing it in prison in Sluys in 1525. The rediscovered
section on 1521–5 was published by Goubaix and Lesmoisne between 1913 and
1924 (Florange (1913, 1924) Introduction).

young).[75] Secondly, though he remained consistently loyal to the king of France, his was a family, not uncommon in the period, of independent princes who changed their allegiance according to the extent to which they felt their services appreciated (the Italian prince of Melfi is another example).[76] As is often the case in such writings, Florange portrays battles as a series of personal valorous encounters rather than as a coherent whole.[77] The inevitable consequence is to distort the picture, though Florange, unlike many of his successors in this genre, was not an old man rancorously defending his record against enemies. Nor is Florange simply a classic chivalric figure. He went to Italy first at the head of a band of adventurer hommes d'armes and ended as a specialist commander of German Landsknechts.[78]

A more substantial *Mémoire* in historical terms, perhaps the classic of its kind in the period of the Renaissance, is the history of the Habsburg-Valois Wars created by Martin du Bellay on the basis of his brother Guillaume's preliminary work (completed *c.* 1555–8, published 1569).[79] Like many writers in this genre Martin du Bellay was an infantry commander who emerged from the lesser nobility of long-standing royal service and rose to the summit as a royal Lieutenant-general. He was mainly concerned with the doings of kings and great lords. Montaigne, who thought his work signally lacking in the 'franchise et liberté d'escrire' necessary for a historian and suggested the reader look elsewhere for a history of Francis I, nevertheless thought

---

[75] Florange (1913), I, 3. At the age 21 left for Italy in 1510 (ibid., 53); Bouchet (1527), chs 3–6.

[76] Florange (1913), I, 238–45. Jean Caracciolo, prince of Melfi, fought first for Charles VIII and Louis XII, then went over to Charles V and finally, disappointed by the Emperor's treatment, took service with Francis I, who made him his Lieutenant-general in Piedmont, where he died in 1550. See Brantôme (1864–96), II, 226–39, esp. 228, and VII, 233.

[77] The most vivid example is Florange's description of the battle of Marignano, (Florange (1913), I, 184–99) and his reception of knighthood from the newly knighted Francis I. He commends the fact that his brother-in-law the comte de Braine was there 'pour son plaisir' (ibid., 191). For his skirmishing with enemies at great odds see Florange (1924), II, 72–3.

[78] He first commanded 11,000 Landsknechts raised by his father, in the Italian campaign of 1513: Florange (1913), I, 113.

[79] Du Bellay (1908–19), introduction. For the composition, see Bourrilly (1905), 376–89. Langey had begun to write a humanist history of Francis I but it was very incomplete on his death in 1543 and his brother Martin reworked it in the form it survives, very much as a military history. The second half of Book IX and Book X are solely Martin's.

it profitable for 'la deduction particuliere des batailles et exploictz de guerre où ces gentilshommes se sont trouvez.'[80]

The world described in these memoirs has been called by Arlette Jouanna an 'utopie guerrière' in which the rewards of military valour were thought to reflect the natural hierarchy, courage automatically bringing with it material reward.[81] As François de La Noue put it, contempt for learning on the part of soldiers had gone hand in hand with the view that 'quand quelqu'un se monstroit sans peur, adroit aux armes, & prompt à se ressentir, que cela suffisoit pour luy acquerir richesse & grandeur.'[82] Blaise de Monluc (d.1577) reveals the ambiguity of these ideas since his *Commentaires* (published 1591) are much the most personal and opinionated of the genre.[83] He shared the chivalric notion that bravery and honorable service were naturally rewarded (though not excessively). In a well-known passage on his youth he recalled that:

> je suis venu au monde filz d'ung gentilhomme, que son père avoict vendeu tout le bien qu'il possedoyt, hormis huict cens ou mil livres de rente ou revenu. Et comme j'ay esté le premier de six freres que nous avons esté, il a failleu que je fisse cognoistre le nom de Monluc, de nostre maison, avecques autant de périlz et hasardz de ma vie que soldat ny cappitaine qu'aye jamais esté.[84]

---

[80] Montaigne (1925), II, 143 (Livre II, ch. X). Montaigne rightly pointed out that what purported to be a history of Francis I that did not mention Mme. d'Estampes was, to say the least, lacking. Du Bellay is certainly much more reticent than Monluc about making observations on the events he chronicles and allows his point to emerge through narrative.

[81] Jouanna (1981), I, 326–7.

[82] La Noue (1967), 232–3. It should be noted that the *Jouvencel* did not necessarily think that the virtuous *homme d'armes* would prosper.

[83] Written in the early 1570s; the first edition, by Florimond de Raemond, in 1592 seriously garbled the text in places. The full text was not available until de Ruble's in the 19th century (Monluc 1864–72) and a fully critical text not until Courteault's in the 20th (Monluc 1963). On Monluc, see above all Courteault (1908) and idem (1909). The commentary of Arlette Jouanna noted previously is very suggestive but the reader will see I have given a rather different emphasis here. The edition I have used is that of Alphonse de Ruble, though I am aware of the superior critical quality of the text edited by Paul Courteault. For a useful overview of Monluc's career, see Knecht (1995) and idem (1999) and La Guardia (1999) 45 *et seq.*

[84] Monluc (1864–72), I, 29–30. He repeated the point in describing his return to France in 1525: 'ou je trouvis mon père assés en nécessité', three quarters of the original family estate of 6000 lt. revenue sold, charged with five children of his father's second marriage and with ten of his own (ibid., 105).

As he recounted it, after service as a page to the duke of Lorraine and as archer in his company (then commanded by Bayard), at the age of 17: 'il me print oppinion que les guerres commenseroint plus-tot en Italie qu'en France, et il me print envie d'aller en Italie, sur le bruict qui couroict des beaux faicts d'armes qu'on y faisoict ordinairement.'[85] Such words echo those of other contemporaries in describing the rush to enlist in the Italian wars. Du Bellay recalled that men joined 'pour leur plaisir et pour acquerir honneur.'[86] In 1525, the young nobility flocked to the northern front 'sans commandement . . . en espoir un chacun de rompre sa lance, ainsi qu'est la coutume le plus souvent des jeunes gentilshommes de France de porter peu d'obéisance à ceux qui les commandent.'[87] Even in the rugged 'guerre guerroyable' on the borders of Picardy, there was scope for 'belles entreprises' and 'faicts d'armes' in involving 'une charge brusque et furieuse' by the gendarmerie.[88] At times, this could impede command as when, at Ceresole in 1544, the court paladins egged on Enghien to a foolhardy cavalry charge or, in Piedmont in 1556, another troop of young princes arrived from court on news of a possible battle but refused to accept Paul de Termes as comamnder when the lieutenant-general Aumale fell ill, because they thought he was beneath them.[89]

---

[85] Ibid., 41. Courteault (1908), 88–89, casts doubt on whether Monluc ever really knew Bayard.

[86] Du Bellay (1908–19), I, 227, II, 67, 83 and III, 392 for similar terms. For other examples of young paladins of the court flocking to the front in search of honourable combat, see ibid., I, 139: Montmorency going to Mézières in 1521 'avec beaucoup de jeunesse de la cour, gens de bonne volunté'; IV, 119: Aumale at Thérouanne in 1543 with 'cent gentilshommes volontaires qui l'accompagnèrent pour leur plaisir'; IV, 201–2: 'la jeunesse de la cour congneut bien que malaisement se passeroit la partie sans qu'il y eust du passetemps, parquoy, selon qu'est la coustume de la noblesse de France, chacun se prepara pour s'y trouver', some without permission; IV 308–13: Boulonnais 1545 (one consequence being the killing of the sieur de Dampierre at the skirmish 'at the mill'). See also Monluc (1864–72), II, 150; and Florange (1913), I, 191.

[87] Du Bellay (1908–19), I, 338. In Piedmont in 1551 the young nobility flocked to Brissac's service and thought it a good idea to provoke a potentially disastrous siege at San Damiano: Villars (1850) 51, col. 1.

[88] As with Aumale at Aire in 1543 (Du Bellay (1908–19), IV, 119–20) or the 'belles entreprinses' at Mézières in 1521 (ibid., I, 142). See Florange on 1521 'ce firent beaucoup d'entreprinse et belle' (ibid., I, 53).

[89] Monluc (1864–72), I, 259, 275 and II, 150–51, 154–60. The men concerned were Enghien, Condé, Nemours and Bonnivet. They were sharply put in their place, though Monluc received the blame.

Monluc's *Commentaires* (written in the light of the then newly published du Bellay *Mémoires*) concentrate almost exclusively on the campaigns he fought in, the time he spent at home clearly thought to
be a complete waste. He claimed to have written his work 'pour
monstrer à tout le monde que je n'ay jamais esté en séjour et que
je n'aye esté toujours aux afferes, où ilz se sont présentés, tousjours
prest au premier son de tabourin. Les jours de paix m'estoinct
années.'[90] His narratives of action show him to have lived in a sort
of exalted state during war, all the more so for the 'reputation' gained
at its conclusion.[91] A key moment in his career he saw as his honourable service for the king in the defence of Siena. The city was
starving and had to capitulate in April 1555 but Monluc's men
marched out 'les picques sur le col', banners flying and accompanied by the old and their allies. Monluc was fiercely proud of the
fact that he had saved his men but never agreed to capitulate with
the enemy: 'Or où trouverez-vous livre qui parle que jamais homme
soit sorty d'une place sans cappitulation.'[92] Passing though Rome
after the siege Siena and receiving the plaudits of the crowd 'Cela
ne me faisoit que d'autant plus eslever le coeur pour acquérir l'honneur; et encore que je n'eusse pas presque d'argent pour m'en
retourner, si me sembloit-il que j'estois plus riche seigneur de France.'[93]
Knighted by Enghien at Ceresole in 1544, at the end of his long
career Monluc could see himself as 'le plus content homme de ce
monde.'[94]

Yet Monluc was far from being an uncomplicated exemplum of
the military utopia; he was after all a specialist infantry commander
who rose to be a royal Lieutenant-general. Foot soldiers were central to warfare by the first half of the 16th century[95] and after some

---

[90] Monluc (1864–72), I, 130–31. See also ibid., 62 on the disgrace for a young
man, while others gain a reputation 'et ce pendant il mange la poule du bon homme
auprès du feu'; and 288: 'Je ne haissois rien tant que ma maison.'
[91] 'Il me sembloict, en ces banquets, que mon corps ne pesoict pas une once, et
que je ne touchois pas en terre' (ibid., 424). His gain of reputation would 'enfler
le coeur.' (ibid., 101). At his return from Piedmont, 'mon nom estoict en réputation bien grande et, pour une choze que j'avois faicte, on m'en vouloict fere à
croire quatre.' (ibid., 431)
[92] For this narrative see Monluc (1864–72), II, 103–9.
[93] Ibid., 125.
[94] Monluc (1864–72), I, 19.
[95] Contamine (1972), 344; idem (1989). For an older study, still valuable, see
Spont (1897).

initial hesitation, a high proportion of noblemen acted as captains of all branches of the infantry.[96] The Venetian envoy Correro observed that the *gendarmerie* had become so admixed with commoners that many noblemen preferred to serve in the infantry.[97] Monluc, after beginning his military career in 1521, quickly decided that his métier was as a commander of *gens de pied* and later as *maître de camp*.[98] Monluc, too, stressed the importance of service to the crown. In his prefatory letter to the duc d'Anjou (later Henri III) he insisted that his rewards had been modest, though he maintained that a soldier's prime duty was that of loyalty to his king: 'Que serions-nous si n'estoict le Roy . . . il nous fault doncques confesser que l'honneur et réputation que nous avons acquize, nous la tenons de Dieu premièrement et du Roy.'[99] Not that he was uncritical of princes; in fact he explicitly blamed the enmity of his master and Charles V: 'ennemis jurés et envieux de la grandeur de l'un et de l'autre; ce qui a cousté la vie à deux cens mil personnes, et la ruyne d'un million de familles.'[100] Nor did he always think he had received his due. Avowedly a failure as a courtier, he found time after time that, though he gained in reputation, this was not always rewarded in substance.[101] In his

---

[96] Louis XII in 1509 aimed to raise 11,000 French infantry and have them commanded by experienced nobles (Jacquart (1987), 156–57).

[97] Tommaseo (1838), II, 148–9. La Noue, on the other hand, in 1580 thought that the main problem with the French infantry was the failure of the nobility to take part in it: idem (1967), XIV, 316.

[98] 'J'avois tousjours eu envie de me jecter parmy les gens de pied' (Monluc (1864–72), I, 47). At least half, and probably most, of the captains of *aventuriers* employed in Piedmont during the winter of 1537 were nobles (Lot (1962), 198–231).

[99] Monluc (1864–72), I, 3, 8–9. See also ibid., 62: 'La première, c'est que vous vous faictes louer et estimer aux grands, et de mesmes par leur rapport serés cogneuz du Roy, de quy nous debvons tous espérer.' In his preface he described himself as 'ung homme de peu et de rien, si ce n'estoict les moyens que le Roy m'a baillés.' He was first and foremost the 'loial et fidelle subject et serviteur du Roy' (ibid., 13). In all this he was, of course, seeking to refute the charge, made by Damville among others, that he had enriched himself irregularly.

[100] Monluc (1864–72), I, 43. Monluc notes with regret that his 'bon maistre' had been badly advised not to relieve Siena (II, 91). In his celebrated address to commanders he adds that 'Les princes sont glorieux, et combattent plus pour la gloire et l'honneur que pour acquest.' (II, 108–9); that they have by 'la plus grande ruse et finesse' convinced their subjects that 'leur plus grand honneur estoit de mourir pour leur service' (II, 116); 'Les roys ont autre coeur que nous; ilz ne pardonnent guières à ceux qui leur font perdre quelque chose, car ilz veulent tousjours gaigner.' (II, 122) and that 'Il n'y a ordre; ils sont nés pour commander, et nous pour servir et obéyr . . . il leur semble qu'encores ce nous est trop d'honneur de mourir pour leurs querelles.' (II, 131)

[101] 'Je feuz toute ma vie mal propre pour ce mestier: je suis trop franc et trop

celebrated description of the Ceresole campaign (in which he magni-
fied his role in the royal decision-making) he claimed to have been
out-manoeuvred after the battle for the honour of riding post-haste
to bring the good tidings to Francis I.[102] Nor was Monluc simply a
protagonist of chivalric values in war. As has been noted, he was a
commander of infantry above all and took a dim view of gallant
and fruitless cavalry attacks. At Ceresole Enghien, on whose abilities Monluc had his doubts, attacked with his gendarmerie, in 'deux
furieuses mais trop inconsidérées charges' a mass of Spanish and
German infantry with the predictably disastrous consequence of its
destruction along with the lords who had flocked to Italy from the
court for the battle; only the steadiness of the infantry saved the
day.[103] When noting the alliance of his master with the Turks in
1543 he simply says 'contre son ennemy on peult de tous bois faire
flesches.' Though he professed distaste for it, he acted as a spy at
Perpignan in 1537.[104] His narrative, as is obvious to any reader, is
designed both as self-justification and a practical manual for the soldier and the commander. He offers advice to the young soldier starting out on his career and in need of reputation in order to attract
men to his service, warns about the difficulties of getting on with
superior commanders and strictly advises against gambling, drink,
avarice and women.[105] While advising his young soldier not to hesitate to risk all in order to gain a reputation, he insists on keeping
a cool head on the battlefield, even though the day may be going
wrong; nothing is worse than panic.[106] He censures over-confidence
before the outcome of the battle is clear,[107] notes the disastrous out-

---

libre, aussi y trouvay-je fort peu d'acquest' (ibid., I, 131). He was never favoured
by Montmorency (ibid.) and managed to make an enemy of Mme. d'Etampes at
the end of Francis I's reign (ibid., 305).

[102] Monluc (1864–72), I, 284–85. For a critique of Monluc's whole narrative, see
Courteault (1908), 152–72, esp. 170 n. 3.

[103] Monluc (1864–72), I, 274–75, Monluc suggests that Enghien was suicidal in
contemplating the loss of the battle. Cf. the account by Florange (1913) I, 93, of
Nemours' senseless charge with only 35 men against 2000 Spaniards at the end of
the battle of Ravenna; and Bouchet (1839) 774, who describes Nemours 'suyvant
sa martiale fureur et se confiant en la riante face de fortune' but 'contre l'oppinion des anciens capitaines et la doctrine de Vegèce.'

[104] Monluc (1864–72), I, 143, 134–35 on spying 'c'est ung mestier trop dan-
gereux et que j'ay toujours hay.'

[105] Ibid., 62, 328, 30–40 (the censure of vices is purely for the practical reason
that they detract from fitness).

[106] Ibid., 62–63, 303–4.

[107] Ibid., 467.

come of attempting to retreat in face of the enemy and advises doing so, if necessary, only under cover of night.[108] When telling the vivid story of the siege of Siena already mentioned, he unashamedly defends his expulsion of the 'bouches inutiles' to almost certain death with the words 'ce sont les lois de la guerre: il faut estre cruel bien souvent, pour venir à bout de son ennemy.'[109] Most notably, he offers comprehensive advice to commanders of fortresses under siege.[110] In short, there is a degree of continuity with the world of Le Jouvencel if not the earlier work of Charny, though perhaps with a clearer emphasis on the practical. For all his lapses of memory and special pleading, Monluc gives a unique insight into the science of war and the art of leading men in battle.[111]

A near-contemporary of Monluc's, François de Rabutin, gives a rather different picture of war though with some similarities. Rabutin spent his adult life in the heavy cavalry of the Nevers company. Unlike Monluc, he was thus a simple soldier who viewed war from the point of view of an ordinary homme d'armes.[112] All the more extraordinary was it, then, that he should have published an extensive account of the campaigns in the the northern and eastern theatres in which he played a part in 1555 and then a continuation in 1559.[113] Like Monluc, he was a serious practitioner of war and

---

[108] Ibid., 470–71. Earlier, during his service with Lautrec in the 1520s he says that 'Il n'y a pas moings d'honneur de fere une belle retraicte' (ibid., 61).

[109] Monluc (1864–72), II, 74. His argument is entirely pragmatic: it would have been better to do it before for that might have saved the town.

[110] Ibid., 110–23. Monluc's main preoccupation was the dishonour of losing a fortress and the necessary bravery for keeping it. He advised his commanders to read the memoirists such as du Bellay and Guicciardini and then above all 'il fault avoir l'esprit tendu à espier ce que vostre ennemy peut faire, et jouer deux rooles, disant à part à vous: si j'estois l'assaillant que ferois-je?' (ibid., 120). Show yourself to your men, he adds, 'le gentilhomme veut estre caressé, mesmement le Gascon.' (ibid., 121)

[111] For an appreciation, see Courteault (1908), 612.

[112] The standard Société de l'Histoire de France text of his Mémoires is Rabutin (1932–44). It is defective in that passages are deleted and the biography is limited. Little is known about him other than that he was probably a bastard of the house of Rabutin and a domestic of François de Clèves duc de Nevers (I, i–ii). 'Petit soldat comme je suis' (II, 28); 'pauvre gentilhomme et simple soldat, je ne puis parler hautement, ne plus ne moins qu'une petite campanelle qui ne peut rendre si haut son qu'une bien grosse cloche' (II, 1–2, proeme to 1559 edn). Compare Brantôme's remark on the hautiness of great princes: 'je n'en metz pas plus gros pot au peu, et n'en lève pas ma bannière plus haute; car les princes sont si glorieux qu'ilz desdaignent tout le monde' (Brantôme (1864–96), X, 102).

[113] As the editor makes clear, Rabutin regarded his literary skills as limited and was eager for a scholar to rework them. Unfortunately, books VII–XI were

thought soldiers should be trained and fit. He blamed the exhaustion of Henri II's army on its march through Alsace in 1552 on the fact that too many 'par le temps de paix et repos s'estoient tant relaschés et abandonnés à leurs aises et voluptés, que ... par peu de peine et travail estoient abatus.'[114] Unlike Monluc he seems to have relished returning home at the end of campaigns[115] and seems to have welcomed the making of peace.[116] Though he shared the customary contempt for peasants who sought to fight back with unorthodox tactics,[117] he took a clearly sympathetic view of the sufferings of the victims of war.[118]

The vicissitudes of civil war which overwhelmed France after 1562 could not fail to have their effect on military thought. Pierre de Bourdeille, abbé commendataire de Brantôme (b. *c.* 1540) served as a young man in the later stages of the Italian wars and in Scotland under Guise patronage. Balked by ill-fortune in his search for new patrons and unsuccessful in attracting serious royal favour, he spent much of the 1560s in series of picaresque adventures against the infidel, fighting at Peñon de Velez in August 1564 and enlisting in a private-enterprise expedition to help the knights of Malta in the great siege.[119] He could not avoid the wars of religion; many Huguenots were his friends but he remained a Catholic and was commissioned by Monluc to raise an infantry company in 1567–68. As commander at Péronne in 1568 he was tempted by his friend Téligny to surrender:

> Alors je fis responce que j'aymerois mieux mourir de cent mortz que de faire un si lasche et vilain party à mon roy que de luy trahir une ville qu'il m'avoit donné en garde et garnison ... Voylà comment il

polished by Bernard du Poey, with the result that they are overladen with 'literary' conceits (Rabutin (1932), I, v–vii). Rabutin is very reliable on what he saw himself but otherwise borrowed extensively from contemporary writings such as Paradin.

[114] Rabutin (1932), I, 61.
[115] He notes his company were given leave 'pour nous aller reposer et rafraischir en nos maisons' in January 1553 (ibid., 188).
[116] See his remarks on the truce of Vaucelles: 'sembloit estre une oeuvre de Dieu ... desquelles beaucoup de personnes espéroient advenir une paix de longue durée et perpetuelle' (Rabutin (1932–44), II, 82–83). Compare with Monluc's hostility to the peace of 1559.
[117] E.g., Rabutin (1932–44) I, 21, 26, 185.
[118] Such remarks are scattered through every book: see ibid., 26, 67–8, 70, 83, 89, 120, 253, 264, 282, 293–4, 297.
[119] See Lalanne (1896), 14–18, 38–45, 92–98.

se fait acquitter des charges qu'on a du roy, quelques mescontentements qu'on aye de luy.[120]

Charles IX appointed Brantôme a *gentilhomme de la chambre* as a reward for this service but after the siege of La Rochelle (1573) he saw little further service in the wars.[121] In 1583, he broke with Henri III over the latter's refusal to pass his brother's office of sénéchal of Périgord, on resignation, to a nephew. Brantôme was enraged above all at what he thought was the king's ingratitude and swore that, if he had a thousand lives, 'je n'en employerais jamais une pour roys de France, et que jamais, au grand jamais, je ne leur fairois service.'[122] He symbolically threw the gold key to the king's chamber into a river. Yet, tempted by service to Spain he refused 'j'en fusse esté maudit à perpétuité.'[123] This conditionality of service has been described as 'une forme très décadente de la chevalerie' and his refusal to enter foreign service 'la naissance du sentiment "national"'.[124] Such distinctions are highly artificial. Brantôme after all would have approved Monluc's earlier remark on kings that they had convinced their subjects by deceit that 'leur plus grand honneur estoit de mourir pour leur service'. To place loyalty to country above 'tous autres debvoirs' he considered an 'abus.'[125]

There is good reason to think that, when Brantôme came to draw up his lives of the great captains some time between 1590 and 1614, he looked back to the Italian wars as a golden age; his father after all began his service with Bayard.[126] Echoing the sentiments of *Le Jouvencel* he thought that 'il n'y a rien si brave et si superbe à voir

---

[120] Brantôme (1864–96), IV, 128.

[121] Brantôme claimed to be one the few who accompanied the body of his 'maistre' Charles IX to Saint-Denis (ibid., VII, 326).

[122] Ibid., V, 205–9, esp. 208; elsewhere: 'l'ingratitude est inexcusable: car faillir à l'obligation que l'on a, ce vice est trop déshonneste' (VII, 249). It is likely that he means here the obligation of the king or commander.

[123] Ibid., V, 211

[124] Grimaldi (1971), 178–79.

[125] Monluc (1864–72), II, 116; Brantôme (1864–96), VII, 232, who goes on to paint a devastating picture of the soldier, required to fight for his country but treated with contempt by his superiors. What loyalty should he have?

[126] Brantôme (1864–96), II, 387. Brantôme recalled Francis I's early years when he was well regarded by his nobility 'car on le voyoit jeune, prest à entreprendre guerre, et libéral pour récompenser les siens; ce que demande fort la noblesse que d'aller à la guerre, et puis en tirer un bon visage et une bon récompense de son roy' (ibid., III, 136).

qu'un gentil soldat, bien en poinct, bien armé, bien leste.'[127] He was
a proud and touchy Gascon sometimes, like Monluc, given to personal violence and he was certainly acerbic about the failings of some
of his contemporaries. Nevertheless, the lineaments of chivalric ideals
continue in the midst of the complex picture of his age. He rejected
categorically the idea that in a civil war it was not necessary to keep
a word given to a rebel or heretic since 'les grandz et braves capitaines... ne viollent jamais les parolles ny promesses.'[128] What is
more, he continued to think that 'Les chevalliers de chevallerie doivent
précéder tous autres; et le nom de chevallier a esté le premier entre
tous les noms d'honneurs... ceste religion de chevallerie a esté dicte
pareillement religion d'honneur.' Brantôme preferred to view all
chevaliers on an equal footing but he praised commoners who through
their own efforts could show themselves worthy of arms.[129] Thus the
military utopia remains, embedded in a realistic world of ambition:

> il n'y a rien qui nourrisse mieux le soldat, de quelque party que ce
> soit, qu'un brave capitaine guerrier et ambitieux; car il n'ayme non
> plus la paix ny le repos que le soldat... car, pour en parler saine-
> ment, le soldat n'advise pas quel vent tire sur le droit et sur le tort
> de la guerre mais où il y a à gaigner; et qui luy ouvre les moyens
> pour avoir du pain, celluy-là est son père.[130]

Like Monluc, Brantôme thought that a certain heedless bravery was
necessary in a young man but after this first flush of youth 'il est
bon qu'il se face sage, s'il veut estre estimé et se rendre capable
d'avoir des charges de son roy.'[131] Writing at the end of the sixteenth century, Brantôme is seriously schizophrenic in his attitude
to chivalry; he shared the view that all forms of war (not just the
courteous) were invigorating and complimented commoners who
showed valour but he still thought the profession of arms the prerogative of the nobleman.[132]

---

[127] Brantôme (1864–96), V, 367.
[128] Ibid., II, 178.
[129] Ibid., VI, 476–77. Fourquevaux supposed that only the worst sort would volunteer for the legions, while Brantôme thought these 'jeunes gens... des villages,
des boutiques, des escolles... des forges, des escuries' had great potential (ibid., V,
367–8). They seem to have been a mixture of men who had already acquired some
experience in the infantry or who were forced to look for employment for various
reasons (Potter (1993), 174–75).
[130] Brantôme (1864–96), VII, 66–67.
[131] Ibid., IV, p. 6.
[132] See the interesting discussion of this in Jouanna (1981), I, 349–51.

The genre of the military biography became a vehicle for contemporary discourse in the hands of Brantôme. It had, though, already been transmuted into a polemical form, now often based on documents retained by relatives, loyal followers or secretaries. Two examples may serve to illustrate this. The biography of marshal Charles de Cossé-Brissac was written by his secretary François de Boyvin-Villars, himself later a chevalier and bailli de Gex. Villars did not publish the book until 1610 but it in fact constitutes a defence of his master's record as governor of Piedmont in the 1550s. Like other such cases it purports to be a sternly factual account of military campaigns founded on authentic documents.[133] In fact, it is a diatribe on the ingratitude of princes for the services of honourable men.[134] Brissac is portrayed as an an intelligent and enlightened commander who abstained from looting enemy country, despite provocation, in the hope, eventually gratified, of reaching an agreement to allow the peasantry on both sides to live their lives normally.[135] Other military biographers in the same generation confirm the picture. For Jean de Saulx-Tavannes, writing the biography of his father the marshal de Tavannes, it was clear that valour alone ('toutefois commune avec les soldats') was no longer enough to serve the king in arms and thus maintain the integrity of the noble order. Training in proper conduct was essential.[136] Tavannes has harsh things to say about the conservatism of the constable de Montmorency and his generation.[137] Beauvais-Nangis, likewise writing the biography of his father, Antoine de Brichanteau, in the 1630s, also demonstrates the tension between honour and the need for reward.[138]

---

[133] Villars (1850), first published 1610. Villars's chronology is often faulty because of his confusion between the paschal and calendar year in the documents he uses.

[134] Addressing France, Villars asserts that the ill-treatment of Brissac 'n'aura jamais puissance d'eschauffer les coeurs de ceux qui voendront après luy à te servir.' For all Brissac's successes 'on ne le vit jamais enorgueillir d'aucun felice succés, ne se donner en proye à l'adversité. Son esprit fut toujours dressé à si dextrement et conscientieusement manier les affaires': Villars (1850), 370–71.

[135] Ibid., 65–6.

[136] Saulx-Tavannes (1838), 60.

[137] 'M. le Connestable . . . monstre avoir eu plus de jugement dans les conseils qu'à la vueue des ennemis' (ibid., 297). La Noue (1967), 332, noted that some had said that since Guise and Montmorency 'n'y ont rien innové, c'est bien signe qu'elle doit estre laissée en usage.'

[138] Beauvais (1862). Beauvais-Nangis wrote the *Mémoires* between 1636 and 1641, almost certainly based on his father's recollections. The tone at first scarcely differs from that of Monluc 70 years before: the need to seek 'occasions d'acquérir de l'honneur' (ibid., 30–31). The reader is admonished to 'marcher toujours en ordre'

It would of course be foolish to suppose that the ideology of chivalry ever formed a template for the actual fighting of war or that biographies served as handbooks for action. In addition to the military memoirs, the period saw the issue of contemporary printed battle reports and many practical handbooks. That there was a market for battle reports is testimony enough to the interest in the subject, though like any journalism they were subject to extreme bias.[139] The handbooks for commanders and soldiers which were written in the period carried on the tradition of Honoré Bovet's *Arbre des batailles* (*c.* 1387) and Christine de Pisan's *Livre de Fayttes d'Armes et de Chevalerye* (*c.* 1408) which were, to a greater or lesser extent, shaped by the reading of the classical works on war, most notably Vegetius.[140] The *Rosier des guerres*, probably dictated by Louis XI to Pierre Choisnet, drew heavily on Vegetius but gave some useful common sense information to the commander on preparing for battle. The work was a largely private one, though, meant as a political testament for the dauphin and, when it appeared in print in 1523, seems to have had little impact.[141] A more typical example was the *Traité sur l'art de la guerre*, a work dictated at the very end of his life by Béraut Stuart, seigneur d'Aubigny (*c.* 1452/3–1508), veteran of the Italian wars who had also fought in Grenada, adversary in battle of the *Gran Capitan* Gonsalvo de Cordoba.[142] Stuart was influenced by Vegetius, as were most of his predecessors, and drew very heavily on Robert de Balsac's

---

(even if it is thought the enemy is distant, p. 19) and 'vous tenir toujours sur vos gardes, et ne croire jamays estre en seureté' (p. 21), to remain impassive under fire (p. 25). Antoine had started his career by a signal act of bravery in the front line at Jarnac: 'il fut remarqué entre les jeunes gents de son aage . . . cette action luy donna grande estime parmy le monde' (pp. 4–5). This, with his father's reputation, had given him entry into the court. The work then goes on as an extended discourse on his father's virtues and the ingratitude of princes.

[139] For a bibliography of such works, see Bib. Nat., *Catalogue de l'Histoire de France* (Paris, 1855–) vol. I under Lb^{28}, Lb^{29}, Lb^{30} and LB^{31}. Printed and manuscript bulletins of troop movements and reports in the form of royal letters appeared in 1494–5. See Pilorgerie (1866), printed example pp. 274–9. There are concentrations of publications in 1494–5, 1543–4 (Ceresole), 1552–3 (siege of Metz and battle of Renty) and 1558–9 (sieges of Calais and Thionville). For an example see Anon. (n.d.) (Bib. Nat. LB^{30} 102).

[140] For an introduction to this theme, see Contamine (1976A). See also the very useful conspectus of French theoretical military writings in the period in Dickinson (1954) xcii–cix.

[141] For a rather defective modern edition see *Rosier des guerres* (1925) ch. VI *passim*. The best discussion of authorship is Stegmann (1985).

[142] For a discussion of the origins and content of this work see de Comminges (1976), "Introduction".

Le Nef des Princes et des Batailles de Noblesse . . . (Lyon, 1502, reprinted Paris, 1525)[143] but the importance of his work is that it is a practical handbook written by a skilled soldier and diplomat which places the emphasis on the professional approach to the command and administration of armies: decisions for war, the role of experienced commanders, the disposition of reserves, reconnoitering and map-making, spies. Much of this is a personal interpretation of the lessons of Vegetius but the emphasis on artillery and its protection is, of course, very much of the time and reflects the importance of this new arm of war in Stuart's own experiences in Italy during the 1490s. In many ways comparable is the *Instruction de toutes manières de guerroyer*[144] of Philippe de Clèves, sieur de Ravestein (1456–1528), a Netherlands prince who entered French service in 1488 and served both Charles VIII and Louis XII in the Italian wars and the Levant. Unlike Stuart, Ravestein, though highly cultured and possessed of a fine library, largely ignored the classical sources and concentrated, except for vague echoes of *Le Jouvencel* and Bovet, on his own experiences. While he appealed to ancient concepts of the just war and crusade and specified the appropriate religious rites, Ravestein was remarkable in fact for ignoring classical precepts on the siting of a battle-line (high ground, sun to the back etc.) taking the view that the mass of infantry (seen as the dominant element of any battle) and the use of artillery was more important. In fact, the strongly practical element is confirmed by the attention paid to the the functions of the 'maréchal des logis' and his use of reconnoitering and to the assembly of statistical information on paper and finally by the annexes concerning the 'art du feu', costs of artillery and supply (left out in the printed version).[145]

The treatises of the Renaissance period continued to combine this practical streak with the principles of chivalry. There were a number of rather slight and routine examples of the genre, such as that by a captain, Michel d'Amboise, in his 1543 *Le guidon des gens de guerre* avowedly drew on the classical sources while adding 'une partie de

---

[143] Balsac was first published in a collection of writings on the education of a prince attributed to Jean Bouchet.

[144] Clèves (1558); original MS in BN, MS Fr. 1244, probably written *c.* 1516 in retirement.

[145] See in particular Contamine (1980). The work is closely related to a MS by Jehan Bytharne, "Livre de guerre, tant par mer que par terre", BN, MS Fr. 3890.

moi-même'.[146] Most famously, of course, Fourquevaux's *Instructions sur le Faict de la Guerre* of 1548 provided a systematic printed hand-book for the military commander.[147] Fourquevaux was profoundly dismayed by what he saw as the corruption and ineffectivess of French armies, brought about, he thought, by godlessness and then idleness and poor training. His solutions involved a combination of models drawn from classical antiquity and his own experience and emphasised the rational organization of an esentially native infantry (like many others he shared a contempt for mercenaries). Above all, he formulated a code of military discipline which predated that issued by Coligny in 1551 as *colonel-général de l'infanterie*.[148]

Finally, the most thoughtful and considered work on war to be written in France during this period, the *Discours politiques et militaires* of the Protestant chief François de La Noue has some remarkable insights to offer. La Noue wrote the *Discours* (first published at Basel in 1587) in detention in the early 1580s and has often been pillaged for his narrative of the first phase of the civil wars. Less familiar perhaps are his ideas on chivalric warfare. La Noue was a proud Breton nobleman who remained convinced that the nobles were the prime actors in war 'ayans l'honneur devant les yeux, souvent mieux faire que les autres qui sont de moindre qualité.'[149] For him, there-fore, it was natural to see the officer class of any army as domi-nated by nobles, but serious thought needed to be given to training and tactics. All honour was due to the Romans, he said, but things had changed.[150] He insisted that cavalry tactics had to change since the old style by which the *gendarmerie* charged *en haie* stemmed from the age of Froissart when it was 'toute composee de noblesse, cha-cun vouloit combattre de front & ne demourer des derniers rangs.' What was needed was to perfect concentrated squadrons and replace the lance with the pistol.[151] His main concern, though, was that war was becoming endemic through the propensity of soldiers to seek employment when fighting ceased. His startling insight is that a state

---

[146] Amboise (1543). Dickinson (1954), p.c., rather harshly described it as 'worth-less'.
[147] For the substance of Fourquevaux's arguments, see the useful summary in Dickinson (1954), lxxxxii–xci.
[148] Fontanon (1611), III, 152–57.
[149] La Noue (1967), XV, 338.
[150] Ibid., 333.
[151] Ibid., 333–4 and XVIII, 357; cf. Monluc (1864–72), III, 484.

has arisen in which nobles 's'y voüent tellement qu'ils font d'une telle profession (qui doit estre comme extraordinaire) une vocation perpetuelle.'[152] War therefore is not a full-time profession for a noble-man, though it may be for commoners who have little else to live on. La Noue was not against the maintenance of a small peace-time army but thought that most soldiers, on demobilisation, should find some other form of employment.[153] In the course of his discussion of the perennial question of arms and letters as qualities for the courtier, La Noue almost exactly repeats Castiglione's story about the courtier who could talk of nothing but war being told he should be shut up in cupboard until it was time to use him.[154] He had already attacked the reading of chivalric romances like the *Amadis*, which he provocatively placed on the same level of Machiavelli: 'quand un gentil-homme auroit toute sa vie leu les livres d'Amadis, il ne seroit bon soldat ne bon gendarme.'[155] The true nobleman of lineage should retire to his estates and cultivate the arts of peace when there is no war. The notion of a permanently militarised nobil-ity was, then, for him not only anathema but a malignant source of civil conflict. La Noue therefore divorces noble virtues and the virtues of the warrior while retaining the value of chivalric honour.

The mentality of chivalry, understood in different ways, was obvi-ously still very much alive in the sixteenth century. It should per-haps be seen primarily as a guide for personal behaviour on the part of those soldiers—primarily nobles—for whom it embodied the principle of honour. For Monluc 'noz vies et noz biens sont à noz roys, l'ame est à Dieu et l'honneur à nous; car sur mon honneur mon roy ne peut rien.'[156] The three forms of didactic military writ-ings discussed here—chivalric, memoir and manual—offered uneven pickings for those anxious to learn a clearly-defined body of knowl-edge yet all of them shared the view that expertise was essential.

---

[152] La Noue (1967), IX, 210.

[153] Ibid., 210–13 *passim* and 235.

[154] Ibid., 235: 'je vous conseille de vous enfermer dans un coffre.' Castiglione (1585), 46 (Castiglione had been available in J. Colin's translation since 1540).

[155] La Noue (1967), VI, 160–76, esp. 175. He was not attacking 'les exercita-tions aux armes' and thought them 'outre le plaisir, honnestes & necessaires.' La Noue's contempt for the *Amadis* was shared by Montaigne (see (1925), II, 130–31, livre II, ch. X). However, it should be pointed out that, with its siege engines, artillery, mines etc., the descriptions of war in the *Amadis* are very similar to those of the memoirists of the 16th century: see Bourciez (1886) 81.

[156] Monluc (1864–72), II, 117.

The chivalric soldier was also a 'professional' in that he needed to act in accordance with the harsh demands of war.[157] The swathes of burnt villages and slaughtered peasants in Artois and northern France between the 1520s and the 1550s, the heaps of corpses on the battlefields of the Italian Wars all testify to the grim realities of war in the period. At Ravenna, one of the hardest fought battles of the age, the Loyal Serviteur gave French losses as 3000 foot and 80 *hommes d'armes*, while the Spanish lost 10,000 infantry and 20 captains.[158] Bouchet wrote of Marignano: 'La meslée fut cruelle et longue . . . et estoyent les Françoys et les Souysses si acharnés à se occire l'ung l'autre, qu'il n'y eust chose qui les peust séparer que l'obscurité de nuyt'; estimates of Swiss casualties are around 15,000 out of 35,000.[159] Finally, at Ceresole, another contemporary observer noted that for a quarter league around the town 'nos chevaulx étoient jusqu'au genoil dedans le sang, et n'eussent sçeu marcher que dessus gens morts'. Estimates of Imperial casualties were 12–15,000 'de toutes nations'.[160]

A tension therefore remained at the heart of the 'professionalisation' of the French army in this period. The royal army was a vast and complex mechanism requiring rational administration but encumbered by layers of tradition, not least to be found in the central importance attributed to the heavily armoured cavalry in military thinking until the third quarter of the sixteenth century. 'Chivalry' still offered an ideology of engagement which could be made to inculcate a spirit of preparedness. Ultimately, though the gentleman amateur in war had a long life before him, the pressures towards a centrally-governed army with clear command structures and chains of command were bound to dilute the concept of chivalry as the yardstick of an independent warrior class and replace it by a more inchoate sense of honour, while the demands of expertise were to be more effectively met from the seventeenth century by military training, academies and scientific manuals.

---

[157] When the death of a soldier such as Teligny is regretted, it is as 'gentil chevalier et homme fort experimenté.' Du Bellay (1908), I, 211.

[158] "Serviteur" (1878), 330.

[159] Bouchet (1839), 786. Barrillon (1879), 125; Du Bellay (1908–19), I, 74.

[160] See Courteault (1908), 168; Du Bellay (1908–19), 227–28.

Bibliography

Primary Sources and Contemporary Writings

Anon. (n.d.) *L'ordonnance de la bataille faicte à syrizolles en Piedmont, avec la defaicte des Espagnols* (n.p., n.d., Bib. Nat. Lb³⁰ 102).

Anon. (1561) *La Harangue de par la noblesse de toute la France* (Paris: 1561).

———. (1576) *Advertissement envoyé à la noblesse de France tant du party du Roy que des rebelles et coniurez* (written 1568, 1576 ed.).

Amboise, Michel d' (1543) *Le guidon des gens de guerre* (Paris: 1543); reprinted Paris, 1878 in the publications of *Journal de la Librairie militaire*.

Beauvais (1862) Beauvais-Nangis, François de Brichanteau, Marquis de, *Mémoires du marquis de Beauvais-Nangis et journal du procès du marquis de la Boulaye*, ed. M. M. Monmerqué and A. H. Taillandier (Paris: 1862).

Barrillon J. (1879) *Journal de Jean Barrillon, secrétaire du chancelier du Prat 1515–21*, ed. P. de Vaissière, vol. I. (Paris: 1879).

Bib. Nat., *Catalogue de l'Histoire de France* (Paris: 1855–), vol. I.

Bouchet, Jean (1839) *Le Panegyric du chevallier sans reproche* [Louis de La Trémoille] (Poitiers: 1527), eds. J. Buchon, Choix de Chroniques (Paris: 1839).

Bovet, Honoré (1883) *L'arbre des batailles* ed. E. Nys (Paris: 1883).

——— (1949) above work, trans. G. W. Coopland, as *The Tree of Battles of Honoré Bonet* (Liverpool: 1949).

Brantôme (1864–96), Pierre de Bourdeille *Oeuvres complètes*, ed. L. Lalanne, 12 vols (Paris: 1864–96).

Castiglione, B. (1585) *Le parfait courtisan*, trans. G. Chapuis (first pub. 1580; Paris: 1585).

Champier, Symphorien (1992) *Les gestes ensemble la vie du preulx chevalier Bayard* (Lyon, 1525), ed. by D. Crouzet (Paris: 1992).

Champollion-Figeac, A. (1847) *Captivité du roi François Ier* (Paris: 1847).

Charny, G. de (1996) *The Book of Chivalry of Geoffroi de Charny: Text, Context and Translation* ed. R. W. Kaeuper and E. Kennedy (Philadelphia: 1996).

Chartier, Alain (1988) "Le Breviaire des nobles", in *Poèmes*, ed. J. Laidlaw (Paris: 1988).

Clèves, Philippe de (1558) *Instruction de toutes manieres de guerroyer tant par terre que par mer et des choses y servantes* (Paris: 1558).

Comminges, E. de (1976) *Traité sur l'art de la guerre de Béraut Stuart seigneur d'Aubigny*, ed. E. de Comminges (The Hague: 1976).

Contamine P., ed. (1983–4) "Un traité politique inédit de la fin du XVᵉ siècle", *Annuaire-bulletin de la Société de l'Histoire de France* (1983–4).

Dickinson, G. (1954) *Fourquevaux's Instructions sur le Faict de la Guerre*, ed. G. Dickinson (London: 1954).

Du Bellay, Guillaume and Martin (1908–19) *Mémoires*, ed. V.-L. Bourrilly and F. Vindry, 4 vols (Paris: 1908–19).

Florange (1913, 1924), Robert de La Marck, sieur de, *Mémoires du maréchal de Florange, dit le jeune adventureux*, eds. R. Goubaix and P.-A. Lemoisne, 2 vols (Paris: 1913–24).

Fontanon, H. (1611) *Les edicts et ordonnances des rois de France* (ed. 1611).

Gaguin, R. (1903) *Epistole et Orationes*, ed. L. Thuasne, 2 vols (Paris: 1903).

Jouvencel (1887, 1889) *Le Jouvencel par Jean de Bueil suivi du commentaire de Guillaume Tringant*, eds. C. Favre and L. Lecestre, 2 vols (Paris: 1887–89).

La Marche (1883–88), Olivier de *Mémoires*, ed. H. Beaune and J. Arbaumont, 4 vols (Paris: 1883–88).

La Noue, François de (1967) *Discours politiques et militaires* ed. F. E. Sutcliffe (Geneva: 1967).

La Sale, A. de (1935) "La Salade", in *Oeuvres complètes*, ed. F. Desonay, Bib. de la Faculté de Philosophie et Lettres de Liège, no. 68 (Paris/Liège: 1935).

Lannoy, Ghillebert de (1878) "Instruction d'un jeune prince", in his *Oeuvres*, ed. C. Potvin (Louvain: 1878).

Llull, Ramon (1972) *Le livre intitulé lordre de chevalerie ouquel est contenue la maniere comment on doit faire les chevaliers et l'honneur qui a eulx appartient et de la dignité diceulx*, pub. by S. Champier and included in his *Recueil ou chroniques des hystoires des royaulmes daustrasie* (Lyon: 1510), ed. V. Minervini (Bari: 1972).

Molinet, Jean (1935–37), *Chroniques de Jean Molinet*, ed. G. Doutrepont and O. Jodogne, 3 vols (Brussels, 1935–7).

Monluc, Blaise de (1864–72) *Commentaires et lettres*, eds. A. de Ruble, 5 vols (Paris: 1864–72).

—— (1963) *Commentaires 1521–1576*, ed. Paul Courteault (repr. Bib. de la Pléiade, Paris: 1963).

Montaigne, Michel de (1925) *Essais*, ed. J.-V. Leclerc, 4 vols (Paris: 1925).

Pannier & Meyer (1877) *Le débat entre les hérauts d'armes de France et d'Angleterre* ed. L. Pannier, P. Meyer (Paris: 1877).

Rabutin, François de (1932–44) *Mémoires*, ed. Taurines, 2 vols (Paris: 1932–44).

Rosier de guerres (1925) *Le Rosier des Guerres. Enseignements de Louis XI Roy de France pour le Dauphin son fils*, ed. M. Diamantberger (Paris: 1925).

Saulx-Tavannes, Jean de (1838) *Mémoires de Gaspard de Saulx . . .*, ed. J.-F. Michaud and J.-J.-F. Poujoulat, *Nouvelle collection des mémoires sur l'histoire de France* (Paris: 1836–54), 1st ser., VIII (1838).

"Serviteur" (1878) *La Très-joyeuse, plaisante et récréative histoire composée par le loyal serviteur, des faicts, gestes, triomphes et prouesses du bon chevalier sans paour et sans reproche gentil seigneur Bayard* (1527), ed. M. J. Roman (Paris: 1878).

Seyssel, Claude de (1961) *La Monarchie de France*, ed. J. Poujol (Paris: 1961).

Tommaseo, N. (1838) *Relations des ambassadeurs vénitiens sur les affaires de France au XVIe siècle*, 2 vols (Paris: 1838).

Villars (1850) *Mémoires de François de Boyvin, chevalier baron du Villars*, eds. J.-F. Michaud and J.-J.-F. Poujoulat, *Nouvelle collection des mémoires sur l'histoire de France* (Paris, 1836–54), 1st ser., X (1850).

Secondary Works

Allmand, C., ed. (1976) *War, Literature and Politics in the Later Middle Ages: Essays in Honour of G. W. Coopland* (Liverpool: 1976).

Allmand, C. (1999) "Entre honneur et bien commun: le témoignage du *Jouvencel* au XVe siècle", *RH* 301 (1999), 463–81.

Anglo, S. (1990) *Chivalry in the Renaissance*, ed. S. Anglo (Woodbridge, Suffolk: 1990).

Baret, E. (1853) *De l'Amadis de Gaule et de son influence sur les moeurs et sur la littérature au XVIe et XVIIe siècle* (Paris: 1853).

Barrière, P.F. (Paris, 1961) *La vie intellectuelle en France du seizième siècle à l'époque contemporaine*.

Blanchard, J. (1989) "Ecrire la guerre au XVe siècle", in *Le moyen français*, 24–5 (1989).

Bourciez, E. (1886) *Les moeurs polies et la littérature de cour sous Henri II* (Paris: 1886).

Bourrilly, V.-L. (1905) *Guillaume du Bellay seigneur de Langey (1491–1543)* (Paris: 1905).

Britnell, J. (1986) *Jean Bouchet* (Edinburgh: 1986).

Broussillon, B. de (1895–1903) *La maison de Laval* (Paris: 1895–1903).

Caron, M. T. (1994) *Noblesse et pouvoir royal en France XIIIe–XVIe siècle* (Paris: 1994).

Cazelles, R. (1960) "La réglementation royale de la guerre privée de Saint Louis à Charles V", *Revue historique du droit français*, 4th ser. 38 (1960), 530–48.

Contamine, P. (1972) *Guerre, état et société à la fin du moyen âge: études sur les armées des rois de France, 1337–1494* (Paris and The Hague: 1972).

——. (1976A) "The war literature of the later middle ages: the treatises of Robert de Balsac and Béraut Stuart, Lord of Aubigny", in Allmand, ed. (1976), cit. above, 102–21.

——. (1976B) "Points de vue sur la chevalerie à la fin du Moyen Age", *Francia* 4 (1976) 255–85.

——. (1980) "L'art de la guerre selon Philippe de Clèves, seigneur de Ravestein (1456–1528): innovation ou tradition?" *Bijdragen en Mededelingen betreffende de Geschiedenis der Nederlanden* 95 (1980), 363–76.

——. (1984) "Les industries de guerre dans la France de la Renaissance: l'exemple de l'artillerie", *RH* 271 (1984), 249–80.

——. (1986) "Les tournois en France à la fin du moyen âge", in *Das ritterliche Turnier im Mittelalter*, ed. J. Fleckenstein (Göttingen: 1986).

——. (1989) "Naissance de l'infanterie française (milieu XVe–milieu XVIe siècle)", in *Avènement d'Henri IV. Quatrième centenaire de la bataille de Coutras* (Pau: 1989), 63–88.

——. (1992) *Histoire militaire de la France*, 2 vols, ed. A. Corvisier Paris: 1992), I, 209–301.

Cooper, R. (1990) " 'Nostre histoire renouvelée': the reception of the romances of chivalry in Renaissance France", in Anglo (1990), cit. above, 195–238.

Corvisier, A. (1976) *Armées et sociétés en Europe de 1494–1789* (Paris: 1976).

Courteault, P. (1908) *Blaise de Monluc, historien* (Paris: 1908).

——. (1909) *Un cadet de Gascogne au XVIe siècle: Blaise de Monluc* (Paris: 1909).

Crouzet, D. (1993) "Un chevalier entre 'les machoires de la mort': note à propos de Bayard et de la guere au début du XVIe siècle", in *La vie, la mort, la foi, le temps: Mélanges offerts à Pierre Chaunu*, eds. J.-P. Bardet and M. Foisil (Paris: 1993), 285–94.

Grimaldi, A. (1971) *Brantôme et le sens de l'histoire* (Paris: 1971).

Hamon, A. (1901) *Un grand rhétoriqueur poitevin, Jean Bouchet (1476–1557?)* (Paris: 1901).

Hauser, H. (1963) *La modernité du seizième siècle* (Paris: 1963).

Huizinga, J. (1960) "The political and military significance of chivalric ideas in the late Middle Ages", in *Men and Ideas* eds. J. S. Holmes and H. van Marle (London, 1960) [repr. of earlier essay, published before *Waning of the Middle Ages*].

——. (1924) *The Waning of the Middle Ages*, trans. F. J. Hopman (London: 1924).

Jacquart, J. (1987) *Bayard* (Paris: 1987).

Jones, M. (1988) *The Creation of Brittany: A Late Medieval State* (London: 1988).

Jouanna, A. (1981) *L'idée de race en France au XVIe siècle et au début du XVIIe* 2 vols (Montpellier: 1981).

Kaeuper, R. W. (1988) *War, Justice and Public Order: England and France in the Later Middle Ages* (Oxford: 1988).

Keen, M. (1965) *The Laws of War in the Middle Ages* (London: 1965).

——. (1977) "Huizinga, Kilgour and the decline of chivalry", *Medievalia et Humanistica* 8 (1977), 1–20.

——. (1984) *Chivalry* (London: 1984).

Kilgour, R. L. (1937) *The Decline of Chivalry as Shown in the French Literature of the Late Middle Ages* (Cambridge, Mass.: 1937).

Knecht, R. J. (1989) "Military autobiographies in sixteenth-century France", in *War, Literature and the Arts in Sixteenth-Century Europe*, eds. J. R. Mulryne and M. Shewring (London: 1989) 3–21.

——. (1995) "The sword and the pen: Blaise de Monluc and his *Commentaires*", *Renaisance Studies* 9 (1995), 104–18.

——. (1999) "Monluc et l'art militaire", in *Monluc, d'Aubigné: Deux épées, deux plumes (Colloque d'Agen, 1996)* (Agen: 1999).

La Guardia, D. (1999) "On the ethos of the noble warrior: Blaise de Monluc's *Commentaires*", *Medievalia et Humanistica* 26 (1999).

Lalanne, L. (1896) *Brantôme, sa vie et ses écrits* (Paris: 1896).

Lot, F. (1962) *Recherches sur les effectifs des armées françaises des Guerres d'Italie aux Guerres de Religion, 1494–1562* (Paris: 1962).

Love, R. S. (1991) " 'All the King's Horsemen': the equestrian army of Henri IV, 1585–98", *Sixteenth Century Journal* 22 (1991), 511–33.

Morgan, D. (1990) "From a Death to a View: Louis Robessart, Johan Huizinga and the Political Significance of Chivalry' in Anglo (1990), cit. above.

Pilorgerie J. de la (1866) *Campagne et bulletins de la grande armée d'Italie commandée par Charles VIII 1494–1495* (Nantes & Paris: 1866).

Potter, D. (1993) *War and Government in the French Provinces: Picardy 1470–1560* (Cambridge: 1993).

——. (1997) *"Rigueur de justice*: crime, murder and the law in in Picardy, fifteenth to sixteenth centuries", *French History* 11 (1997), 265–309.

Spont, A. (1897) "La milice des francs-archers, 1448–1550", *Revue des questions historiques* (1897).

Stanesco, M. (1988) *Jeux d'errance du chevalier médiéval* (Leiden: 1988).

Stegman, A. (1985) *"Le Rosier des guerres*: testament politique de Louis XI", in *La France de la fin du XVᵉ siècle—Renouveau et apogée*, eds. B. Chevalier and P. Contamine (Paris: 1985) 313–23.

Thomas, A. (1889) "Les états généraux sous Charles VII", *RH* 40 (1889), 72–5.

Vale, M. (1981) *War and Chivalry: Warfare and Aristocratic Culture in England, France and Burgundy at the End of the Middle Ages* (London: 1981).

Vayssière, A. (1874) *Le pas des armes de Sandricourt* (Paris: 1874).

Wood, J. B. (1996) *The King's Army: Warfare, Soldiers and Society During the French Wars of Religion, 1562–1576* (Cambridge: 1996).

Wright, N. A. R. (1976) "The *Tree of Battles* of Honoré Bouvet and the laws of war", in Allmand (1976), cit. above, 12–31.

Zeller, G. (1943) *Le siège de Metz par Charles-Quint* (Nancy: 1943).

CHAPTER SEVEN

CHIVALRY, MILITARY PROFESSIONALISM AND THE EARLY TUDOR ARMY IN RENAISSANCE EUROPE: A REASSESSMENT

Luke MacMahon

When reading studies of English military history in the early sixteenth century one often receives the impression that Henry VIII and the nobility which prosecuted his wars alike saw war as little more than a game. Henry's central motivation, at least where his invasions of France were concerned, was to match and hopefully outdo his ancestors, Edward III and Henry V.[1] The opportunity to participate personally in the campaigns provided an additional incentive, permitting Henry to take part in the grandest of tournaments, bringing closer the dream of unseating his great rival, Francis I on a genuine battlefield.[2] Modern day critics argue that Henry's sense of chivalry and competitive nature not only led him into ill-advised wars with England's perennial enemy but drove him to set unrealistic objectives, stopping little short of a complete dismemberment of France. What made the king's ambitions all the more spurious, they claim, was the means at his disposal with which to achieve them. To quote Helen Miller, 'Fundamentally the "army royal" was an old fashioned force, raised by quasi-feudal methods, fighting with out of date weapons for an anachronistic cause.'[3] Millar in his study of Tudor mercenaries and auxiliaries is no less damning: 'as unskilled as they were inexperienced in the arts of war ... the conclusion that English armies were inferior to their counterparts on the continent can hardly be escaped.'[4] Unlike his European counterparts Henry

---

[1] As Scarisbrick observed more than thirty years ago, 'It is damaging historical surgery that cuts [Henry] off from his ancestry—Edward I, Edward III and Henry V—for they surely were his models.' Scarisbrick (1997) 23.

[2] For a recent re-assessment of just how important Henry's rivalry with Francis was, see Richardson (1995), *passim*.

[3] Miller (1986), 142.

[4] Millar (1980), 4–5, 16.

lacked a professional army and was thus compelled to hire mercenaries and borrow auxiliaries from his allies before launching any
campaign. Constrained by hidebound notions of honour and chivalry
that were equally influential amongst the gentry and nobility chosen
to command his armies, the king, so the argument goes, repeatedly
dispatched expeditions to the continent consisting of amateur soldiers, who with their lack of training and archaic weaponry were woe-
fully mismatched against the new professional armies of the renaissance.

The aim of this paper is to demonstrate that much of the criticism levelled at Henry and the armies he dispatched abroad is at
the very least exaggerated. I will show that, contrary to the impression given by some historians, many aspects of the early Tudor army
were far from sub-standard. If the bulk of the king's army was never
'professional' in the senses of the word identified in the Introduction
to this volume, there were nevertheless certainly key elements of it
that warranted favourable comparison with their European equiva-
lents. However, the standard of the soldiers who made up Henry's
armies and the way in which they were armed makes up only half
the picture. Also in question is the use to which they were put; the
validity of the king's military objectives and strategy, and the tactics
of his generals. Were Henry and his officers prisoners to outmoded
notions of warfare and did their adherence to ideas of chivalry make
them incapable of carrying out modern campaigns? I believe not.
While there is clearly evidence to demonstrate that Henry and his
captains were highly conscious of their knightly honour, and where
possible eager to act in accordance with the traditions of chivalry as
it applied to war, they by no means felt compelled to do so. Both
in terms of strategy and tactics I hope to show that it was the
demands of politics and the dictates of common sense that most
often prevailed in the conduct of Henry's wars.

Before continuing a point on terminology would seem to be in
order. Central to this study will be the contention that important
elements of the armies dispatched by Henry to France were, by contemporary standards, of a reasonable quality; this is not to say they
were 'professional' soldiers. I intend to apply the term 'professional'
to two groups of men. The first and least ambiguous of these were
the large numbers of mercenaries employed by Henry during his
wars with France. Such men earned their livelihood through war,
they were organised into cohesive bands with an internal command
structure, the existence of which was not predetermined by the advent
or length of an individual conflict. The second group consisted of

those smaller bodies of men organised, equipped and employed by
the crown both in times of peace and war, specifically the king's
bodyguard and those men that served in the king's coastal and border garrisons. Central to the professional status of both groups is the
permanent nature of their service and their organisation as military
units. Much of the chapter will be concerned with an assessment of
individuals who might best be described as 'experienced' or 'knowl-
edgeable' and whom in certain cases can justifiably be called military veterans or experts. To call such men 'professional soldiers' would
be inaccurate since in addition to their military activities they served
Henry as courtiers, ambassadors, local administrators and political
advisers. Undoubtedly military service was for many of Henry's nobility the task of choice and one that large numbers were admirably
suited to perform, yet the demands and limitations of early modern
government ensured that it was denied to them as a profession.[5]

                                I

At first glance there seems much in the English armies of the early
sixteenth century with which one might find fault. Most obviously
the lion's share of men recruited to serve in Henry's campaigns had
little or no military experience. As J.J. Goring observed, 'the great
majority of the men who served in the armies of the early Tudor
period were not professional soldiers, in the normal way a soldier
was merely a man who had been obliged (sometimes against his will)
to serve in an army.'[6] In most cases these men were drawn from
the retinues and tenantry of the nobility and clergy and mustered
through the quasi-feudal practice of indenture. As members of the
nobility and gentry the captains and petty captains chosen to officer
the king's armies had at least received military training, but this
should be carefully distinguished from military experience in which
many were pointedly lacking. Furthermore, English soldiers continued to be armed with the weapons with which their fourteenth and
fifteenth century ancestors had fought, the bill and longbow. Key
components of the renaissance army such as heavy cavalry, pikemen

---

[5] For a useful assessment of what military professionalism in the early modern
period actually meant see, Hale (1987), 127–52
[6] Goring (1955), 227.

and arquebusiers seem to be conspicuous by their absence. Even the manner in which Henry's lightly armed and lightly armoured soldiers were organised, in huge formations or battles, on occasion numbering more than ten thousand, were unwieldy and out of step with current military thinking.

In fact such an analysis while not incorrect is nevertheless far from complete. If many of the officers in Henry's army lacked military experience then many more were veterans of numerous campaigns. Henry's most active general, Thomas Howard, third Duke of Norfolk, enjoyed a military career that lasted almost fifty years. Before his final command as one of the two generals entrusted with the siege of Montreuil in 1544, he had led campaigns in Ireland, Scotland and France which varied from punitive raids to full scale invasions. In Henry's wars with France he had directed sieges and led amphibious operations. Acting as a military governor he had defended the Anglo-Scottish border and sought to bring order to Ireland. He fought with his father at Flodden and ten years later directed the forces that halted the admittedly somewhat timorous Duke of Albany in his plans to lead a Franco-Scottish army into northern England.[7]

John Wallop, given command of the English expeditionary force dispatched by Henry to aid the Low Countries in 1543 had devoted much of his life to soldiering. He fought against France in 1512, 1513, 1522 and 1523. In 1515 he took part in a Portuguese expedition launched against North Africa, before returning to England to join Thomas Howard on campaign in Ireland. Additionally, he served as high marshal of Calais from 1524 to 1530, deputy of Calais castle from 1529 to 1532 and captain of Guisnes from 1541. Like all Tudor servants Wallop was called upon to perform a wide range of tasks, but undoubtedly he was first and foremost a soldier.

If few of Henry's generals could match Norfolk and Wallop for experience some were not far behind. John Russell, Norfolk's fellow general at the siege of Montreuil, fought in France in 1513 before being appointed a captain in the Tournai garrison where he remained until 1518. He fought at the brief but bloody battle of Morlaix in 1522 and spent much of the next three years in the Imperial camps of Charles V and his ally the Duke of Bourbon.[8] Of course, it can

---

[7] Head (1995), 21, 29, 32–42, 54–59, 62–66.
[8] Willen (1981), 6–9.

hardly be claimed that all commanders were selected by the king on the criteria of military expertise or experience. Henry's great favourite, Charles Brandon, attended his first campaign in 1513 and as high marshal was second only to the king. Yet for all the responsibility the novice general was given—he was entrusted with the organisation and discipline of the army and given personal command of 3,000 men—he took little part in the direction of overall strategy.[9] Furthermore, he was surrounded by experienced soldiers on whom both he and Henry could confidently rely. Among them was George Talbot, 4th Earl of Shrewsbury, lieutenant of the forward battle in which Henry himself rode. Thought by Wolsey to be as 'active a captain as can be chosen within your realme, mete convenable and necessary to be appointed for the ledinge of an armye', Talbot had fought at the battle of Stoke in 1487 and accompanied Henry VII on his abortive invasion of France in 1492.[10] Other such veterans included, Charles Somerset, lieutenant of the rear battle, Rhys ap Thomas, captain of the English light cavalry, Edward Poynings and William Lord Sandys.[11] No doubt Brandon had much to learn but then he hardly lacked for teachers. Similarly, when he was given personal command of the 1523 expedition to France, in addition to being able to rely on the experience of Floris d'Egremont, count van Buren, the Burgundian commander, he was also supported by men such as Wallop and Sandys.[12] By the time he took command of the siege of Boulogne in July 1544 Suffolk was an experienced general in his own right.

The great majority of officers in the Tudor army simply held the rank of captain or petty captain and their experience and ability varied as widely as the responsibilities with which they were entrusted. In nearly all cases drawn from the gentry it was simply a case of translating the civil authority they enjoyed as landlords and magistrates to the military forum. Such thinking was especially applicable when the individual in question could field a sizeable personal retinue since the tenets of military discipline could be reinforced by the more long standing obligations owed by a tenant, retainer or client to his landlord or patron. Inevitably this basis for selection led to

---

[9] Gunn (1988), 17–18.
[10] Bernard (1985), 5.
[11] Cruickshank (1969), 29–33.
[12] Gunn (1986), 603.

the appointment of men lacking military experience who were in certain cases quite unfit for command. The Welsh chronicler Ellis Gruffudd was particularly vocal about such men and in particular one Master Hussey, 'a fat-bellied lump of a man, big in body and authority, lacking in sense and a coward at heart.'[13] Dispatched by the Duke of Norfolk to escort a supply train to Montreuil, Gruffudd described how against all advice Hussey led his men into a French ambush that resulted in heavy casualties and the loss of much food and drink.

Yet if it is undeniable that many of the captains in Henry's armies may have been unsuitable and certainly lacked military experience, then it is also true that considerable numbers served in several campaigns and were often highly competent. In the same passage in which he criticises Hussey, Gruffudd concedes that 'there were many amongst the host both gentlemen and common soldiers', who possessed the experience and knowledge to organise a large escort and make efficient use of the artillery that accompanied it.[14] Before being given command of the 1543 Landrecy expedition John Wallop had served as an officer in six earlier campaigns. Edward Poynings, in command of 600 men in the 1513 invasion of France had fought with Henry VII at Bosworth, acted as military governor in Ireland and led two expeditions to the Netherlands.[15] Francis Bryan, who fought his last battle as a captain of cavalry at Pinkie in September 1547, fought against France in 1513, 1522, 1523 and 1544. William Fitzwilliam, not only served in the campaigns of 1513, 1522 and 1523, he was also deputy respectively of Calais and Guisnes castles and Henry's vice admiral and later lord admiral.[16] To these names one might add Anthony Browne, Nicholas Carew, Richard Wingfield and Thomas Cheyne. All members of the privy chamber, Henry relied on these men not only to command his garrisons and officer his armies, but also to carry out a wide range of sensitive missions both at home and abroad. Yet as table one shows the list of men who performed if not frequent then at least repeated military service was by no means limited to the small circle of the king's favourites.

---

[13] Gruffudd (1949), 62.
[14] Ibid., 65.
[15] Palmer (1994), 15–26; Nichols (1846), 8–9.
[16] Vodden (1972), I, *passim*.

Table I: Officers who served in Multiple Campaigns

Name	1512	1513	1522	1523	1543	1544	Scotland	Garrison Duty
Baynton, Edward					*	*	1523	Spear at Guisnes
Berkeley, Maurice	*	*	*					deputy Calais Castle[17]
Bowes, Robert				*				
Bray, Edward		*	*			*		lieutenant of Calais
Browne, Anthony		*				*		
Bryan, Francis		*	*	*		*	1523	
Carew, George					*	*		captain of Rysbank
Carew, Nicholas		*	*				1523	
Cheyne, Thomas		*		*		*		
Cornwall, Richard	*		*	*	*			
Cornwall, Thomas	*	*						
Curson, Robert		*	*	*				captain of Hammes
Ellerker, Ralph						*	1513, 1522, 1533	marshal of Calais marshal of Boulogne
Fitzwilliam, William		*	*	*				deputy Calais Castle deputy of Guisnes
Fortescue, Adrian		*	*	*				
Gage, John		*				*	1542	captain of Guisnes, comptroller of Calais
Grey, Leonard	*		*	*				
Guildford, Edward	*		*	*				marshal of Calais
Jerningham, Richard		*	*					marshal of Tournai deputy of Tournai
Jerningham, Robert			*	*				captain of Newen Bridge
Kingston, William	*			*			1513	
Palmer, Thomas			*		*			high porter Calais, lieutenant Newen Bridge
Poynings, Edward	*	*						deputy of Calais governor of Tournai
Poynings, Thomas					*	*		
Raynsforth, John		*	*		*	*		
Ryngeley, Edward		*					1523	marshal of Calais comptroller of Calais
Russell, John		*	*			*		spear at Calais captain at Tournai
Sandys, William	*	*	*	*				treasurer of Calais deputy of Guisnes

---

[17] For a comprehensive list of officers serving the various garrisons located in the Calais Pale see, Grummitt (1997) 219–228.

(table cont.)

Name	1512	1513	1522	1523	1543	1544	Scotland	Garrison Duty
Skeffington, William		*	*	*				
Ughtred, Anthony	*	*						marshal of Tournai marshal of Berwick
Wallop John	*	*	*	*	*			deputy Calais castle, high marshal Calais, deputy Guisnes
Wingfield, Richard		*	*	*				deputy Calais castle, high marshal Calais

Although table one is by no means an exhaustive list of those men who served as officers in multiple campaigns it does highlight the fact that Henry could and did rely upon a corps of experienced men to furnish his armies with high and middle ranking officers. Although it would be inaccurate to call such men 'professional' soldiers the continuity of their military service ensured their suitability to lead the king's armies.

In addition to the court nobility repeatedly chosen to serve abroad, Henry was able to make use of the long serving officers in command of the English garrisons on the French and Scottish frontiers. Robert, Lord Curson, captain of Hammes castle in the reign of Henry VII served with the young king in 1513 and with both Surrey and Suffolk in the 1520s.[18] Richard Jerningham, who took part in both the 1513 and 1522 French campaigns, was successively marshal, treasurer and deputy of Tournai between 1514 and 1519.[19] Maurice Berkeley a captain in the 1512, 1513 and 1522 expeditions served as deputy of Calais castle between 1520 and 1523. Edward Guildford, deputy of Calais for much of the 1520s also fought in 1522 and 1523. Thomas Palmer served as both high porter of Calais and lieutenant of Newen Bridge, before joining the Landrecy campaign in 1543 and attending the siege of Boulogne the following year. Other Calais stalwarts who fought as officers in the king's wars included Robert Jerningham, Thomas Poynings and Edward Baynton. Nor need there be any doubt about the military experience of these men. Although it is the major expeditions and occasional battles of

---

[18] G. E. C. (1910–40) III, 579.
[19] Cruickshank (1973), pp. 44, 46, 54, 96–97 and 100.

Henry's reign that monopolise the attention of later historians, contemporary accounts repeatedly describe the frequent tussles between
the garrisons of the Calais Pale and their rivals in the Boulonnais.
Thus in 1514, Richard Whetehill and Nicholas Vaux sallied forth
from Calais to rescue a hard pressed English raiding party only to
narrowly escape capture themselves when they were pursued by a
force of 1500 French cavalry.[20] Eight years later Whetehill, now captain of Hammes, was less fortunate when seeking to drive off a
French raiding party he was lured into an ambush in which a number of his men were killed and he was first injured and later taken
captive.[21] In the early 1520s, Edward Guildford and William Lord
Sandys led several raids into the Boulonnais including one in June
1522 when at the head of nearly 1500 men they ravaged the province
and burned the town of Marguison.[22] Among the many forays led
by the somewhat reckless Thomas Palmer, for whom border brawl-
ing seems to have been a *raison d'être*, was a small excursion in
February 1523, when at the head of sixty men he fought a pitched
battle with eighty Frenchmen killing three and capturing 25.[23] None
of these encounters produced results of any strategic value, what they
demonstrate is that the men who commanded Henry's border garrisons were capable soldiers, used to leading relatively large bodies
of men with considerable experience of fighting and killing.

To a lesser degree Henry also used the expertise of those captains usually reserved for defence of the Scottish border in his wars
against France. Anthony Ughtred, a captain in the army sent by Henry
VII to Ireland in 1496 and as a Yorkshire landowner primarily
involved in the fighting on the Anglo-Scottish border, nevertheless
served in France during 1513. Robert Bowes, another member of
the Yorkshire gentry, and a veteran of Henry's northern difficulties,
having only just secured his release from Scottish captivity, joined
John Wallop in France and served with distinction in the Landrecy
campaign of 1543. Although Ralph Ellerker spent the lion's share
of his military career defending the Anglo-Scottish border, joining
his father and brothers at Flodden and serving with the forces mustered against the threatened Scottish invasions in 1522 and 1533,

---

[20] *L&P Henry 8th*, I, ii, no. 2049, Richard Wingfield to Wolsey, 25 Feb. 1514.
[21] Hall (1809) 651.
[22] Ibid., 641.
[23] Ibid., 651.

he nevertheless died in France, the victim of a French ambush in
April 1546. That many of the men, particularly those chosen as petty
captains, lacked military experience and expertise can hardly be dis-
puted. Yet the long held consensus on this point has done much to
obscure the fact that within the armies of early Tudor England
there was also present useful numbers of men with considerable military experience and skill, capable of providing a functional command structure.

II

So much for the leadership of Henry's armies; what of the rank and
file? Again it is undeniable that a significant proportion of the men
who served in Henry's armies were unskilled novices, or as Gruffudd
somewhat ungenerously described them; 'men with base hearts who
would rather go home to their mothers and fathers, some to plough
and thresh, others to follow the cart and hedge dig and live nig-
gardly'[24]—farmers with mail-shirts and longbows. However, this rather
unprepossessing group of warriors only ever constituted a part of the
king's invasion forces that always consisted of a variety of military
types, reflecting a wide spectrum of competence and experience. At
the heart of every expeditionary force dispatched from England could
be found a corps of native professional soldiers. From his father
Henry inherited the Yeomen of the Guard.[25] In permanent service
to the crown each yeoman was paid 12*d* a day whether at court or
on campaign and provided with livery, arms and probably their
armour.[26] It seems likely that they underwent regular military training, particularly with the longbow, and on occasion themselves provided training for others.[27] Their numbers fluctuated throughout

---

[24] Gruffudd (1944), p. 39.
[25] This paragraph is largely based on information found in Hewerdine (1998),
pp. 90–100.
[26] In 1496 Charles Somerset, then captain of the Guard, paid £27 10s for 110
sheaves of arrows and a further £18 6s 8d for 110 bows. In 1505 John Heron,
treasurer of the chamber, paid one John Vandelf £200 for making 200 rich jackets for the king's guard: ibid., 36.
[27] Thus there is a record in the earl of Rutland's accounts for the payment to
"Holland of the Guard' for the training of one of the earl's servants with the longbow: ibid., 85.

Henry's reign. At his accession, they numbered roughly 200 rising to 600 in 1513 but by the close of the reign this figure had contracted to 125. As the king's guard this force attended Henry on both his 1513 and 1544 campaigns, but their military activities extended far beyond the provision of a royal escort. Of the 600 men who accompanied Henry to France in 1513, 400 remained behind as part of the 5,000 strong garrison left in Tournai. More than thirty years later 185 men were chosen to join the garrison the king's second conquest, Boulogne. In 1520 almost half of the 500 men taken by the Earl of Surrey to Ireland were drawn from the king's guard. Fifty yeomen participated in the battle of Morlaix in July 1522 and a further 200 took part in Surrey's raid on Picardy later in the year. They also served with Henry's navy. During 1512 and 1513 numbers of the Guard took part in the amphibious operations launched against the Breton coast, such as the force of fifty that sailed with the *Sovereign* in August 1512 and the compliment of 191 who joined the crew of the *Great Nicholas* between May and July 1513. Members of the Guard also officered some of Henry's most prestigious ships among them Thomas Jermyn, master of both the *Harry Grace a Dieu* and the *Mary Rose* in the 1520s and Thomas Ranger, captain of the *Marie Fortune* in 1546. In addition to the Yeomen Henry established two further forces. In 1510 the King's Spears were brought into existence. Made up from noble families this short-lived force—it was disbanded in 1515—not only attended the king but provided officers for both the army and navy.[28] Finally, in 1539 Henry created a 50 strong force, the Gentlemen Pensioners. As with the King's Spears this force was drawn from the nobility. It served as a single unit in the 1544 campaign before being dispersed to provide officers for key areas such as the garrisons at Portsmouth and the Isle of Wight.[29]

Another source of professional and semi-professional soldiers upon which Henry could draw was England's border garrisons. Foremost of these were the garrisons stationed in the Calais Pale. For much of the reign, of neither a uniform standard nor number, as we have already seen the soldiers serving in and around Calais were nevertheless no strangers to active service. Furthermore, reforms following in the wake of Sir William Fitzwilliam's commission held in

---

[28] Goring (1955), 232–34.
[29] Ibid., 238–41.

August 1535 did much to improve standards in Calais. Soldiers were forbidden to take secondary jobs to augment their pay, officers were no longer permitted to accept payment for admitting men to the retinue and the size of the garrison was regulated at roughly 800.[30] Under the direct control of the crown and denied the distractions of a civilian lifestyle, as one historian has observed, 'The Calais act had gone a long way to providing a permanent professional army for the defence of the Pale.'[31] Of course since the *raison d'être* of the Calais garrisons was to defend the Pale against attacks by the French its aggressive potential was necessarily limited; that is not to say that it did not play a prominent part in all three of Henry's wars with France. The vanguard of Henry's middleward during the 1513 campaign was composed of spears and mounted archers drawn from the Calais garrison, while the king's artillery train consisted in part of ordnance drawn from the Pale's forts and was under the command of Sir Robert Carew, lieutenant of Calais Castle.[32] Of the 14,000 men that invaded France under the Duke of Suffolk in 1523 nearly 1,700 were drawn from Calais.[33] Although by no means all 1,700 were in permanent government employ the large number of 'adventurers' drawn to the Pale by the prospect of war had considerable potential. Thus Hall describes, 'the M men proper and hardy', under John Wallop's command, who, 'having litle wages or none, lived alonely on their aventure, wherfore of some they were called adventurers, and of some they were called Kreekars'.[34] During the campaign Wallop's men ravaged the countryside and supplied the army with livestock and other victuals. Not under pay, these men had to live on what they could scavenge; hardly the basis for a disciplined force but one can hardly question their dedication. Although numbers taken from Calais for Wallop's 1543 expedition are unclear, the general's personal retinue came to 100 footmen and 20 horsemen, and at least one document suggests that as many as 2,000 of the 5,000 strong army may have been drawn from the forces currently picketed in the Pale.[35]

---

[30] Grummitt (1997), 155.
[31] Ibid., 156.
[32] Cruickshank (1969), 60–67.
[33] Gunn (1986), 599.
[34] Hall (1809), 669.
[35] *L&P Henry 8th*, XVIII, i, no. 832: List for the army of Flanders, 1543.

Outside Calais the number of men in permanent service was small, perhaps forty at Berwick and at the height of the invasion scare in 1540 another 170 in the coastal forts between Gravesend and Portsmouth.[36] Yet from the English marches of the Anglo-Scottish border Henry did have access to considerable numbers of men, which, if not in permanent service to the crown were by no means lacking in military experience. Drawn from the tenancies of great magnates such as the Percy earls of Northumberland and the Dacres of Greystoke, and very probably from the considerable numbers of border outlaws who made their livings through the rustling of live-stock, these lightly armoured horsemen known as demi-lances or spears, were of enormous use to the king in his wars against France. They could be deployed as scouts or foragers, used to disrupt enemy supply lines and harry the wings and rear of an opposing army, while in the event that the opposing army should be routed, they were ideally suited to press the attack and inflict maximum damage. At the Battle of the Spurs in August 1513, Henry's light horsemen under the leadership of Rhys ap Thomas, skirmished throughout the day with their French counterparts and succeeded in stopping them from bringing any support to the main body of the French army.[37] In October 1543, upon seeing John Wallop deploy his light cavalry on a reconnaissance mission around Landrecy, the emperor him-self—surely a man qualified to judge—remarked, 'Par ma foy, voyla de gens qui vont de grand courraige, et ils semblent tresbien les Alarbes d'Affrice.'[38] The final invasion of France launched in June 1544 provided few opportunities for open combat in which to test Henry's light cavalry. Yet amongst the thousands of English light cavalry present in the Boulonnais were 1000 demi-lances and 500 mounted arquebusiers sent by the earl of Hertford from Scotland. These men had been involved in both pitched battles and brutal attritional raids, they were highly skilled and combat hardened; undoubtedly a match for their French rivals.[39]

A further aspect of the English armies dispatched to France that deserves serious consideration is their use of artillery. In an age when

---

[36] Goring (1955), 241–245.
[37] Hall (1809), pp. 550–551; Cruickshank (1969), 116.
[38] *SP Henry 8th*, IX, p. 524 (*L&P Henry 8th*, XVIII ii, no. 291), Wallop to Henry, 2 Oct. 1543.
[39] *L&P Henry 8th*, XIX I, nos. 508, 531, 634.

war was coming increasingly to revolve around long drawn out sieges
the armies Henry sent to France all contained large, modern forces
of artillery. When Henry came to the throne he inherited reasonable quantities of modern ordnance stockpiled by his father at Calais
and in the Tower,[40] stores that the new king rapidly built upon and
continued to do so throughout his reign. In addition to the famous
twelve Apostles, the English artillery train in the 1513 campaign
included a further six bombards, heavy artillery designed to breach
walls, 120 organs, light anti-personnel guns, and almost 180 other
pieces, the calibres of which filled the ballistic spectrum between
these two extremes.[41] With this impressive train Henry reduced two
cities, Therouanne and Tournai. Ten years later his lieutenant, the
Duke of Suffolk, put his master's ordnance to even more formidable effect. Although we lack numbers for the 1523 artillery train
there is plentiful evidence of its impact. In under a month the towns
and cities of Braye-sur-Somme, Ancre, Corbie and Montdidier were
reduced by English guns as well as numbers of strategic forts such
as Belle Castle. The joint Anglo-Burgundian force came within fifty
miles of Paris, and was halted not by stoic French defence but by
the weather and supply line difficulties.[42] Once again in 1544 Henry
brought an artillery train to France quite the equal of any that his
European rivals could field. Containing over a hundred heavy calibre pieces alone, in two months these bombards, cannons, demi-
cannons and culverins, launched nearly 24,000 balls against the walls
of Boulogne and Montreuil.[43] That neither city fell to assault reflected
the changing balance in favour of modern defensive fortifications
with which every would-be besieger now had to contend.[44] That
Boulogne did finally capitulate on September 14 no doubt owed
much to the terrible pounding it had received from the English
artillery. The forces Henry sent to France between 1513 and 1544
always possessed plentiful stores of artillery, the most devastating
and sophisticated weapon available to renaissance armies.[45] In this

---

[40] According to David Grummitt, 'by the end of the fifteenth century Henry
VII's use of artillery appears to conform to that characteristic of the early modern
state': Grummitt (2000), 269; see also Fissel (2001), ch. 1.
[41] Cruickshank (1969), 65–67.
[42] Gunn (1986), 609–618.
[43] L&P Henry 8th, XIX i, no. 272(13); MacMahon (1992), 60–62.
[44] Parker (1996), 6–24; Duffy (1979), 43–57; Hale (1965).
[45] Although this work is primarily concerned with the activities of Tudor armies

respect early Tudor armies were no more primitive than their European counterparts.

III

Finally, we come to the mercenary and auxiliary forces that the king included in all his campaigns against France. In 1513, 7,000 mercenaries augmented Henry's 24,000 strong army. In 1523 the emperor supplied his English ally with 6,000 auxiliary troops evenly divided between foot and horse. Finally, in 1544 a combination of mercenaries and auxiliaries added more than 4,500 cavalry and 5,300 infantry to Henry's last invasion of France, bringing his total strength to over 42,000 men.[46] Thus in 1513 nearly 30% of the army sent to France was composed of mercenaries, in 1523, 43% of Suffolk's army consisted of Burgundian auxiliaries while in 1544 the number of mercenaries and auxiliaries in Henry's army represented 23% of the overall force. Regardless of the percentages, however, the indisputable fact is that Henry never undertook a continental invasion without the support of large numbers of highly trained soldiers. The great majority of mercenaries employed were German pikemen, while the auxiliaries supplied by the emperor consisted of heavy Burgundian cavalry and arquebusiers. In short Henry bought and borrowed the types of soldiers which social and technological developments in England had ensured remained in short supply. This has led to some strange and woolly thinking on the part of certain historians.[47] It

---

in France, it is also worth pointing out that artillery came to play an increasingly important role in England's wars with Scotland. According to Gervase Phillips, 'from the 1523 campaign onwards trains of what can legitimately be described as field artillery accompanied many large scale raiding forces into Scotland': Phillips (1999), 142. The most conspicuous use of such weapons came shortly after Henry's death in September 1547 when Protector Somerset deployed a coastal bombardment against a Scottish army at Pinkie to withering effect: ibid., 183–86; Oman (1937), 358–368. Eleven years later similar tactics were employed by a squadron of English warships at the Battle of Gravelines to the great benefit of their Habsburg allies: ibid., 279–80.

[46] Millar (1980), 45–46.

[47] Thus, Gilbert John Millar argues that English armies sent to the continent were amateur in nature because they required the support of mercenaries and auxiliaries, Millar (1980), 15–25. Yet regardless of what they were when they left English shores, the addition of many thousands of mercenaries before they entered France must by default have turned Henry's armies into semi-professional forces.

would be difficult to dispute that combinations of pikes, handguns
and heavy cavalry increasingly dominated continental battles in the
sixteenth century. Nor can it be argued that the armies that Henry
was able to muster should he need to fight battles in England would
primarily consist of bills, longbows and light cavalry. Yet the only
real threat to the English throughout the majority of the reign was
the Scottish—a threat that the battles of Flodden, Solway Moss and
Pinkie would suggest they were equipped to deal with. On those
occasions when Henry chose to go to war in Europe he made sure
he had large numbers of the requisite types of soldiers to fight a
modern war. It is surely irrelevant that when he sent armies to
France the pikemen were drawn from Germany, the heavy cavalry
from the Low Countries, and the arquebusiers perhaps from Italy.
The point is, when the English fought in France they possessed all
the elements one would expect to see in a renaissance army.

Of course, much of the criticism relating to the nature of early
Tudor armies is based on comparisons with their Habsburg and
Valois rivals. Any re-evaluation must therefore include at least a brief
assessment of these 'modern' renaissance forces. It would certainly
be hard to deny that Charles V had at his permanent disposal large
numbers of well-trained soldiers. However, I would like to raise a
note of caution concerning the calibre of the Burgundian heavy cavalry lent to Henry by the emperor. As Millar himself concedes there
is little evidence to demonstrate that these forces served the king
well or otherwise.[48] Drawn from the Burgundian nobility one may
reasonably assume that like their English counterparts they devoted
much of their lives to the development of equestrian and martial
skills. Yet this is not to say that their ability on the field of battle
was any less variable than that of Henry's own nobility. Henry
received the assistance of Burgundian auxiliaries not because they
were necessarily superior to his own heavy cavalry, but because they
were far more numerous. Whether the cavalry loaned by Charles V
to his ally was good, bad or indifferent is unclear, and more research
is certainly needed in the area.

Nevertheless, from his grandfather, Ferdinand of Aragon, Charles
had inherited excellent light cavalry known as *genitors*, as well as considerable numbers of arquebusiers and pikemen many of whom gained

---

[48] Millar (1980), 172.

military experience in the battles of the Great Captain, Gonsalvo de Cordoba.[49] During the 1530s, Charles instituted a reorganisation of his Spanish forces, combining pikes and arquebuses in 3,000 strong units known as *tercios*. First employed in Italy then later, most infamously in the Netherlands, these large highly trained units came to enjoy a reputation that equalled both the German landsknechts and Swiss pike phalanxes.[50]

In theory, Francis too possessed a large well-trained standing army. At its heart were the *gens d'armes* of the *compagnies d'ordonnance*, the French heavy cavalry. By the reign of Francis I this cavalry was organised into companies of 100 that actually consisted of forty *gens d'armes* each supported by two pages, and sixty archers.[51] Although there is little reason to doubt the quality of these soldiers, the numbers the French king was able to draw upon at any given time must raise doubts. Thus, in 1523 the strength of the *compagnies d'ordonnance* stood at less than 4,000 heavy cavalry and roughly 6,000 archers.[52] A far greater number of trained soldiers than Henry could hope to muster but then they had far longer frontiers to defend against two invading armies. It will be recalled that in 1523 the Duke of Suffolk began his invasion of northern France with roughly 14,000 men, yet the number of professional soldiers in Picardy and the Boulonnais at the time was less than 350 heavy cavalry and roughly 500 archers![53] Twenty years later as Henry prepared to enter France with more than 40,000 men, Francis allotted 800 *gens d'armes* to defend Picardy and the Ile de France; he could spare no more since he had to defend himself from a similar incursion on his eastern frontier from the emperor.

Furthermore, unlike Charles, Francis did not possess large numbers of highly trained infantry. Like Henry, he possessed garrison troops—no doubt in considerably larger numbers—upon which he could rely in both peacetime and war. Yet equally like his English rival, when war did come he needed to greatly augment this permanent force, and, at least till the early 1530s, he appears to have done so through conscription of the general population. The drawbacks

---

[49] Oman (1937), 53–56.
[50] Ibid., 59–61.
[51] Potter (1993), 159–161.
[52] Ibid., 160.
[53] Ibid.

of such a process were clearly demonstrated by Francis' efforts in the early 1530s to establish a permanent infantry force to complement the *compagnies d'ordonnance*. His efforts met with little success. In 1531 four legions, each containing 6,000 men were created, however, low officer ratios and irregular pay ensured that these new standing forces were plagued by poor discipline.[54] From a military perspective, lack of artillery support and engineers weakened their potential.

The truth is that neither Charles nor Francis possessed anywhere near the numbers of professional soldiers necessary to conduct a large-scale war over a prolonged period of time. In answer to the problem they employed mercenaries, not like Henry, in the thousands and for months, but in the tens of thousands and for years. The French army at Pavia in February 1525 numbered roughly 28,000 of which 10,000 were Swiss and 6,000 were German.[55] In 1542, of 70,000 men under French arms no less than 43,000 were Swiss and German pikes, 4–5,000 Italian cavalry and at least 2,000 horse from Cleves.[56] A muster roll for the forces of Charles V in Italy in July 1536 includes 2060 German cavalry and 24,080 German infantry.[57] The first point to make is that numbers like these clearly show that Charles and Francis had many more professional soldiers at their command than ever Henry did. The second point is that they chose to all but bankrupt themselves hiring foreign soldiers because their native armies were inadequate—or if one prefers, insufficiently professional. They therefore differ from their English counterpart not so much in nature as in degree.

It would be difficult not to concede that a gap did exist between England and her continental rivals, or that early Tudor armies still had a long journey ahead of them before the term professional could reasonably be applied. Alternatively, to picture the forces dispatched to France by Henry solely as disorganised amateurs, suitably equipped for a war taking place in the mid-fifteenth century is equally misleading. Each campaign was led by a small number of highly experienced officers who had under their command not only thousands of inexperienced recruits but also bodies of battle hardened infantry

---

[54] Oman (1937), 162–163.
[55] Hale (1985), 63; Oman (1937), 187.
[56] Phillips (2000), 52.
[57] Oman (1937), 61.

and cavalry. Every expedition was dominated by sieges and for these Henry's armies were well prepared. However, in the event that the invaders were challenged to battle they could rely on the support of foreign pikemen, arquebusiers and heavy cavalry. Perhaps the most important reason that no English army suffered a defeat at the hands of the French during the reign of Henry VIII was the preoccupation of Francis I with the greater threat of his Habsburg rival. However, a further explanation is that the quality of the English forces dispatched to France, if not the equal of their Valois opponents, were sufficiently good to deter the French from challenging them in battle.

IV

If one accepts that the military resources available to Henry VIII were not perhaps as inadequate as others have suggested, the question remains how effectively did the English king make use of them? To what degree did the ideals of chivalry continue to control the thoughts and actions of the king and his nobility in the military arena? Finally, were Henry's objectives merely the product of anachronistic ambitions, or realistic goals attainable with the resources at his disposal?

Certainly in Europe, although it would be unwise to dismiss the impact of chivalry in the conduct of early modern warfare, it would be difficult to deny that its role was steadily diminishing. Certainly renaissance princes and the nobility that accompanied them to war often remained eager to fulfil the knightly paradigm defined by the codes of medieval chivalry, as David Potter showed in the previous chapter. Unfortunately the pace of military change made this increasingly less feasible. Malcolm Vale provides a neat summary of these changes:

> The impersonality of war increased, and it was intensified by the centralised organisation of newly founded standing armies in France, Burgundy and some Italian states; by the greater numbers and degree of specialisation involved, and the disciplinary measures that were consequently necessary.[58]

---

[58] Vale (1981), 147.

An essential aspect of chivalry had always been the cult of the individual, the idea that single knights could, by the performance of heroic deeds and worthy acts make a difference. The exponential growth of army sizes, the growing importance of gunpowder weapons, the repeated success of large infantry formations and the growing dominance of siege warfare swiftly eroded this principle. The dreadful consequences of indulging one's chivalric desires were amply demonstrated in February 1525 when a heavy French defeat at Pavia was converted into a military disaster by the capture of Francis I. Princes might remain eager to lead their nobility in battle, but as the drawn out sieges and inconclusive manoeuvrings of the later Habsburg-Valois wars demonstrated they had largely learned to suppress these martial urges in grudging acceptance of the dictates of modern warfare.

What then of Henry and his nobility? Certainly, the king's decisions to go to war with France owed much to his desire to demonstrate to his princely rivals and to his own people that he was a warrior king, the equal of both his European contemporaries and his English ancestors. Whatever he believed he could realistically achieve by going to war with France, Henry repeatedly spoke and acted as though his ultimate objective was at the very least a return to the post-Agincourt days of Henry V. In 1512 he pressed Julius II to issue a papal brief recognising him as the rightful king of France. Eleven years later the Duke of Suffolk, presumably at the king's direction, compelled the populace of each town that fell to him to swear fealty to Henry as king of France. In both 1523 and 1524, Henry was insistent that the rebel Duke of Bourbon recognise his title to the French throne. In 1528 the emperor's ambassador at the English court passed on a request from the king that Charles' soldiers should avoid devastating the French countryside as in doing so it was Henry's country they were actually damaging.[59] Declarations of war against France delivered by the English herald centred on complaints about incursions into the Calais Pale, attacks on English shipping, the suspension of pension payments, and aid given to the Scots;[60] for the most part valid complaints that no doubt

---

[59] Gunn (1987), 37–41.
[60] BL, Cotton MS, Caligula D.VIII, fo. 220 (*L&P Henry 8th*, III ii, no. 2292), Declaration of war by Clarencieux king-at-arms, 29 May 1522.

irritated the king considerably. Even so, these were just the legal justifications Henry needed to go to war. Unquestionably a key part of what drove him to make these issues *causus belli* rather than potential bargaining counters to extract concessions from Francis was the king's belief in his historic duty to bring back the glory days of Agincourt and Crecy, to restore England's continental empire and place himself amongst the pantheon of great warrior princes.

It is also clear that Henry enjoyed war since it offered him a stage of unparalleled magnificence upon which to display the prowess and virtue for which one might look in a knight and a king. This is no more apparent than in Henry's first campaign in France. The king disembarked at Calais:

> appareilled in almayne rivet crested and his vanbrace of the same, and on his head a chapeau montayn with a riche coronal, the fold of the chapeau was lined with crimsyn saten and on that a riche brooch with the image of Sainct George. Over his rivett he had a garment of white cloth of gold with a redde cross.[61]

Once disembarked he led a procession about the city that ended at the church of St Nicholas where he stopped to ask God's blessing for the coming campaign. The night of his departure from Calais and despite the inclement weather he made a point of touring the camp just as Henry V had reputedly done nearly 100 years before.[62] In preparation for the anticipated battle in front of Therouanne he ordered his tents to be erected and his army gathered in full battle array, despite the potential loss of surprise that such a display would inevitably cause.[63] His conduct towards the clutch of illustrious captives garnered after the rout of the French at Spurs was magnanimous, allowing several of them go free after the payment of generously low ransoms.[64]

Neither Henry's second nor third war against France offered the same opportunities for such personally chivalrous behaviour. The king was absent from both the 1522 and 1523 expeditions. Finally, although Henry's presence on the 1544 campaign was every bit as tangible as the heaviest pieces of English artillery, the expedition was

---

[61] Hall (1809), 539.
[62] Scarisbrick (1997), 35.
[63] Cruickshank (1990), 113.
[64] Richardson (1995), 34.

dominated by the sieges around Boulogne and Montreuil and offered
almost no opportunities for the practically inert monarch to act as
he had thirty years before. Even so, one can find occasional examples when it is clear that Henry's tactical and strategic considerations were influenced by a desire to promote and protect his honour
and by a keen wish to conform to traditional ideals of chivalry. In
1521 when, under Imperial pressure, the king toyed with the idea
of sending 6,000 archers to the emperor's aid, he clashed with Wolsey
over who should lead the force. Sweeping aside the cardinal's concerns that a general drawn from the aristocracy would not only be
expensive but also conspicuous, he argued that, 'it can not stonde
wyth hys honor to sende ony personage off lower degree than an
erle owt off hys realme with the sayde army.'[65] The following year
the instructions given to the Earl of Surrey for his expedition into
the Boulonnais urged him to do as much damage in the province
as possible with the specific objective of luring the French into battle.[66] No doubt part of the thinking behind these instructions was
based on the relative numbers of the Anglo-Burgundian and French
forces in north-eastern France and the opportunities that might arise
should the allies win a decisive victory in the Boulonnais. Yet, it is
also reasonable to assume that Henry was spoiling for a fight and
was eager for the chance to see his forces best their perennial foe.
The *chevauchee* could inflict terrible damage on wide areas of enemy
territory, and, at least in the mind of the prince who set it in train,
demonstrate the cost of provoking his wrath, but the only people
upon whom it made a lasting impression were the individuals upon
whom it was unleashed. Finally, in the run-up to the 1544 campaign Henry argued with both the emperor and his own advisers
about his decision to accompany his army on campaign. As the
Imperial ambassador, Eustace Chapuys, reported to Charles, the
king's councillors were eager for him to remain in England both
over concerns for his safety and fears that his presence might do
much to slow the campaign down.[67] Nevertheless, Henry was adamant,
that if Charles was going to lead his armies against France then he
would do likewise, and he would do it because honour demanded

---

[65] *SP Henry 8th* I, 25 (*L&P Henry 8th*, III ii, no. 1454), Pace to Wolsey, Aug.
1521.
[66] BL, Cotton MS, Galba D.VIII, fo. 264 (*L&P Henry 8th*, III ii, no. 2526),
Wolsey to Surrey, 9 Sept. 1522.
[67] *L&P Henry 8th*, XIX I, no. 324, Chapuys to Charles, 13 Apr. 1544.

that he should.[68] It would seem that the king was quite prepared to hamper the English campaign to protect his honour and indulge his interest in war.

There is also evidence to suggest that in their approach to war the nobility were still very much influenced by the ideals of chivalry. At least two of Henry's leading officers, Thomas Lord Darcy and John Wallop, performed the ultimate act of chivalry and participated in crusades. In 1512 Darcy armed 1,000 men at his own expense and led them on an expedition to North Africa. Four years later Wallop gained leave of the king to join a Portuguese campaign, again launched against the Moors of North Africa.[69] Nearer to home, Henry's wars with the French offered ample opportunity for members of the gentry and aristocracy to emulate their knightly forbears. Upon hearing news of the death of Thomas Knyvett in 1512, Edward Howard apparently vowed that he would not look upon the king's face until he had revenged himself of his friend's death.[70] Less than a year later Howard was himself killed as a result of a foolhardy attack on a larger French naval force.[71] In September 1522 William Lord Sandys wrote to Henry in glowing terms of the destruction his forces had wreaked in the Boulonnais.[72] Even so, when describing the destruction of a church in Lodingham, Sandys felt it necessary to justify his actions by explaining that the building had been so heavily fortified, 'that it was more like a fortress than a house of God.'[73] At the outset of the Landrecy campaign Wallop gave the Privy Council an account of a joust that took place between six of his own officers and a similar number of French gentlemen:

> For tholde acquaynetance I had with the Captayne of Therwaine I sent him a letter of visitacion . . . the effect of my said letter was, that seyng he wold send owt no greter nombre to skyrmishe with us, if he had any gentlemen under his charge that wold breke any staves for theire ladis sake, I wold the next morning appoint 6 gentlemen to mete with them.[74]

---

[68] Ibid. no. 530, Chapuys to Charles, 18 May 1544.

[69] Gunn (1987), 43.

[70] BL, Cotton MS, Titus B.I, fo. 90 (*L&P Henry 8th*, I i, no. 1356), Wolsey to Foxe, 26 Aug. 1512.

[71] Loades (1992), 55–56.

[72] BL, Cotton MS, Galba D.VIII, fo. 265 (*L&P Henry 8th*, III ii, no. 2530), Sandys to Henry, 10 Sept. 1522.

[73] Ibid.

[74] *SP Henry 8th*, IX, 459 (*L&P Henry 8th*, XVIII i, no. 979), Wallop to the Privy Council, 31 July 1543.

In the ensuing combat, one of the Englishmen was badly hurt when a lance punched through his armpit with such force that on passing through his body it split his mail-coat on the other side. Too ill to continue the campaign, the man was left in French care at Therouanne, after which Wallop and his army began the business of laying waste to the French countryside in earnest.[75] At the close of the expedition whilst skirmishing with a French force two young gentlemen, Edward Bellingham and George Carew, along with the stalwart campaigner, Thomas Palmer, were captured.[76] Wallop's efforts to discover the fate of the three men were greatly aided by his old rival, Marshal Odart du Bies. The French general not only helped him locate them, but even proffered advice on how the English general should go about negotiating with their Italian captor to gain their return at the lowest possible price.[77]

Yet the Landrecy campaign also offers perhaps the best example of how generals such as Wallop, for whom the ideals of chivalry still clearly mattered, were capable of viewing war from a professionally detached perspective. Early in the campaign Wallop's dispatches describing raids against a number of castles and abbeys contain a palpable note of satisfaction, not only because of the extensive damage being caused, but because the officers under his direction, men like Thomas Poynings and Robert Bowes, were orchestrating the destruction with such efficiency.[78] Later reports to Henry's secretary, William Paget, contained detailed accounts of new artillery and ammunition being used by the emperor's forces at the siege of Landrecy.[79] Wallop enjoyed discussions with Charles about styles of camp fortification and varying types of light cavalry.[80] At the close of the expedition he noted to Henry, that, 'he was never in war where there was so much for youth to learn both at the being before Landrecy, and then at the Emperor's coming with horse and foot

[75] Ibid.

[76] *SP Henry 8th*, IX, 538 (*L&P Henry 8th*, XVIII ii, no. 345), Wallop to Henry, 6 Nov. 1543.

[77] *SP Henry 8th*, IX, 543 (*L&P Henry 8th*, XVIII ii, no. 365), Wallop and Bryan to Paget, 10 Nov. 1543.

[78] *SP Henry 8th*, IX, 452 (*L&P Henry 8th*, XVIII i, no. 960), Wallop to the Council, 27 July 1543.

[79] *SP Henry 8th*, IX, 527 (*L&P Henry 8th*, XVIII ii, nos. 293, 310), Wallop to Paget, 22 and 26 Oct. 1543.

[80] *SP Henry 8th*, IX, 522–527 (*L&P Henry 8th*, XVIII ii, no. 291), Wallop to Henry, 21 Oct. 1543.

of all nations.'[81] Wallop clearly enjoyed the expedition on two levels: it gave him the chance to do battle with the old foe; to participate in a rather dangerous game against opponents towards whom he does not seem to have harboured any great ill-feeling. It also afforded him the opportunity to see war done properly. In charge of a relatively small force, with numbers of experienced officers under his command he was able to direct an efficient, well-organised campaign. Under such circumstances the medieval knight and the early modern professional soldier could happily co-exist. The warrior nobility of early Tudor England could be chivalrous *and* professional.

V

If one must concede that for Henry and his nobility both the motivation to go to war and the manner in which they conducted themselves once on campaign owed something to tradition and the ideals of chivalry, there are also indications that the king's military objectives were based on sound strategic thinking. Of course, it might well be argued that it was a shame Henry felt the need to go to war at all. What might have been achieved at home with the reserves left to the king by his father, or the great riches plundered from the dissolution of the monasteries? Such questions are grossly anachronistic. Henry was a renaissance prince and the pursuit of glory through war represented the norm at that time.[82] Yet within this context it can be argued that certainly in his latter two wars against France Henry's true objectives were militarily achievable and potentially beneficial to the English position on the continent.

Although Suffolk's 1523 campaign was ultimately transformed into an ambitious invasion with Paris as it objective, this was not the plan that the king originally favoured. In September 1523 Henry pointed out to Wolsey the inherent difficulties of a full-scale invasion of France. He predicted that the large artillery train needed for such an expedition would become bogged down in difficult terrain; as Suffolk's army penetrated further into France so it would be

---

[81] *SP Henry 8th*, IX, 550 (*L&P Henry 8th*, XVIII ii, no. 384), Wallop to Henry, 14 Nov. 1543.
[82] Admittedly, a small but much respected body of opinion, spearheaded by men such as Erasmus, More and Vives, queried this idea.

increasingly difficult to victual; given the lateness of the season the
English would encounter ever harsher conditions inevitably provoking the rank and file to demand the campaign's end and a return
to England; and finally, the invasion would put an intolerable strain
on the king's finances.[83] Instead Henry urged an attack on Boulogne,
a strategically sensible objective, far less likely to stretch English
resources beyond their breaking point. On this occasion he permitted himself to be swayed by Wolsey and his Habsburg allies upon
whom he was so dependent for military and logistic support. As a
result he at least had the satisfaction of seeing his predictions
come true.

When Henry next came to invade France the situation was reversed.
This time he openly committed himself to another march on Paris,[84]
while remaining quietly resolved that his army would attempt nothing more than an attack on one or two strongholds in north eastern France. Consequently, he did less to help his Imperial ally than
he had in the two previous campaigns and succeeded in making the
biggest conquest of his reign. If, as Henry's remarks in 1523 would
seem to suggest, Boulogne, and perhaps Ardres and Montreuil, were
the preferred objectives of the king's later wars with France then his
strategy, when others did not prevail upon him to alter it, was by
no means foolish. In seeking to capture Boulogne as well as Montreuil,
which I have argued elsewhere was a genuine objective of the 1544
campaign,[85] Henry was attempting to make a substantial and useful
addition to England's toehold on the continent. Unlike the ephemeral
conquests of the 1523 campaign the proximity of Boulogne and
Montreuil both to Calais and the Burgundian territories of his allies
ensured that the king would not be obliged to relinquish these prizes
when autumn drifted into winter. What is more, the arguments for
attacking such towns were not limited to a need for the king to emulate his ancestors and really annoy the French. The fall of Boulogne
and Montreuil would effectively double the size of the Calais Pale,
and in a manner that would not prove easy for the French to reverse.
Should Henry's ambitions remain unslaked by two such useful conquests, and the possibility did exist, then how much better would

---

[83] *SP Henry 8th*, I, 135–140 (*L&P Henry 8th*, III ii, no. 5346), More to Wolsey,
20 Sept. 1543.
[84] *L&P Henry 8th*, XVIII ii, no. 526, Anglo-Imperial treaty, 31 Dec. 1543.
[85] MacMahon (1992), 40–45.

his position be to renew the war the following year from a much extended beachhead and deeper incursion into French territory? As Steven Gunn has observed,

> the expansion of the Pale, whether by the capture of Boulogne or Ardres . . . or the cession of Boulogne or other towns in a peace settlement . . . was the most sensible aim of English aggression against France.[86]

In the event the siege of Boulogne proved a greater drain on English resources than had been anticipated, Montreuil failed to surrender, although not it should be stressed for want of commitment on the part of the English, and Charles, not unreasonably, made peace with Francis, leaving Henry to fight on alone. Consequently the English, rather than pressing home the advantage in 1545, found themselves on the defensive. What conclusions should one draw from the final year of England's war with France? For all that we have been told that England's armies were laughable by comparison to their French rivals, they managed to hold Boulogne in the face of their enemy's undivided attention. Francis was unable to wrest the town from Henry's grasp, firstly, because it was defended by a reasonably competent army, and secondly, because the king's final military objective was one that could be effectively re-fortified and easily supplied from Calais and the Low Countries.

It would be difficult to refute the argument that England would have done better to remain aloof from the Habsburg-Valois wars, but it is important to keep the 'folly' of Henry VIII in proportion. Francis I beggared his country and exposed it to terrible deprivation in a thirty-year effort to make good his claim on Milan, a claim derived from a marriage between Louis duc d'Orleans and Valentina Visconti formed a hundred years before the French king came to the throne.[87] For his part, Charles V concentrated his efforts on restoring the boundaries of his Burgundian inheritance to their extent at the time of his great grandfather, Charles the Bold. These efforts culminated in the outrageous demands of the Treaty of Madrid, so excessive that the French king, upon whom they were imposed, had no compunction about repudiating them once free of Spanish captivity.[88]

---

[86] Gunn (1987), 33.
[87] Knecht (1994), 62–64.
[88] Brandi (1939), 223–33.

Just as importantly, their excessive nature ensured that Francis gained wide international sympathy and support for an act that under other circumstances would have been viewed as reprehensible. Thus was the victory of Pavia squandered. In the latter part of his reign Charles devoted himself to the imposition of imperial authority over his German subjects the like of which had not been seen in centuries. Seeking to impose a religious status quo thirty years past, by the use political authority dead long before, Charles was ultimately forced to accept the humiliating Peace of Augsburg, which was not only a partial acceptance on the emperor's part of the protestant religion, but an acknowledgement of the individual sovereignty of the German princes.[89] By comparison the ambitions of Henry, the real ambitions of expanding the English foothold in north-eastern France, seem both plausible and level-headed.

One could hardly contend that the English armies of the early sixteenth century in modern terms were professional or were used, certainly in Europe, for purposes of any great strategic merit. But then a large proportion of the forces against which they might potentially be ranged were not truly professionals either, so the mismatch, at least in terms of quality was never especially great. In any case the question is moot. Henry only went to war with France when she was in no condition to fight back, hardly chivalrous but commendably opportunistic. It would be difficult to argue that had Francis I truly devoted himself to the conquest of the Calais Pale he would not have achieved his goal. But rather than consolidate the natural boundaries of France he pursued his Italian dream and spent more than 40 per cent of his reign in ruinously expensive and largely inconclusive wars with Charles V. In turn Henry indulged himself, and when not being otherwise misled attempted to expand England's last foothold in France. Seen in this perspective, the king's armies seem neither so puny and amateurish, nor his folly so great, as many scholars would have us believe.

---

[89] Ibid., 549–73, 625–29.

Bibliography

Bernard G. W. (1985) *The Power of the Early Tudor Nobility: A Study of the 4th and 5th Earls of Shrewsbury* (Brighton: 1985).

Brandi K. (1939) *Charles V* (London: 1939).

Cruickshank C. G. (1966) *Elizabeth's Army* (Oxford: 1966).

——. (1973) *The English Occupation of Tournai* (Oxford: 1973).

Duffy C. (1979) *Siege Warfare: The Fortress in the Early Modern World, 1494–1660* (London: 1979).

Fissel M. C. (2001) *English Warfare, 1511–1642* (London: 2001).

G. E. C. (1910–40) *The Complete Peerage*, ed. H. A. Doubleday *et al.*, 14 vols (London: 1910–40).

Goring J. J. (1955) "The military obligations of the English people, 1511–1558", unpublished PhD thesis (University of London: 1955).

——. (1975) "Social change and military decline in mid-Tudor England", *History* 60 (1975) 185–197.

Gruffudd E. (1944) "Suffolk's expedition to Montdidier, 1523", trans. M. B. Davies, *The Bulletin of Faculty of Arts, King Faoud I University* 2 (1944).

——. (1949) "The enterprise of Paris and Boulogne", trans. M. B. Davies, *The Bulletin of Faculty of Arts, King Faoud I University* 7 (1949).

Grummitt D. (1997) "Calais, 1485–1547: A Study of early Tudor politics and government", unpublished PhD thesis (University of London: 1997).

——. (2000) "The defence of Calais and the deployment of gunpowder weaponry in England in the late Fifteenth century", *War in History* 7 (2000) 253–72.

Gunn S. J. (1988) *Charles Brandon, Duke of Suffolk, c. 1484–1545* (Oxford: 1988).

——. (1986) "The Duke of Suffolk's march on Paris in 1523", *EHR* 101 (1986) 596–634.

Hale J. R. (1965) "The development of the bastion, 1440–1534", in, *Europe in the Late Middle Ages*, ed. J. R. Hale, J. R. L. Highfield and B. Smalley (London: 1965).

——. (1985) *War and Society in Renaissance Europe, 1450–1620* (London: 1985).

Hall E. (1809) *Chronicles* (London: 1809).

Head D. M. (1985) *The Ebbs and Flows of Fortune: The Life of Thomas Howard, Third Duke of Norfolk* (Athens, Georgia: 1995).

Hewerdine A. R. (1998) "The Yeomen of the king's Guard, 1485–1547", unpublished PhD thesis (University of London: 1998).

Howard M. (1976) *War in European History* (Oxford: 1976).

Knecht R. J. (1994) *Renaissance Warrior and Patron: The Reign of Francis I* (Cambridge: 1994).

Loades D. (1992) *The Tudor Navy, an Administrative, Political and Military History* (Aldershot: 1992).

MacMahon L. (1992) "The English invasion of France, 1544", unpublished MA thesis (University of Warwick: 1992).

Millar G. J. (1980) *Tudor Mercenaries and Auxiliaries, 1485–1547* (Charlottesville, Virginia: 1980).

Miller H. (1986) *Henry VIII and the English Nobility* (Oxford: 1986).

Nichols J. G. (1846) ed., *The Chronicle of Calais in the Reigns of Henry VII and Henry VIII to the Year 1540* (Camden Society: 1846).

Oman C. (1937) *The Art of War in the Sixteenth Century* (London: 1937).

Palmer W. (1994) *The Problem of Ireland in Tudor Foreign Policy, 1485–1603* (Woodbridge, Suffolk: 1994).

Parker G. (1996) *The Military Revolution: Military Innovation and the Rise of the West, 1500–1800* (Cambridge: 1996).

Philips G. (1999) *The Anglo-Scots Wars: A Military History* (Woodbridge, Suffolk: 1999).

Potter D. L. (1993) *War and Government in the French Provinces, Picardy, 1470–1560* (Cambridge: 1993).

Richardson G. J. (1995) "Anglo-French Political and Cultural Relations during the Reign of Henry VIII", unpublished PhD thesis (University of London: 1995).

Rodger N. A. M. (1999) *The Safeguard of the Seas: A Naval History of Britain* (London: 1999).

Scarisbrick J. J. (1997) *Henry VIII* 2nd edn. (London: 1997; orig. edn., 1968).

Vale M. (1981) *War and Chivalry, Warfare and Aristocratic Culture in England, France and Burgundy at the end of the Middle Ages* (London: 1981).

Vodden D. F. (1972) "The correspondence of William Fitzwilliam, Earl of Southampton", unpublished MPhil thesis, 2 vols (University of London: 1972).

Willen D. (1981) *John Russell, First Earl of Bedford: One of the King's Men* (London: 1981).

CHAPTER EIGHT

CHIVALRY AND PROFESSIONALISM IN ELECTORAL SAXONY IN THE MID-SIXTEENTH CENTURY

Helen Watanabe-O'Kelly

This volume poses questions about the survival into early modern times of medieval notions of chivalry, about the introduction and development of the technology of war, about the self-understanding of the officer class and about the increasing professionalisation and specialisation of the soldier. If it is difficult to answer these questions with regard to a nation state such as France or England, it is impossible to do so with regard to the disparate collection of territories that made up the Holy Roman Empire. Instead this article focuses on one territory, Electoral Saxony, and in particular on the activities of one ruler, Elector August (1526–1586, r. 1553–1586). He was a modern prince in his intense and practical interest in science and technology, and his cabinet of curiosities and his library, founded around 1560, bear witness to that interest. It is therefore not surprising that he hired Italian architects to improve the fortification of his capital city of Dresden in the new Italian manner and that he collected firearms and works on fortification techniques. What is surprising is that as late as 1584 he commissioned a manuscript tournament book that portrayed him as a knight in armour in the jousts that he had ceased to practise in 1566. Both these images of August— as man of science and technology and as latter-day knight—were carefully cultivated by his successors. They formed part of the myth of August as founder of the Dresden court and of the fortunes of the Albertine Electors of Saxony.

While the first of these images, that of moderniser and technocrat, seems natural, indeed admirable, to us today, the second, which bears witness to the active cultivation at so late a date of the concept of the knight, is much harder to understand. The question therefore for us to answer is what interests it served.

Electoral Saxony in the Sixteenth Century

The House of Wettin, whose ruling dukes became Electors of Saxony in 1423, divided its territory into two in 1485 in the so-called Leipzig Partition ('Leipziger Teilung'). According to this, the Ernestines, descendants of Elector Ernst (1441–1486), retained control of Torgau, Wittenberg, Gotha, Coburg, Jena, the Vogtland and Weimar, which they made their capital city. The cadet branch, descendants of Ernst's brother Duke Albrecht (1443–1500) and therefore known as Albertines, kept the territories of Meissen and Thuringia, with such cities as Dresden, Chemnitz, Freiberg and Leipzig. It was the Ernestines who were the original protectors of Luther and it was their territory that could claim to be the cradle of the Reformation. The Albertine lands did not become Lutheran until 1539, when Duke Heinrich (1473–1541) introduced the Reformation on his accession.

It was Duke Heinrich's son Moritz (1521–1553) who won the Electorship of Saxony for the Albertines, a title they kept in perpetuity, acquiring at the same time a large tranche of Ernestine land including Wittenberg and Torgau. Having fought with his fellow Protestant princes in the Schmalkaldic League, Moritz changed sides and supported the Emperor Charles V against it in 1545, defeating his cousin, the Ernestine Elector Johann Friedrich, at the battle of Mühlberg in 1547, though with strong Imperial assistance.[1] Moritz changed sides again, fighting against the Emperor on behalf of the Protestants in 1552. He forced the Emperor to sign the Treaty of Passau which ultimately brought about the Peace of Augsburg in 1555, thus assuring the legal rights of Protestants within the Empire. It was Moritz who made Dresden the capital city of the Albertines and the focus of its court. He was killed at the battle of Sievershausen in 1553, fighting against Albrecht Alcibiades of Brandenburg-Kulmbach, a former ally.

Moritz was succeeded by his brother August, whose 33–year reign established Dresden as a cultural centre and enlarged the Duchy. August secured his own claim to the Electorship at the Treaty of Naumburg in 1554.

---

[1] Blaschke (1983).

The Fortification of Dresden

The short reign of Moritz and the much longer one of August show several of the characteristic features of increasing military professionalisation—the concentration of responsibility for defence in the hands of the prince rather than of the citizens, the increasing employment of professional soldiers, the growth in importance of specialists, particularly artillery experts and fortification engineers, and the introduction of new fortification techniques from Italy. Developments in the city of Dresden show this very clearly.

Dresden was one of the first cities to be equipped with bastions in the so-called old Italian manner.[2] This began in 1545 under Moritz, who had seen Donato de Boni's fortifications in Antwerp, the first time the old Italian manner was implemented north of the Alps.[3] Moritz hired the Dutchman Caspar Vogt von Wierandt, in whose company he had visited Antwerp and Ghent, to be his fortification engineer, architect and artillery specialist. Wierandt designed a ring of eight bastions around Dresden, seven of which were finished at Moritz's death in 1553. August commanded Wierandt to complete the projected eighth bastion, which he did by 1555. August confirmed Wierandt in his post which he held until his death in 1560. August too had also visited the Low Countries and had seen the fortifications there.

How advanced this ring of bastions round Dresden was from a German perspective is confirmed by looking at the great German compendium of military lore by Fronsperger.[4] The work is dedicated to Emperor Maximilian II (the dedication is dated 1565) and covers every aspect of military organisation and of the conduct of war in ten books. Books 4 and 8 deal exclusively with artillery and explosives, while book 7 discusses siege warfare and fortification. The section on the construction of fortifications (fos. CLXIIIb–CLXVIIb) envisages only round towers and does not mention bastions. This is confirmed by the numerous woodcuts throughout the treatise which, with the exception of that after fo. CCXIb, depict circular towers and curved curtain walls.

---

[2] Papke (1997) and Castor (2000).
[3] See Simon Pepper's chapter in this volume, above, p. 133.
[4] Fronsperger (1571).

In other ways too, Dresden was progressive from a military point of view. Moritz had garrisoned the city with a standing troop of 400 men, extracting contributions towards their upkeep from the citizens. He had equipped the fortifications with 76 pieces of artillery and employed fifty specialists to man them.[5] This trend towards the removal of responsibility for defence from the citizens of Dresden continued under August, who appointed Melchior Hauffe as commander of the fortress in 1558 during August's absence abroad. Hauffe was a highly experienced professional soldier who had taken part in the siege of Vienna in 1529, had served in Northern Italy and the Netherlands and been a captain since 1552. In 1563 Hauffe was named Wierandt's successor as 'Oberzeug- und Baumeister', that is, he was given overall responsibility for the defence of the fortified city. The post of commander of the fortress of Dresden, always filled by the Elector's appointee, existed from here on in perpetuity and again confirms the concentration of military responsibility in the hands of the prince.[6] The importance August attached to the defence of his capital city can also be judged by the fact that he commissioned Wierandt in 1558 to build a new arsenal or 'Zeughaus' in Dresden.

It was clear by the mid 1560s that the existing fortifications needed considerable improvement, so August imported Italian architects to modernise them. One of the earliest was a Brescian, Giovan Battista Buonomia, who was employed from 1566 to 1571.[7] His contract states that he was engaged not only as a sculptor and designer of court festivities but also as a fortification engineer and architect. It seems that there were tensions between his ideas and those of two other native specialists of importance who were also in the Elector's employ at this time, the 'Hauszeugmeister' or artillery specialist Enderle Hess and the engineer and architect Paul Buchner, who was later responsible for a number of building projects in Dresden.[8] In 1569, however, August succeeded in attracting to Dresden a fortification specialist of European renown, Rocco Guerini, Conte di Linar (1525–1596).

As Castor points out, Rocco di Linar represented a new type of architect—an aristocrat, a man of education and polish, a diplomat

[5] Papke (1997), p. 51 and p. 60 resp.
[6] Papke (1997), p. 63 and Castor (2000), p. 111.
[7] Dombrowski (2000), p. 71.
[8] Papke (1997), p. 64.

and a courtier.[9] Born in Maradia in Tuscany as Rocco Quirino di Linar, he is said to have been educated with Cosimo de' Medici. He first worked as a fortification engineer at the court of Alfonso II in Ferrara in 1539 but then, following a family feud, fled to France where he had a spectacular career for almost twenty years in spite of his Huguenot sympathies. As the leader of a Huguenot rebellion in 1567 he had to flee and first joined the prince de Condé, who recommended him to Count Palatine Johann Casimir. He subsequently went to Calvinist Heidelberg, to the court of Friedrich, Elector Palatine, and then in 1569 to Lutheran Dresden as architect and artillery specialist, where he remained until 1578, when August released him into the service of Elector Johann Georg of Brandenburg. Even after the official end of his service in Saxony, he was retained (and paid) by August as a special adviser. During his time in Dresden, Rocco di Linar's wide experience and many talents were fully utilised. He advised the Elector on mining, minting and forestry, he took charge of the building work on the palaces in Freiberg and Augustusburg and advised on the improvements to other residences such as those at Sitzenroda and Lochar. In the spring of 1572 he was sent on a diplomatic mission to Florence, Ferrara and Mantua and on his return brought gifts to Elector August which, as Marx has shown, initiated an exchange of presents between the two courts.[10]

Most relevant to the present discussion is his large-scale improvements to the fortifications of the city according to the most advanced conceptions of the day, that is, according to the new Italian manner.[11] Linar built two huge modern bastions instead of the three oldest small bastions to the north-west of the fortified area round the palace. His chief problem here was the necessity to build a dam in order to be able to extend the fortifications out over the old city moat which was connected to the Elbe and the much smaller Weisseritz. All of this had to be pushed through against the suspicions of the native German specialists and of the citizens of Dresden, who feared flooding from the new dams.[12] Linar succeeded in his endeavours, however, before leaving for Brandenburg in 1578, where

---

[9] Castor (2000), p. 112.
[10] Marx (2000, b).
[11] See the detailed discussions by Papke (1997), p. 66 f. and Castor (2000), 115 f.
[12] Papke (1997), p. 67, quotes from the archival documents.

one of his principal achievements was the fortification of the fortress of Spandau.

After Linar's departure for Brandenburg, August took another Italian specialist into his service, the Neapolitan engineer Carlo Theti (1529–1589). This appears to have occurred in about 1581, though his first official contract was not made out until 1584. He was the author of the treatise on fortification techniques entitled *Discorsi di fortificationi* (Rome 1569) which ran into subsequent editions in 1575 and 1589 respectively. August considered the art of fortification so important that he asked Theti to teach it to his heir, Christian I. In addition, Theti was sent to Florence in 1585 as a Saxon envoy.[13]

August's Interest in Technology

That August should be aware of and concerned to make use of the newest fortification techniques fits in with his interest in science and technology in general. This is exemplified particularly clearly in his cabinet of curiosities or *Kunstkammer*, founded in 1560, and in his library. Whereas other *Kunstkammern* founded at around the same time, such as those in Vienna, Munich or Innsbruck, present a combination of natural objects (*naturalia*), which bear witness to the multifariousness of nature, and man-made objects (*artificialia*), which give testimony to the ingeniousness of man, August's *Kunstkammer* was a scientific and technological museum.[14]

The bulk of the objects in it consisted of scientific instruments, scientific books, and tools of all kinds. Of the eighty-five groups of objects catalogued in the first inventory of the *Kunstkammer* compiled by the custodian, David Ußlaub, in 1587, a year after August's death, about twenty-three groups were devoted to scientific instruments and clocks and about twenty-four to all kinds of tools.[15] The collection was not merely for show, since we know that August sat and worked in the midst of it. Indeed the name given to the first and most important room of the seven in which the collection was stored

---

[13] Marx (2000, b).

[14] For a much fuller treatment of August's scientific interests, including his library and his other collections, see my monograph *Court Culture in Dresden* (Palgrave).

[15] Ußlaub (1587). This is kept in the Grünes Gewölbe in Dresden.

makes this very plain, for it is called 'Meines gnedigsten Churfürsten und hern Reiß Cammer und kleinem Gemach'—that is, 'the small room in which my Most Gracious Elector and Lord did his drawing'. In fact, each room in the *Kunstkammer* had desks and writing implements in it, so that one could work there.

August's interest and his knowledge were not just passive. He was a mapmaker and the collection focuses strongly on mapping the heavens and the earth. He was an ivory turner and thus master of an important technical skill using a machine, the turner's lathe, and the objects he produced were kept in the collection. He was interested in gardening and surgery and the Armoury in Dresden still preserves his own gardening tools and surgical instruments from the *Kunstkammer*. He was also clearly interested in the technical aspect of gunnery. In the second room in the Kunstkammer were six separately-listed groups of instruments and drawings relating to this branch of knowledge.[16] They include tools and instruments relating to gunnery, artillery and explosives, designs for cannon and morters and various kinds of ball and shot. A further collection of splendid handguns was housed in the Armoury.

The *Kunstkammer* also contained in the same room an important collection of 288 numbered volumes quite separate from the books in the Electoral Library.[17] Apart from about thirty-seven volumes of engravings and a small number of illustrated festival books, costume books, books of heraldry and some miscellaneous items, it is a scientific collection which complements the scientific instruments. Works of Renaissance mathematics and astronomy which provide the theoretical underpinning for architecture, ballistics and gunnery are prominent. Regiomontanus is represented (nos. 55, 59, 137, 144, 147) and so are Heinrich Grammaticus (written as Schreiber, no. 210), Georg Peuerbach (nos. 35, 39, 100), Johann Schöner (nos. 41, 48) and Johannes Stöffler (nos. 145, 164). Orontius Finaeus's *Promathesis* (no. 28) and his *Geometria practica* (no. 210) are listed, as are Jakob Kölbel's work on surveying (no. 212), Balthasar Scultetus's *Gnomonice*, Johannes de Sacro Bosco (nos. 227, 247, 259), Georg Joachim Rheticus (no. 128) and Copernicus (nos. 86, 167). We find here Walther Rivius (nos. 48, 46, 47, 50, 62), Erasmus Reinhold's Prutenic Tables (nos.

---

[16] Ußlaub (1587), fos. 142a–159b.
[17] Ibid., fos. 165a–196b.

134, 135, 143), Gemma Frisius (nos. 85, 168) and Tilemann Stella (no. 106), Junctinus (nos. 226, 227) and Caspar Peucer (nos. 244, 247, 250) and the Saxon arithmetician Adam Ries (nos. 197, 286).

These books also betray an intense interest in architecture and perspective. We have Vitruvius in several editions (nos. 119, 200) in addition to Giovanni Battista Bertani's version of the *Opera Ionica* (no. 22), the commentary by Daniele Barbaro (nos. 72, 83) and Walther Rivius's German translation (no. 67). We have Sebastiano Serlio (no. 20), Pietro Cataneo (no. 33) and Girolamo Cataneo (nos. 76, 162), Giovanni Battista Benedetti (no. 34), Cosimo Bartoli (no. 173) and Giovanni Battista Carelli (nos. 125–126) and such notable German writers on the subject as Wentzel Jamnitzer (nos. 17, 257, 263), Johannes Lencker (no. 78) and Albrecht Dürer (nos. 44, 54, 59, 89).

Direct evidence of August's interest in fortification techniques can, however, be gleaned from two inventories of his library taken during his lifetime, in 1574 and in 1580 respectively. August had begun to collect books from about 1556 and we know from archival records that he took advice from the professors of the Universities of Wittenberg and Leipzig but also chose books himself from the catalogues of the German Book Fairs.[18] The first inventory is entitled: 'Registratur der bücher in des Churfürsten zu Saxen Liberey zu Annaburg'—(inventory of the library of the Electors of Saxony at Annaburg).[19] Annaburg was the ducal residence near Torgau to the north-west of Dresden, and a favourite of Duke August and his wife Anna, after whom it was named. That the books were kept there at this date rather than in the palace in Dresden indicates that this was a collection for the personal use of the Elector and his family rather than for prestige or show. The organisation of the library underlines this. The collection is neither that of a bibliophile nor of a scholar and is therefore organised according to a system which reflects the Elector's interests. Of the 1,721 volumes the inventory lists, the majority are in the vernacular and all the vernacular (mostly German) works are listed together before the Latin works. How easily Elector August read languages other than German is open to question.

---

[18] See the article 'Sächsische Landesbibliothek, Dresden' (1997). This library is now called the Sächsische Landesbibliothek, Staats- und Universitätsbibliothek (hereafter SLUB).

[19] It dates to 1574 and is preserved today in the SLUB at Bibl. Arch. I B vol. 20.

War in all its manifestations was clearly of great interest to August, as one would expect for the ruler of such a large and important territory as Electoral Saxony during a century of great confessional tension. We find works to do with military matters in three different sections in the inventory. Under 'Historica' we find a list of accounts of various battles at fos. 44a and b, there is a separate section of military books entitled 'Kriegsbucher von allem was dem zugehorig' (Military books dealing with everything belonging to [war]) from fo. 61a to fo. 64a, and works on fortification appear in the section on architecture ('Architectur, Perspectiva, Kunststuck etc.' (fos. 87a and b). The forty-three military books listed include several works by Leonhard Fronsperger (quoted respectively as 'Vom Krigsregiment funff bücher' (fo. 61a), 'Besatzung, ein kurtzer bericht wie Stät Schlösser oder Flecken mit Krigsvolck sollen gesetzt sein. Das sie sich fuer dem feinde erhaltenn mögen. Mit einer austeilung, was einem Menschen einen jeden tag an Brot und Fleysch . . . erhalten künden', (fo. 61b), 'Vom kaiserlichen Krigsrechten Malefitz unnd schuldthandeln' (fo. 62a) and 'Krigsbuch anderteil vonn wagenburg umb die feldläger' (fo. 62a)—works that afterwards were amalgamated into his great compendium of 1571). Also listed on fo. 61a is what is clearly Reinhard the Elder, Count of Solms-Lichtenstein's manual on fortification techniques: *Eyn gesprech eynes alten erfarnen kriegssmans vnd bawmeysters mit eynem jungen hauptmann: welcher massen eyn vester bawe fürzuonemen unnd mit nütz des herren mög vollenfürt werden*, printed in Mainz by Schöffer in 1535, and Sextus Julius Frontinus's *Strategmaticon* in German translation, possibly that published in Mainz by Schöffer in 1532 (fo. 62b). Other works on fortification are harder to identify, e.g.,'Ein bericht etzlicher Krigsgebeud von pasteien Bollwerg Wäll unnd graben' and 'Ein buch eine Festung zu besetzen zuerhalten unnd widerumb wie dieselbe zugewinnen in welscher sprach' (fo. 63a). At fos 63a to 64a in the same section there is a whole series of books on artillery by Walter Rivius, Fronsperger, and other unnamed authors. The only Latin work in this section is Giacomo Lanteri's *Libri duo de modo substruendi terrena munimenta ad urbes atque oppida . . . quibus aditus hosti praecludatur,* etc.—Venice 1564) (fo. 64a).

In the section on architecture we find on fo. 87a Albrecht Dürer's *Unnderricht zu befestigung der Schloß Stedte unnd flecken,*Vitruvius in French and an unidentified work called 'Wie man Festungen bawen unnd dieselbe wider beschissen sol', which the inventory tells us was in Italian.

The 1580 inventory is very similarly organised to that of 1574 with most of the same categories, though the order is different and titles are given in a much more shorthand way.[20] From the fact that the total number of works has grown to 2,354, we can see that the Elector was purchasing books at the rate of about a hundred a year. One of the categories that increased in the course of the six years between the first and second inventories was Italian works on fortification.

In the military books section in the 1580 inventory ('Kriegsbucher') we find what can be identified as Girolamo Cataneo's *Tauole breuißime per sapere con prestezza quante file vanno al formare una giustissima battaglia* (Brescia 1563), while the architecture section (fo. 51b) has been augmented by what are clearly Girolamo Maggi and Jacomo Fusto Castriotto's *Della fortificatione delle Città* (Venice 1564), Abel Foullon's *Descrittione, et vso dell'Holometro per saper misurare tutte le cose* (Venice 1564), Girolamo Cataneo's *Libro nuouo di fortificare, offendere & difendere* (Brescia 1564) and Guillaume Du Choul's *Discorso sopra la castrametatione, et disciplina militare de' Romani . . . tradotto in lingua Toscana per M. Gabriel Symeoni*. Whether this is the edition published in Lyons in 1556 or that in Padua in 1558 is not specified. The same work is also listed in the military books section. The architecture section also includes *Ciuitates Orbis terrarum* by Georgius Braun and Franz Hohenberg, (Cologne 1575), which is easy to identify, but 'Del modo di misura', 'Libro del misurar con la vista', 'Contrafet aller furnemsten Festung in der welt', and 'Allerley festungen, porten und wappen', which are not. But in general we can see that, in the 1570s, during the decade that Rocco di Linar was in his service, August was assiduously collecting works in Italian on fortification techniques and must therefore have been studying the subject himself.

All of this presents the picture of a modern, forward-looking prince with a personal interest in science and technology and its practical application for his territory. August was, however, concerned simultaneously to put forward precisely the opposite image and did so by having recourse to the myth of chivalry.

---

[20] SLUB Bibl. Arch. I vol. 21.

August as Knight in Armour

Jousting, in which two knights in armour and on horseback charge each other with lances, is a tournament exercise that mimics the lance charge of the heavy cavalryman on the battlefield. In order to make it safer the tilt barrier was invented—a wooden fence which separated the two knights and made it more likely that the lance would shatter on impact rather than penetrate the opponent's armour. In the tilt the lances were often also rebated so as to make them less deadly. But central to both jousting and tilting was the man-to-man collision of two riders in heavy armour, each riding a war-horse bred for strength rather than speed, each aiming to unseat his opponent by knocking him off his mount by sheer force (though of course accuracy of aim and dexterity were also needed).[21] In spite of the growth in importance of the pike and the crossbow in actual warfare and the steady development of firearms, the heavy cavalryman wielding a lance was still an important factor on the battlefield up to the middle of the sixteenth century. It is therefore not surprising that Elector August, like other princes of his day, should assiduously practise jousting into the second half of the sixteenth century.[22] Between 1543 and 1566, indeed, we know that August jousted at least 55 times and was only unhorsed in five of these encounters. The jousts took place in the course of twenty-eight different tournaments, fourteen of them in Dresden (in 1543, 1545, 1551, 1553, 1554, 1555, 1556, 1557, 1558, 1559, 1563, 1564 and 1566). These were held to celebrate such events as christenings (for instance, those of Moritz's son Alexander in 1554 and of his own daughter Dorothea in 1563) or to honour important visitors such as Archduke Ferdinand of Austria in 1556 or the Emperor Maximilian II in 1564. Other tournaments took place either in Saxony in such places as Torgau (in 1548 for the wedding of Ernst, Duke of Braunschweig-Grubenhagen, and Margarethe, Duchess of Pomerania, and in 1562), Meissen (1549) or Leipzig (in 1561 for the wedding of Willem I, Prince of Orange-Nassau, to his niece Anna) or in neighbouring territories such as Merseburg (1544), Weissenfels (1551) or Weimar (1555). August also participated in tournaments further afield. For instance he went to Minden in 1545 for the wedding of his sister Sidonie to Erich II,

---

[21] Anglo (1988).
[22] Schnitzer (1999), p. 349 f.

Duke of Braunschweig-Calenberg, he visited Copenhagen in 1557 and again in 1559 for the coronation of his brother-in-law Fredrik II as King of Denmark, Celle in 1561 for the wedding of Wilhelm, Duke of Braunschweig-Lüneburg, to his sister-in-law Dorothea, Princess of Denmark, and Berlin in 1560 for the wedding of Julius, Duke of Braunschweig-Lüneburg to Hedwig, Margravine of Brandenburg. He was in Berlin again in December 1561 for Wilhelm of Rosenberg's wedding.

After the middle of the sixteenth century, however, the function of the cavalryman on the battlefield changed.[23] Because of the development of the pike, the crossbow and the firearm, the cavalryman now needed to be more mobile and more agile, be able to ride faster horses of Arab blood and be more versatile in the use of a range of weapons from lance to sword to handgun. Tournament contests that demonstrated and trained speed and sureness of aim now superseded the joust and the tilt. The most popular of these was the running at the ring. In this exercise the rider galloped up the lists towards a small metal ring divided into fields hanging above shoulder height between two pillars and attempted to carry it off on the point of his light wooden lance. He was awarded points according to which of the fields he pierced. Speed of movement and sureness of eye were more necessary for success than sheer strength.

In 1574 the court at Dresden staged a running at the ring for the first time instead of a joust or tilt.[24] It was put on for the carnival season on 23 February and conformed to emerging European practice in that all the participants were costumed and that many groups of contestants were accompanied by floats or festival cars.[25] As was usual in such contests, the participants processed onto the lists before the competition to show off their floats and costumes. (Armour was now unnecessary, since the contestants were no longer competing against each other.) They were divided into groups or 'inventions', each one usually consisting of the contestant with attendants on

---

[23] For a more complete account of this development see Watanabe-O'Kelly (1990).

[24] It is depicted in the illustrated manuscript account by Daniel Bretschneider the Elder (1550–1623) (Bretschneider 1574). This magnificent manuscript is an oblong folio of 98 leaves, in pen, ink, wash, gouache and gilding on paper.

[25] Compare, for instance, the running at the ring held in Vienna in 1571 for the wedding of Karl, Archduke of Austria, and Maria, Duchess of Bavaria. The official account is Wirre (1571). See Watanabe-O'Kelly (1992) for more information about tournaments at European courts in general.

horseback or on foot, riders and musicians. August's tournament practice thus kept pace with international trends, which in turn were dictated by advances in actual warfare.

How surprising it is, therefore, that in 1584, two years before his death, August should commission a manuscript tournament book recording his success in the now outdated jousts in which he had not taken part for almost twenty years. He had his court painter Heinrich Göding portray him as a knight in armour practically invincible as a jouster. The tournament book is in oblong folio and consists of fifty-five sheets of parchment with gouache paintings.[26] It is entitled:

> Vorzeichnus vnd warhafftige eigentliche Contrafacturen aller Scharff rennen vnd Treffen, so der Durchlauchtigste hochgeborne Fürst vnd Herr Herr Augustus Hertzog zu Sachßen etc. vor vnnd inn S. Churf. G. Churfürstlichen Regierung mitt sonderlicher geschicklichkeit auch großer Lust vnnd verwunderung aller Zuseher gantz Ritterlich vnd rühmlich gethan vnd verbracht hat auch Zu wes Zeitt an welchem ortt vnnd mitt was Personen ein Jedes Rennen geschehen, Zu Ewigem löblichem gedechtnus S. Churf. G. geübtem mannlichen Ritterspielen deroselben Posteritet also fürgestellet.
>
> (Register and actual true depictions of all the jousts à outrance and à plaisance that the most noble and exalted prince and lord, lord August Duke of Saxony, previous to and during his Electoral reign executed with especial skill in a most chivalrous and praise-worthy fashion and to the great delight and amazement of all observers. With the date and place and with what persons each joust was carried out. To the eternal praiseworthy memory of the manly knightly exercises executed by his Electoral Highness hereby presented to posterity.)

This manuscript suffered so badly in World War II that it can no longer be examined. We can gain some idea of it from the fourteen double pages reproduced from it in 1910 by Erich Haenel and from the details he gives of the whole work.[27] Each double-page spread depicts a joust between Elector August and another knight and contains a small panel documenting where and when the contest took place, who unseated whom and who August's adversary was. Just as the title of the whole work lays great stress on the person of August himself, on his manly prowess and on his knightly persona as a jouster, so do the depictions. In the fifty-five courses depicted, August

---

[26] SLUB Mscr. Dresd. J 44.
[27] Haenel (1910).

was unseated only five times. The paintings thus show us again and again August magnificent on horseback, looming over his opponent, who is shown sprawling on the ground or is hanging in an undignified manner half off his horse. The text panels emphasise August's superiority as a contestant, for we read time and time again after August's adversary is named: 'der ist alleine gefallen' (he alone was unseated). Once, at a tournament in 1551 in Weissenfels, the text tells us that August ran against Otto von Ebeleben but 'wegen der geule ist nichts draus wordenn' (because of the horses nothing came of it).[28] Nonetheless, so we are told, they continued fighting on foot and Ebeleben was brought to his knees. August has again demonstrated his manly prowess. In Copenhagen in 1557 the knight Georg Lucke broke his lance in two against August but the text tells us that Lucke was the only one to be unhorsed.[29] The tournament book thus shows August as an individual who in his own person is brave, strong, skilful and indomitable. Furthermore, the tournament book shows him demonstrating his personal strength and prowess all over northern and central Europe. At the time the manuscript was completed, we should remember, August was an elderly man with a white beard who walked with the aid of a stick, as can be seen in the famous portrait of him by the court painter Cyriacus Reder dating to 1586.[30]

The Tournament Book Tradition

In commissioning a beautifully illustrated tournament book August was drawing on an established German sixteenth-century tradition.

The Emperor Maximilian I (1459, r. 1508–1519) provided subsequent rulers with a model of image-making that was not surpassed in its extensiveness, grandeur and consistency for many centuries. He commissioned a whole series of works that portrayed him as a knight participating in various sorts of chivalric combat and for the execution of which he drew on the services of the foremost artists of his day and used both manuscript and the new art of printing in this endeavour. The richly-illustrated verse romance known as the

---

[28] Plate no. 17 in the MS; Haenel (1910), p. 40.
[29] Plates nos. 37 and 38 in the MS; Haenel (1910), p. 44.
[30] Cyriacus Reder, Kurfürst August von Sachsen. 1586. Oil on canvas. Rüstkammer Dresden, Inv. no. H 92.

Theuerdanck was published in 1517 (we know that a team of twenty artists and writers were engaged in its production) and was one of the works in August's library.[31] Two other works were intended for publication but were unfinished at Maximilian's death. One of them is the courtly verse epic *Freydal* (begun in 1502), for which there are 255 drawings of which some were made into woodcuts, and which depict Maximilian's participation in various tournaments. The *Weißkunig* is a prose novel illustrated with 236 woodcuts which portrays Maximilian as the hero setting out to woo his lady.[32] In all of these works, Maximilian presents himself as a chivalric hero under various pseudonyms. He also commissioned an actual tournament book, an illustrated manuscript by Hans Burgkmair the Elder (1453–1530), completed by his son Hans Burgkmair the Younger (c. 1500–c. 1560) in 1555.[33] This tournament book is in three parts. The first presents a kind of illustrated catalogue of fifteen different kinds of tournament contest, rather than depicting encounters between individuals, and the only date mentioned is 1511. The second part presents a number of late fifteenth-century tournaments in which Maximilian took part, while the third part added by Hans Burgkmair the Younger in 1553 describes tilts for the wedding of Graf Jakob von Muntfurtt and Katharina Fugger. Unlike the narrative works mentioned above and unlike August's tournament book, therefore, this tournament book is not focussed exclusively on the person of Maximilian.

Much more similar to August's are two tournament books from Saxony and one from Bavaria. The first of the Saxon works is the tournament book of Johann the Constant (b. 1468, r. 1525–1533) covering tournaments he took part in between 1487 and 1527.[34] It is very extensive and depicts 125 courses. Though all the depictions give the names of the contestants, only the first fifteen give the outcome, telling us that Duke Johann was unhorsed only once. The second Saxon tournament book is that of Duke Johann Friedrich the Magnanimous (1503–1554, r. 1532–47) and dates to 1543. This

---

[31] Maximilian (1517). It was beautifully printed to look like a manuscript and appears in the 1574 inventory of August's library (SLUB Bibl. Arch 20) on fol 55a as 'Teurdancks gefehrliche geschichte und taten reimweis'.

[32] This was not printed until 1775.

[33] Hefner-Alteneck (1853).

[34] Das Turnierbuch Johanns des Beständigen (Mscr. Dresd. J16) is also in the SLUB in Dresden but inaccessible because of war damage. Some of the illustrations are reprinted in Haenel (1910).

consists of 146 representations of tournaments on 334 pages (that is, on 167 leaves of paper). Again, only the names of the contestants are given and the outcome is not indicated at all. The tournament book of Wilhelm IV, Duke of Bavaria (b. 1493, r. 1508–1550), dates to 1541 and consists of 35 parchment sheets.[35] It depicts Duke Wilhelm in thirty-one tournaments from 1510 to 1524. Again, the text does not usually tell us which combatant was victorious. August himself also owned an unidentified manuscript tournament book. Among the works in his *Kunstkammer* was a work simply labelled 'Ein gar alt thurnirbuch von allerley alten Rüstungen und Kührißen, wie dieselben vor alters geführet worden' (A very old tournament book with all kinds of old suits of armour and cuirasses, as they were used of yore).[36]

A printed work that August had in his library was the famous compendium of thirty-six medieval tournaments between 938 and 1487 by the herold Georg Ruexner or Rixner.[37] The original edition appeared in 1530 in Simmern and was dedicated to Johann II, Pfalzgraf von Pfalz-Simmern. So popular was this work that it was reprinted in 1532, 1566, 1570, 1578/9 and 1586 and it was the 1566 edition that August owned.[38] The focus in Ruexner differs from that of the manuscript tournament books in that it is on the group, not on the individual. Both the illustrations as well as the text are concerned with the tournament as the defining activity of a noble class, whose lineage makes them 'turnierfähig', that is, entitled to take part in a tournament because they have sixteen quarterings. This genealogical aspect is picked up by those manuscript tournament books that are even later than August's, for instance, Codex

---

[35] Schenckh (1541). Its actual title is: Hierinnen seyen beschrieben vnnd aigenntlich vertzaichnet alle gestäch, Rennen vnnd ritterspil, So der durchleüchtig furst, mein genediger herr hörtzig Wilhelm in seinem leben vom anfanng bis zum endte besitzlich, Ritterlich vnnd Vällig verpracht vnnd gethan hat, auch mit wem vnnd wie vnnd an welichem tag, auch in was form, gestalt vnnd libereyen mit Rossen, deckhen vnnd geschmuckten allennthalben, wie dann die gesechen worden sein, diß ist alles hie nach mit Varben lauter ausgestrichen vnnd gemaldt etc. There is another copy or version on paper in the Bayerische Staatsbibliothek in Munich at Cod germ 1929.

[36] Ußlaub (1587), fo. 166b.

[37] Ruexner (1566).

[38] SLUB Bibl. Arch 20 fo. 47a makes clear that Ruexner's compendium and the account of the tournament staged in Vienna in 1566 by Archduke Maximilian are part of the same volume, so this is therefore the 1566 edition.

Rossianus 711 in the Vatican Library.[39] These works depict the same thirty-six tournaments as in Ruexner and indeed are based on his book. Usually, however, they were put together for a single family (e.g. that of von Helmstatt) to document their participation in tournaments over centuries or for a tournament society (e.g. the Kraichgauer Ritterschaft).[40] The focus here is not on the combat as such (we never even see the points of the lances or find out who was victorious or not) but rather on the devices and coats of arms. These late tournament books are thus not at all comparable to August's.

Indeed, it would appear from the above that his tournament book is *sui generis*, unusual not just in that it is so late for a princely tournament book, but also for the insistent emphasis it places on the prowess and person of August himself. It is not chivalric combat *per se* that is being celebrated nor the society which gave rise to it but the bravery and skill of one man. If it is surprising that August should construct this myth for himself so late in the century, it is even more striking that his successors should develop and publicise it further.

The Myth of Elector August

Elector August died in 1586. His son Christian I (b. 1560, r. 1586–1591) was another forward-looking prince deeply interested in the most modern impulses to come from Italy. His short reign began in February and by April he had already given orders to gather the necessary stonemasons and other craftsmen for the construction of a new stables in Dresden, an Italianate Renaissance building with *sgraffito* decoration.[41] The foundation stone was laid already on 6 June 1586 and the building was completed by 1588.[42] This U-shaped building, situated in the centre of Dresden next to the Palace, could house 128 horses on the ground floor and was one of the most magnificent stable buildings in the Empire in its day.[43] The new stables were intended as a symbol of the modernising aims of the new Elector.

---

[39] Published as facsimiles with an afterword by Kurras (1963) and (1996).
[40] Kurras (1992), p. 15.
[41] May (1992).
[42] Müller (1700), p. 192.
[43] See Götz (1964).

Though the actual architects were the local men Paul Buchner and Hans Irmisch, some of the inspiration at least came from Giovanni Maria Nosseni (1544–1620), another Italian architect who had been brought to Dresden by Elector August in 1575, and who was influenced by the buildings he had seen in Florence. In addition, Nosseni designed the so-called Long Corridor or 'Langer Gang' (also built between 1586 and 1588), an arcade of twenty-one arches 100 metres long with a covered upper storey linking the Stables with the Palace. Christian I made this upper storey into a portrait gallery celebrating his ancestors. It was lined with life-size paintings of the Wettins going back quite fictitiously to 90 BC. Accompanying each portrait was a motto and a depiction of that Wettin's famous deeds. Each generation of subsequent Electors added its own portraits to the gallery. The diplomat and art dealer Philipp Hainhofer visited it in 1629 and described the portraits of the then ruler Johann Georg I and his four sons.[44] Anton Weck in his description of the Stables published in 1680[45] lists the fifty portraits up to and including Johann Georg II. The 'Long Corridor' was thus a continuing monument to the Electoral family.

For this space celebrating the dynasty, Christian I also commissioned twenty-nine wooden panels depicting the jousts in which Elector August had taken part between 1543 and 1566, the same ones that are celebrated in the tournament book. They were all by Heinrich Göding, are datable to 1589/90 and were based on Göding's own paintings in the tournament book.[46] In contrast to the latter, the panels, which hung under the windows in the gallery, place each pair of knights in an architectural setting, for instance, in a town square, and position other figures round about as seconds or onlookers. Nine of the panels still survive today in the Armoury (Rüstkammer) in Dresden.[47] The windows of this gallery looked down onto a courtyard called the Stallhof, closed off on three sides by the Stables and on the fourth by the Langer Gang. The Stallhof was designed to accommodate the running at the ring. The first such contest took place there in 1588 and the bronze pillars which we see there today

---

[44] Hainhofer (1629), p. 189.
[45] Weck (1680).
[46] Bäumel (1995), pp. 6–9.
[47] Bäumel (1995), pp. 80–84. *Vermißte Kunstwerke* (1990), pp. 50–53, gives descriptions of the remaining twenty panels which are missing since the war.

date from the year 1601. As Schnitzer points out, the gallery func-
tioned into the eighteenth century as a kind of royal box from which
special guests could watch equestrian contests in the courtyard below.[48]
There was therefore a connection between the depictions of August
jousting and the runnings at the ring and at the head taking place
below.

But the really significant thing is that these depictions should have
been commissioned at all and should have been placed in such a
prominent position. They were clearly drawn to the attention of visitors. The above-mentioned Philip Hainhofer comments on the paintings and on the fact that August ran fifty-five times and was only
unhorsed on five occasions.[49] He can only have known that if told
it on his guided tour. The official account of the Dresden *Kunstkammer*
by Tobias Beutel in 1671 and of the city of Dresden by Anton Weck
in 1680 also pick out these paintings for comment. Beutel emphasises that one of the contestants unhorsed by August is the future
Emperor Ferdinand I, while Weck stresses that these were difficult
knightly exercises ('mühesamer Ritterlicher Ubungen').[50] August was
thus being celebrated a hundred years after his death as a doughty
knight of yore.

But posterity, exemplified by the same two writers, also saw August
as a master of science and technology. The *Kunstkammer*, for instance,
turned into a monument to its founder, with at least one portrait of
him in every room, as we can see from the inventory of the contents taken in 1640. This is corroborated by the account of the
Kunstkammer given by Weck. Weck begins his description of it by
telling us that August's portrait is in every room because he is 'ein . . .
in Mechanicis und Mathematicis wohlerfahrener Potentat und Herr/
gleichsam dieses wichtigen Wercks Fundator und Urheber' (a ruler
most learned in technology and mathematics, both the founder and
'onlie begetter' of this important collection).[51] Beutel too, in his
account of the *Kunstkammer*, announces it as August's legacy to posterity, telling us that it was founded in 1560.

One of the founding legends of the Wettins as Electors of Saxony
was thus of Elector August both as modern man and also as late

[48] Schnitzer (1999), p. 348.
[49] Hainhofer (1629), p. 190.
[50] Beutel (1671), fo. J4ʳ; Weck (1680), p. 58.
[51] Weck (1680), p. 34 f.

medieval knight. In the former role he was a moderniser, in the forefront of the technical and scientific developments of his day, and thus looking to Italy, but as the latter he aligned himself in a consciously anachronistic piece of image-making with the Germanic chivalry of his ancestors. Chivalry, which celebrated individual heroism and strength and which distinguished the armigerous knight from the foot-soldier or the military technician, was needed as part of the panoply of power of the prince precisely because real warfare was becoming the business of the well-drilled regiment, of the professional soldier and of the specialist. Where is the glory for the prince in conducting a siege in which the artillery specialist and the fortification engineer determine the outcome? The myth is the necessary concomitant for him of the new reality. In the case of the Elector of Saxony, guardian of Lutheranism, leader of the Protestant cause in the Empire, one must at least ask whether his image as knight in armour had in addition an essential quality of 'Germanness', at a period when Protestants sought to appear to be the only true Germans.

Bibliography

Primary Sources

Beutel, Tobias (1671) *Chur=Fürstlicher Sächsischer stets grünender hoher Cedern=Wald/ Auf dem grünen Rauten=Grunde Oder Kurtze Vorstellung/ Der Chur=Fürstl. Sächs. Hohen Regal=Wercke/ Nehmlich: Der Fürtrefflichen Kunst=Kammer/ und anderer/ Seiner Chur=Fürstl. Durchl. hochschätzbaren unvergleichlich wichtigen Dinge/ allhier beyder residentz Dreßden/ Aus schuldiger Danckbarkeit zu GOtt/ vor so grosse/ dem Durchleuchtigsten Chur=Hause Sachsen/ verliehene Wohlthaten und Schätze . . .*, Dresden: gedruckt bey den Bergischen Erben. Anno 1671.
Bretschneider, Daniel (1574) Contrafactur des Ringrennens, So . . . Augustus Hertzogk zu Sachsen, des heiligen Römischen Reichs Ertzmarschalch vnd Churfürst . . ., den 23 February 1574 im Fastnacht alhier zu Dreßden im Churfürstlichem Schlosse gehalten, SLUB Mscr. Dresd. K 2.
Hefner-Alteneck, Joseph von (1853) *Hans Burgkmairs Turnier=Buch*, ed. Joseph von Hefner-Alteneck (Frankfurt: 1853). Facsimile (Dortmund: 1978).
Fronsperger, Leonard (1571) *Von Kayserlichem Kriegßrechten, Malefitz und Schuldhändlen, Ordnung und Regiment sampt derselbigen und andern hoch oder niderigen Befelch, Bestallung, Staht und Empter, zu Rosß und Fuß, an Geschütz und Munition, in Zug und Schlachtordnung.* Frankfurt a.M.: Hieronymus Feyerabend, gedruckt von Martin Lechler 1571.
Hainhofer (1629) *Des Augsburger Patriciers Philipp Hainhofer Reisen nach Innsbruck und Dresden*, ed. by Oscar Doering, Vienna: Carl Graeser, 1901.
Maximilian I, Holy Roman Emperor (1517) *Die geuerlicheiten vnd einsteils der geschichten des loblichen streytparen vnd hochberumbten helds vnd Ritters herr Tewrdanncks*, Nürnberg: Johann Schönsperger 1517. By Maximilian I and Melchior Pfinzing with woodcuts by Hans Schäufelin, Leonhard Beck and Hans Burgkmair the Elder.
Maximilian I, Holy Roman Emperor (1755) *Der Weiß Kunig. Eine Erzehlung von den*

Thaten Kaiser Maximilian des Ersten. Von Marx Treitzsaurwein auf dessen Angeben [sic] zusammengetragen, nebst den von Hannsen Burgmair dazu verfertigten Holzschnitten. Herausgegeben aus dem Manuscripte der kaiserl.königl. Hofbibliothek. Wien 1775.

Müller, Johann Sebastian (1700) *Des Chur= und Fürstlichen Hauses Sachsen/ Ernestin= und Albertinischer Linien/ Annales von Anno 1400. bis 1700 . . .,* Weimar/ in Verlegung Johann Ludwig Gleditsch Buchhändlers in Leipzig/ Anno 1700.

Ruexner, Georg (1566) *Thurnier Buch. Von Anfang, Vrsachen, vrsprung, vnd herkommen, der Thurnier im heyligen Römischen Reich Teutscher Nation/ Wie viel offentlicher Landthurnier/ von Keyser Heinrich dem ersten dieses Namens an/ biß auff den jetztregierenden Keyser Maximilian den andern/ unsern Allergnädigsten Herrn/ und in welchen Stetten die alle gehalten/ Auch durch welche Fürsten/ Graffen/ Herren/ Ritter/ und vom Adel/ dieselben jeder zeyt/ besucht worden. . . .* Frankfurt am Main:Sigmund Feyerabend 1566.

Schenckh (1541) *Das Turnierbuch Wilhelms IV. Von Bayern.* Text by Hans Schenckh, paintings by Hans Ostendorfer, 1541 (cgm 2800 Bayerische Staatsbibliothek, Munich). Reprinted in black and white in: *Miniaturen aus Handschriften der Kgl. Hof- und Staatsbibliothek in München,* ed. Georg Leidinger, Munchen 1912. 3 Abt. 1–2.

Ußlaub, David (1587) Inventarium uber des Churfürsten zu Sachsenn und Burggrauen zu Magdeburgk etc meines gnedigsten hern Kunst Cammernn in Ihrn Churf. Gnaden Schloß und Vehstunge zu Dreßden: Wie desselben Vornehme sachen, Kunststücke und Zugehoriger Vorradt iedes besondern Sortirt und Ordiniert wordenn und nachuolgendenn Orten Zubefinden. Inuentirtt vnd aufgericht Anno 1587.

Weck, Anton (1680) *Der Chur=Fürstlichen Sächsischen weitberuffenen Residentz=und Haupt=Vestung Dresden Beschreib: und Vorstellung/ Auf der Churfürstlichen Herrschafft gnädigstes Belieben in Vier Abtheilungen verfaßet/ mit Grund; und anderen Abrißen/ auch bewehrten Documenten erläutert durch Ihrer Churfürstlichen Durchl. zu Sachsen/ etc. Rath/ zu den Geheimen: und Reich=Sachen bestalten Secretarium und Archivarium Antonium Wecken.* Nürnberg/ In Verlegung Johann Hoffmanns/ Buch: und Kunsthändler/ Gedruckt daselbst bey Christian Sigismund Froberger. Anno MDCLXXX.

Secondary Literature

Anglo, Sydney (1988), 'How to win at tournaments: the technique of chivalric combat', *The Antiquaries Journal* 68 (1988), 248–64.
——. (2000) *The Martial Arts of Renaissance Europe* (New Haven and London: 2000).
Bäumel, Jutta (1995) *Die Rüstkammer zu Dresden. Führer durch die Ausstellung im Semperbau* (Munich, Berlin: 1995).
Blaschke, Karlheinz (1983) *Moritz von Sachsen, ein Reformationsfürst der zweiten Generation* (Göttingen: 1983).
Castor, Markus (2000), 'Rocco di Linar und die *Mathematica Militaris* der Dresdner Fortifikation in italienischer Manier', in *Elbflorenz. Italienische Präsenz in Dresden 16.–19. Jahrhundert,* ed. Barbara Marx (Dresden: 2000), 101–34.
Dombrowski, Damian (2000) 'Dresden-Prag: Italienische Achsen in der zwischenhöfischen Kommunikation', in *Elbflorenz. Italienische Präsenz in Dresden 16.–19. Jahrhundert,* ed. Barbara Marx (Dresden: 2000), 65–99.
Götz Wolfgang, *Deutsche Marställe des Barock,* (München, Berlin: 1964).
Haenel, Erich (1910) *Der sächsischen Kurfürsten Turnierbücher* (Frankfurt a.M:. 1910).
Kurras, Lotte (1963) *Turnierbuch der Kraichgauer Ritterschaft* (Munich: 1963).
——. (1992) *Ritter und Turniere. Ein höfisches Fest in Buchillustrationen des Mittelalters und der frühen Neuzeit* (Stuttgart, Zurich: 1992).
——. (1996) *Das grosse Buch der Turniere. Alle glanzvollen Ritterfeste des Mittelalters* (Stuttgart, Zurich: 1996).

Marx, Barbara (2000, a) *Elbflorenz. Italienische Präsenz in Dresden 16.–19. Jahrhundert*, ed. Barbara Marx (Dresden: 2000).

——. (2000, b) 'Künstlermigration und Kulturkonsum. Die Florentiner Kulturpolitik im 16. Jahrhundert und die Formierung Dresdens als Elbflorenz', in Bodo Guthmüller (ed.), *Deutschland und Italien in ihren wechselseitigen Beziehungen in der Renaissance*, (Wiesbaden: 2000), 211–97.

May, Wolfgang (1992) 'Die höfische Architektur in Dresden unter Christian I.', in *Dresdner Hefte* 29 (1992), 63–72.

Papke, Eva (1997) *Festung Dresden. Aus der Geschichte der Dresdner Stadtbefestigung* (Dresden: 1997).

'Sächsische Landesbibliothek, Dresden' (1997) in Bernhard Fabian (ed.), *Handbuch der Historischen Buchbestände in Deutschland*, vol. 17 Sachsen A-K, ed. Friedhilde Krause (Hildesheim, Zurich, New York: 1997).

Schnitzer, Claudia (1999) *Höfische Maskeraden. Funktion und Ausstattung von Verkleidungsdivertissements an deutschen Höfen der Frühen Neuzeit* (Tübingen: 1999).

Vermißte Kunstwerke (1990). *Vermißte Kunstwerke des Historischen Museums Dresden* (Dresden: 1990).

Watanabe-O'Kelly, Helen (1990) 'Tournaments and their Relevance for Warfare in the Early Modern Period', *European History Quarterly* 20 (1990), 451–63.

Watanabe-O'Kelly, Helen (1992) *Triumphall Shews. Tournaments at German-Speaking Courts in their European Context 1580–1730* (Berlin: 1992).

CHAPTER NINE

SOLDADOS PLATICOS AND CABALLEROS: THE SOCIAL DIMENSIONS OF ETHICS IN THE EARLY MODERN SPANISH ARMY*

Fernando González de León

The scholarship on early modern Spanish theory of war is quite rich, especially in the field of *jus ad bellum* (theories and questions concerning the legitimacy of war) and its application to the conquest of America. The various approaches and systems of humanist pacifists such as Juan Luis Vives and neo-scholastic theologians and founders of international law of the School of Salamanca such as Francisco de Vitoria and and Francisco Suárez, have been the subject of excellent studies. In addition, intellectual historians have explored the portrayal of the sixteenth century Spanish soldier and his evolving ethos in contemporary novels and treatises, while others, including literary critics, have examined with varying degrees of historical rigor and plausibility the perspectives extant in the writings of leading chroniclers and conquistadors.[1]

This essay will take a new and different path. Leaving aside the New World context, the *jus ad bellum* controversies, as well as the pronouncements of civilian theorists and literary authors, it will focus instead on *jus in bello*, the ideals and practices of war proposed and enforced by members of the Spanish military during the longest armed conflict of the early modern era: the Eighty Years War in the Netherlands (1567–1659). As Geoffrey Parker points out, practitioners very seldom wrote about campaign ethics, but in the case of the Low Countries war we can rely on a large number of memoirs as well as polemical and technical treatises produced by Spanish

* I wish to thank Professor Geoffrey Parker who read a draft of this essay and offered his suggestions for improvement.
[1] For the only a few of the most prominent examples of this vast scholarship see the introduction by Anthony Pagden and J. Lawrance to Vitoria (1991), Rivera de Ventosa (1986), Pastor Bodmer (1992) Fernández-Santamaria (1977) and Puddu (1984).

officers and military officials that allow us to compare theory and practice at a depth almost unique in the context of early modern Europe.[2] Based on those sources, this essay will examine the evolution of theoretical and applied Spanish military codes of conduct in their attitude towards civilians and the enemy and will suggest that, though overlooked by recent scholarship, they evolved mainly in accordance with the social composition of the leadership of royal armies and reflected its values.[3]

I. *Precedents and Antecedents, 1481–1567*

The origins of the early modern Spanish military date back to the late fifteenth century when Ferdinand of Aragón and Isabella of Castile, the Catholic Kings, united their forces for the conquest of Granada (1481–1492). Their armies were still an ad hoc collection of foreign mercenaries, seignorial levies (including the forces of the crusading orders of Santiago, Alcántara and Calatrava), local militia and royal troops, most of them led by a landed aristocracy imbued with late medieval ideals of chivalry.[4] The war against the Muslims in Granada was a major social occasion in which the leading Castilian and Aragonese nobles showed off their finest weapons, clothes, and luxurious hospitality.[5] In battle, order, cohesion and discipline, or at least the modern understanding of those terms, were often lacking. Throughout the conflict, individual Spanish noblemen or groups of them left their encampment and went out to engage their Muslim

---

[2] Parker (1994) note 36. Parker's article, though general in scope, is particularly useful for the Spanish context. For two recent explorations within the English and French contexts see Donagan (1988) and Chagniot (1992).

[3] This enterprise has, as far as I am aware, never been carried out before. Gutmann (1980) and Parker (1994) generally overlook social factors in the ameliorating trend they detect in seventeenth century war and focus on other agents such as civilian control of the military. A more complete examination of military mores as practiced by professionals towards each other, though highly worthwhile, lies beyond the reach of this essay. For an examination of the influence of political and military factors on campaign ethics see Parker (1994). For the ideology of the *tercios*, broadly considered, see Quatrefages (1983) 383–399 and Más Chao and Sánchez de Toca (1993).

[4] For an excellent detailed analysis see Albert D. McJoynt's Introduction to Prescott (1995) 13–56.

[5] Prescott (1995) 184–185. For the practice of chivalry in late medieval Castile see Firoozye (1974) 51–66. Garate Córdoba (1967) is also useful.

counterparts in single combat without regard for the overall outcome of the campaign. The Christians probably suffered more casualties in this type of fighting than in the regular siege of Granada, and although King Ferdinand frowned upon it, the custom survived for at least another half century after the fall of the last Muslim outpost in Western Europe.[6]

Certain traditions inherited from the long medieval struggle against Islam, the *Reconquista*, received strong confirmation in this conflict, among them the crusading identification of the cross and the sword, the monarchy and the Catholic religion. However, the war and subsequent royal ordinances led to the rise of artillery, light cavalry and infantry, contributed to the atrophy and incipient obsolescence of heavy cavalry, seigniorial levies and municipal militias and brought into question the leadership role of the high aristocracy in the new royal army. Thus it was not the cavalry but the infantry that formed the backbone of the expeditionary force that don Gonzalo Fernández de Córdoba, 'the Great Captain', took to Italy to fight against the French in 1495.[7]

The Italian Wars (1495–1559), especially its first three decades, marked the emergence of the early modern Spanish army. The Great Captain and his principal subordinates and successors Pedro Navarro and don Fernando de Avalos, Marquis of Pescara, introduced the pike, the arquebus and the musket (which the Spaniards pioneered) and made the infantry the army's most important branch. They also encouraged self-control, discipline and group cohesion among their soldiers and on occasion (though certainly not as a matter of policy) rejected enemy challenges to individual combat.[8] The Spanish army (particularly its infantry) came to be manned largely by the lowest ranking noblemen of the *hidalgo* class and commoners, groups that had no qualms about firearms, the use of 'devious' tactics such as ambushes and the avoidance of battle for the sake of wearing out an enemy.[9] In spite of these changes, the aristocratic way of war, at least in the early campaigns, remained a vibrant option and the treatment of prisoners, especially superior noble officers, was generally quite punctilious. Within the cavalry, challenges (*desafíos*) that led

---

[6] Prescott (1995) 221.
[7] Quatrefages (1983) 1–120.
[8] Hall (1997) 166–179.
[9] Puddu (1984) 58.

to duels, group clashes and tournaments, which Spanish commanders sometimes encouraged and condoned, continued to take place
outside regular organised combat as for instance during the French
blockade of Barletta in 1502–1503.[10] Not surprisingly, noble horsemen remained prone to undisciplined bursts of enthusiasm that sometimes produced disasters such as the cavalry sallies against the French
at the battle of Ravenna (1512).[11] However, after the ordinances and
reforms of 1534, when Emperor Charles V created the infantry
tercio or regiment and the early modern Spanish army acquired its
classic structure, discipline markedly improved. Challenges and single combat, as well as the chivalric ideals that inspired them, became
less prevalent and imperial forces consistently more effective.[12] At the
same time, attitudes towards the enemy hardened considerably. For
instance, in August 1543 Spanish and Italian troops sacked and
burned the city of Dúren in Germany, slaughtering most of its inhabitants and in 1555 don Fernando Alvarez de Toledo, Duke of Alba,
methodically massacred French garrisons in northern Italy.[13]

The works of Spanish military ethics written during this forma-
tive era clearly reflect this transitional mentality. Staunch advocates
of the code of chivalry such as Juan López de Palacio Rubios, author
of the *Tratado del Esfuerzo Belico Heroico* [Treatise on Heroic and
Military Enterprise] (1524), decried the use of deceitful tactics and
long-range weapons, regarded war mainly as a stage for individual
heroism and advised soldiers not to jeopardise their honour for any
reason or cause including the monarch or Spain itself.[14] The military model extant in most contemporary chronicles and novels as
well as in many treatises is that of the *caballero esforzado*, or enter-
prising knight who wages what Raffaele Puddu calls 'courteous warfare', a type of campaigning that allowed for private aristocratic
moments of confrontation and courtesy towards the enemy in co-
existence with, yet outside, the boundaries of regular combat.[15] Writers
of this school emphasised the ethical judgement and moral respon-

---

[10] Ibidem 45–63.
[11] On the battle see Oman (1937) 130–150.
[12] On these reforms see Quatrefages (1983) 49–104 and Oman (1937) 51–62.
For the Spanish army's discipline and cohesion see Williams (1972) 20.
[13] On these events see Más Chao and Sánchez de Toca (1993) 119 and Maltby
(1983) 94.
[14] Puddu (1984) 52–53.
[15] Ibidem 46–47.

sibility of the individual soldier for his actions in accordance with 'natural law, and the common and public rights of people' which in some cases could override 'the laws of the fatherland, the good of the Republic, or the authority or command of the King'.[16]

As the century progressed, the tendency to criticise, marginalise and discard the old ways of war and replace them with tougher attitudes became more pronounced, though the change was gradual and subtle. Even Palacio Rubios had pointedly included the caveat that commanding officers were exempt from the ethical demands of the code since they were not expected to fight in person and Imperial secretary Alfonso de Valdés, in his *Diálogo de Lactancio* also known as *Diálogo de las Cosas Ocurridas en Roma* [Dialogue on the Events in Rome] (1527) presented the protracted sack of the papal city by the troops of Charles V in May of that year as divinely ordained punishment for the sins of the Catholic church. Critics of the code such as the humanist philosopher Juan Ginés de Sepúlveda, in his *Democrates* (1535), dedicated to his patron the Duke of Alba and subtitled *Diálogo Sobre la Compatibilidad Entre la Milicia y la Religión Cristiana* [Dialogue on the Compatibility Between the Military and Christianity], rejected single combat and duelling as contemptible gladiatorial shows.[17] The most thorough Spanish military treatise of the early half of the century, Francisco de Pedrosa's *Arte y Suplemento Remilitar* [Complement of Military Art] (1541) warned its readers that war had to be fought with 'honourable means' but included an entire section on stratagems and tricks.[18] Seven years later, Juan Quixada de Reayo's *Doctrina del Arte de la Cavalleria* [Doctrine of the Art of Cavalry] contained little reference to chivalric ethics or tactics, pointing the way to the purely technical treatise of the late century.

II. *The Dutch Revolt, 1567–1609*

With few exceptions, it was civilian intellectuals and not career soldiers or Spanish military officials who wrote the most important *jus in bello* treatises in the first half of the century. The participation of

---

[16] The words are Fortunio García de Ercilla's in his undated manuscript *Materia de Guerra*, quoted in Puddu (1984) 52.

[17] Sepúlveda (1963) 287–294.

[18] Puddu (1984) 61 Pedrosa (1541) Libro V.

members of the military establishment in these controversies came as a result of King Philip II's struggle to put down the Dutch Revolt and Calvinism in the Netherlands. The outbreak of the conflict in 1566 occurred at a time when Spanish commanders had begun to arrive at a remarkable state of self-conscious professionalism geared, as is almost always the case in modern history, towards the creation of a group identity based on expertise and efficiency and a specialized career path.[19] The emergence of this new professional mentality had eroded the old chivalric code enough to allow the military, religious and political features of the Revolt to bring into sharper focus crucial questions such as the proper treatment of enemy soldiers and prisoners of war, rebellious towns and their populations.

The architect of the Spanish political and military reaction to the Dutch Revolt was the Duke of Alba, the first Captain General (1567–1573) of what would become the Spanish Army of Flanders. In 1567 his forces arrived in the Netherlands and the Duke set out to crush the Calvinist rebellion by all available means. Alba's tactics and professional ideas were remarkably goal-oriented and implied a radical rejection of the old code of arms with its scruples and breaks on aggressive action. The Duke's deeds and words as well as the treatises penned by his successors and subordinates to justify them, came to be known as 'the School of Alba'. Though perhaps counterproductive in the long run and a source of useful propaganda for Spain's detractors through much of modern history, this 'school' nurtured the production of theoretical works by *tercio* officers and officials and contributed to one of the most fruitful periods in the history of European military ethics.

The practice came before the theory, at least in the 1560s and 70s. At a time when high aristocrats monopolised the officer corps of all other European armies, Alba surrounded himself with a general staff distinguished by its many *hidalgo* and commoners, men like Julián Romero, Cristóbal de Mondragón, Sancho de Londoño, Francisco de Valdés and Sancho Dávila, with few or no class connections to the chivalric ethos and who owed their position primarily to their efficacy on the field.[20] Alba, who encouraged their profes-

---

[19] For a succinct explanation of military professionalism see David Trim's Introduction to this volume.

[20] On the social origin of Alba's high command see González de León (1991) Chapter I. It should be noted that none of them used the aristocratic "don" before their names.

sionalism and taught by example, was an austere and focused warrior with a keen understanding of the technical aspects of his trade. He was, for instance, the first General to make the musket a standard infantry weapon and he was widely praised for his attention to the latest fortification techniques. As a matter of tactical principle Alba avoided field battles and preferred, as in the 1568 campaign, to wear out the enemy with dilatory manoeuvres, harassing skirmishes, frequent ambushes and sneak attacks under cover of darkness. He rejected the arguments of those who considered such methods inglorious and maintained the propriety of his tactics, especially in fighting rebels who deserved no better.[21] Quite predictably, when the Dutch commander William of Nassau challenged him to battle and proposed an exchange of prisoners of war, the Duke not only refused but also hanged the heralds that brought the message.[22] Consequently, for almost twenty years challenges, ransoming, single combat and the other trappings and protocols of aristocratic campaigning vanished almost completely and the war became progressively more brutal.

Alba was known as a stern disciplinarian who severely punished his soldiers' spontaneous outbreaks of violence against civilians.[23] However, in order to put down the Dutch Revolt as soon as possible and obviate the endless task of subduing rebel enclaves one by one, the Duke extended his campaigns into the winter. It elevated the combat readiness and professionalism of his officers but alienated them from local civilian life even more than they naturally were and made them more ready to regard the local population as enemies. In addition the Duke began to apply what he called 'terror', that is, acts of exemplary toughness against the rebels designed to intimidate them into immediate surrender.[24] The laws of war as they

---

[21] For Alba's combat doctrine in theory and practice see Ossorio (1945) 280–282, 386–387, 397, 430, 432 and Mendoza (1922) 435–436 and 441–442.

[22] For the episode of the herald see the slightly different versions given by Williams (1972) 79 and Mendoza (1922) 429–430. Given his attitude towards rebels and heretics, Alba's decision to hang the Dutch envoys was entirely predictable and consistent with his earlier declarations during a similar situation in 1546 in Germany. See Avila y Zúñiga (1924) 414 and Núñez Alba (1890) 48. For another incident in which a Dutch herald was shot see Mendoza (1922) 464.

[23] For Alba's disciplinary strictures see Londoño (1943) 20–21 and 72. See also his break-up of an entire *tercio* in 1568 for conducting a private campaign of vengeance against the inhabitants of Heiligerlee in Mendoza (1922) 427.

[24] Alba (1952) III 219–221: Alba to Philip II 2–20–1572 and Ibidem 250–253 Alba to Philip II 28–11–1572.

were commonly understood at the time usually granted a town mercy if it capitulated before the enemy had surrounded it with artillery but rebels were normally excluded from such guarantees.[25] Alba, filled with 'a personal hatred for heretics and traitors', would issue no terms or give quarter to towns that had voluntarily joined the Revolt once he had begun military preparations to take them by force. That was the point of no return beyond which, he warned, there would be only expropriation, extermination and repopulation by foreigners.[26]

Siege warfare began in earnest in the spring of 1572, when dozens of places declared for William of Orange. In September of that year the Army of Flanders pillaged Valenciennes but, for strategic reasons, Mons received terms of surrender.[27] Three weeks later Mechelen (Malines), abandoned by its rebel garrison, was sacked for 'three good days' by Spanish troops, as the Duke sardonically put it, 'in order to refresh them a little'.[28] Zutphen suffered a similar fate and in Naarden the soldiers massacred almost the entire population, burned the town, knocked down its walls and 'flattened everything' (as Alba said on another occasion).[29] After the capitulation of Haarlem in July 1573 Alba ordered the execution of most of the garrison,

---

[25] Parker (1994) 46–51.

[26] Alba (1952) III 502–504 Alba to Philip II 31-8-1573 and for Alba's view of the laws of war, Ibidem 331–338 Alba to Philip II 16–4–1573 and 462–464 "A las villas rebeldes de Flandes" 16–7–1573. For a discussion of Alba's motives, a topic that deserves much further attention, see Maltby (1983) 238–42 and Parker (1994) 49.

[27] For the sack of Valenciennes see Alba (1952) III 128–130 Alba to Philip II 1–6–1572. For the terms given to Mons see Mendoza (1922) 469–470, *Codoin* (1880) LXXV 99–102 "Capitulaciones Tocantes a la Restitución de Mons" 19–9–1572 and Maltby (1983) 237–238. In addition to Alba's need to concentrate his troops elsewhere, the fact that Mons was not defended by rebels may have played a role in his decision. According to Williams (1972) 106–107 royal troops had pillaged Rotterdam in April.

[28] On the events at Mechelen see *Codoin* (1880) LXXV 123–129 "Relación de Cinto Calbi . . . 16–10–1572" 110–114, Ibidem "Copia de Carta Autógrafa del Secretario Estéban Prats, Fecha en Bruselas a Ultimos de Noviembre de 1572," Vázquez (1879–1880) LXXIII 102 and the modern perspectives of Parker (1981) 141 and Maltby (1983) 240.

[29] For the events at Zutphen and Naarden see *Codoin* (1880) LXXV 130–150 "Lo Sucedido Desde el Saco de Malinas Hasta que se Asedió a Harlem" 14–12–1572, Parker (1981) 141–142. For Alba's use of the term "flatten" see Ibidem 161. For his account of the events at Naarden see Alba (1952) III 259–264 Alba to Philip II 19–12–1572.

though he forbade a sack in exchange for payment and spared the majority of townsmen as a special mercy.[30]

No one had any reason to be surprised. The Duke had applied his policy to battles and other field clashes right from the opening of hostilities in 1568. Respect for prisoners of war did not apply to rebels, thus Alba placed rewards on the capture of enemy officers 'dead or alive', took few prisoners (except to interrogate them) and routinely killed most of those he and his commanders seized regardless of rank or status. Once he had them drawn and quartered.[31] Alba's terror led to the immediate unconditional surrender of several major strongholds and for years to come the Dutch would abandon whenever possible fortresses in danger of falling to the *tercios*.[32] However, the resistance of Dutch towns and field forces left with no chance to escape stiffened out of desperation and the certainty that surrender would not save them from what they called 'the furie of Duke d'Alva.'[33] As a result, the royal reconquest of rebel areas slowed down considerably.

Almost at once the war settled into a cycle of brutality and reprisals in which the Dutch paid the Spaniards back in the same coin and with interest. Although the Army of Flanders included Italian and German as well as locally recruited troops, the rebels picked out Spanish prisoners for immediate execution or for torture and mob killings, the latter a procedure in which the Spaniards never engaged.[34] The Dutch too occasionally sacked captured cities, though with less

---

[30] For Haarlem's surrender see Alba (1952) III 458–459 Alba to Philip II 14–7–1573 and *Codoin* (1880) LXXV 242–243 "La orden que dió don Fadrique de Toledo al Conde de Bossu para la entrada en Harlem" undated.

[31] See for instance *Codoin* XXX (1857) 438–443 "Carta autógrafa del maese de campo D. Sancho de Londoño al duque de Albuquerque" 26–4–1568, Ossorio (1945) 391, Mendoza (1922) 412, 413, 426–427, 437, 446, and 480–481 and Alba (1952) III 139–142 Alba to Philip II 13–6–1572. The "fortunate" ones the Duke sent to the galleys: Ibidem 418–423 Alba to Philip II 7–6–1573.

[32] This was usually the case (almost regardless of the size of the besieging force) when the garrison had the chance to escape under cover of darkness. For some of the many examples see Mendoza (1922) 428, 452–453, 457, 477, 496, 515, 523, 529, 530 and *Codoin* (1880) LXXV 199–200 "Copia de Capítulo de Carta del Duque de Alba ... 16–4–1573."

[33] For the quote, supposedly by Count Louis of Nassau see Williams (1972) 85. See also Parker (1981) 160 and Maltby (1983) 243.

[34] For instances of this see Parker (1990) 217, Parker (1981) 133, Trillo (1592) Book I 28–29v, Ossorio (1945) 360 and Mendoza (1922) 427. See the Duke's account of the torture of Captain Hernando Pacheco in Flushing in Alba (1952) III 112–120 Alba to Philip II 23–5–1572, Mendoza (1922) 494 for the drowning of the entire

legal support than the Spaniards.[35] In addition they involved the civilian population in attacks on the Spanish soldiery and pressed peasants and townspeople into service regardless of age or gender which, of course, turned them combatants (as well as rebels) in the eyes of the Spanish.[36] They not only targeted the person of the Duke of Alba and hanged his officers and relatives but were notorious as well for their disregard of the accepted norms of siege warfare.[37] For instance, during the siege of Haarlem, while negotiating their possible surrender, the defenders let in reinforcements and then resolved to go on fighting.[38] When the Spaniards flung over the walls the head of a Dutch Captain, the besieged responded with seven Spanish ones.[39] In addition, they made it a point to taunt and goad the Spaniards by defiling religious images and vestments and torturing to death members of the Catholic clergy (as well as Spanish soldiers) in plain view of the besiegers.[40] Furthermore, they frequently broke their word. Some of the soldiers executed after the fall of Haarlem had violated their earlier vow given at Mons to stop fighting the royal armies and those Alba pardoned after promising to leave the Netherlands rejoined rebel garrisons instead.[41] One of the most provocative violations of the old code of war was false parleys, either the product of confusion among the defenders or a deliberate ploy

garrison of the royal fortress of St. Maartensdijk in May 1573, after it had surrendered and Williams for the killing of prisoners taken by the Dutch at the naval battle of Reimerswaal in January 1574 in Williams (1972) 152.

[35] For the Dutch sack of Roermond see Alba (1952) III 171–174 Alba to Philip II 28–7–1572.

[36] Alba also tried to involve civilians in the war: Ibidem 466 Alba to Francisco de Valdés 20–7–1573.

[37] Parker (1981) 136. For the case of a Spanish Sergeant Major hanged by Count Louis of Nassau at Heilegerlee in May 1568 see Trillo (1592) 29v. See also Williams (1964) 55.

[38] Ossorio (1945) 435. Perhaps the best Spanish account of the siege is Book Nine in Mendoza (1922) 479–493 and the most thorough modern presentation is Maltby (1983) 243–261.

[39] *Codoin* (1880) LXXV 169–174 and 183–184: "Capítulos sacados de cartas escritas por un capitán que está en el campo sobre Harlem a un amigo suyo . . ." 12 to 24–1–1573 and "Copia de Carta que Estéban de Prats Escribió al Secretario Albornoz" (undated).

[40] This happened not only at Haarlem but elsewhere. See Mendoza (1922) 473, 488, 527, and Alba (1952) III 418–423 Alba to Philip II 7–6–1573.

[41] Mendoza (1922) 492, and Alba (1952) III 446 Juan de Albornoz to Gabriel de Zayas 19–7–1573, Ibidem 471–474 Alba to Philip II 28–7–1573 and Ibidem 491–496 Alba to Philip II 30–8–1573. For another instance of broken promises see Mendoza (1922) 497–498.

to lure senior royal commanders out of their trenches under pretense of negotiating a capitulation only to shoot at them with better chance of success. If the town later fell, as happened to Naarden in 1572 and Neuss in 1586, it would be inevitably sacked, maybe levelled, and their garrisons and inhabitants killed to the last person, which would add to the reputation of 'the savage war-dogs of Spain'.[42]

Despite these extenuating circumstances and the fact that his all-out policy was based on the strict observance of contemporary military ethics, Alba's actions provoked tremendous criticism both in Spain and the Low Countries and contributed to his recall in late 1573 as well as to an official investigation that damaged the careers of some of his subordinates.[43] The dour and blunt old Duke became a stock villain and his name a synonym of wanton cruelty in anti-Spanish propaganda, history and art down almost to our own day.[44] What is often overlooked is that his immediate successors at the head of the Army of Flanders were no gentler. Though they maintained a more peaceful demeanor, toned down their language and refrained from personalizing the conflict, they were arguably harsher because, unlike Alba, they did not punish spontaneous outbursts against civilians, had less control over their troops, and made no distinction between towns that had willingly rebelled and those held down by Dutch garrisons.[45]

---

[42] For Naarden see Mendoza (1922) 477 and for Neuss, Vázquez (1879–1880) LXXIII 193–197. [Obviously this version of the events at Naarden in 1572 differs from Parker (1981) 142. See also Maltby (1983) 244–245]. The derogatory reference to the Spaniards is from Dutch propaganda, quoted in Parker (1981) 127. For another example of false parleys in October 1575 see Mendoza (1922) 535–536 and for the royal commanders' fear of coming out of their trenches to negotiate see Vázquez (1879–1880) LXXII 119–120.

[43] Parker (1994) note 49 and Maltby (1983) 267. For a Spanish critique of Alba's rule see the opinions of a prominent political thinker in *Codoin* (1892) CII 473–476 "Discurso de [Fadrique] Furio Ceriol Sobre la Quiete [sic] de Estos Estados" (undated). For English praise see Williams (1972) 142.

[44] See for instance, Goethe's and Beethoven's *Egmont*, Schiller's and Verdi's *Don Carlos*, Donizetti's *Il Duca d'Alba*, the list goes on. A study on Alba's image through the centuries, still to be produced, might yield interesting conclusions about attitudes towards traditional Spain, Counter-Reformation Catholicism and all the Duke stood for and symbolized.

[45] For an instance of Alba's verbal harshness, in this case a vow during the siege of Alkmaar "not to leave a single creature alive but to knife them all" see Alba (1952) III 491–496 Alba to Philip II 30–8–1573.

Alba's replacement as Captain General, don Luis de Requeséns (1573–76), despite failed negotiations with the rebels to obtain the release of a captured General and the exchange of a small number of Dutch prisoners, allowed his forces to sack enemy cities such as Oudevater and exterminate their garrisons and ordered the execution of prisoners of war.[46] He also endorsed and sent to Madrid for approval the high command's plan to break the dikes, flood large areas of the rebellious provinces and end the Dutch Revolt with one crushing blow.[47] Although Philip II vetoed the project out of concern for its propagandistic repercussions, calculated brutality remained a basic tactic, especially after Requeséns' sudden death in March 1576 when the Spanish high command, left leaderless and harassed by the local authorities, decided to take matters into their own hands.[48] In the autumn of 1576 the general staff led by Sancho Dávila responded to the provocations of the civilian government in Brussels by intensifying the policy of terror. The pillaging of Maastricht in October 1576 (described by a Spanish apologist as having been carried out 'with great moderation') and the sack of Antwerp in November occurred before the arrival of don John of Austria, the new Captain General (1576–1578).[49]

---

[46] For the capture of Maximilien de Henin, Count of Bossu and royal Governor of Holland and Zeeland and the ransoming of some thirty Spanish prisoners see Mendoza (1922) 497–498 and 505. Negotiations for the release of Count Bossu, like the peace talks of which they formed part, fell apart in July 1575 and had to be revisited in 1577. [Parker (1981) 166–167 and Mendoza (1922) 551–554]. In the meantime, the Count remained captive and eventually joined the Revolt. Although the Dutch retained (and did not hang) Bossu as a valuable bargaining chip, there is much evidence that the treatment of enemy towns and garrisons did not improve. In the summer of 1575 the English garrison of The Hague was spared against the advice of many of Requeséns' aides and only through the personal intercession of Bernardino de Mendoza who wanted to facilitate his diplomatic mission to Queen Elizabeth. [Mendoza (1922) 515–516]. However, Buren and Oudevater were sacked [Ibidem 526, 528] and in October of that year Spanish troops refused to allow surrender negociations with the French commander of the fortress of "Bommenee" in the island of Schouwen, mounted an unauthorized assault and ultimately slaughtered the entire garrison. [Ibidem 537–538]. On Requeséns position on the handling of prisoners see BZ Carpeta 100, 61 Requeséns to Cavalry General don Alonso de Vargas 25–10–1574 demanding that Dutch captives be killed not ransomed. Obviously I disagree with Parker's assertion that the capture of Bossu marked a watershed in the treatment of prisoners in this war, in Parker (1994) 55.

[47] Parker (1998) 136–138, Cornejo (1580) Book II 60 and Mendoza (1922) 523–524.

[48] According to Mendoza the policy of gentleness to deal with the rebellion was proven "a great illusion, since experience demonstrated . . . that only the remedy of arms could cut off such as a cancer." Mendoza (1922) 539.

[49] Trillo (1592) Book II 86.

The Spanish Fury at Antwerp rivalled the sack of Rome of 1527 as one of the most appalling events of the century, roughly equivalent to the twentieth's Dresden, Hiroshima and Nagasaki. The term 'fury' may suggest a wild outbreak of irrational elan but the five-day rampage in the streets of Antwerp was calmly prepared by the senior officers gathered in the city's huge citadel.[50] It extracted a toll in lives, property and confidence from which Antwerp, then one of the world's major commercial and financial centres, never fully recovered. Though Spanish commanders argued (with some justification) that the sack had not been an atrocity against civilians but a regular engagement leading to a superb military triumph, the resulting outcry (and propaganda bonanza for the Dutch) further blackened the reputation of the *tercios* and forced Philip II to withdraw them from the Netherlands.[51] In a concession almost unique in its time, the monarch agreed to the demands of the local representative assembly, the States General, for a full investigation 'of our military commanders and their subordinates who in any manner or form might have committed crimes either in the Low Countries or in their vicinity' and pledged 'to carry out justice be it in our said Low Countries or in our Spanish kingdoms, or elsewhere we may find it more convenient'.[52]

A second official inquiry into the actions of the Spanish military as well as the first general exchange of prisoners in the war resulted from this agreement but the King sent the *tercios* back to the Low Countries later that year to put down another outbreak of rebellion. Although some of the key figures of the Alba High Command, especially those with close family or personal connections to Duke of Alba such as Sancho Dávila, main instigator of the sack of Antwerp, were not allowed to revisit the scene of their 'victories', their absence did little to alter the army's treatment of the enemy in 1578.[53] Diest received terms of surrender but don John may have ordered the execution of hundreds of prisoners captured at the battle of Gembloux.

---

[50] See for instance AGS E 568, 141 Gerónimo de Roda to Philip II 26–10–1576 as well as Mendoza (1922) 543–549.

[51] For the Spanish version of the events at Antwerp see AGS E 569, 183 Gerónimo de Roda to don John of Austria 9–11–1576. For a thorough though biased modern version see Génard (1875).

[52] Mendoza (1922) 557.

[53] AGS E 568, 222 Lo que en substancia me dijo el cardenal de Granvela que acordase al señor don Juan (undated).

His troops also slaughtered the garrison of Zichem as well as most of the inhabitants of Dahlen, a town that Alba's commanders had spared a decade earlier.[54] A Spanish civilian observer, shocked by such 'great cruelty' concluded 'that the wars in these provinces are worse than they have ever been'.[55]

Some of the campaign memoirs and treatises of military science and law published by Spanish officers and officials of the Army of Flanders during this era provided powerful explanations for these actions. One of Alba's cavalry commanders, don Bernardino de Mendoza, put forth perhaps the most interesting justifications in his *Comentarios de las Guerras de los Paises Bajos* [Commentaries on the Wars in the Low Countries], published in 1591 but composed in the 1570s.[56] Overall Mendoza found little to criticise in the policies of the Duke of Alba and his high command. In fact, he questioned the motives, orthodoxy and loyalty of those who accused the *tercios* of brutality. It was Calvinist heresy that had started and fueled the Revolt 'and not as some have suggested, the excesses of the Spanish army, even if there had been some'.[57] A university-trained gentle-man, Mendoza drew occasional implicit parallels between the impe-rial armies of the Romans and the Spaniards, both engaged in civilising struggles against northern barbarians and artfully combined examples from ancient history with pragmatic, legal and religious arguments to vindicate questionable deeds.[58] Thus he excused the hanging of heralds as a necessary act meant to drive a wedge between the native Catholic and Protestant parties in a kind of conflict in which, as Caesar's *Civil Wars* indicates, ties of family and clientele

---

[54] Petrie (1967) 317, *Codoin* XXX (1857) 438–443 "Carta autógrafa del maese de campo D. Sancho de Londoño al duque de Albuquerque" 26–4–1568 and Vázquez (1879–1880) LXXII 101–103 and 130. Spanish accounts of Gembloux are conflicting but in view of the record and the biases of the chroniclers I am inclined to believe that don John showed no mercy. For alleged Dutch ethical violations that year see Porreño (1899) 273–274.

[55] Quoted in Quatrefages (1983) 390–391.

[56] Mendoza began his work in the early 1570's as a daily record of Alba's cam-paigns (1567–1573) and later extended it to include the first ten years of the war during which he fought at the head of a cavalry company. See Mendoza (1922) 389 "Al Rey Nuestro Señor," dated January 2, 1573 as well as 404, 441, 444–445.

[57] Ibidem 476.

[58] See for instance his account of the Spanish defeat of Heiligerlee in May 1568 which he subtly juxtaposes to the Roman catastrophe at Teotoburger Forest in 9 A.D. Mendoza (1922) 416–417. On Mendoza's life see DeLamar Jensen (1964).

often interfere with energetic campaigning.[59] 'Reason of war' (a recurrent term meaning the primacy of necessity over ethics) and the upholding of 'the reputation of the King's army', would amply justify a ruthless drive for complete victory, since '*soldados pláticos* [understand] that in cases of war weapons and the sword are the lawgivers'.[60] Rebellious towns like Mechelen *ipso facto* deserved to be sacked, but even if superior officers had wished it, it would have been impossible to prevent unpaid soldiers from taking advantage of a victory except at the cost of a crucial loss of authority and respect among the troops.[61] Although his treatise is not an exercise in circumstantial ethics, Mendoza seems particularly concerned with shifting responsibility for the most troubling incidents of the war from the officers to the soldiers, the enemy or the conditions of siege warfare. For example, in describing the horrors at Haarlem, Mendoza suggests that it was the terrible circumstances of the siege that brutalised the Spaniards, that after months in the trenches the soldiers regarded the siege as 'each one's own personal revenge' and would have disobeyed orders to lift it.[62]

Other *tercio* officials apparently did not feel this need to justify Spanish conduct on a piecemeal basis. Balthazar Ayala, Judge Advocate of the Army of Flanders argued in his *De Iure et Officiis Bellicis et Disciplina Militari* [On the Law of War and the Duties Connected with War and on the Military Discipline] (1582), that the laws of war did not apply to rebels because hostilities against them were not real wars but police actions against outlaws in which to keep promises, respect emissaries and property and treat prisoners kindly were optional behaviours.[63] Even in regular wars, ethical boundaries were quite elastic since 'necessity often makes that lawful which otherwise would have been unlawful'.[64] Thus clemency towards defeated enemies, though generally desirable, could and should be put aside when necessary, such as for instance when razing a city could cower an

---

[59] Ibidem 429–530.
[60] Ibidem 477 and the quote in 537.
[61] Ibidem 471.
[62] Ibidem 484 and 486. He makes a similar case for the killing of an enemy garrison in Schouwen in October 1575, and for the sack of Antwerp. Ibidem 537–538, 542–550.
[63] Ayala (1912) 11, 59–60, and 90.
[64] Ibidem 107.

enemy and end a war more quickly.[65] These were also the views of another army official, Luis Valle de la Cerda who in his *Avisos en Materias de Estado y Guerra* [Observations in Matters of State and War], written in 1583, used massive classical and biblical erudition to affirm that the Spanish army had both the duty and the right to fight the Revolt free from traditional ethical restraints and that to criticise its actions or propose peace was naive and harmful since it undermined the self-confidence of the military.[66]

The works of Ayala and others have traditionally been studied exclusively for their political and legal perspectives even though their contents suggest other more pragmatic professional objectives.[67] For instance, the title and subject matter of Ayala's book reveal his concern to explain the war plainly and realistically and to coordinate ethics with the creation of an efficient and disciplined army.[68] In this sense his work does not belong to the neo-scholastic tradition of Vitoria and Suárez but instead falls squarely within what was at the time a new and growing literature, the genre of the 'perfect officer'. In the late sixteenth century, new ideals of military professionalism, or the increasingly common notion among Spanish officers and theorists that soldiers ought to be primarily *soldados pláticos*, disciplined military technicians rather than old-fashioned *caballeros esforzados*, began to marginalise the debate over the morality of the military response to the Dutch Revolt and gave rise to an abundant professional literature.[69] In treatises intended primarily for the education of the 'perfect' career soldier, technical writers in search of discipline and efficiency criticised and proposed outlawing the most disruptive aspects of the chivalric ethos. *Tercio* commander Sancho de Londoño in his *Discurso sobre la Forma de Reducir la Disciplina Militar a Mejor y Antiguo Estado* [Discourse on the Way to Reduce Military Discipline to its Ancient and Better State) (published in 1589 but written twenty years

---

[65] Ibidem 135. This view stands in sharp contrast with that of Diego García de Palacio who restricted the killing of a city's defenders to those who, in an assault, refuse to give up peacefully. García de Palacio (1583) 87vis.

[66] See for instance Valle de la Cerda (1599) 23–24, 31–40, 62–67, 89–93.

[67] See for example, Peralta (1964).

[68] See "Preface Concerning the Law of War" in which Ayala maintains the inseparable nature of military law and discipline. Ayala (1912) i–ix. Furthermore, only Book I deals exclusively with military law. The other two parts pertain to the duties and privileges of military rank.

[69] For an overview and analysis of the vast professional and technical output of Spanish officers in the late sixteenth century see González de León (1996).

earlier) asked his soldiers to work themselves quietly into a fury before attacking but called for the execution of anyone who provoked the enemy or went out to fight in single combat.[70] Others among his colleagues, following in the footsteps of Niccolo Machiavelli, eschewed even the Christian call for mercy and love of enemies.[71] The ideal soldier needed to lay religious qualms aside and understand the nature and demands of his trade. 'The day a man picks up his pike to become a soldier is the day he ceases to be a Christian', declared one of the officers responsible for the plan to break the dikes, Francisco de Valdés, in the genre's most influential work, the *Disciplina y Espejo Militar* [Mirror of Military Discipline] (1586).[72]

Another veteran of the Army of Flanders, Catholic priest and royal military consultant Bernardino de Escalante, offered similar moral advice.[73] In his *Diálogos del Arte Militar* [Dialogues on Military Art] (1583), Escalante tackles one of the central questions of modern *jus in bello*, the responsibility of soldiers and officers for their actions in war and provides a rather surprising answer. Neoscholastic theorists and Erasmian humanists had rejected the legitimacy of wars among Christians and as late as 1583 a layman jurist like Diego García de Palacio in his *Diálogos Militares* [Military Dialogues] (1583) counseled military personnel to disobey orders when they believed a war to be unjust. However, Escalante, who held up obedience as the supreme martial virtue, defended the primacy of discipline over ethics in war.[74] Thus when it is asked whether soldiers jeopardised their salvation by fighting against other Christians in an unjust war, Escalante responds: 'Indeed not, since the soldier is obliged to serve his Prince and defend his designs, and it is not his task to examine whether a

---

[70] Londoño (1943) 84 and 88.

[71] See the plagiarized version of Machiavelli's *Art of War* by Salazar (1590) 6.

[72] Quoted in Parker (1994) 44. For the work's publishing history see González de León (1996) 68.

[73] On Escalante see José Luis Casado Soto's introduction to *Discursos* (1995) 19–77.

[74] Escalante (1595) 23v. The disagreement, though one of degree, is nonetheless crucial. García de Palacio argues that the responsibility for determining the morality of a conflict belongs to the king and his council and that soldiers and officers must generally obey their orders. However,

if it is evident that the war is unjust, either because it does not meet the necessary criteria [for justice] or due to the presence of evidence and signs of its injustice sufficient to engender a highly probable conclusion that [the war] contravenes reason and justice, it would then be illicit to fight even if Prince ordered it because in such case the enemy would be innocent and as such we cannot kill him even when authorized by our Princes, neither do we then owe subjection

war is just or unjust as long as it is not against the Catholic Church'.[75] In the 1580s and 90s the founders of the 'perfect officer' genre, working along this line of reasoning, advocated automatic discipline and created an almost mechanistic ideal of the technical expert, a *soldado plático* or practical and pragmatic soldier who took pride in his effectiveness and kept away from moral judgements as matters properly belonging to other authorities. Then they abandoned the field of martial ethics and dedicated their works primarily to the technical aspects of their craft (tactics, ballistics and fortification) thus pushing the moral dimensions of war further backstage.[76]

Historians tend to attribute the harsher tone and message of Spanish military ethics in the late sixteenth century largely to the need to respond to the challenge of the Dutch Revolt (or to rebellion in general).[77] This view is only partially correct. As we have seen, Spanish military ethics had considerably hardened both in theory and practice in the mid-sixteenth century *before* the start of the troubles in the Netherlands. Although the Revolt undoubtedly contributed to a stiffening of attitudes towards the enemy and to the justification of measures inconceivable in other tactical contexts, it was not the only (or perhaps even the major) factor in this evolution. At least as important was the development of a professional discourse dedicated to the creation of an efficient military and focused primarily on the defence of experience and expertise over high social origin. Not surprisingly, the soldier-authors most willing to put aside the niceties of chivalry and justify the tough handling of enemies were those engaged in the construction of this technocratic officer model. Writers of this sort of military education manual such as Londoño, Valdés, Mendoza, Escalante and others, inspired by the examples and doctrines of the Duke of Alba, criticised not only essential chivalric practices and notions but also the nobility's claims to innate military merits and leadership rights.[78] And vice-versa, those like García de Palacios who

---

or obedience to our rulers since their commands oppose those of a superior Prince who is God to whom we owe primary loyalty and who commands us not to kill persons we know to be innocent.
García de Palacio (1583) 17vis–18.

[75] Escalante (1595) 22v.

[76] For this trend compare Lechuga (1603) with Lechuga (1611).

[77] See Parker (1994) 44.

[78] For instance, Escalante insists that high ranks should not automatically be the prerogative of "sons of noble parents" but should fall instead "to captains and old soldiers who have served well." Escalante (1595) 4v. See also Mendoza (1595) 52–53.

remained loyal to the traditional belief in the essential value of noble pedigree in the military, normally held fast to the scruples of chivalry.[79] In other words, advocates of unrestrained warfare were generally those who favored the lifting of social barriers to advancement in the military, probably because they regarded the old traditions and practices as class attributes of the high aristocracy and hindrances to their own professional success. All of these authors, with the sole exception of Mendoza, were either *hidalgos* or commoners who had joined the *tercios* to advance in society and who admired the Duke of Alba's meritocratic standards of promotion, his goal-oriented tactics and his legendary toughness towards the enemy.

In the 1580s practice once again outran theory, and while members of the Spanish military establishment in the Netherlands affirmed their commitment to total war against the rebels, the actions of the Army of Flanders and its leaders began to moderate. A key to the campaign success of Alexander Farnese, Prince (and later Duke) of Parma, Captain General from 1578 to 1592, was his ability to soften and modulate Alba's terror policy. To be sure, the torture, mutilation and killing of prisoners though increasingly rare still took place in the early years of his command and as late as the mid-1580s soldiers occasionally vented their anger on the peasantry, especially when provoked.[80] Furthermore, as the governor of Karpen had the opportunity to learn, Dutch officers who refused to surrender could still expect death and Spanish commanders gave no quarter to iconoclasts or when the enemy killed a particularly popular officer. For instance, following the clash on Steenbergen dike in June 1583, the Spaniards, furious over the slaying of Captain Carlos Menéses, slaughtered more than 1200 Dutch and French troops. However, a significant incident took place after the battle. French Marshall Armand de Gontaut, Lord of Biron, challenged the Prince of Parma to a duel between twelve French and Spanish champions and, in a drastic departure from standard procedure, the Captain General accepted the *defi* or challenge. The proposed encounter did not take place but Parma's gesture heralded the return of chivalry to this conflict.[81]

---

[79] García de Palacio (1583) 37–37vis. See also Alava y Viamont's *El Perfeto Capitán*, which defends the importance of pedigree for military command and argues for milder style of campaigning. Alava y Viamont (1590) 4–22v.

[80] Vázquez (1879–1880) LXXII 188, 421, 431–432, 473.

[81] For the execution of the Dutch governor of Karpen see Vázquez (1879–1880)

Under Parma's leadership treatment of the enemy became markedly gentler. Although the Dutch maintained their merciless handling of Spanish prisoners (drowning them at Maastricht in 1579, for instance), and the *tercios* still sacked most enemy towns, (including those that capitulated without assault), the Prince began to seek prisoner exchanges and to issue surrender terms to some garrisons that had resisted well beyond the traditional cut-off point of artillery emplacement.[82] In another significant gesture, he pardoned the life of a French officer sent by the Dutch to assassinate him during the siege of Antwerp in 1585.[83] The rebels did not immediately correspond to Parma's new policy, but it seems likely that his chivalrous overtures weakened their resolve to mount heroic last stands. For instance, in August 1585 Antwerp surrendered on unusually generous terms that included an exchange of prisoners and temporary guarantees to heretics with property in the city.[84] The Captain General scrupulously complied with his side of the agreement and other towns followed Antwerp's lead.[85] Thus in the 1580s the Spanish reconquest of the southern Netherlands gathered considerable momentum as Dutch soldiers and townspeople learned that they could trust the Duke of Parma not to slaughter them merely for revenge, profit or terror.

Gradually, the Duke's gallantry became a normative example for his subordinates and adversaries as both sides began to demonstrate increasing levels of mutual respect and courtesy.[86] In 1590 even an

---

LXXII 178. For execution of iconoclasts after the capture of Steenwick, Ibidem 398–399. For the projected meeting of French and Spanish champions see Ibidem 420.

[82] One of the earliest instances of prisoner exchange I have found is in *Codoin* (1880) LXXV 274–276 "Copia de Carta Original del Duque de Parma al Ilustrísimo Señor don Pedro de Toledo" 10–12–1579.

[83] For the case of Maastricht see Vázquez (1879–1880) LXXII 188. For surrender terms granted by Parma see for instance the case of Dendermonde in August-September 1584 in Ibidem 511–512. For the incident with the would-be assassin, Ibidem 68.

[84] For the terms of the surrender of Antwerp see Vázquez (1879–1880) LXXIII 85–94.

[85] See for instance the terms given to Saint Gertruidenberg in April 1589 in Coloma (1922) 16–17.

[86] Even in his dealings with subordinates, Parma knew how to put to good use his mastery of dramatic chivalric gestures. At a critical moment for his leadership, when rumors began to circulate within the high command blaming him for the failure of the Armada, he gathered his officers in the main square of Dunkirk and promised "to satisfy anyone who blamed him ... not as Captain General of the armies of Philip II his uncle, but as Alexander Farnese." Vázquez (1879–1880) LXIII 349, 352. Rumors had it that Parma had dragged his feet in getting his

old soldier of fortune of the Alba mould such as Colonel Francisco Verdugo, who used to boast that he was 'Francisco (Francis) to the good and *verdugo* (executioner) to the evil' sent his herald to challenge Count William of Nassau, the Dutch governor of Friesland.[87] By then chivalric notions had spread to the Dutch officer corps. Contrary to the opinion of scholars who have posited a 'bourgeois' Dutch officer corps, aristocratic ideals of honour led Dutch commanders to engage in chivalric exhibitions and challenges.[88] Increasingly frequent exchanges of prisoners called *cuarteles* or 'quarters' began in the late 1580s and early 1590s and towards the end of the decade the Army of Flanders initiated the *cuartel general* or routine ransoming of captives according to a set scale that varied in accordance to rank and social status.[89] Contact with the French military during the Army of Flanders' intervention in the French Wars of Religion in the 1590s further consolidated these practices.[90]

Nevertheless, this renewed emphasis on the old ethics of war did not imply a rejection of the sharp pragmatism of the school of Alba and its technical officer manuals. It was, like Parma's generous policy towards captured cities, carefully crafted for campaign success. Unlike the *caballeros esforzados* of yore, the Duke and his commanders subordinated their chivalric impulses and moments to their tactical and strategic objectives. Thus when in August 1590 Henry of Navarre, head of the French Huguenots and King of France, tried to lure Parma out of his fortified positions around Paris by challenging him to battle, Farnese ordered his officers not to respond to French provocations and asked the herald to tell the Prince of Bearne [Henry] that I have come to

> France with this army you see only to free her if I can from the heretical oppression from which she ails, and that in accordance with the

---

army ready to be shipped across the Channel. See Parker (1998) 229–250 for the context of this dispute.

[87] Coloma (1922) 107 and Vázquez (1879–1880) LXXIII 465–466.

[88] For some examples see Vázquez (1879–1880) LXXIII 365–367, 394–395 and 465. Oestreich (1982) 68–69 argues otherwise.

[89] For examples of courtesy between enemies see Villalobos (1612) 130, 154, 155 and Coloma (1922) 125. For *cuarteles*, a practice that seems to have begun with the ransoming of the Spanish soldiers of the failed Armada see Coloma (1922) 9, 82, 85, 114, 116, 122, as well as Parker (1994) 52, Parker (1990) 169–170 and Martin (1988).

[90] See for instance Williams (1972) lx–lxi.

will of the King my lord I will put into the execution of this mission
all the possible care and diligence, that I will seek the shortest route
to achieve this goal and that if I find that it means fighting a battle,
I will do it without fail.[91]

Moreover, Parma was not loath to introduce new and deadlier
weapons against enemy cities; the Army of Flanders was the first to
use incendiary bombs in the siege of Wachtendonck in 1588.[92] In
brief, what Captain Alonso Vázquez called the 'school of Parma'
consisted, (among other doctrines and practices), of a well-balanced
synthesis of chivalry and professionalism.[93]

Parma's return to chivalry was of a piece with the changing social
composition of the officer corps. Numerous young aristocrats from
Spain's most prominent grandee families such as the Prince of Asculi,
the Duke of Pastrana and the Duke of Osuna, joined the Army of
Flanders in mid and late 1580s leading a Spanish commander, Carlos
Coloma, to exult 'that there was no memory of having seen such
numerous and splendid nobility the Netherlands since Charles V ab-
dicated his crowns [in 1555]'.[94] Some of them came to the Netherlands to take part in the 'Enterprise of England' and others were
ransomed from the Dutch after the defeat of the Armada or joined
the *tercios* lured by Parma's courtly charisma and triumphs. Gradually these noblemen began to push aside the *hidalgos* and commoners
of the officer corps in all aspects of the profession from salaries to
promotions, despite the very sharp protests of the authors of the
'perfect officer' genre.[95] By the mid-1590s the transformation of the
high command was well advanced, the Generals of the three major
branches and many *tercio* and garrison Governors were high aristocrats while men like Verdugo and Mondragón were regarded as
relics 'more rare than unicorns' according to one official.[96]

The presence of these *caballeros* had a profound impact upon the
culture of the *tercios* and contributed to the revival of genteel meth-

---

[91] Coloma (1922) 33–34. For a similar version of Parma's words see Vázquez
(1879–1880) LXXIII 499–502.
[92] Van der Essen (1933–1937) V 248.
[93] For the "School of Parma" see Vázquez (1879–1880) LXXIV 360.
[94] On these arrivals see AGS E 589, 116 Parma to Philip II 6-5-1585; AGS E
604, 67 Count of Fuentes to Philip II 3-5-1593; Vázquez (1879–1880) LXIII
333–335, 415–416 and Coloma (1922) 7, 19.
[95] See for instance Marcos de Isaba (1594) among many others.
[96] AGS E 605, 56 Esteban de Ibarra to Martín de Idiáquez, 4-5-1593.

ods of warfare in the Netherlands since, unlike their predecessors, they did not depend on their professional success for their social and financial security and could afford to exercise greater restraint.[97] As Carlos Coloma proudly pointed out, 'the Spanish nobility would not consent to the killing of women and children' even during an assault.[98] These were the officers who in the 1590s and early 1600s extended the aristocratic practice of ransoming to soldiers on all sides regardless of nation or social status, who worked to end the customary sacking of captured cities and eventually helped eliminate the mutinies that had inflicted so much harm on the civilian population.[99] This aristocratic humanisation and regulation of campaign ethics was evident in two of the most prominent military treatises of the 1590s. The most important technical work written by a nobleman, don Diego de Alava y Viamont's *El Perfeto Capitán* [The Perfect Captain] (1590) contains veiled criticism of Alba's policy and specifies that it is not 'the severity that destroys cities' that a leader should demonstrate but justice, clemency, magnanimity, fortitude and host of other moral virtues and Cristóbal Mosquera de Figueroa's *Comentario en Breve Compendio de Disciplina Militar* [Commentary and Brief Compendium of Military Discipline] (1596) insists on the legalistic conduct of campaigns.[100] With this change in values and behaviour in mind, authorities in Madrid proposed new training procedures for noble officers more in keeping with their values and social origin than the strict garrison drill and regimentation of the Alba school.[101] Thus councillors of state sometimes advocated a return to more genteel methods of combat preparation such as courtly jousts and tourneys, even as an old hard-bitten soldier, Miguel de Cervantes, took aim at the new vogue for chivalric fighting in his *Don Quixote* (1605 and 1615).[102]

In the early seventeenth century Spanish campaign narratives which had earlier excoriated the Dutch and unconditionally defended Spanish actions adopted a more detached attitude, ceased to approach the

---

[97] For incidents of old-fashioned irregular group combat and undisciplined charges see Coloma (1922) 91, 97–98.

[98] Ibidem 116.

[99] For a major example of restraint see the case of Cambray in October 1595 in Coloma (1922) 124–125. On mutinies see Parker (1990) 185–206. For the stabilizing influence of the aristocracy in the Army of Flanders see González de León (1991) chs I, III.

[100] Alava y Viamont (1590) 4–22v and Mosquera de Figueroa (1596) 34v–38.

[101] See for instance AGS E 2023, 60 Consulta del Consejo de Estado 18–1–1603.

[102] Cervantes (1615) Chapter I 2–2v and Chapter VI 19v–22v.

conflict as 'the Dutch Revolt' and began to consider it as 'the Low Countries War'.[103] Ironically, the emphasis of the 'perfect officer' genre on professional excellence as a *sine qua non*, originally mustered in defence of total war against the Dutch, had generated a new standard of evaluation for friends and enemies beyond the traditional political and religious dichotomies of rebellion versus loyalty and orthodoxy versus heresy.[104] The two major tendencies of intramural Spanish military discourse, the professional and the chivalric, merged during these years to yield a new perspective on the Dutch. The memoirs of *tercio* officers now faulted unethical Spanish behaviour and presented the Dutch as exemplary soldiers from whom all professionals could learn. For instance, Alonso Vázquez describes with admiration Maurice of Nassau's use of deceit to capture Zichem in 1591, and Carlos Coloma praises the Dutch General, criticises the Spanish killing of prisoners of war, and condemns as vile traitors rightly executed those who in 1598 conspired to hand over Breda to the Army of Flanders![105] The tone and message of these memoirs suggest that Spanish officers and government officials were beginning to acknowledge the rights of their foes, not only on a human, social or personal level but also in the political sense. It is no coincidence that one of the most extreme advocates of total war against the Calvinist republic, Luis Valle de la Cerda, chose to issue his truculent tract in 1599, even though it had been penned sixteen years earlier. As the author of the *Avisos* realised (besides 'observations' the title can also mean 'warnings'), the humane treatment of the Dutch (as well as the death of Philip II the previous year) had opened the door to a possible cessation of hostilities. Events proved him right. The return of chivalric ideals and the establishment of value-neutral professional standards helped the Spaniards see the Dutch not as heathen rebels but as regular adversaries subject to the protection of the laws of war, thus paving the way for Spain's *de facto* recog-

---

[103] Two of the most detailed eyewitness accounts date from this period. Coloma's memoirs were first published in 1625 but as the dedication to don Diego de Ibarra on page 1 indicates, they were written in 1609. Vázquez' wrote his in 1616 as is obvious from his reference to Parma's death: Vázquez (1879–1880) LXXII 8.

[104] This new standard was latent in the letters of the Duke of Alba and his high command, although their view of the Dutch as rebels and heretics remained uppermost. See for instance *Codoin* LXXV (1880) 193–198 "Copia de carta original de don Fadrique a Su Excelencia [Alba]" 10–4–1573, and Alba (1952) III 281–282 Alba to don Diego de Zúñiga 17–1–1573.

[105] Vázquez (1879–1880) LXXIV 42–43 and Coloma (1922) 114, 174, 180, 185.

nition of the legal status of the Republic in the terms of the Twelve
Years Truce (1609–1621).[106]

III. *The Eighty Years War, Second Phase 1621–1659*

The second half of the war is perhaps less interesting from the point
of view of the history of ethics since it consisted primarily of the full
working out of the process of aristocratisation already in evidence
in the 1590s and early 1600s. The changing outlook of the Generals
in charge had by the 1620s stripped the campaigns in the Low
Countries of most of their ideological content and ferocity and, in
marked contrast with neighbouring conflicts in England and Germany,
this became perhaps the most restrained war of the century. As in
early decades, the social composition of the officer corps had great
impact on military ethics. At sea, where the nobility was largely
absent from privateering campaigns, the drowning of prisoners and
non-combatants continued well into the 1620s.[107] However, on land
chivalric mores reigned supreme as aristocrats came to dominate
almost completely the officer corps and high command, especially
after the arrival of don Fernando of Austria, Cardinal-Infante of
Spain in 1634. The young and dashing Captain General came surrounded by a large retinue of grandees and attracted to his banner
the flower of the local nobility. By 1636 the army's general staff
could boast of no less than twenty-eight titled noblemen or almost
its entire roster.[108]

A command culture of etiquette, pose and grand gesture now per-
meated the entire corps replacing the religious fervour, grim fru-
gality and single-minded focus on victory that earlier leaders had
practised and prescribed.[109] From the perspective of grandee commanders, war was not a crusade or a means to social advancement
but a theatre of personal honour and, as one of them put it, a form

---

[106] For the negotiations surrounding this recognition and what it entailed see
Parker (1981) 239–240.
[107] In the 1630's, as Flemish privateering fell under the supervision of Iberian
aristocrats these practices ceased. Stradling (1992) 40–41, 45 and 87–88.
[108] Vincart (1873) 111.
[109] See for instance Londoño (1943) 61–65 and 70–73 and Alava y Viamont
(1590) 34vis–39.

of 'entertainment'.[110] Thus individual autonomous action such as challenges and single combat remained acceptable and sieges such as Breda's in 1624–25 or Roermond in 1637 became social events, opportunities to greet distinguished foreign visitors or hold parades and other celebrations.[111] The nature of these proceedings clearly shows itself in the works of painters and engravers such as Pieter Snayers and Jacques Callot, as well as in the most famous iconographic depiction of the Eighty Years War, Diego de Velázquez's *Surrender of Breda* (plate 7) in which a victorious royal commander, Ambrogio Spínola, puts on a grand display of chivalric generosity towards his Dutch counterpart, Justin of Nassau, on the latter's capitulation of the important city of Breda. Spínola accepts the keys to the city from the defeated Justin and, in a magnanimous gesture, does not allow him to kneel and instead touches his shoulder in a sign of camaraderie, while the siege works, with all their sordid and technical associations, fade into the background. The canvas, finished in the spring of 1635 for the new royal palace of El Buen Retiro, represents the Spanish crown's official embrace of the chivalric ethos in the war in the Netherlands.[112]

Velázquez's masterpiece also illustrates the evolution of the written self-portrait of the Spanish soldier. In the 1620s the technical treatises of the 'perfect officer' genre as well as the realistic memoirs of Mendoza, Vázquez and Coloma gave way to the genteel narratives of Jean Antoine Vincart, whose works for the most part avoid the horrors and hardships of war and show instead the noble manner in which the officers conducted themselves on campaign, their personal panache, the size of their retinue and the luxury of their equipage.[113] The relatively few works of military ethics published during this era formulated a new ideal of martial behaviour more in accordance with the chivalric ethos. Magnanimity was, of course, a well-known chivalric virtue and at least one author undertook the

---

[110] See the analysis of the Spanish Captain General after the battle of Rocroi in AGS E 2059 don Francisco de Melo to Philip IV, 25–4–1643.

[111] For singular combat see Vincart (1958) 59–60. For visits to the siege of Breda, which at one point created such a distraction in the royal camp that almost allowed the Dutch to break the siege see Rodríguez Villa (1893) 61. For the visit of the Duke of Neoburg to the Cardinal-Infante at the siege of Roermond see Vincart (1891) 36–37.

[112] On the Velázquez' painting as well as other pictorial representations of the Breda campaign see Vosters (1973) 1–127.

[113] For a similar French perspective see Chagniot (1992) 31.

formation of the new '*el soldado magnánimo*' or magnanimous soldier, scrupulous in his observance of the rules of war.[114] In this process, the crucial notion of 'reputation' evolved from a goal-oriented to a procedure-based concept. It had earlier been a matter of results (success or failure), but it now became closely connected with ethics and appearance.

As Velázquez and other artists understood, the culture of command that became prevalent in the second half of the war involved a self-conscious humanisation of military ethics. Civilians and non-combatants, town dwellers and peasants, were now under the official protection of the army in the person and staff of the Superintendent of Military Justice (a post created in 1594 specifically for this purpose) who regularly investigated and tried even Generals charged with brutality, extortion or pillage.[115] Adversaries received similar consideration. No sacks of enemy cities took place over four decades of constant sieges (1621–1659) and the Army of Flanders, despite the occasional excesses of its enemies, almost without exception spared the lives of Dutch and French garrisons even when their surrender followed withering artillery exchanges, long encirclement and fierce assaults.[116]

Such magnanimity became possible as the nature of the Low Countries war changed. The social priorities of aristocratic commanders (who wished to repair their trains, mind their estates, or

---

[114] However, the first "*prenda*" or talent is "*Estudioso.*" Pizarro de Carvajal (1649) 11–14v. The rest are religious and moral qualities. See also the fascinating range of ethical problems studied in the ostensibly technical work of a Spanish Captain, Medina (1650) 247–258.

[115] For the creation of the office see AGS E 2222, 29 Philip II to Archduke Ernest of Austria, 2–12–1594 and González de León (1993). For cases of officers accused of various abuses against the local population in 1651 see AGR TM 175, especially the files pertaining to a prominent Spanish General, don Esteban de Gamarra (AGR TM 175 unfol. "Consulta de Su Alteza" 29–12–1651). Fear of reciprocity, which as Parker points out, was a major factor in the humanization of the treatment of enemy populations was clearly not at work here. For a series of events in which reciprocity did play a role see note 120 below.

[116] In their 1636 invasion of France the Spanish did not retaliate for the worst atrocity of the second half of the war, the French sack of Tirlemont in June of the previous year: Vincart (1958) 134–136. For a significant Dutch instance of restraint see their recapture of Breda in 1637 in which the besiegers lobbed thousands of shells at the town and lost hundreds of soldiers, but did not harm the Spanish garrison. Israel (1989) 258. The sole Spanish exception I have found to the policy of restraint is the surprise attack on Mardyke in 1645 in which hundreds of French soldiers were killed. Vincart (1877) 578.

appear in court during the winter season) put an end to year-round campaigns and reintegrated the army's general staff into peaceful life for at least part of the year dulling its professionalism but making it less likely that officers would regard civilians as aliens or enemies. Furthermore, protracted sieges such as had taken place in the early half of the war at Haarlem (1572–1573) or Ostend (1601–4) became increasingly rare in the 1620s and 30s and disappeared altogether in the 1640s and 50s.[117] Concepts or heroism and loyalty also evolved. In the sixteenth century it had been official doctrine that a Governor, unless ordered otherwise, had the duty to die defending his fortress.[118] In contrast, aristocratic siege etiquette allowed the besieged to sue for terms when their outer works had been breached (or were about to be), or after an initial assault or threat thereof or if reinforcements did not arrive after an agreed number of days.[119] Normally the military personnel of captured towns departed under escort with their weapons and even some artillery pieces.[120] Officers and soldiers taken in battle, skirmishes and surprise assaults were still held for ransom or exchange, though sometimes royal commanders, in magnificent demonstrations of generosity and individual initiative, released their aristocratic captives without consulting with anybody and without financial preconditions.[121]

The enemy usually reciprocated these courtesies, often releasing common soldiers and junior officers and granting the most prominent prisoners who had given their word of honour not to escape, total freedom of movement while they waited to be ransomed.[122]

---

[117] For the noble officer's reluctance to campaign during the winter see for instance the case of the loss of the crucial border enclave of Fort Schenkenschans: AGS E 2287, Philip IV to the Cardinal Infante, 11–12–1635, AGS E 2051, 25 Consulta del Consejo de Estado 17–6–1636 and AGS E 2052 Errores cometidos en Flandes despues de la muerte del Marquez de Aytona y toma del fuerte de Schencq, 19–4–1637.

[118] See for instance Vázquez (1879–1880) LXXIV 94.

[119] Alava y Viamont (1590) 104–105v argues that surrender when besieged is not dishonorable. The shortest term I have found is three days, in the case of the capitulation of Corbie to the French in 1636. Vincart (1873) 84. For other cases see Vincart (1877) 505, 507, 521–523, 526.

[120] In the mid-1640's the French, aware of the difficulties the Army of Flanders faced in replenishing its troops, began to refuse surrender terms to Spanish garrisons in order to hold them prisoners. The indignant Spaniards reciprocated and normalcy returned. See Vincart (1877) 501, 563, 566, 585 and Vincart (1913) 106, 115, 120, 152, 154.

[121] For instances of this see Vincart (1891) 53–54, and Vincart (1913) 114.

[122] See for instance the case of don Alvaro de Vivero, brother of the Count of

These *caballeros* lived more like honoured guests than enemies or captives, their stay in Paris or The Hague enlivened by hunts, dinner parties or visits from friends and colleagues.[123] Some were even allowed to return to the Spanish Netherlands to lobby for their ransom or attend private functions.[124] In fact, as some Generals recognised, in this war-in-lace the fate of the noble prisoner of war had become almost desirable.[125] However, there were exceptions. In 1638 a particularly stubborn resistance by a Spanish Captain in Chatelet so irritated the Marquis of La Meilleraye that he had him put to death. The French Marshall probably considered such obstinacy rude: the town's commanding officer, who had argued for surrender, received splendid treatment.[126]

Cushioned by the certainty that the enemy shared his values and attitudes, secure in his professional and social position and extremely jealous of his individual autonomy, the aristocratic warrior of the second half of the war sometimes carried his punctilio to extremes. In 1637 a local nobleman, *tercio* commander Charles Stassin, Lord of Everlange and Governor of the town of Damvillers on the French border, turned back a supply convoy and reinforcements that arrived after he had given to a French commander his word of honour to capitulate. Damvillers and its garrison surrendered in plain sight of a relief army, and although the Governor had to face a military tribunal he managed to elude any penalty for his remarkable behaviour.[127] A similar occurrence took place at La Bassé a decade later

---

Fuensaldaña, captured by the French in 1637, and released on his word of honor to attend a private function. Don Alvaro kept his word and returned to captivity to await ransoming. Novoa (1877–1886) LXXVII 280.

[123] See the case of Count Jan van Nassau, Cavalry General of the Army of Flanders who went hunting with his relative, the Dutch General Frederick Henry of Nassau in 1630 in Orange (1733) 120–121, and 145. See also the case of the Prince of Ligne, captured at Lens in 1648 and allowed to receive the visits of Spanish Generals. Vincart (1880) 520.

[124] See note 125 below for the case of don Gabriel de la Torre.

[125] AGS E 2066 Marquis of Castelrodrigo to Pedro Coloma 5–9–1646 and Ibidem Ottavio Piccolomini to Philip IV 10–9–1646.

[126] Cevallos y Arce (1880) 196–197. Don Gabriel de la Torre, spent nearly two years in Paris and was released after promising to return if the costs of his stay in an aristocratic mansion were not paid by the King. His debts amounted to 4000 florins which were duly paid out of the army's budget. AGR SEG 226, 1 Cardinal-Infante to Philip IV 1–10–1640; AGR SEG 226, 3 Relacion de los servicios de don Gabriel de la Torre, n.d.; AGR SEG 651, 3–9 Junta de Hacienda 4–5–1640.

[127] AGR SEG 217, folios 532 and 563 Philip IV to the Cardinal-Infante 12–12–1637 (2 letters) and folio 565 Philip IV to Peter Roose 12–12–1637.

when a Spanish Colonel refused to break his vow to the French besiegers.[128]

Incidents like these indicate that, from a practical point of view, the officers' adherence to noble etiquette could have negative consequences when rigidly applied to sieges. The same held true of battles. The Duke of Alba based his tactics on the practice of engaging the enemy in ambushes and skirmishes and avoiding large clashes whenever possible. However, the grandee Generals of the 1630s and 40s with their predilection for honour and appearance sought out decisive battles as the proper stage for their grand gestures and poses.[129] Though it remained essentially a war of sieges, the highest number of field battles in the entire conflict took place in the last twenty-four years: Avein, 1635, Kallo, 1638, Honnecourt, 1642, Rocroi, 1643, Lens, 1648, Rethel, 1650, and the Dunes, 1658. Except for Kallo, (which was not really a field battle but a messy series of skirmishes), all involved the French, who shared similar values, and many were fought in a style and for reasons that included but went beyond strict tactical necessity.[130] For instance, the man who succeeded the Cardinal-Infante as Captain General of the Army of Flanders, don Francisco de Melo, Marquis of Tordelaguna, led the *tercios* to an unnecessary and risky confrontation with the French army at Rocroi in May 1643.[131] Melo, a thorough product of the chivalric culture of command, allowed the French army to come close and fall into combat formation and then refused to give his troops a sheltered position in the field because, 'the courage of a General of the King of Spain could not allow him to show fear by hiding behind a marsh'.[132] The ensuing clash gave the army leaders the opportunity they sought 'to act like who we are', as the young Cavalry General,

---

[128] AHN E 978 Cargos que se hazen al Coronel don Francisco del Hierro ... 19-7-1647.

[129] They also sought such opportunities outside regular combat. See for instance in 1650, the case of Captain Arias Gonzalo who in order to save "the reputation of His Majesty's cavalry" and "win honor and fame" charged against a numerically superior French force and was mortally wounded. The aristocratic French commander rendered homage to his body and sang his praises. Vincart (1880) 528-529.

[130] On Kallo see Israel (1982) 259. In its social composition and values the French high command most closely resembled the Spanish one; see Lynn (1997) 248-281. For the values of the French military nobility see Smith (1996) 37-49.

[131] See Parker (1990) 260-261.

[132] Vincart (1880) 430.

the Duke of Albuquerque, put it.[133] Even when clearly beaten, the Spanish commanders refused to withdraw their *tercios* and surrendered only when offered terms (normally given only to fortresses).[134] It was the army's finest moment but also its most disastrous defeat: thousands of soldiers and dozens of noble officers proved their courage and panache but lost their lives and damaged beyond repair the Spanish cause in the Netherlands.[135]

Despite the human toll of Rocroi and other battles (which pales in comparison to the massacres of the first half of the war), the seventeenth century aristocratisation of the army's senior command appears to be the most important humanising influence on the conflict in the Netherlands. In fact it could be argued, that at least in the context of the Eighty Years War, it was the driving force behind the process of 'deconfessionalisation' and 'spread of reciprocity' that Geoffrey Parker correctly identifies as two major factors in the growth of martial restraint in seventeenth century Europe.[136] The noble commander contemplated war through social lenses and his sense of elitist belonging, group solidarity and *noblesse oblige* cut across religious and political boundaries and overrode most other considerations. A renascent chivalric ethos exerted a moderating influence on the more ethically flexible notions of professionalism, confessionalism, nationalism, and dynastic loyalty as well as on the increasing deadliness of weaponry. In this sense it became more significant to the ethics of war in the early modern era than it had been in its medieval heyday, when rival models of military behaviour were largely absent.

Sources and Bibliography

I. *Archival Sources*

Archivo General de Simancas, Estado. (AGS E), Simancas, Spain.
Archivo Histórico Nacional, Estado (AHN E), Madrid, Spain.
Archives Generales du Royaume, Secretarie d'Etat et de Guerre (AGR SEG) and Tribunaux Militaires (AGR TM). Brussels, Belgium.
Biblioteca Zabálburu (BZ), Madrid, Spain.

---

[133] Ibidem 434.
[134] Dávila Orejón (1684) 91–94.
[135] AGS E 2059 Consulta del Consejo de Estado 3-7-1643. For further details see González de León (1991) Chapter IV.
[136] Parker (1994) 53–55.

II. *Primary Printed Sources*

Alava y Viamont, Diego de (1590) *El Perfeto Capitan* (Madrid: 1590).
Alba, Duke of (1952) *Epistolario del III Duque de Alba don Fernando Alvarez de Toledo* 3 vols (Madrid: 1952).
Avila y Zúñiga, Luis de (1924) *Comentario de la Guerra de Alemania* in *Biblioteca de Autores Españoles* vol. 21 (Madrid: 1924). (Originally published in Antwerp, 1550).
Ayala, Balthazar de (1912) *Three Books on the Law of War and On the Duties Connected with War and on Military Discipline* (Washington DC: 1912). (Originally published in Latin in Douay, 1582).
Cervantes, Miguel de (1615) *Segunda Parte del Ingenioso Cavallero Don Quixote de la Mancha* (Madrid: 1615).
Cevallos y Arce, Lorenzo (1880) *Sucesos de Flandes en los Años de 1637, 38, 39 y 40* in *Varias Relaciones de los Estados de Flandes 1631 a 1656* (Madrid: 1880) 129–318.
Codoin: Colección de Documentos Inéditos Para la Historia de España 113 vols. (Madrid: 1842–1895).
Coloma, Carlos (1922) *Las Guerras de los Estados Bajos*, in *Biblioteca de Autores Españoles*, XXVIII (Madrid: 1922). (Originally published in Antwerp, 1625).
Cornejo, Pedro (1580) *Origen de la Civil Disensión de Flandes* (Turin: 1580).
Dávila Orejón, Francisco (1684) *Política y Mecánica Militar* (Brussels: 1684). (Originally published in Madrid, 1669).
Escalante, Bernardino de (1595) *Diálogos del Arte Militar* (Brussels: 1595). (Originally published in Seville, 1583).
——. (1995) *Discursos de Bernardino de Escalante al Rey y sus Ministros* (Laredo: 1995).
Garcia de Palacio, Diego (1583) *Diálogos Militares* (Mexico City: 1583).
Isaba, Marcos de (1594) *Cuerpo Enfermo de la Milicia Española* (Madrid: 1594).
Orange, Frederick Henry, Prince of (1733) *Memoires* (Amsterdam: 1733).
Lechuga, Cristóbal (1603) *Discurso del Cargo de Maestro de Campo General* (Milan: 1603).
——. (1611) *Discurso de la Artillería* (Milan: 1611).
Londoño, Sancho de (1943) *Discurso Sobre la Forma de Reducir la Disciplina Militar a Mejor y Antiguo Estado* (Madrid: 1943) (Originally published in Brussels, 1589).
Medina, Juan de (1650) *Tratado Militar* (Milan: 1650).
Mendoza, Bernardino de (1922) *Comentario de los Sucedido en las Guerras de los Paises Bajos*, in *Biblioteca de Autores Españoles*, XXVIII (Madrid: 1922). (Originally published in French in Paris, 1591 and in Spanish in Madrid, 1592).
——. (1595) *Teórica y Práctica de la Guerra* (Madrid: 1595).
Mosquera de Figueroa, Cristóbal (1596) *Comentario en Breve Compendio de Disciplina Militar* (Madrid: 1596).
Novoa, Matías de (1877–86) Historia de Felipe IV, Rey de España in *Codoin*, LXIX, LXXVII, LXXX, LXXXVI (Madrid: 1877–1886).
Núñez Alba, Diego (1890) *Diálogos de la Vida del Soldado* (Madrid: 1890) (Originally published in Cuenca, 1589).
Ossorio, Antonio (1945) *Vida y Hazañas de don Fernando Alvarez de Toledo, Duque de Alba* (Madrid: 1945) (Originally published in Salamanca, 1669).
Palacio Rubios, Juan López (1941) *Tratado del Esfuerzo Bélico-Heróico* (Madrid: 1941). (Originally published in Salamanca, 1524).
Pedrosa, Francisco de (1541) *Arte y Suplemento Remilitar* (Naples: 1541).
Pizarro de Carvajal, Alvaro Joseph (Count of Torrejón) (1649) *Prendas del Soldado Magnánimo* (Toledo: 1649).
Porreño, Baltasar (1899) *Historia del Serenissimo Señor Don Juan de Austria* (Madrid: 1899).
Quixada de Reayo, Juan (1548) *Doctrina del Arte de la Cavalleria* (Medina del Campo: 1548).
Salazar, Diego de (1590) *De Re Militari* (Brussels: 1590). (Originally published in Alcalá de Henares, 1536).

Sepúlveda, Juan Ginés de (1963) *Demócrates Primero*, in *Tratados Políticos* (Madrid: 1963) (Originally published in Latin in Lérida, 1571).

Trillo, Antonio (1592) *Historia de la Rebelión y Guerras de Flandes* (Madrid: 1592).

Valdés, Alfonso de (1952) *Dialogue of Lactancio*, in John E. Longhurst and Raymond MacCurdy (eds.), *Alfonso de Valdés and the Sack of Rome* (Albuquerque, New Mexico: 1952) (Originally published in Venice, 1545).

Valle de la Cerda, Luis (1599) *Avisos en Materias de Estado y Guerra* (Madrid: 1599).

Vázquez, Alonso (1879–1880) *Los Sucesos de Flandes y Francia del Tiempo de Alejandro Farnese*, in *Codoin* (Madrid: 1879–1880), vols. LXXII, LXXIII and LXXIV.

Villalobos y Benavides, Diego de (1612) *Comentarios de las Cosas Sucedidas en los Paises Baxos de Flandes* (Madrid: 1612).

Vincart, Jean Antoine (1958) *Les Relations Militaires des Années 1634 et 1635* (Brussels: 1958).

———. (1873) *Relación y Comentario . . . desta Campaña de 1636* in *Codoin*, LIX (Madrid: 1873).

Vincart, Juan Antonio (1891) *Relación de la Campaña de Flandes en 1637*, in *Codoin*, XCIX, (Madrid: 1891).

———. (1880) *Relación de la Campaña del Año de 1643*, in *Codoin*, LXXV (Madrid: 1880).

———. (1877) *Relación de la Campaña del Año de 1645*, in *Codoin*, LXVII (Madrid: 1877).

———. (1913) *Historia de la Campaña de 1647 en Flandes*, in Antonio Rodríguez Villa, *Artículos Históricos* (Madrid: 1913) 93–159.

———. (1880) *Relación de la Campaña del Año de 1650*, in *Codoin*, LXXV (Madrid: 1880).

Vitoria, Francisco de (1991) *Political Writings* (Cambridge: 1991).

Williams, Sir Roger (1972) *The Works of Sir Roger Williams* (Oxford: 1972).

III. *Secondary Sources*

Chaignot, Jean (1992) "The Ethics and Practice of War Amongst French Officers During the Seventeenth Century," *War and Society*, 10, no. 1 (1992), 19–36.

Donagan, Barbara (1988) "Codes and Conduct in the English Civil War", *Past and Present* no. 118 (1988) 65–95.

Fernández-Santamaria, J. A. (1977) *The State, War and Peace. Spanish Political Thought in the Renaissance 1516–1559* (Cambridge: 1977).

Firoozye, Barbara (1974) "Warfare in Renaissance Castile", unpublished PhD thesis (University of California: 1974).

Garate Cordoba, José María (1967) *Espíritu y Milicia en la España Medieval* (Madrid: 1967).

Génard, Pierre (1875) *La Furie Espagnole* (Antwerp: 1875).

González de León, Fernando (1991) "The Road to Rocroi: the Duke of Alba, the Count-Duke of Olivares and the High Command of the Spanish Army of Flanders in the Eighty Years War, 1567–1659", unpublished PhD thesis (The Johns Hopkins University: 1991).

———. (1993) "La Administración del Conde-Duque de Olivares y la Justicia Militar en el Ejército de Flandes, 1567–1643", *Investigaciones Históricas* 13 (1993) 107–129.

———. (1996) "Doctors of the Military Discipline: Technical Expertise and the Paradigm of the Spanish Soldier in the Early Modern Period", *Sixteenth Century Journal* 27 (1996) 61–85.

Gutmann, Myron P. (1980) *War and Rural Life in the Early Modern Low Countries* (Princeton: 1980).

Hall, Bert S. (1997) *Weapons and Warfare in Renaissance Europe* (Baltimore, Maryland: 1997).

Israel, Jonathan (1989) *The Dutch Republic and the Hispanic World 1606–1661* (Oxford: 1989).

Jensen, DeLamar (1964) *Diplomacy and Dogmatism. Don Bernardino de Mendoza and the French Catholic League* (Cambridge, Massachussets: 1964).

Lynn, John A. (1997) *Giant of the Grand Siècle. The French Army, 1610–1715* (Cambridge: 1997).

Maltby, William S. (1983) *Alba. A Biography of Fernando Alvarez de Toledo, Third Duke of Alba 1507–1582* (Berkeley, California: 1983).

Martin, Paula (1988) *Spanish Armada Prisoners* (Exeter: 1988).

Más Chao, Andrés and Sánchez de Toca, José (1993) "La Piedad y la Furia", in *La Infantería en Torno al Siglo de Oro* (Madrid: 1993) 95–128.

Oestreich, Gerhard (1982) *Neostoicism and the Early Modern State* (Cambridge: 1982).

Oman, Charles (1937) *A History of the Art of War in the Sixteenth Century* (London: 1937).

Parker, Geoffrey (1981) *The Dutch Revolt* (New York: 1981).

——. (1990) *The Army of Flanders and the Spanish Road 1567–1659* (Cambridge: 1990).

——. (1994) "Early Modern Europe", in Michael Howard, George J. Andreopoulos and Mark R. Shulman (eds), *The Laws of War* (New Haven, Connecticut: 1994) 40–58.

——. (1998) *The Grand Strategy of Philip II* (New Haven, Connecticut: 1998).

Pastor Bodmer, Beatríz (1992) *The Armature of Conquest: Spanish Accounts of the Discovery of America, 1492–1589* (Stanford, California: 1992).

Peralta, Jaime (1964) *Baltasar de Ayala y el Derecho de la Guerra* (Madrid: 1964).

Petrie, Charles (1967) *Don John of Austria* (New York: 1967).

Prescott, William H. (1995) *The Art of War in Spain. The Conquest of Granada 1481–1492* (repr., London: 1995).

Puddu, Raffaele (1984) *El Soldado Gentilhombre* (Barcelona: 1984).

Rivera de Ventosa, Enrique (1986) "El Tema de la Paz en Erasmo y Vives Frente a la Escuela de Salamanca", in *El Erasmismo en España* (Santander: 1986) 376–391.

Rodríguez Villa, Antonio (1893) *Ambrosio Spinola, Primer Marqués de los Balbases* (Madrid: 1893).

Quatrefages, René (1983) *Los Tercios* (Madrid: 1983).

Smith, Jay M. (1996) *The Culture of Merit. Nobility, Royal Service, and the Making of the Absolute Monarchy in France, 1600–1789* (Ann Arbor, Michigan: 1996).

Stradling, R. A. (1992) *The Armada of Flanders* (Cambridge: 1992).

Van der Essen, Leon (1933–1937) *Alexandre Farnèse, Prince de Parme, Gouverneur Gènèral des Pays-Bas, 1545–1592*, 5 vols (Brussels: 1933–1937).

Vosters, Simon A. (1973) *La Rendición de Breda en la Literatura y el Arte de España* (London: 1973).

CHAPTER TEN

ARMY, SOCIETY AND MILITARY PROFESSIONALISM IN THE NETHERLANDS DURING THE EIGHTY YEARS' WAR

D. J. B. Trim

It is common in modern military historiography to regard the Dutch Republic during the late-sixteenth and seventeenth centuries as the birthplace of military professionalism. Moreover, it is also common to identify the officer corps of the republic's army as predominantly bourgeois, to which is attributed that early development of professionalism, reflecting the view that Dutch society more generally was less influenced by the chivalric ethos than its European counterparts. There is, in consequence, a widespread perception that military professionalism developed in the Netherlands *because* of a lack of noble and thus, implicitly, chivalric input into the Dutch army (the *staatse leger*). The example of the United Provinces, then, seems to support the contention that the decline of chivalry indeed goes hand in hand with—or is even a necessary prerequisite to—the development of military professionalism.

However, such a conclusion is insecure, because it is based on a very thin evidential foundation. There are few authoritative secondary works on the Dutch army before *c.* 1700 and those that exist are not sufficiently founded in archival material. Moreover, recent revisionist studies of early-modern Dutch political society emphasise the lasting power of the nobility in the Netherlands and the similarity of its culture to other European nobilities. The following brief survey of secondary literature on war and society in the Netherlands, tested against a selection of primary sources, does not verify an alternative scenario, but it does show that the existing orthodoxy is, at best 'not proven'. More research needs to be done both on the role of the nobility in the Dutch Republic and on the development of military professionalism in the early-modern Netherlands.

I

The provinces of the Netherlands found much of the early part of
their 'Eighty Years' War' for independence from the Spanish Monarchy
(1568–1648) a real struggle. The decade following the repudiation
of the Habsburgs by the States-General of the United Netherlands
(1581) was particularly difficult for the new Dutch Republic, but it
survived, despite the assassination of its original leader, William 'the
Silent', Prince of Orange (1533–84). By the 1590s the Republic was
no longer dependent on the English military aid that had been necessary to survive the late 1580s and the *staatse leger* was transformed
by a series of remarkable reforms. So profound was their effect and
so copied were they throughout Europe that they are widely regarded
as trigger, or at least integral part, of a 'military revolution' during
the seventeenth century.[1]

The celebrated programme of reform that commenced in the 1590s
was initiated chiefly by the republic's Captain-General, Maurice of
Nassau (1567–1625, from 1618 Prince of Orange), his cousins William
Louis of Nassau-Dillenburg (1560–1620) and John of Nassau-Siegen
(1561–1623), and his brother and successor as Captain-General,
Frederick Henry, Prince of Orange (1584–1647)—all active and adept
soldiers. The reforms encompassed organisation, administration, tactics, arms and equipment, logistics, and military justice. What emerged
was an army with a remarkable degree of uniform proficiency, which
was highly standardised in equipment and drill, and subject to formal regulations, administered by central, bureaucratic authority, to
an extraordinary extent by the standards of the time.[2] As part of
this process, the reforms established a clear hierarchy for a permanently embodied officer corps, paid (by the standards of the time)
regularly and well, whose standard body of expertise had been systematised and which was more efficient. Thus, the reforms achieved,
or put into place structures that made it possible to achieve, four of
the seven key criteria of a profession for the *staatse leger*'s officer corps.[3]

---

[1] Parker (1988), ch. 1; Feld (1975B), 428–29; Rothenburg (1986); Weigley (1993),
9–14. For the most accessible introduction to the literature debating the existence
and periodisation of an early-modern 'military revolution' see the essays collected
in Rogers (1995).
[2] Wijn (1934); Parker (1988), 18–23; Israel (1995), 252–53, 265–70, 294–95; van
der Hoeven (1997), 36–43, 76–82.
[3] See above, pp. 6–11.

What also emerged was an army in which units had been down-sized in comparison to other forces of the period—the consequence of tactical innovations themselves made in order to maximise developments in technology. As McCullough observes: 'These smaller, more articulated units required a required a closer degree of control, which called for more and better-educated officers.' Moreover, even before the troops reached the battlefield, not only individual soldiers but, as Parker points out, 'entire tactical units' required repeated drilling in order to learn 'to perform the motions necessary for volley-firing both swiftly and in unison'. These motions, which involved pikemen as well as musketeers, were laid out in drill-books, planned and written by Maurice, William Louis and John of Nassau, published by the States-General of the Republic and periodically updated (and lavishly illustrated—for examples, see plates 5, 6). Thus, it was not just that well-trained officers were required if troops were to be used most effectively in combat. The universal use of set manoeuvres meant that even a naturally brilliant officer could not simply have stepped into a combat situation and handled his unit. He himself needed to have been instructed in and to be familiar with (ideally by having drilled the rank and file) what was in effect a formal tactical doctrine, determined by a central authority as a matter of policy.[4]

The reforms thus not only created a more bureaucratic army, with structures typical of a profession. The reforms also necessarily engendered amongst the majority of officers an approach that can fairly be characterised as 'professional' (at least in the adjectival sense), since they effectively privileged the values associated with a profession.

II

All in all, it is not surprising that M. D. Feld believed the very 'concept of military professionalism first emerged in the Netherlands... in the course of the revolt against the Hapsburg monarch', or that Russell F. Weigley associates the Dutch Republic with 'the birth of

---

[4] McCullough (2001), 370. Parker (1988), 19–20. See Rothenburg (1986), 37–45; Feld (1975B), 423–28; Zwitzer (1997), 37–38; Puype (1997), 76–81. The best known of the drill-books was that for infantry: de Gheyn (1607); there is a modern English edn in facsimile, de Gheyn (1986).

Military Professionalism'.[5] This view is perhaps overstated, but clearly contains much truth. As we have seen, the military career in the Netherlands by the 1620s exhibits many of the markers of a profession. By many criteria, then, the Dutch army had certainly undergone a process of professionalisation,[6] one of the first in Europe, regardless of whether it yet been truly professionalised.

Many scholars attribute this significant development to the nature of Dutch society. The traditional, textbook view of the Netherlands during its 'golden age' is that its nobility was in decline and of little significance in politics, which was dominated not by landed aristocrats, but by the bourgeois magistrates of the booming commercial towns, particularly in Holland, who had 'played the leading part in the birth of the Dutch Republic'. In consequence, 'commerce dominated both politics and religion', with all other values (including, even especially, those of the cult of chivalry) subordinated to the desire of the burgher-oligarchs of Amsterdam and the neighbouring cities to increase trade and profits. Thus, its culture 'was bourgeois rather than aristocratic'; indeed, 'the dominant social and political class, the urban merchant oligarchs, had a positive aversion to military careers in any form.'[7] Given this supremacy of the urban bourgeoisie and their disdain for the military vocation of the nobles which they had superseded, it was natural for Feld to conclude that a native 'military tradition was almost entirely absent'. His wider conclusion is also unsurprising: that 'the creation of the first modern army and earliest rationalized form of military administration occurred not in the context of the major powers of the time but in a relatively backward and decidedly unmilitary society'.[8]

For Feld and others who have followed his work, this was not a coincidence. Rather, it was *because* the nobility was of relative unimportance in the Netherlands and *because* the Dutch were less imbued with the associated aristocratic value system (including the chivalric ethos) that military professionalism could develop in the Netherlands. An integral part of this process of professionalisation was the exclu-

---

[5] Feld (1975A), 193; Weigley (1993), 9 *et seq.*

[6] Compare with my "Introduction", above, pp. 13, 17.

[7] Van Nierop (1997), 83; Green (1952), 358–59 at 359; Parker (1984), 140–41, at 141. See also, e.g., Bush (1967), 325; Feld (1975B), 420–23; Cornette (1993), 102.

[8] Feld (1975B), 421, 419, also 433.

sion of members of the Dutch nobility from the Dutch republic's war-making process. In Feld's initial essay on the subject, this argument was implicit—he maintained that in the Netherlands during the Eighty Years' War, the war-making role of the nobility was superseded by the new Dutch state and he associated this with the emergence of military professionalism.[9]

In a subsequent article, his argument was developed and made more explicit. The nobility's belief 'that a soldier fought for glory and from a sense of duty to his sovereign', with 'the gratitude of his ruler and the property of his enemies' his chief reward meant that war-financing was not planned sensibly in the early part of the revolt. Because the Dutch Republic, even by the turn of the seventeenth century, was 'dominated by a merchant class', its rulers accepted 'maintenance of commerce and credit . . . as a worthwhile end in itself. Investment in an armed force was regarded as one of the fixed expenditures of that trading company in extended form, the Dutch city.'[10] In the area of tactics, too, the reforms were incompatible with the chivalric ethos of the nobility, for 'quantification of firepower made command a technique for managing violence rather than an example of heroic leadership'.[11] After all, though in other countries 'subordination among officers was impeded by considerations of social status', with nobles 'apt to resent taking orders from anyone, including nobles of lower rank' (all accurate observations), in the Netherlands the absence of noble input into the army 'facilitated the imposition of a rational command structure' (Feld's choice of the loaded term 'rational' is interesting).[12] Feld particularly suggests that the use 'on a systematic basis' of 'the engineering, artillery, and quartermaster branches' of an army *first* took place in the Dutch Republic because in other countries nobles looked down on such 'forms of military expertise' because they 'were based on technical knowledge' and/or 'did not involve direct combat'. Since such branches were 'staffed by officers of nonnoble extraction' (who, the implication is, were looked down on in most national armies but not in the Dutch) the United Provinces had an advantage in these areas.[13] 'The Dutch

---

[9] Feld (1975A), 193.
[10] Feld (1975B).
[11] Ibid., 428.
[12] Ibid., 433. It was certainly the case that differences in social rank could hinder the exercise of military command: e.g., Boynton (1967), 103–4.
[13] Feld (1975B), 433–34.

military officer was thus preeminently a technocrat. He was not an aristocrat' and both his authority and his military role 'depended not so much on what he was supposed to be [i.e., from inherent nobility] as on what he was supposed to know.' All in all, not only was the *staatse leger* by 1610 'a new kind of armed force', it was because there was no support amongst wider society for 'aristocratic military prejudices' that this was so. As Feld concludes, the United Provinces' 'most innovative military contribution . . . may well have been that it was uniquely dominated by the middle class'.[14]

Feld's influence can be seen on subsequent scholarship. H. L. Zwitzer in his study of 'de militie van den Staat', emphasises the bourgeois nature of the majority of the *staatse leger*'s officers and implies at least an association between this and their professionalism.[15] Weigley, whose general history of early-modern European warfare is itself much cited, draws partly on Feld. Weigley asserts that it was because so few nobles fought for the Revolt that the Dutch 'had to build a new kind of army'. He explicitly characterises the 'relative absence of aristocratic pretensions among Dutch officers' as beneficial to the army's efficiency and an aid in the process of professionalisation triggered by the Nassaus' reforms (e.g., by aiding in 'establishing a modern military rank structure'). This was not least because (Feld's influence here is obvious), whereas other armies collectively slighted the 'technical branches that demanded a mathematical education . . . because noblemen did not . . . [have] the necessary education', Dutch artillerists and engineers did not have to worry about being anyone's social inferior.[16] John Keegan, whose authorities include Weigley, argues that adopting 'stereotyped, almost mechanical drill-movements' led to a 'surrender of individuality' and of 'personal freedom' by officers; the Nassaus' 'reforms . . . accelerated the process'.[17] Most recently, Richard D. Brooks, is categorical: a large part of Maurice's military achievement was that he 'substituted the legionary for the preux chevalier as the ideal soldier.'[18]

It is necessary to place such views in context. Since the pioneers of sociology in the late nineteenth century, social and political sci-

---

[14] Ibid., 435, 433, 439.
[15] Zwitzer (1991), esp. ch. 6.
[16] Weigley (1993), 10–1, and 546 (citing Feld).
[17] Keegan (1993), 343–44.
[18] Brooks (2000), 75—restating Hale (1985), 130, but applying it specifically to the Netherlands.

entists (including Feld) have been fascinated by the rise of the modern nation-state as an impersonal construct, existing in and of itself, and dependent on its right to monopolise the use of force, wielded through military institutions—frequently perceived as incompatible with traditional, medieval political society.[19] A consequence of this association of the state with military force is that scholars often assume that a high degree of military organisation and efficiency indicates a decline in traditional, chivalric values.

This may seem logical. Many studies demonstrate that early-modern aristocratic values were defined by pride in lineage and highly individualistic self-sufficiency; recourse to arms was the ultimate arbiter of honourable status. Early-modern nobles, like their medieval forebears, 'were individual warriors, loaning their persons and/or troops to the service of their prince, partly from personal loyalty to him, partly for the good of the common weal, and partly in order to obtain honour.' However, the reality of early-modern society was that legitimacy 'did not only derive from the power of the relatively weak state, but also from the honour inherent in every member of the nobility.'[20] The power of the nobility effectively came from its military capability; the chivalric ethos exalted martial ability and success. In consequence, as many recent studies of medieval warfare show, and as the essays in this volume bring out, although individualism and fixation on honour might sometimes hamper the handling of operations by chivalrous warriors, their tactical and logistical acuity was often great, and they tended to adopt technological or tactical innovations very readily.

Nevertheless, there is still a widespread assumption that professionalisation of the military could occur only once individualistic aristocrats, obsessed with the honour culture produced by the chivalric ethos, ceded their predominant place in the officer corps to men of bourgeois origins. Ironically, this owes much to the historiographical orthodoxy about the nature of the Dutch army during the period of the wars of religion and the Thirty Years' War, so that these assumptions are self-feeding. Yet studies of the Dutch army in this period are insufficiently anchored in primary sources. Thus, there is

---

[19] See, e.g., Amussen (1995), 2; Greene (2000), 15, 43; Feld (1975A), 191 and (1975B), 419; cf. Tönnies (1955), 250–53; Durkheim (1971), 194, 211.

[20] See Trim (2002A), 83–88, 95 and (2002B), 83–85, at 84.

a danger of an over-mighty scholarly edifice being erected on shaky
foundations.

III

There are unfortunately few archivally-based studies of military developments in the United Provinces during the Eighty Years' War, even
though a central role in European history is ascribed to them by
proponents of a seventeenth-century military revolution, and consequently by theorists of state development, as well as by historical
sociologists such as Feld. There are authoritative modern studies,
both narrative and analytical, of how armies were organised and war
waged by France,[21] Spain,[22] England,[23] and the Ottoman Empire,[24]
in the second half of the sixteenth and first half of the seventeenth
centuries. There are no equivalent studies for the Netherlands.[25]
Works on war and society, such as Marjolein 't Hart's impressive
study of war, politics and finance during the Dutch Revolt do not
fill this gap; nor does Jonathan Israel's magisterial history of the
Dutch Republic, which though an admirable source for the political, social and economic *context* to Dutch military operations, treats
military matters themselves very superficially (as we will see).[26] There
are articles and chapters in volumes of essays, of course, but again,
collectively they do not match the volume of work for other countries in this period.

Such works as do exist are not authoritative. A history of *Het
Staatsche Leger* was produced by the Netherlands General Staff in the
first decades of the seventeenth century, but the first three volumes—
covering the period identified by Parker and Feld as critical—contain little analysis and are not strong on narrative. They print abstracts
of a large number of original documents and give lists of officers,
commissions and strengths, but while they are reliable as sources of

---

[21] Lot (1962); Potter (1993); Wood (1996); Lynn (1997); Parrott (2001).
[22] Parker (1972); González de León (1991).
[23] Davies (1963); Cruickshank (1966); Boynton (1967); McGurk (1997); Fissel
(2001).
[24] Finkel (1988).
[25] I exclude works published before World War II and on military theory—such
works could of course also be multiplied for other national military historiographies.
[26] Hart (1993); Israel (1995).

data, their interpretations (when offered) are not.[27] One of the works on which Israel draws is a book by C. M. Schulten and J. W. M. Schulten on *Het Leger in de Zeventiende Eeuw* ("The Army in the Seventeenth Century"). What few readers in English will appreciate is that this is a very slender book of only just over 100 pages, one in a series of popular, textbook histories.[28] The volume edited by Marco van der Hoeven is a collection of essays: although some are specialist studies based on primary research, others are not of a high scholarly standard.[29]

This situation is all the more remarkable, since there *are* substantial works on the early-modern Dutch army and its campaigns, but from later in the epoch. As well as Olaf van Nimwegen's excellent monograph on the War of the Spanish Succession, there is also the history of the Republic's army by H. L. Zwitzer.[30] Even this latter work is problematic. His expertise is evidently on the 1690s and eighteenth century. When Zwitzer writes of what he knows, he can be taken as authoritative. However, his book's sub-title ("The Army of the Republic of the United Netherlands") implies that it covers from the 1570s to the end of the Dutch Republic in 1795. To be sure, he does incorporate the sixteenth and seventeenth centuries into his account. What is masked by his thematic approach (since sections dealing with the earlier period are sprinkled throughout the text) is that *only* his statements on the very late seventeenth-century and the eighteenth-century army are based on archival research. For the sixteenth century and almost the whole of the seventeenth century he synthesises from *Het Staatsche Leger*, studies of other countries and general surveys of military history in Europe, along with a few specialist articles. The same is true even of his contribution to van der Hoeven's volume: though titled "The Eighty Years' War", the specific facts and figures on Dutch recruiting and troop strengths (for example) come from the first decade of the eighteenth century.[31] The essay also contains no references. In sum, the veneer of authority given by Zwitzer's solid research on the army of William III and

---

[27] ten Raa & de Bas (1911–15).
[28] Schulten & Schulten (1969).
[29] Van der Hoeven (1997). For the volume's weaknesses (and strengths), see the review in *Dutch Crossing* 22 (1998), 167–69.
[30] Van Nimwegen (1995); Zwitzer (1991).
[31] Zwitzer (1997), 46.

after should not mask the superficial nature of his treatment of the first century of the Dutch army.

It is notable that Israel, in dealing with 'Dutch Military Reforms and their European Significance', draws on a smattering of printed primary sources, the Schultens, Zwitzer and Geoffrey Parker's *The Military Revolution* (itself a synthetic overview).[32] That these are his authorities for such a crucial subject is a good insight into the state of historical literature on the Dutch army of the Eighty Years' War.

IV

The apparently impressive historiographical consensus on the nobility in the Dutch Republic is also now subject to question. Unlike the Dutch army, there is an authoritative book on the Dutch nobility: Henk van Nierop's seminal *Van ridders tot regenten*, published in English translation by Cambridge University Press.[33] However, despite its availability to Anglophone readers, van Nierop's arguments are taking time to penetrate the wider world of scholarship, indoctrinated as it has been for decades with the centrality of the bourgeois to the Netherlands in the sixteenth and seventeenth centuries. In this context, therefore, it is worth stressing van Nierop's conclusions on the period up to the end of the Eighty Years' War: 'There was no "crisis" of the Holland nobility. The history of the nobility in the age of the Dutch Revolt is a success story'. The nobility's 'social prestige had not declined' and their political power also endured.[34] These conclusions have been reinforced by subsequent more focused studies.[35]

However, van Nierop almost ignores the Dutch nobility's military role. He devotes only a handful of pages to it in his monograph, while in a paper on the role of the nobility in the early Revolt he deals with their military activities in less than a page of text.[36] This signals, or so it may be assumed, that the Dutch nobility, if still important, were nevertheless militarily disengaged. In fact, it may

---

[32] Israel (1995), 267 *et seq*.
[33] Van Nierop (1990) and (1993).
[34] Ibid., 221.
[35] E.g., van Nierop (1999).
[36] Van Nierop (1990), 17, 167–70 and (1997), 94–95.

simply reflect that generations of Dutch historians have focused on social and economic history; or the deeply unfashionable nature of military history in the Netherlands—a situation that is only now changing.[37] Nevertheless, even van Nierop's revisionist account of the Dutch nobility leaves open the possibility that it indeed played little part in the *staatse leger*, just as Feld, Zwitzer and others have argued.

In the absence of anything approaching an officer list for the *staatse leger* in this period it is impossible to be categorical about the involvement of the Dutch nobility in their Republic's army. What emerges from a survey of relevant primary and secondary sources, however, is that the nobility's ethos was equally as martial as their European counterparts at the beginning of the crucial period examined by Feld (1589–1609): 'civilianization' is just as much a myth in the sixteenth-century Netherlands as elsewhere in Christendom.[38] There are also clear indications that the culture of the Netherlands in general and of its nobility in particular was highly influenced by war; and that the chivalric ideal affected the actions even of the architects of 'professionalisation'.

V

Because of the problematic nature of the sources, it is hard to reach any firm conclusions about the great mass of officers. What is clear, though, is that Dutch nobles were far from uninterested in war.

Little is known of the *bandes d'ordonnance* in the Low Countries, but they seem to have been recruited and constituted like those in France—that is, their rank and file were virtually entirely nobles, chosen by the great aristocrats who were the captains (for whom captaincy of an *ordonnance* company was a much sought-after honour)—and they had been an important part of the military resources of the Netherlands in the years before the Revolt.[39] This remained the case right up to the creation of the United Provinces in the late 1570s.[40] Even outside the organised *bandes*, the 'tenants and

---

[37] Zwitzer (1991), 9–13.
[38] See p. 16 above, in 'Introduction'.
[39] Parker (1977), 49–50; cf. Parker (1972), 25.
[40] E.g., Gachard (1854), 11, William of Orange, proposal to the States-General,

dependants' of the nobles 'formed a major source of the private armies they led into the service of the States-General or Spain.'[41] Regardless of whether circumstances had changed by the end of the sixteenth century, the Dutch nobility was in its nature as martial as its counterparts elsewhere in Europe. As van Nierop, indicates, this explains why Protestant craftsmen and merchants who fled Spanish persecution in the 1560s and early 1570s generally supported the rebellion only through money, whereas refugee nobles actively pros-ecuted hostilities against the Spanish. Both simply carried on their lifestyle in exile: those who traded used their profits to fund and supply those who fought—but certainly the members of Dutch sec-ond estate at this point still conceived of themselves as being those in society who fought. At this stage, they were in effect, both in their own eyes and those of the urban bourgeois, 'the profession-als'.[42] This was not only true of those nobles who fought for William of Orange and the rebellious States-General. It was also true of the many nobles who remained loyal.

There was no pacifistic tradition prior to the Revolt. If the nobil-ity of the Netherlands did disengage from war it must have hap-pened in the 1580s and 1590s. In fact, however, Dutch aristocrats continued personally to invest heavily in the war effort against Spain right through to the seventeenth century. It is true that the num-bers of aristocrats serving *in the ranks* ('edelluyden') declined consid-erably. Early in the revolt, the proportion of aristocratic rankers found in surviving muster rolls is as high as 7.07 per cent, though it is also as low as 1.09 per cent and probably was usually at the lower end of this spectrum. However, from the reforms of the 1590s there was no longer any provision for them at all in the official establishments of foot companies.[43] There is thus some evidence that the central government was trying to rationalise rank hierarchy, but without knowing more about the subalterns of the States' forces it is impossible to say that there were fewer noble *officers*, as opposed to gentlemen rankers. Indeed, the sharp distinction between the stand-

---

29 Aug. 1577; PRO, SP 83/4, no. 53, memorandum of Ambassador William Davison, Dec. 1577.

[41] Wilson (1970), 49–50.

[42] See van Nierop (1997), 94–95.

[43] Trim (2002B), 280. For the relevant regulations see ARA, Collectie Aanwinsten 877 (for 1595), Archief Raad van Staat 2476, pp. 91–92 (for 1599), and Archief Adrian Bogaers 46, unfoliated (for 1599 and 1623).

ing army and the celebrated civic militias of Dutch cities, which were drawn from the merchants and wealthier artisans (with the other local troops, the *waardegelders*, raised from those of still lower social status), suggests that the officers of the *staatse leger* collectively had different social origins—and thus were predominantly noble, rather than bourgeois.[44]

Nor is it the case that nobles were found as officers only in the horse and foot units of the army. As we have seen, the notion has been advanced, *inter alia* by Feld and Weigley, that aristocrats viewed 'the engineering, artillery, and quartermaster branches' with disdain. This was probably never true: indeed, 'medieval captains as a group were enthusiasts for gunpowder technology, in the use of which they proved themselves quite adept'.[45] Simon Pepper in this volume has shown how a profession which we would instinctively associate with the bourgeois (that of the military engineer-cum-architect) was in fact not divorced from the chivalric culture of the nobility.[46] The same is true, at least in the Netherlands, of officers of artillery and of logistics. The 'artillerists and engineers' of 'the Dutch army . . . were the social equals of just about everyone else' *because* most of them were nobles.[47]

Under Prince Maurice, the *staatse leger* had a sequence of great aristocrats as generals of the artillery, including Charles de Levin, Lord of Famars, Pieter van der Does, Johan van Duyvenvoorde, Karel van Wijngaerden, and Willem Adriaan, count of Hornes and Lord of Kessel.[48] At the more junior level, of five commanders of artillery of the garrison of Ostend, which endured a famous siege from 1601–4, four were infantry captains of whom at least two were nobles, while the fifth is described as a 'nobleman of the ordinance'— evidently nobles continued to serve in the ranks in the artillery, if not in the infantry. This is further evidence that the reason for their removal in the reforms of the 1590s was to rationalise the rank structure, not because of a shortage of, or antipathy to, nobles.[49]

Members of the second estate also continued to serve as engineers—mastery of the necessary mathematical knowledge was part

---

[44] See Wagenaar (1997), 211, 227; Israel (1995), 442–48.
[45] Trim (2002A), 71–72.
[46] Ch. 5, above.
[47] *Pace* Weigley (1993), 11.
[48] ten Raa & de Bas (1913), 265–66 and (1915), 14.
[49] ten Raa & de Bas (1913), 275–76: 'edelman van het geschut'.

of their education rather than otherwise.[50] In addition, Dutch nobles
recognised the importance of logistics: the interest of the élites in
this vital area may well have been a major factor in the United
Provinces' military success. The systematisation of the system of logistics was, as we have seen in chapter 1, an indication of the army's
increasing professionalism.[51] It began, however, even before the reforms
of the Nassaus' in the 1590s, originating under Aernt van Dorp,
master of the logistics train for the States-General in the early 1580s.
His papers survive—many of his letters were published in the late
nineteenth century,[52] but many of the documents relating to his management of the logistics in the early 1580s remain accessible only in
manuscript. They show his genuine interest in, methodical approach
to and adeptness at handling of, campaign supply.[53] Yet van Dorp
was one of the greatest nobles in what became the United Provinces
and he was a man who very much subscribed to the noble (and
chivalric) ethos. He not only used his and his family's estates to
finance the rebellion, he was prepared to finance a particular campaign against the city-state of Mechelen by William of Orange,
because his property litigation records were all stored there![54] Clearly,
for many of the Dutch nobility at the time Maurice became Captain-
General, individual exigencies remained an important consideration
in war.

VI

This should not come as a surprise. Dutch culture was neither as
bourgeois nor as pacifistic as Victorian-era Dutch historians and art
historians, themselves products of bourgeois culture and *mentalité*, perceived it to be.

The great Dutch cultural historian, Johan Huizinga, writing in the
early years of the twentieth century, marginalised the significance of
war to the culture of the Netherlands in 'the golden age', declaring

---

[50] E.g., ch. 8, above; and Guy (1990), 421–22. See also *New DNB, s.n.* Thomas
Lovell and John Ogle, for examples of aristocratic soldiers in the Dutch army with
an interest in engineering.

[51] Above, p. 17.

[52] Van Dorp (1887–88).

[53] Key collections of documents are, e.g., ARA, Archief van Dorp 971, 973, 986.

[54] Van Nierop (1990), 107–8.

that land warfare did not agree with the Dutch national character. As Zwitzer observes, this tell us more 'about Huizinga's . . . interpretation of Dutch history' than it adds 'to our knowledge of Dutch culture in the seventeenth century.' Indeed, Dutch fascination with the events of the Eighty Years' War 'found expression in works of art, in many songs, in books and in poetical works', as well as in numerous pictures, though (thanks not least to Huizinga), paintings of naval actions are better known than those of land actions.[55]

Dutch society and culture was not only more martial than many textbooks and surveys indicate it was also more influenced by noble values. Gordon Kipling, in his superb study of the interplay of sixteenth-century English and Dutch culture, emphasises how William of Orange's propagandists of the 1570s and 1580s portrayed his cause in terms of traditional Burgundian martial culture. They presented William himself, and other leaders of the Revolt, as the embodiment of chivalric virtues.[56] William's sons, Maurice and Frederick Henry, not unnaturally lived up to this and it was reflected in the political culture of even the urban bourgeoisie. The city council of Haarlem in 1620 commissioned a large allegorical painting that emphasised 'the Christian virtues' and martial prowess of all the leading members of the house of Orange. Engravings of Maurice and Frederick Henry, depicted at moments of martial triumph, were popular in the following decade.[57] It is true, as Feld points out, that Maurice's lifestyle was not princely and that, in H. H. Rowen's words, 'the vanity of titles was not one of his vices'.[58] Frederick Henry, however, lived not so much like a prince as a king. His court was one of splendid magnificence, he himself a patron of painters, designers, architects, gardeners, poets and philosophers—in short, he lived exactly as expected of a great noble and was, as Israel puts it, 'one of Europe's leading courtly figures'.[59] Moreover, leading members of the households of both Maurice and Frederick Henry were aristocratic soldiers—French, English and German, as well as Dutch—whose traditional values accorded with their princes' own aristocratic ethos.[60]

---

[55] Zwitzer (1997), 53, 54.
[56] Kipling (1977), 160–63.
[57] Israel (1995), 460.
[58] Feld (1975B), 434; Rowen (1990), 50.
[59] Israel (1995), 486, also 534, 586.
[60] See Rowen (1990), 41; Cornette (1993), 108–9.

It is true that in the 1640s a number of Dutch pamphleteers alleged a sharp contrast between Frederick Henry and his subjects—between princes who lived for war and merchants who sought peace in order that trade might flourish. This was, however, a rhetorical strategy used against the Prince by his political opponents in the provincial States at a time of war-weariness, when Frederick's magic touch that had brought a string of victories in the late 1620s and early 1630s had deserted him.[61] It would be a mistake, therefore, to put too much weight on these sources. All in all, as J. L. Price argues: 'The culture which developed in the Dutch state in the last decades of the sixteenth and in the course of the seventeenth century was to an extent in the thrall of the past: this is shown in the conservative ethos of politics as well as in the influence of traditional forms and values in painting and literature. . . . Similarly, there [was] no direct challenge to the aristocratic value system that was dominant in the rest of Europe.'[62]

We can say more, however, than simply that nobles fought and that they came from a society that was still imbued by traditional aristocratic (and hence chivalric) values. The Dutch nobility's approach to war was informed by the chivalric ethos and it influenced their actions. Dutch nobles in Feld's critical 1589–1609 period and after were keen to demonstrate prowess and courage and to obtain recognition from the community of honour for their individual achievements. Chivalric values thus influenced the conduct of operations.

Jan Orlers, a prominent Leiden publisher, in 1610 published an important book—*Den Nassauschen Lauren-crans* (or "The Laurels of Nassau").[63] This is a record of all the campaigns waged by Maurice of Nassau from the time he succeeded William of Orange until the Twelve Years' Truce commenced in 1609. As owner-manager of a print shop in one of the commercial towns of Holland, Orlers could not better represent the supposed 'middle-class' ethos that Feld saw as guiding developments in the *staatse leger*. Yet this member of the urban bourgeoisie constantly praises actions of heroic, individual mar-

---

[61] Maland (1980), 175–78.
[62] Price (1994), 52.
[63] Orlers (1610). An English translation was published three years later: Shute (1613). However, it was made from the French edition, published in 1610, and whether for this or other reasons, a number of sections in the original are missing or inaccurately translated, so the Dutch edn is to be preferred.

tial prowess. This may or may not reflect his own world-view and precisely which sections of Dutch society Orlers aimed the book at is not clear, but what is clear he took for granted that they, at any rate, bought into the chivalric value system.

Moreover, the number of incidents recorded among "The Laurels of Nassau" makes it clear that Orlers is not describing a theoretical, or nominal, value system, found only in literature. The eminent Dutch cavalry commander Marcelis Bacx was one of Maurice of Nassau's circle of trusted commanders for some twenty years, an expert in the most up-to-date cavalry tactics; he is a clear example of the developing influence of military professional values. But he did not therefore abandon the values of chivalry. Instead, when confronted with a mounted enemy champion (an Albanian), near Bergen in 1589, Bacx engaged him in single combat as the hero of a chivalric epic might have done. He was victorious and his deed praised among "The Laurels of Nassau".[64]

Orlers emphasises the participation of Dutch aristocrats as gentlemen volunteers in the Earl of Essex's Anglo-Dutch expedition to Cadiz in 1596.[65] Essex's adherence to the values of the cult of chivalry was well known at the time (indeed, he is often regarded as a throwback to a previous era because of it); he was popular in the Netherlands (which is itself suggestive) and remained popular even after his premature death.[66] In choosing to relate the service of the numerous Dutch 'voluntaries' (in English parlance), Orlers privileges not professional values but rather, by implication, those of the knight-errant, seeking great adventures regardless of the hierarchy of rank. The heroic death of Captain Baldwin Meetkerke is described in laudatory terms and Orlers also recounts the knighting by Essex of four Dutch nobles.[67]

Orlers also lauds in traditional, heroic, chivalric terms, not only the generals but also the officers and soldiers of the States' army who contributed to great victories, such as those at Turnhout (1597) and Nieuwpoort (1600). Turnhout, for example, is termed 'a lordly victory'[68] and Orlers stressed how 'the counts Hohenlo and Solms,

---

[64] Orlers (1610), 64.
[65] Ibid., 109.
[66] I am obliged to Dr Paul Hammer for this information.
[67] Orlers (1610), 113.
[68] Ibid., 117: 'een herrlicke victorie'. Shute (1613) 200, translates it as 'gallant

with [Sir Francis] Vere (whose horse was slain that day under him) and [Sir Robert] Sidney were highly honoured for their wisdom and honour, also other captains and commanders that had valiantly behaved themselves, especially Bacx . . . with all their officers and soldiers.'[69] Similar examples could be multiplied.

Orlers was not alone in praising traditional, chivalric values. The seventeenth-century chronicler Wouter van Gouthoeven associated 'inborn bravery of mind' with 'the exercise of arms and virtues', which he commended to the townsmen of Holland, Zeeland and Utrecht. An anonymous pamphleteer of 1608, writing on 'the triumph of war', likewise asserted that common men could only be made noble 'through brave deeds'.[70] He was effectively linking courage and nobility, just as the literature of chivalry had done for centuries.[71]

Equally, the surrender of Breda, memorably pictured by Diego de Velázquez, 'represents the Spanish crown's official embrace of the chivalric ethos in the war in the Netherlands', as González de León pointed out in the last chapter,[72] but it also encapsulates Dutch adherence to the same world-view (see plate 7). Justin of Nassau, handing the key to the city to the victorious Spínola is dressed more simply than the magnanimous victor, but this probably reflects his age—it is the fashion of two different generations that is counterpointed, rather than that of two different societies. Justin was a full participant in a chivalric ritual and if the Dutch are, on this occasion, the recipients of Spínola's 'chivalry', there had been many occasions in the preceding thirty years when the boot had been firmly on the other foot—and first Maurice and then Frederick Henry (Justin's cousins) were no less punctilious in their observation of the chivalric courtesies than was Spínola in 1625.

---

victory'. A modern equivalent would be 'magnificent victory', but as Kipling (1977), 28–29, 61, points out, in the early-modern period 'magnificence' was a cardinal chivalric virtue—thus, lordly conveys the original sense well.

[69] Orlers (1610), 117: 'De Graven van Hohenlo & van Solms meete heeren Ridderen Vere, diens paert onder hem gheschoten werdt, & Sidney, werdt groote eere toegeschreven van haer voorsichticheyt ende vroomheyt . . .'. Shute (1613), 200.

[70] Van Gouthoeven, *D'Oude chronyke ende historiën van Holland, Zeeland ende Utrecht,* 2nd edn (The Hague: 1636), 119, and anon., *Den Triumph vanden oorloch ende de misprijsinghe vanden peys seer genoechlijck ende cortswijlich om te lesen enz* (Leiden: 1608), fo. B2ᵛ, both quoted in van Nierop (1993), 29.

[71] Compare p. 29 above, in 'Introduction'.

[72] Above, p. 260.

Conclusion

Chivalry was not, then, irrelevant in the Netherlands during the Eighty Years' War. The *staatse leger* certainly had many professional qualities. Military professionalism probably developed earlier and more substantially in the Dutch Republic than elsewhere. It did not, however, arise because of a lack of bellicosity in the Dutch nobility or Dutch society more generally.

Dutch nobles were still very much a presence in the army and they still adhered to the chivalric ethos long after the nobility had allegedly abandoned traditional martial values and retreated into decline and after the army had supposedly been transformed by middle-class professionalism. Because the nobility dominated the officers' ranks, the social potential inherent in the Nassaus' reforms was not realised in this period. Military professionalism developed in the Netherlands in this period to an unusual extent. Perhaps this was *in spite of* the enduring importance of the chivalric ethos. However, it certainly did not develop because the chivalric ethos was moribund.

Bibliography

Amussen, S. (1995) "Punishment, Discipline, and Power: The Social Meanings of Violence in Early Modern England", *Journal of British Studies* 34 (1995) 1–34.

Boynton, L. (1967) *The Elizabethan Militia, 1558–1638* (London/Toronto: 1967).

Brooks, R. (2000) "The Military Renaissance 1500–1650", in *The Times History of War*, ed. R. D. Brooks (London: 2000; St. Helens: 2000) 62–81.

Bush, M. (1967) *Renaissance, Reformation and the Outer World* (London: 1967).

Cornette, J. (1993) *Le Roi de Guerre: Essai sur la souveraineté dans la France du Grand Siècle* (Paris: 1993).

Corvisier, A. (1976) *Armées et sociétés en Europe de 1494 à 1789* (Paris: 1976).

Cruickshank, C. (1966) *Elizabeth's Army*, 2nd edn (Oxford: 1996).

Davies, C. (1963) "Supply Services of English Armed Forces 1509–1550", unpublished DPhil thesis (University of Oxford: 1963).

van Dorp, A. (1887–88) *Brieven en onuitgegeven stukken van jonkheer Arend van Dorp*, ed. J. B. J. N. van der Schueren (Historisch Genootschap, Utrecht, new ser., nos 44, 50).

Durkheim, E. (1971) *Selected Writings*, ed., trans. and intro. A. Giddens (Cambridge: 1971).

Feld, M. (1975A) "Military Professionalism and the Mass Army", *Armed Forces and Society* 1 (1975), no. 1, 191–214.

——. (1975B) "Middle-Class Society and the Rise of Military Professionalism: The Dutch Army 1589–1609", *Armed Forces and Society* 1 (1975), no. 4, 419–42.

Finkel, C. (1988) *The Administration of Warfare: The Ottoman Campaigns in Hungary, 1593–1606*, Zeitschrift für die Kunde des Morgenlandes, XIV (Vienna: 1988).

Fissel, M. (2001) *English Warfare 1511–1642* (London & New York: 2001).

Gachard, M. (1854) *Correspondance de Guillaume le Taciturne, Prince d'Orange*, 6 vols., ed. M. Gachard (Brussels, Leipzig & Ghent: 1847–57), IV.

de Gheyn J. (1607) *Wapenhandelinghe van roers, musquetten ende spiessen* (The Hague: 1607).

———. (1986) *The Exercise of Arms: A Seventeenth Century Military Manual*, ed. D. J. Blackmore (London: 1986).

González de León, F. (1991) "The Road to Rocroi: The Duke of Alba, The Count-Duke of Olivares and the High Command of the Spanish Army of Flanders in the Eighty Years' War", unpublished Ph.D thesis (John Hopkins University: 1991).

Green, V. (1952) *Renaissance and Reformation* (London: 1952).

Greene, C. (2000) "The Cultural Significance of Interpersonal Violence, With Special Reference to Seventeenth-Century Worcestershire", unpublished PhD thesis (University of Warwick: 2000).

Guy, J. (1990) *Tudor England* (Oxford: 1988; paperback edn, 1990).

Hale, J. (1985) *War and Society in Renaissance Europe*, paperback edn (London: 1985).

't Hart, M. (1993) *The Making of a Bourgeois State, War, Politics, and Finance during the Dutch Revolt* (Manchester: 1993).

van der Hoeven, M. (1997), ed., *Exercise of Arms: Warfare in the Netherlands, 1568–1648* (Leiden, New York & Köln: 1997).

Israel, J. (1995) *The Dutch Republic: Its Rise, Greatness, and Fall 1477–1806* (Oxford & New York: 1995).

Keegan, J. (1993) *A History of Warfare* (London: 1993).

Kipling, G. (1977) *The Triumph of Honour: Burgundian Origins of the Elizabethan Renaissance*, Publications of the Sir Thomas Browne Institute, General Ser., 6 (Leiden: 1977).

Lot, F. (1962) *Recherches sur les effectifs des armées françaises des Guerres d'Italie aux Guerres de Religion 1494–1562*, Bibliothéque générale de l'École Pratique des Hautes Études, 6e section (Paris: 1962).

Lynn, J. (1997) *Giant of the Grand Siècle: The French Army 1610–1715* (Cambridge & New York: 1997).

McCullough, R. (2001) "Military Theory: Early Modern, 1450–1800", in *Reader's Guide to Military History*, ed. Charles Messenger (London & Chicago: 2001) 369–72.

McGurk, J. (1997) *The Elizabethan Conquest of Ireland* (Manchester: 1993).

van Nimwegen, O. (1995) *De Subsistentie van het Leger: Logistiek en Strategie van het Geallieerde en met Name het Staatse Leger tijdens de Spaanse Successieoorlog* (Amsterdam: 1995).

Maland, D. (1980) *Europe at War 1600–1650* (London & Basingstoke: 1980).

van Nierop (1990) *Van ridders tot regenten: De Hollandse adel in de zestiende en de eerste helft van de zeventiende eeuw*, 2nd edn (Amsterdam: 1990).

———. (1993) *The Nobility of Holland: From Knights to Regents, 1500–1650*, trans. Maarten Ultee (Cambridge: 1993).

———. (1999) "The Nobility and the Revolt of the Netherlands: Between Church and King, and Protestantism and Privileges", in *Reformation, Revolt and Civil War in France and the Netherlands 1555–1585*, ed. P. Benedict, G. Marnef, H. van Nierop and M. Venard, Koninklijke Nederlandse Akademie van Wetenschappen, Verhandelingen, Afd. Letterkunde, [new ser.], 176 (Amsterdam: 1999) 83–98.

Orlers, J. (1610) *Den Nassauschen Lauren-crans . . .* (Leyden: 1610). English edn 1613, see Shute, cited below.

Parker, G. (1972) *The Army of Flanders and the Spanish Road* (Cambridge: 1972; repr. with corrections, 1990).

———. (1977) *The Dutch Revolt* (London: 1977).

———. (1984) *Europe in Crisis 1598–1648* (London: 1979; 4th impression with revisions, 1984).

———. (1988) *The Military Revolution: Military Innovation and the Rise of the West 1500–1800. The Lees Knowles Lectures 1984* (Cambridge: 1988).

Parrott, D. (2001) *Richelieu's Army: War, Government and Society in France, 1624–1642* (Cambridge: 2001).

Potter, D. (1993) *War and Government in the French Provinces: Picardy 1470–1560* (Cambridge: 1993).

Price, J. (1994) " 'By Their Fruits Shall Ye Know Them': The Cultural Legacy of the Revolt", *De Zeventiende Eeuw* 10 (1994) 47–56.

Puype, J. (1997) "Victory at Nieuwpoort, 2 July 1600", in *Exercise of Arms: Warfare in the Netherlands, 1568–1648*, ed. Marco van der Hoeven (Leiden, New York & Köln: 1997) 69–112.

Rogers, C. (1995) *The Military Revolution Debate: Readings on the Military Transformation of Early Modern Europe*, ed. C. J. Rogers (Boulder, Colo.: 1995).

Rothenberg, G. (1986) "Maurice of Nassau, Gustavus Adolphus, Raimondo Montecuccoli and the "Military Revolution" of the Seventeenth Century", in *Makers of Modern Strategy from Machiavelli to the Nuclear Age*, ed. P. Paret *et al.* (Princeton: 1986) 32–63.

Rowen, H. (1990) *The Princes of Orange: The Stadholders in the Dutch Republic* (Cambridge: 1988; paperback edn, 1988).

Schulten, C. & J. Schulten (1969) *Het Leger in de Zeventiende Eeuw* (Bussum: 1969).

Shute, W. (1613), trans., *The Triumphs of Nassov: or, a description and representation of all the victories both by land and sea, granted . . . to . . . the Estates Generall of the United Netherlands Provinces* (London: 1613)—English edn of Orlers (1610) cited above.

ten Raa, F. & F. de Bas (1911–15) *Het Staatsche Leger 1568–1795*, I, *1568–1588*, II, *1588–1609*, III, *1609–1625* (Breda: 1911, 1913, 1915).

Tönnies, F. (1955) *Community and Association*, trans. C. P. Loomis (London: 1955).

Trim, D. (2002A) " 'Knights of Christ'? Chivalric Culture in England, *c.* 1400–*c.* 1550", in *Cross, Crown and Community: Religion, Government and Culture in Early Modern England, 1400–1800*, ed. Peter J. Balderstone and D. J. B. Trim (Oxford, Bern, New York & Frankfurt-am-Main: 2002) 67–102.

———. (2002B) "Fighting 'Jacob's Warres'. The Employment of English and Welsh Mercenaries in the European Wars of Religion: France and the Netherlands 1562–1610", unpublished PhD thesis (University of London: 2002).

Wagenaar, P. (1997) "The 'Waardegelders' of Den Haag", in *Exercise of Arms: Warfare in the Netherlands, 1568–1648*, ed. M. van der Hoeven (Leiden, New York & Köln: 1997) 211–30.

Weigley, R. (1993) *The Age of Battles: The Quest for Decisive Warfare from Breitenfeld to Waterloo* (London: 1993; orig. edn, Indianapolis: 1991).

Wijn, J. (1934) *Het krijgswesen in den tijd van Prins Maurits* (University of Utrecht: 1934).

Wilson, C. (1970) *Queen Elizabeth and the Revolt of the Netherlands* (London: 1970).

Wood, J. (1996) *The King's Army: Warfare, Soldiers, and Society during the Wars of Religion in France, 1562–1576* (Cambridge: 1996).

Zwitzer, H. (1991) *"De Militie van den Staat": Het leger van de Republiek der Verenigde Nederlanden* (Amsterdam: 1991).

———. (1997) "The Eighty Years War", in *Exercise of Arms: Warfare in the Netherlands, 1568–1648*, ed. Marco van der Hoeven (Leiden, New York & Köln: 1997) 33–55.

CHAPTER ELEVEN

THE OFFICER CORPS AND ARMY COMMAND IN THE BRITISH ISLES, 1620–1660

Martyn Bennett

I

The development of a professional officer corps was essential to the establishment of a national army in the seventeenth century. Experience of combat and of army life in general was considered important to the successful management of armies, but it was not the only consideration. Armies raised in the British Isles reflected the social structure; from the private man to the commander in chief in an army which mirrored society. They often also reflected the geography. Officers and soldiers for home service wherever possible were selected on the grounds that they would have had, what have then been then called an 'interest' in the area in which they would be stationed. Property holders or owners were desirable soldiers: their military rank reflected their social position. This policy was somewhat adulterated in the armies raised for service abroad, but some elements of it remained: the officers reflected the social structure and the recruitment followed a similar pattern to that for home service. The wars between 1639 and 1653 saw recruitment begin along similar lines, but the continuation of the wars tended to alter long held principles. Yet, even at the outset of the most cataclysmic home war for over a century and a half, principles of regionalism and social rank remained a paradigm.

This essay will examine the recruitment and the structure of officer corps in armies raised during the early seventeenth century within the British Isles. It will focus on some armies in particular and raise questions about the structures of others. Whilst the essay will concentrate upon one royalist regional army during the first civil war, it will set this in the context of other armies including: Count Mansfeldt's expeditionary force; the Cadiz expedition; the Duke of Buckingham's intervention in France's religious conflicts; the Bishop's

Wars; the army raised for service in Ireland in 1641–2; and briefly the New Model Army. Professionalism in the armies raised during the first half of the seventeenth century developed largely from experience of warfare, but a sense of class could also create a form of *esprit de corps*: The officers' revolt of 1624–5 suggests that even a newly created cadre of officers could develop a sense of professional identity. Military experience, even if brief, was considered a premium in most cases. There were exceptions during the 1620s but the 1640s saw the experienced professional soldier as a necessity.

II

Even though there had been no expeditionary forces dispatched to Europe during James Stuart's reign as King of England, Ireland and Wales troops from Britain had served in garrisons in the Low Countries until 1615. However, for about nine years state sanctioned military experience was largely confined to garrisons within the British Isles. By 1624 James VI and I's policy of non-intervention had been eroded. Troops were raised in England for service in Holland and Germany under Count Ernst de Mansfeldt in 1624. In 1625 Sir Edward Cecil led a doomed expedition to Cadiz and in 1627 troops were recruited for service against the French under the Duke of Buckingham. In total orders for the conscription of 50,000 men were issued during the 1620s, 28,000 between 1624 and 1627 alone.[1] In these cases the soldiers were unpopular amongst the communities upon which they were billeted whilst awaiting transportation to Europe. In some case the troops initiated a crime-wave where they were billeted, such as occurred at Dover in 1624–5 when troops, raised for service under Count Mansfeldt, could not be controlled by their in experienced officers.[2] Eventually this unpopularity made itself felt in political circles and formed part of the basis for the Petition of Right in 1628.

In 1624, 8,000 soldiers were raised in England and 4,000 ordered to be raised in Scotland for a military expedition in Lower Germany under Count Mansfeldt. These would be organised into six regiments, three of which would be commanded by members of the

---

[1] Stearns (1972) 4.
[2] Everritt-Green (1859) 439.

English nobility and three by members of the gentry.[3] At the same time 2,250 foot and 230 horse were raised for service in Ireland in case the unsettled state of northern Europe caused trouble there.[4] The troops for Mansfeldt were to be selected in twenty-four counties and sent to Dover by the traditional leaders of the county military community, the lord lieutenants and their deputies. This gave recruitment a firm basis in county levies, even if these were broken down later. The men selected were not those usually commanded by the lord lieutenants. Rather than the husbandmen and yeomen who made up the trained bands, the levies for Mansfeldt seem to have been labourers and skilled craftsmen and perhaps unfortunate but for the authorities, timely, visitors to the counties from which they were dispatched.[5] Indeed, agricultural tenant farmers, beloved of the trained bands were specifically excluded for enlistment in 1624 and 1627 as were members of the trained bands themselves. There were exceptions; the Leicestershire 1624 Mansfeldt levy did contain a significant proportion of husbandmen, although the Isle de Rhe levy of 1627 did not.

In 1624 the Privy Council and monarch who were canvassed by friends and associates seeking places for individuals nominated the initial selection of officers, the colonels and first captains. Some of these recommendations were no doubt on the grounds of social status rather than experience but in some cases experience counted. Secretary of State Edward Conway suggested a place for a Dutchman, Van Hutton, because of his military experience and because as the expedition would serve in the Low Countries, it would be a good idea to have someone who spoke the language.[6] The captains proved to be a wilful group; demonstrating a sense of their worth and standing. They were not content with the conditions of their commissions: they were expected to pay for their soldiers' coat and conduct money out of their own pockets. Another annoyance was that they were not told what their pay-rates were to be, because the Privy Council simply did not know. This had been left to Mansfeldt and he lost the necessary records at sea. Colonels and first captains wished to have the right to appoint the junior officers, but the Privy Council

---

[3] One of them, James Hay, Lord Doncaster was a Scot with English titles.
[4] Everritt-Green (1859) 394.
[5] Ibid., 361, 362; Fissel, (1994) 227–230.
[6] Everritt-Green (1859) 391.

wanted to retain that right itself. The officers were probably unhappy at not being allowed to chose the soldiers themselves and thus ensure the quality of the recruits. There was a good deal of corruption in the counties where deputy lieutenants who would not have to lead the men in battle accepted bribes from able-bodied recruits to get themselves off the rolls. In some places the deputies were also over recruiting to secure similar bribes from the 'extras'. George Villiers, Duke of Buckingham, eventually got Mansfeldt to cover coat and conduct out of his advance. Although he supported the officers' desire to select their juniors, he was unable to get the council to loosen its grip on appointments and it issued commissions right down to the rank of ensign and most of the nominees for captain sent by the royal court were accepted.[7] The pay rates were set at 'States' rates' in other words whatever was the going rate in the United Provinces.[8] The problem of the quality of recruits was not resolved for this expedition, but in later ones, captains were allowed input into recruitment. In some cases there appears to have been a failure to employ experienced men. A number of Scottish officers with several years experience of serving under Mansfeld had come to London expecting appointments to captain Scottish regiments. However after six months in the capital they had been completely ignored and were left destitute and begging for help.[9]

The 1625 Cadiz expedition was led by an officer corps, which although it contained a number of experienced men, was dominated by inexperienced gentry nominated by the Duke of Buckingham.[10] Even though a general problem underlying all of these expeditions was that they were led by 'company and regimental commanders with little if any combat experience and often no practise with their new units', the Privy Council had gone to great efforts to bring experienced officers back from Mansfeldt's failed expedition in the United Provinces with their troops.[11] Two thousand men, one fifth of the total to be raised for the Cadiz expedition, were to be shipped back from the Low Countries to England for the campaign. Two thousand new recruits from the northern counties were to be sent from

---

[7] Ibid., 394, 395.
[8] Ibid., 391–392; Stearns (1972) 14–15.
[9] Everritt-Green (1859) 464, 511.
[10] Firth (1992) 3–4.
[11] Wheeler (1999), 72.

Hull to the Low Countries to replace the regiments recalled for Cadiz.[12] At the same time officers due to serve with Mansfeldt, but still in England, were asked to serve instead with the Cadiz force. Secretary of State Conway asked several men to change their plans including the Earl of Essex, who was to become vice admiral of the expedition, and Ralph Hopton, a Somerset colonel with considerable experience in continental warfare.[13] However, Buckingham's men dominated the officer cadre and their inexperience, particularly in logistics, told: the troops returned home after a failed campaign.

Charles I embarked on intervention in French domestic religious issues. Levies were raised for expeditionary forces to be sent to rescue trapped Huguenots. In England fewer husbandmen were recruited to the Rochelle forces as the Leicestershire levy demonstrates. This is explained by the fact this levy was to participate in a spring campaign when husbandmen would be busy with the sowing: Mansfeldt's campaign was scheduled for winter after the harvest when the husbandmen were comparatively idle. The Isle de Rhe regiments were reconstructed for Buckingham's La Rochelle expedition and a total force of 8,000 created with additional conscripts. Twenty companies of men from Ireland were also to be raised, half of them to be veterans of Cadiz. From Scotland, 2,000 men were to be led by the Earl of Morton and sent to await transportation at the Isle of Wight.[14]

III

The 1630s were marked by very little military activity until the end of the decade when unprecedented numbers of troops were raised for war within the British Isles. In 1637 King Charles I's attempt to introduce some uniformity to the disparate churches in his three kingdoms inspired rejection followed by revolt, war and revolution in Scotland. In 1639 Charles sought to impose his will on Scotland with military forces. The Scots reacted by creating an army of their own.

The Scottish forces raised for the Bishop's Wars were created almost from scratch. In Scotland there was a system of periodic

---

[12] Everritt-Green (1858) 23.
[13] Ibid., 27 49.
[14] Everritt-Green (1854) 428.

exercising of men of military age known as Wapinschaws or weapon-showings. This would be done on a shire or burgh basis under the supervision of the local nobility and laird class (for this paper very roughly analogous with English and Welsh upper gentry). However, this practise had gone into abeyance. The principle reason for this was Scotland's lack of an enemy. Good relations with continental powers and a firm alliance with France had minimised the threat from across the sea: the last wars with over seas powers had happened been centuries before the reign of James VI. The principal enemy had been England and the wapinschaws had been kept up because of this fractious relationship. During the reign of Elizabeth I of England the relationship between Scotland and England had stabilised and wapinschaws decreased in number. After the Union of Crowns of 1603 the need for them had almost disappeared, very few were ordered between the Union and 1638.

A new friend also involved making new enemies and so wapinschaws were necessary during Charles I's reign as English foreign policy led to wars with France and Spain. Therefore wapinschaws were held in 1625 for Count Mansfeldt's campaign and two more in 1627 leading to the creation of the Earl of Morton's regiment which was shipped to the Isle of Wight before being embarked for the La Rochelle campaign.[15] The principle behind the raising and administering of troops in Scotland was local: shires and burghs provided the structural basis. Beyond any general wapinschaws ordered by the Council, the militia could be a matter of communal or civic pride. Perhaps the only place where wapinschaws were common was Edinburgh where they were annual between 1607 and 1637. Other burghs may have held their own, but information is lacking. Edward Furgol is sceptical of the value of the Edinburgh musters, because whatever body of troops was mustered in Edinburgh during the pre-war years it had no apparent military impact during the wars years.[16] The military expeditions sent into unruly parts of the kingdom during the early Seventeenth century were a peculiar feature of Scottish governance. Numbers of troops were sent to deal with the unruly Western isles and Highlands on fourteen occasions after the Union of Crowns, but these involved hundreds, not thousands of recruits.[17]

---

[15] Ibid., pp. 428, 435, 489; 530; Furgol (1991) 1.
[16] Furgol (1991) 1.
[17] Ibid., 1–2.

The military experience thus gathered was confined to a very small group.

The lack of this training and experience also implied a lack of leadership training amongst the Scottish noble and laird class. The largest pool of trained and experienced Scotsmen were serving abroad in the armies fighting in the continental wars of religion. To recover this lost asset the Covenanters through their *de facto* government began recalling experienced men from the continent in late 1638. The most prominent was Alexander Leslie who was given command of the army and its noble colonels. Leslie's comrades in arms were to be given a specific role: all regiments raised for the war in 1639 were to have veterans placed alongside those men placed in command for social reasons. Each colonel would have veterans as lieutenant colonels and majors: in each company there would be an experienced ensign and two veteran sergeants. This would balance the need to have an officer corps which reflected the social order; each colonel could appoint family or clan members to the posts of captains and lieutenants: and one that was capable of training and leading the inexperienced recruits. The first Bishop's War was not to prove a good training ground for the Scottish soldiers. There would have been ample time for drill as the forces converged at the danger areas, the West Coast near to Wentworth's Irish forces, Aberdeen and the border with England; but there was little fighting. Except for the battle at Aberdeen, the most action the army saw was a spot of English-chasing near Kelso. The same practise was followed in the second Bishop's War in 1640. However, perhaps on the principle that the nobles had learned the trade as they went the tight control over the command structure tended to dissipate during the later wars.

The structure of the army followed a distinct regional pattern. In the first Bishop's War regiments of foot were recruited almost wholly within shires, like that of the Earl of Dalhousie's regiment raised in Midlothian. Or in parts of shires like Sir George Buchanan of Buchanan's regiment of foot raised in west Stirlingshire. The same pattern prevailed a year later although some regiments could, of course have a much more localised recruitment pattern: Sir Donald Campbell of Ardnamurchan's foot was raised on or close to his own estates only.[18]

---

[18] Ibid., 19–21, 40.

Although the Covenanter government had interfered with the appointment of officers and had established a completely new system of recruitment and logistical support, the traditional regionalism was still in place in the Bishop's Wars.

The English forces ranged against the Covenanters in 1639 were drawn almost entirely from a regional structure, which stretched back to the reign of Henry VII, and adapted by Elizabeth I during the 1580s. The system of county based forces, known as trained bands, had replaced the recruitment of armies through retainers and temporary commissions which sufficed until the Wars of the Roses. The only major change to the organisation was the institution in the 1580s of lord lieutenants and deputy lieutenants as a command structure for the county based militia. This structure replaced the earlier use of special commissions of array issued to men of local standing (often embracing JPs). The two Bishop's Wars left this revised structure intact, utilising the trained bands under the command of the deputies and the lord lieutenants.[19] There was a different approach in the second of these wars. Financial, rather than military, considerations influenced Charles I to experiment with resurrecting commissions of array. This was not to do with the command structure, instead the funding arrangements of the commission levied troops more certainly placed the financial burden of maintenance of the trained bands on the county, rather than on the Treasury.

There were also however units of impressed soldiers which were made of men from groups of counties rather than county-based units. The counties were not always contiguous ones: Lord Grandison for example, impressed men from Leicestershire, Gloucestershire and Worcestershire.[20] Mark Fissel has demonstrated that the social background of the two sets of soldiers thus raised for Charles's second war was markedly different. The trained bands were traditionally comprised of yeomen, husbandmen, traders and craftsmen. The impressed levies rarely mustered a husbandman in some areas, although Northamptonshire levies did have a backbone of husbandmen at its core.[21] These were more similar to 1620s levies for ser-

---

[19] Fissel (1994), contains an excellent discussion of the levying of troops in England and Wales: see pp. 178–214 in particular.
[20] Ibid., 224.
[21] Ibid., 226.

vice abroad than to the normal county-based forces assembled for home defence.

The leadership of the trained bands was firmly based on social position. Professional soldiers were usually confined to the muster-masters and to the non-commissioned officers.

Trained band colonels were the lord lieutenants, members of the aristocracy, often like the Earl of Essex or the Earl of Huntingdon, in charge of more than one county. There was the beginning of unofficial hereditary principles appearing, even though the office had been established less than sixty years. Successive Earls of Huntingdon had commanded in Leicestershire and Rutland. Even when the suitability of the fifth earl had been questioned the solution had been to appoint his heir, the future sixth earl, to share the post with him.[22] The lord lieutenants appointed their deputies who with the expertise of the mustermasters to guide them captained the trained bands. Charles I's attempt to create an 'Exact' or 'Perfect Militia' would have had benefits for the officer corps of 1639. The enthusiasm of the king for military affairs suggested in a portrait from the 1640s, in which he is pictured with his Secretary-at-War, Sir Edward Walker (1612–77), was unfortunately never sustained before the exigencies of the 1640s (see plate 8). If Charles and the Privy Council had not lost interest in the early 1630s the 'schools of arms' for junior officers and non-commissioned officers may have paid off. As it was only about half the counties in England and Wales had continued regular musters into the 1630s. One thing would not have changed regardless of the failure to perpetuate the Exact Militia: it was essentially a gentry-led militia with relatives and client gentry filling the posts. The Earl of Huntingdon and Lord Hastings, his son, appointed the younger son Henry to a captaincy in their band.[23] At the outset of the civil wars in England this principle was to be followed, despite the probability that the Bishop's Wars were lost because of the inexperience of Charles's generals and regimental commanders.[24]

---

[22] Historical Manuscripts Commission (1932) II 71.
[23] Stocks (1923) 300.
[24] Wheeler (1999) 75.

IV

Before the armies were raised in England and Wales for the civil wars, another pair of armies was raised in Britain, this time for service in Ireland. On the night of 22 October 1641 several castles in Ulster were captured by force of arms or by treachery and thus began the Irish Rebellion. For the next few months, much of government business in Edinburgh and London was taken up with creating and funding armies to ship over to put down the rebellion.

In November 1641 almost as soon as news of the rebellion in Ireland reached the governments in Westminster and Edinburgh attention turned to raising forces to send out there. In Scotland the Ulster Army was created, with the intention that it be led by the victorious general Alexander Leslie, now elevated to the peerage as the Earl of Leven by the king he had defeated. Two and half thousand of them arrived in Ulster before their commander in late April 1642 under Robert Monro. This army had been raised in a different manner to those raised for the two most recent wars. For a start the government did not appoint veterans to second the nobles who dominated the high level commissions. This caused resentment amongst the now unemployed professionals dragged from their long-term careers in Europe and now suddenly rendered unemployed by the swift military defeat of Charles I and no less swift political defeat which precipitated the withdrawal from England and the disbandment of the Covenanter Army.[25]

Moreover, whilst regionality seemed to dictate the formation of regiments such as that of the Marquis of Argyle's foot which was raised in Argyll and the adjacent isles, this was not universal. The Earl of Eglinton's regiment was raised in a far less specific area of 'south west lowlands', probably Ayrshire, Renfrewshire and Lanarkshire. Other regiments, like Leven's own were raised from a combination of places: his was chiefly from south of the Tay but Captain George Gordon's company came from far-away Sutherland. As the war dragged on, any regionalism reflected Ulster geography if it continued at all. Sir Duncan Campbell of Auchinbreck's troop of horse did not come from Argyll at all, but initially from the lowlands and then from Ulster settlers. This tendency was exacerbated by the need

---

[25] Furgol (1991) 5.

to recreate units following the acceptance of the Cessation of September 1643 by some regiments. One thing which did give the Ulster Army some form of regional uniformity, was the fact that most units came from southern Scotland, although the Earl of Lindsay's regiment broke ranks by coming wholly from Fife.

The English forces raised for the war in Ireland probably followed the traditions of the 1620s rather than the recent general principles seen in the two Bishop's Wars as far as the social status of the rank and file went. On regionality though even though this was an expeditionary force, tradition was to some extent adhered to.[26] The first regiment sent to the Lords Justices at Dublin was Sir Simon Harcourt's Foot: all 1,100 men were raised in Cheshire. Harcourt was an experienced officer, having fought in Europe and in the Bishop's Wars. It is less clear where other regiments came from, although it is likely that they were enlisted largely in the west of England. Sir Charles Vavasour was commissioned to raise a regiment half in England and half in Ireland. In December 1641 this was altered and the regiment was to be raised wholly in England: the second half from Devon and Cornwall. It is likely that many later units sent to Ireland, including Lord Forbes's levies came from the West Country too.

V

The examination of one of the royalist regional armies demonstrates how the combination of social and geographical origins was carried into the civil war officer corps. It also demonstrates how this was not entirely incompatible with the development of the professionalised officer, even in the royalist armies.

Ian Gentles has recently argued that the royalist armies had an initial dismal record, which changed only when they were replaced with professionals and soldiers of fortune.[27] This study questions his claim. Royalist officers became a professionalised officer corps as the war progressed, using their rapidly gained experience of large scale battles, garrison duty and local policing to develop skills and management training necessary to lead men in war. The first civil war

---

[26] Ryder (1985) np.
[27] Gentles (1998) 108.

should have been fought on traditional lines; neither side was initially prepared to raise troops in an extraordinary manner. The battle over control of the militia between the king and parliament centred
on control of the traditional functionaries; Parliament seemingly having forgotten its qualms about the office of lord lieutenant. The
upshot was Parliament's issue of the Militia Ordinance on 11 March
1642, which gave it control over the appointment of lord lieutenants
(as well as innovating a radical system of government through ordinance). The king responded by establishing an alternative method
of raising the trained bands, not with an alternative to the trained
bands. Charles for the second time resurrected the commissions of
array. With the assistance of county men he drew up lists of potential supporters in each county and sent them out. There were two
motives behind the commissions, one was probably financial: the
shortage of cash in 1640 which prompted the use of the commissions then was nothing compared to the king's pecuniary circumstances in the spring of 1642 when he was divorced from all funding.
The other was social. The king's army had to be commanded by
the social elite, men with proven standing and experience of local
administration and government, as a mark of the 'righteousness' of
the cause. It also offered the possibility of recruiting the lord lieutenants and their deputies displaced by the Militia Ordinance. In
James Scott Wheeler's view, this was storing up problems for later:
it prevented the rationalisation of his forces during the first civil war
as it was difficult to prise the aristocracy from places of honour such
as military command.

Professor Ronald Hutton has argued that the commissioners of
array were generally well chosen, but this may be more true of the
area covered in his book *The Royalist War Effort*, than a universal
phenomenon.[28] In the five midlands counties of Derbyshire, Leicestershire, Nottinghamshire, Rutland and Staffordshire they were not:
out of 128 appointees, 77 (60%) probably never lifted a finger to
support their king's war effort.[29]

Whether or not the commissions of array largely failed to mobilise
the aristocracy and gentry, they failed militarily: they did not succeed in mustering the militia effectively. Neither did Parliament's

---

[28] Hutton (1982) 5.
[29] Bennett (1987) 49 and passim.

lieutenancy. Peter Newman's argument about the trained bands failing to turn out for the king being because they resented his interference in their command structure holds for their reaction to Parliament's lieutenants too.[30] It was left to individual commissioners in the north and east midlands to continue their recruitment work after being given personal commissions. The forces thus raised were to supplant the trained bands, but there were attempts to maintain many of the principles associated with them.

On 11 June 1642 Henry Hastings, the second son of the 5th Earl of Huntingdon, had carried a Commission of Array to his home county of Leicestershire.[31] This was one of the earliest of the commissions intended to reassert Charles I's control over the trained bands in England and Wales. Whilst the nominated commissioners were enjoined to organise and call out the militia they were not to maintain them as a standing force.[32] It is clear that in some parts of the country at least Charles was nominating the very men displaced from the job by Parliament's Militia Ordinance. In Leicestershire and Rutland the Earl of Huntingdon led the commissions having been displaced by the Earl of Stamford in the former and the Earl of Exeter in the latter. In Nottinghamshire, Lord Newark led the commission having been replaced in the Militia Ordinance by the Earl of Clare. Former deputy lieutenants, like Henry Hastings, were also likely to be returned to their posts by the commissions.[33] A main benefit to the king was the retention of financial responsibility by the counties as it had been in 1640. There was also the probability that the king's intention was to return to deputyships men who had gained some military experience during 1639–40 and perhaps the 1620s.

Across the country, the commissions tended to meet with a combination of confusion and apathy. In Leicestershire Hastings, possibly exceeding his authority by recruiting Derbyshire mineworkers, attempted to muster the trained bands on 23 June 1642. The attempt failed as the rival Militia Ordinance deputies, the county High Sheriff, Archdale Palmer and officers sent by parliament combined to frustrate

---

[30] Newman (1993) 259.
[31] Gardiner (1978) 245–247.
[32] BL, Additional MSS 34217, fo. 70: Instructions to the Northamptonshire Commissioners of Array.
[33] Bennett (1987) 25–31.

the muster at Horsefair Leas at Leicester.[34] There were similar failures across the country as the trained bands refused to turn out for either side in numbers sufficient to make them an option. The regional principle of the trained band was not to be eschewed even if its command structure was. The commissioners who had demonstrated their loyalty were retained. Charles had based his first attempt to raise an army on the basic feudal principle of loyalty: natural law and the laws of the kingdom justified service to the king. The trained bands should have assembled in his name because of the traditional personal bonds of loyalty between the subject and the king.[35] This should have enough to circumvent the issue of who commanded them. However the trained bands were men of the 'middling sort', often artisans for whom the bonds of feudalism had long been irrelevant. Moreover, many of the trained bandsmen would be politicised in their own right. If not generally then perhaps by the events of the past two years in which they had been used as weapons in a conflict by a king with whose religious policy they did not agree.

Henry Hastings, the man who brought the first commission of array in the north Midlands went on to command the royalist forces in the region, first as colonel-general from the end of February 1643 and then as lieutenant-general from October that year. Hastings may have been promoted again as by June 1645 he had command over George Lisle who had been appointed lieutenant-general under him.[36] Within the counties under his control, Hastings had an army based in a series of garrisons that served several purposes. The central purpose was to hold onto the counties of Derbyshire, Leicestershire, Nottinghamshire, Rutland and Staffordshire: this it was able to do with varying success during the whole war. Its effective territorial control increased from February 1643 until the end of the year, but decline followed the Battle of Marston Moor (2 July 1644). A second purpose was to assemble as a field or flying army to serve either within its own boundaries or outside: it did so at the successful relief of Newark (18–22 March 1644) and at the catastrophic defeat at Denton (31 October 1644). The third chief purpose was to act as

---

[34] Historical Manuscripts Commission (1930) II, 84; Rushworth (1721–1722), III, 1, 670; Nichols (1804) III, 2 Appendix 4, 24.

[35] Ibid., 21, 26.

[36] Historical Manuscripts Commission (1930) II, 94–95; BL, Harleian MS 986, Note Book of Richard Symonds, fo. 92; Newcastle (1886) 63; Long (1871) 104.

reinforcements for other commanders outside the region: the relief of York and Marston Moor campaign (June-July 1644) or its involvement in princes Rupert and Maurice's West Midland and Marcher County campaign in spring 1645, are examples of this work.[37]

It is to the officer corps of this army that the attention of this chapter now turns. The original data for this analysis was collected some years ago in an attempt to explore the nature of the royalist war effort and to reconstruct the narrative of the war in the region.[38] This renewed analysis follows two impeti; the need to reassess the professionalism within the army command and to re-examine the officers in the light of more recent explorations of the nature of royalism and the regional structure of the civil war armies. Peter Newman has argued convincingly, and along the lines of Gerald Aylmer and J. P. Kenyon, that royalism was more an emotional response to the political world of 1640–41 than a political theory.[39] This of course is somewhat offset by David Smith's analysis of the creation of a genuine political and theoretical constitutional royalism.[40] However, Newman deals principally, as he says with the notion that if there was not a theoretical royalism then there certainly was a militant royalism.

Re-examination of the North Midlands Army both supports and qualifies Newman's position.[41] Newman's 1993 work centres upon the 564 royalist colonels he identifies as serving during the period 1642–1660. He analyses these according to social status, geography and religion. It is possible to analyse Hastings's small army along these lines. This assessment will however include the officer corps from the top, lieutenant-generals (two) down to cornets and ensigns the lowest commissioned ranks in the horse and foot respectively. This is a total of 357 men. As George Lisle served with the army for less than a fortnight because his command imploded immediately

---

[37] I have covered these campaigns in my thesis and alluded to them elsewhere: Bennett (1987), chs 5–6. There is no satisfactory published account of Henry Hastings's command.

[38] Bennett (1987) ch. 4.

[39] Newman (1993) passim; Aylmer (1987); Kenyon (1988) 39.

[40] Smith (1994) passim.

[41] I gave the army this name in 1982–86 and no one has yet challenged it: it is both more accurate and less of a mouthful than the alternative 'the flying army of Ashby de la Zouch'. Of course it was not a name that any of the activists of 1642–46 would have recognised. In view of Newman's assertions about regionality, it has been given more credibility.

after the Battle of Naseby (14 July 1645), we shall leave him out of the accounting. This leaves just one general, Hastings, and 355 others serving in the forces placed under Hastings's command between 1642 and 1646.[42]

Twenty-three men, including Hastings, served as colonel during the first civil war. Their regiments were undersized and grossly top heavy with officers in some cases. For, even if companies and troops were undersized in terms of other ranks, they were almost certain to have a full (and expensive) complement of officers. They compare well with the overall figures presented by Newman. Few were heirs to noble titles, only one of them, Sir John Fitzherbert of Norbury would succeed to a title, representing 4% as compared with Newman's 6.3% for the colonels as a whole.[43] The majority were untitled gentry 16 (69%) compared with Newman's figure of 67%. There were two others who had no specific title but were from noble families, Hastings (a second son) and Ferdinando Stanhope (a fourth son of the Earl of Chesterfield). The majority clearly come from what Newman categorises as the *nobiles minores* as opposed to *nobiles majores*.

There is however a notable shift from Newman's presentation of the royalists when we look at a broader perspective of status and turn to family. Newman rightly identifies the high level of commitment shown by the royalist heads of families who committed themselves to militant royalism. The typical royalist he argues was 'solid, comfortable, respectable and conservative gentleman' with 'obligation of family and often, property to consider . . . a country gentleman approaching or in early middle age'.[44] There were few heirs to families in Newman's analysis and he described them as rare (17.4% heirs as opposed to 54.4% heads). In the north Midlands Army there were far more balance proportion: 30.4% heads of family and 34.7% heirs. There was also a marked difference in the proportion of younger sons amongst the colonels: 26%. The inclusion of the two men who were less identifiable to any of these groups would not unduly disturb the balance between the three sections which is clearly different to Newman's overall findings.

In terms of age, the North Midlands Army colonels are less convincingly middle or approaching middle age, that Newman's

---

[42] For Lisle see Newman (1993) 182–4 and Newman (1981) 235.
[43] Metcalfe (1885) 103; Brighton (1981) 25.
[44] Newman (1993) 137, 310.

examination of the whole group would suggest. Of the 14 colonels whose ages are definitely known, their average age in 1642 was 30. This was younger even than the average age of the Northern Army colonels under Newcastle, which was 35. Five of Hastings's colonels were in their early forties, four, including Hastings, in their thirties and five in their twenties. This was a young man's army.

Examining the professionalism of the officer corps has to be seen as part of an examination of political and administrative experience. The colonels as a whole demonstrate a variety of experiences, two had been MPs, five had been high sheriffs, three JPs, and seven had attended university and three, Inns of Court. The incomplete nature of lists of deputy lieutenants makes it difficult to assess how many of the colonels had actually served in a war even as brief as the Bishop's Wars. Only six: Henry Hastings, Sir John Fitzherbert, John Freschville, Harvey Bagot, Thomas Leveson, and Isham Parkyns seem to have been involved with the trained bands.[45] Although two other colonels had pre-civil war military experience: one, Christopher Roper had served in the Ulster-based regiment of Lord Moore in 1641.[46]

The question of developing professionalism is a subject of some importance. As shown above the Scottish Covenanters sought to deliberately include experienced soldiers into their regiments in 1639 and 1640. That this was done in the royalist forces was also well known. The earl of Newcastle's appointment of the Scots soldier James King, later Lord Eythin is an often-cited example. The North Midlands witnessed similar appointment, John Henderson an experienced soldier was charged with establishing the Newark garrison and spearheading the campaign to seize Nottinghamshire whilst technically working with the militarily inexperienced High Sheriff John Digby of Mansfield Woodhouse.

Schooling in the military arts received 'on the job' was the basis for later promotion. Several of the colonels were promoted into the rank during the war. William Neville was possibly originally commissioned as a captain in Henry Hastings's Horse in the summer of 1642, but took over his father's regiments in spring 1643. John Freschville served as a captain until sent back to Derbyshire in 1643.

---

[45] The original research only revealed five. Isham Parkyn's role as a deputy lieutenant was identified by Stuart Jennings (1991) This should appear as an article; 'Colonel Isham Parkyns: Nottinghamshire's Forgotten Royalist' mss. ref. p. 4.

[46] Historical manuscripts Commission (1899) 140.

John Shallcross served as lieutenant colonel to John Milward before taking over the regiment after the Battle of Marston Moor. The Bagot brothers, Richard and Harvey both entered a military career as captains in Lord Paget's foot. Richard was the fourth son of Sir Harvey Bagot and Harvey the second son. When the Bagots were sent back into their own county after the Battle of Edgehill it was Richard, with military experience on the continent who commanded: his elder brother, with only a captaincy in the trained bands served as his lieutenant colonel. When Richard died of wounds after the Battle of Naseby, Harvey took over as colonel.[47] John Lane served first as a captain in Lord Digby's regiment before being granted a commission to raise his own regiment.[48] John Barnard had been in Ferdinando Stanhope's regiment as major of horse. At some time in 1644 he was commissioned colonel, possibly after Ferdinando's death in November 1644. By January 1645 Barnard was governor of Abby Cwm Hir in Radnorshire. After surrendering the garrison he took over Canon Frome in Herefordshire. The Army of the Solemn League and Covenant massacred him and his soldiers there in the summer of 1645.[49] Ferdinando Stanhope may have begun his service as a captain in 1642.

Hastings's own regiment proved to be a military academy. Colonel Neville and Colonel Christopher Roper passed through it to colonelcies of their own regiments. Sigismund Beeton, the only colonel Newman identifies as a plebeian, passed through Hastings's foot as a captain before having his own regiment under the Marquis of Newcastle.[50] Barnabus Scudamore also served as major in Hastings's horse before moving on to Hereford where his brother was governor. He had served as captain in the Bishop's Wars and helped Hastings raise Leicestershire troops during the summer of 1642. Other field officers had served in Hastings's regiment or in other North Midland Army regiments as regimental officers before being promoted. Some may have moved on to field command elsewhere. Hastings's regiment had a high number of officers claiming to be troop captains when in 1661 Charles II decided to offer financial

---

[47] Bennett (1987) 345–350.
[48] Ibid., 350–351.
[49] Ibid., 342–344; Newman (1981) entry no. 72.
[50] Bl, Harleian MS 986, fo. 93; Newman (1981), entry no. 94; Newman (1993) 128; Bennett (1987) 323.

remuneration to former officers financially ruined by the war.[51] His regiment of horse had three lieutenant colonels, six majors and 29 captains. His regiment of foot had 12 captains. Whilst casualties could easily account for the over population of foot regiment captains (a full size regiment should have had seven commanding their own companies and three companies belonging to the colonel, lieutenant colonel and major, led in the field by captain lieutenants: that is ten companies in all. Hastings's Horse was a different matter there should only be three captains and three captain lieutenants, not 29 captains.[52]

The divergence from Newman's findings develops as this examination descends through the ranks. The 20 lieutenant colonels almost all came from the *nobiles minores*. There was one knight, 10 esquires and two gentlemen. Seven cannot be ascribed social rank. The family status of much of this group cannot be determined; there were seven heirs, and five younger sons amongst those who can. Their administrative, political and educational experience was limited to university and Inns of court attendance: six at the former and four at the latter. The lieutenant colonels of foot were less experienced and socially established than their comrades in the horse. As for age, ten can be ascribed an age at the start of the war: the average age was just 27. Two lieutenant colonels were in their early forties, two in their thirties, five in their twenties and one, Thomas Neville, just seventeen.[53]

The majors continue the downward trends. Out of thirty, 17 left almost no records other than brief service details. Of the rest, seven were esquires, three gentlemen, one a yeoman (although also labelled cow-gelder), one a clerk and another an apprentice before the war. Two were heirs; six were younger sons, the rest unknown. Amongst the regimental officers the majority were so obscure as to be untraceable, the more so as we descend the ranks to cornet and ensign. Of the 92 captains of horse, 58 are untraceable. Those that can be ascribed social rank; they are mostly *nobiles minores*, along with two ministers, a glover and an attorney. However, as 23 were heirs and one was a head of family, it shows that the level of commitment was high. Captains of foot were from lower down the social scale.

---

[51] PRO, SP28/69, 19: List of officers claiming to the £60,000 etc.
[52] Bennett (1987) 316–325.
[53] Cockayne (1902) III, 203; Bennett (1987) 326; Newman (1981) entry no. 1040

Firstly, there were only sixty-two who could be traced. This may be a result of their vulnerability when compared with their mounted comrades, and also that the regiments of foot were all undersized and less of a desirable career for the young gentleman. Only eleven can be identified: an esquire, five gentlemen, a barrister, an apothecary, a tailor and two shoemakers. Only eight can be ascribed familial position, six were first sons and two younger sons. Five had been to university and two to Inns of Court. Only sixteen men served as captain lieutenants: four were gentlemen, three of them heirs and had been to university and one to the Inns of Court: the rest are unidentified. Of the lieutenants, only six out of 35 from the horse and two of the 24 from the foot can be identified. Of the lowest commissioned six of the 33 cornets and none of the 25 ensigns can be identified.

Newman argued that even after several years of war regionalism was still important to the royalist colonels.[54] This is certainly true of the North Midlands Army. Only four of the colonels came from outside the five counties under Hastings. One of these was Gervaise Lucas and he was from adjacent Lincolnshire, Francis Whortley was a Yorkshireman and the other two only became colonels by leaving the area. Most of the lieutenant colonels served in the home county; all of the Lieutenant colonels of horse did and two of the foot lieutenant colonels. Only two of the regionally located majors of horse were outsiders and four of the eight so identified of the foot majors were. Fifty-six of the captains of horse were in their home county or one adjacent to it as were the majority of identified captains of foot. The captain lieutenants and lieutenants, cornets and ensigns who can be located within a county were chiefly serving in their own counties.

This may not be something that distinguishes the north Midlands royalist colonels or the whole officer corps at all. It would appear to be common to most armies raised for home service in the British Isles. The Scottish armies in the Bishop's Wars were raised with strong regional ties. The Army sent into England in 1644 was similar. It was heavily regionalised if not county-based throughout. Horse regiments were drawn from grouped counties: the Earl of Balcarres's Horse was from Fife, Mearns and part of Aberdeenshire. Others

---

[54] Newman (1993) 18.

were raised on a presbytery basis like the Earl of Dunfermline's Foot or on a stewartry base like Colonel Hugh Fraser's Foot. There was even one burgh-based regiment the Edinburgh Foot. There were exceptions, like the College of Justice Foot of Lord John Sinclair composed of apprentices, student clerks, writers resident in Edinburgh, but in reality drawn from across the country.[55]

Analysis of the North Midlands Army in the context of other armies offers several insights into professional military service in the first civil war. Clearly, Peter Newman's analysis of the colonels as a whole hides subtleties. The North Midlands Army only thoroughly supports one of his chief conclusions about the colonels: that of regionality. This is important. The fact that these were younger men than the stereotypical royalist commander goes hand in hand with the relative inexperience of the field officers and the obscurity of the regimental officers. There are notable trends that may pervade the untraceable men. One noticable feature was the high proportion of all the officers who heirs and sometimes heads of families. It is possible that, because this continues within the ranks of the socially obscure officer, we are looking at men who are only obscure to the eyes of those accustomed to looking at the upper echelons of society either in the 1640s or at the end of the twentieth century. Their close ties to their region underlines this. They would not be obscure in their own locality. They may well have served in minor office. There is a great enough dearth of information about the members of grand juries, village offices, and county minor administrators to hide many more officers than staffed the North Midland Army. Officers were not selected from obscurity, they would have had to prove themselves in some way: local office, service in the trained bands would be some level of proof. Distinguished service abroad would not have necessarily entailed social prestige at home. The North Midlands Army would become a professional army as the war progressed and its officers tutored by those with experience. The service record of the army would see to the training process: Edgehill, Marston Moor and Naseby all involved North Midlands' men. The relief of two sieges of Newark, the siege of Lichfield, smaller battles at Hopton Heath, Cotes and Denton and countless skirmishes all within four years provided experience. The army could well have

---

[55] Furgol (1991) 114, 124, 133, 137, 141.

been seen as a profession, for many of these men were of small estate. Only 43.5 per cent of the field officers and small minority of regimental officers compounded for their estates, were fined at the end of the war, or sought to avoid sequestration and composition by inclusion within surrender terms.[56] This was a career. It may not sit well with Newman's assertion that the defence of the king (royalism) was feudal, for these men were fighting with little to lose. Perhaps they had much more to gain. Can we be entirely sure that these men with a small stake in pre-war society were only fighting to defend what little they had? Would it not be more likely that they were fighting with at least half an eye open to the main chance? These young royalists were probably fighting to establish themselves and their families in the higher echelons of local, county and even, for a few of them, national government.

VI

The young royalist blades of the North Midlands Army lost the war and with it their chance of social, political and economic advancement.[57] Only one army became almost a guarantor of success. The New Model Army was the most politically influential of the civil war armies in the early seventeenth century. There were others. The Scottish Whiggamore and the Western Association forces were influential in Scottish politics 1648–1653. The attitude of the Catholic Confederation of Kilkenny's provincial armies was politically important between 1642 and 1648. But in the end the New Model defeated all of these armies and their politics.

The New Model Army came together as the result of two crises in the Parliamentarian cause at the end of 1644. Firstly military stagnation: the gradual diminution of the Earl of Essex's authority had resulted in the creation of several armies led by officers who regarded themselves as being independent of the nominal commander in chief. The defeat of Essex at Lostwithiel further reduced his standing and when the three main armies south and east of the Trent were brought together in autumn 1644, the command structure fragmented. Neither

---

[56] Bennett (1987) 155, 162, 168.
[57] Even after the Restoration they were, as a group, unsuccessful in attaining much in the way of social advancement, Bennett (1987) 122.

the Earl of Manchester nor Sir William Waller would subordinate themselves to Essex and Essex probably feigned an illness, which kept him from working with either of them as equals. Not surprisingly this had an effect on the campaign which they were brought together to fight. Despite outnumbering the king's army at the second Battle of Newbury and despite an ambitious and almost successful strategy to crush the royalists, tactical fractiousness destroyed cohesion and the king escaped. Moreover, Charles was able to outplay the three commanders in the weeks following the battle.

The second push towards restructuring was closely linked to the first. In the heated atmosphere of recrimination Manchester accused his second-in-command, Oliver Cromwell of insubordination. It was a two pronged attack: Cromwell was blamed for the humiliations which followed Newbury because he had refused to pursue the royalists' forces, but he was also charged with bringing into the army officer corps men of radical religious outlook. Cromwell himself was proud of being a gentleman, and was happy to be depicted in traditional heroic (indeed, chivalric) guise (see plate 9), but he valued commitment and competence over confessional conformity or lineage. He counter-attacked his commander with suggestions that Manchester was unwilling vigorously to pursue the war, because he apparently saw no point in defeating a king whose political position was assured even in defeat. This dual impetus so mired in politics ensured that the creation of the officer corps and the army itself would be highly political. Even if J. S. A. Adamson is correct and the creation of the army was the result of old baronial or feudal conflicts between Essex and his enemies, political outlook was still a dominating principle behind the appointment of officers.[58]

Of the 193 appointments to the army officer corps, the House of Lords questioned 57 on religious and political grounds: they objected to Independents and proposed their substitution by Presbyterians and relations of the earl of Essex or his proteges. Ian Gentles argues that attempted interference would have outweighed military considerations, because some of the Lords' nominees were less experienced than those they would have replaced, despite the Lords' declaration to the contrary.[59] When the list was finally passed unaltered a major

[58] Adamson (1990).
[59] Gentles (1992) 16–21.

change had taken place, not only had the old leadership been replaced but around 300 men who had provided a backbone of experience in the original parliamentarian armies had been displaced. Scottish officers, with experience in the continental wars and the Bishop's Wars were now unemployed and for a while unable to get home because their arrears had not been paid. Defeat for the Lords had allowed radical officers and those opposed to the establishment of a Presbyterian church to remain in the army. However, Fairfax had under his command a considerable number of men whom the Lords approved of, they had only questioned 30% of the total number. With the exception of the Scottish officers, the principle behind the creation of the new army weighs heavily towards experience rather than other considerations.

Principles of regionality disappeared to a great extent. Regiments in parliamentarian armies had been raised in similar ways to royalist forces, with locally known figures raising regiments in their own county or region. The New Model Army blended these old regiments together even the most cohesive of the old field armies, The Eastern Association Army was dissolved into the new force. The horse, with a strength set at 6,600 was raised easily from the horse regiments of the three armies: Essex's, Manchester's Eastern Association Army and Waller's. The foot was another case, only 7,226 could be mustered from the old forces (the bulk, 6,626, from Essex's and Manchester's). There was of course the need to conscript new soldiers. The bulk of the demand for 7,174 foot and 1,000 dragoons was regional, 2,500 from London and its environs, Norfolk, Suffolk, Essex and Kent, Parliament's hinterland had to raise a thousand each. These conscripts who came in reluctantly, slowly and never in the expected numbers, were not kept in regional groups, but spread out amongst the undersized regiments already established. Even so as Ian gentles points out the majority of New Model foot were pressed men dragged from the south-east in 1645 and from the south-west in 1646. A smaller number were raised from Midland counties in the later stages of the war.

VII

The stage was being set in the British Isles for a national standing army. The civil wars had, as they progressed broken down many of the presumptions of military structure in Britain. To some extent, both regionalism and social structure were being eroded as principles behind home service by the time the New Model Army was created. Professionalised officer corps were in being, based on experience gained in warfare. At the beginning of the conflict in 1639 the Covenanters had created an army which both mirrored the social structure and accommodated the need to have experienced professionals in place throughout the army. That this was regarded as a temporary expedient is demonstrated by the gradual erosion of this principle as early as 1641–2 when the officer corps of the Army of Ulster was created from the socially elite, even if led by the successful Earl of Leven. The English never fully incorporated this principle, although professional soldiers were found throughout the English/Welsh forces during the period. When the royalists and parliamentarians raised their armies in 1642 both used professionals, but their main preoccupation was social class and then regional attachment. Officers had to be recognised figures in their own land, even if at the lower commissioned levels their land was encompassed by parish boundaries. That military experience could be overridden by social or political principles is demonstrated by the House of Lords' willingness to sacrifice officers of proven standing for less experienced men it considered socially acceptable. The New Model Army was in the end to destroy many of these principles. Even if it was an army drawn heavily from south of the Trent, the regiments had lost any local cohesion after the massive conscription drives of 1645–1646 filled under strength regiments with conscripts. Many of the New Model Army officers became professional soldiers, with military careers stretching over fifteen years by the time of the Restoration. The examination of the North Midlands Army suggests that, even if regionalism remained strong in a small royalist army, professionalism was not unique to the New Model Army: Many royalist officers had chosen a military career before 1645 and were to pursue them in later wars at home and abroad.

Bibliography

Primary Manuscript Sources

British Library, Additional MS 34217, fo. 70: Instructions to the Northamptonshire Commissioners of Array.

British Library Harleian MS, 986, Note Book of Richard Symonds.

Public Record Office, SP28/69, 19, List of officers claiming to the £60,000 etc, granted by his Sacred Majesty for the Relief of his Truly Loyal and Indigent Party.

Primary Printed Sources

Everritt-Green, M. (1858), ed., *Calendar of State Papers Domestic Series 1623–1625* (London: 1859).

——. (1858), ed., *Calendar of State Papers Domestic Series 1625–1626* (London: 1858).

——. (1854), ed., *Calendar of State Papers Domestic Series 1627–1628* (London: 1854).

Gardiner, S. R. (1978), ed., *Constitutional Documents of the Puritan Revolution* (repr., Oxford, 1978).

Historical Manuscripts Commission (1899) *Manuscripts of the Marquis of Ormonde* (London: 1899).

——. (1932) *The Manuscripts of Reginald Rawdon Hastings* II (London: 1932).

Long, C. E. (1871), ed., *Diary of the Marches of the royal Army, During the great Civil War, kept by Richard Symonds* (London: 1871).

Newcastle, Duchess of (1886), *Life of William Cavendish, Duke of Newcastle* (London: 1886).

Stocks, H. E. (1923) *Records of the Borough of Leicester, 1603–1689* (Cambridge: 1923).

Rushworth, J. (1721–22) *Historical Collections*, III (London: 1721–1722).

Secondary Sources

Adamson, J. S. A. (1990) "The Baronial Context of the English Civil War" *TRHS*, 5th ser., 40 (1990).

Aylmer, G. (1987) "Collective Mentalities in Mid-Seventeenth-Century England, ii. Royalist Attitudes", *TRHS*, 5th ser., 37 (1987).

Bennett, M. (1987) "The Royalist War Effort in the North Midlands, 1642–1646", unpub. PhD thesis (Loughborough University: 1987).

Brighton, J. T. (1981) *Royalists and Roundheads in Derbyshire* (Bakewell: 1981).

Cockayne, G. E. (1902) *The Complete Baronetage* (Exeter: 1902).

Firth, C. H. (1992) *Cromwell's Army* (repr., London: 1992).

Fissel, M. (1994) *The Bishops' Wars: Charles I's campaigns against Scotland 1638–1640* (Cambridge: 1994).

Furgol, E. M. (1991) *A Regimental History of the Covenanting Armies, 1639–1651* (Edinburgh: 1991).

Gentles, I. (1992) *The New Model Army In England, Ireland and Scotland, 1645–1653* (Oxford: 1992).

——. (1998) "The Civil Wars in England", in *The Civil Wars: A Military History of England, Scotland and Ireland*, eds. J. P. Kenyon and J. Ohlmeyer (Oxford: 1998).

Hutton, R. (1981) "The Structure of the Royalist party", *HJ* 23 (1981).

——. (1982) *The Royalist War Effort* (London: 1982).

Jennings, S. (1991) "Bunny and Bradmore, 1640–1690: Change and Continuity in an Age of Revolutions", unpublished MA thesis (Nottingham University: 1991).

Kenyon, J. P. (1988) *The Civil Wars of England* (London: 1988).

Metcalfe, W. C. (1885) *A Book of Knights, 1426–1600* (London: 1885).

Newman, P. (1978) "The Royalist Army in the North of England", unpublished DPhil thesis (University of York: 1978).

——. (1981) *Royalist officers in England and Wales 1642–1660* (New York: 1981).

——. (1983) "The Royalist officer Corps as a Reflection of the Social Structure", *HJ* 26 (1983).

——. (1993) *The Old Service: Royalist regimental colonels and the civil war, 1642–46* (Manchester: 1993).

Nichols, J. (1804) *History and Antiquities of the county of Leicester*, III, ii (Leicester: 1804).

Ryder, I. (1985) "The English Army for Ireland, 1641–1642" (unpublished paper).

Smith, D. (1994) *Constitutional Royalism and the Search for a settlement, c. 1640–1649*, (Cambridge: 1994).

Stearns, S. (1972) "Conscription and English Society in the 1620s", *Journal of British Studies* 11, no. 2 (1972).

Wheeler, J. S. (1999) *The Making of a World Power: War and the Military Revolution in Seventeenth Century England* (Stroud: 1999).

Young, P. (1967) *Edgehill, 1642, The Campaign and the Battle* (Kineton: 1967).

——. (1970) *Marston Moor, 1644, The Campaign and the Battle* (Kineton: 1970).

——. (1985) *Naseby 1645, The Campaign and the Battle* (London: 1985).

——. (1974), ed., *Newark upon Trent: The Civil War Siegeworks*, (London: 1964).

POSTSCRIPT:

THE LAST GASP OF CHIVALRY?

CHAPTER TWELVE

SHOOT THEM ALL: CHIVALRY, HONOUR AND THE CONFEDERATE ARMY OFFICER CORPS

Mark A. Weitz

The antebellum American South conjures up images of wealthy aristocratic planters roaming huge cotton plantations living in a world dominated by men where honour held real meaning. For many people this era of American history saw the South as the custodian of the last vestiges of chivalry, where men protected the weak, held justice and God above all else, and lived lives that resembled characters from a Sir Walter Scott novel, where winning was important, but so was showing mercy to a beaten foe. As the South embarked upon the struggle with the North that ultimately destroyed many of its pre-war institutions, its men readily answered the call to arms. Many of the most educated in the South would find a place among the Confederate army's officer corps. Some had already been officers in the United States Army and relinquished hard earned commissions to return and defend the honour of their respective states. Others had never known military service, but their civilian honour compelled them to serve their country. It is easy to look at men like Jeb Stuart and Stephen Ramsuer and conclude that the chivalry that remained a part of Southern society before the war must have followed these men into battle and influenced not only how they fought, but how those under their command waged war. However, the image conveyed by the cape and plume-hatted Stuart belies the role that chivalry actually played. In reality Southern chivalry was never that of British novels and any notions of chivalry that were taken into the conflict did not survive the rigours of modern war.

To be sure, honour remained an important aspect of the Confederate officer corps. However, its most common manifestation came in the dedication to military duty these men demonstrated. When Confederate officers led men into battle any remnants of a chivalric code disappeared as both they and their men struggled to adapt to the rigours of a war that left little room for mercy or deference, either between enemies or among one's own comrades.

The chivalric ethos in the South was at best a distant cousin of
that depicted in traditional notions of chivalry and warfare. Southern
chivalry has been described as 'gentility,' and was in reality more of
a code for men of the upper class in civilian life, than a set of rules
to be observed in combat. Gentility defined the roles of the aristocratic planter and his circle. In turn it also dictated the conduct of
everyone beneath him, from other free white men of varying classes,
to women, and finally to the vast ocean of slaves that populated the
South. The most important aspect of this code was male honour, a
man's reputation or standing among his peers. Affronts to honour
demanded immediate retribution or an apology, and disrespect toward
a woman within a man's family or kinship network could also be a
stain on a man's honour. However, most questions of honour seldom involved women, but more often centred around business, gam-
ing, or some other disparagement to family or personal reputation.
Ironically, duelling, the institution most often associated with 'civilised'
combat, seldom displayed the type of mercy for either the victor or
the vanquished that one would expect from participants in a chivalric trial by combat. The victor was often feared thereafter and never
quite as welcomed as he once had been. The defeated lived, if at
all, in shame.[1]

What did serve as an enduring aspect of gentility was the respect
shown by the upper classes for free white men in the classes below
them. Nowhere was this more apparent than in the manner in which
prominent members of the community exercised leadership. Leadership
in civilian life was an act of accommodation. Other men followed
the upper classes because of who they were in the community, but
at the same time they insisted on being treated with a certain degree
of respect by those they followed. Many men of the lower classes
followed their civilian community leaders into war, and as will be
seen, Southern chivalry was responsible for the enthusiastic response
to the call to arms by Southern men. Honour, regardless of class,
compelled men to fight. The test of combat would be a test of not
only their manhood, but of the South's collective honour, and the
community exerted a strong pressure for every man to do his duty.
During the crisis period leading up to Fort Sumter, prominent
Southerners like future general, John Gordon, argued that Southern

---

[1] Wyatt Brown (1986) 27, 41–62, 152.

chivalry demanded that the South fight because the North's actions toward it were an affront to its honour.[2]

A common military mind set among members of the Southern officer corps is hard to define, not because there is no record of who served as officers, but because there were so many, and at different times. In all 425 general officers served in the Confederate Army of whom 109 rose to the rank of major general or higher. Only twenty-seven attained the rank of lieutenant general and but eight reached the level of general, with Robert E. Lee being the only man to serve as commander in chief.[3] Below these men lay a vast, and ever changing collection of officers who served as company, regiment and brigade commanders. Not only is the officer corps extremely large, but the literature on Confederate officers while growing in recent years, is still limited to a handful of these men, even among the very elite. William Hardee, for example, not only wrote the manual of arms that became the text book for training Civil War soldiers, but he served admirably as a corps commander in the Army of Tennessee. However, he wrote so little in the way of personal correspondence or diaries, that even today we know very little of his personal side.[4] Nevertheless, even with the limited sources and narrow focus of the secondary literature, by examining records of some of the more obscure officers, and by closely scrutinizing the material on the more illustrious leaders, a clear military ethos among the Confederate officer corps emerges. The code that dominated their conduct had few of the traditional aspects of chivalry, and for the most part it forsook both the major tenants of the knight's code, and abandoned those aspects unique to Southern chivalry

Although most of the Confederate officer corps came from the higher levels of Southern society, its wartime conduct would be dictated more by where these men went after leaving home than the influence of home itself. Of the 425 general officers, 146 graduated from West Point Military Academy, ten attended West Point but did not graduate; forty-two others went to some type of military college, either as officers in the regular army, or as students in a state military academy like the Virginia Military Institute, or the Citadel;

---

[2] Ibid., 28–29, 122–23, 234–44; Gordon (1903) 18–25.
[3] Wakelyn (1985) 74; Hall (1898) xi–xiii.
[4] Hardee (1853) was the standard manual. The only biography we have of Hardee is Hughes (1965).

while 142 future Confederate general officers spent time in a prestigious Southern college or university and a handful attended a prestigious non-military institution in the East. In short, most of the upper echelon of the Confederate officer corps attended college, and virtually every man that rose to corps or army command went to West Point. Only 'civilian' generals Wade Hampton and John Gordon would ever hold even temporary corps commands. This is not to say that only West Point and college educated men were good commanders. Patrick Cleburne, perhaps the best general in the western theater and among the best of the war learned warfare as a British enlisted man and did not come to America until he was an adult.[5]

College, and West Point in particular, did several things that helped eventually shape the Confederate officer corps warfare ethos. First, both military and non-military school developed these men's minds and characters. It exposed them to intellectual endeavors that would one day help them cope with many of the problems presented by military command. In particular, higher education placed them under pressure to perform, mostly from family and their own peers at school. The ability to cope with pressure helped develop their decision making skills for a time when outcome would become the sole criterion in combat. Secondly, these men formed important relationship networks and friendships that would later facilitate the development and acceptance of a particular military ethos. Finally, West Point developed a peculiar military mind set, where men followed direct orders irrespective of any prior civilian relationship. More important, the military was not some road to glory or political office, but a profession; one that exacted long hours away from family at assignments in obscure parts of the country. For many of the West Point graduates that became high ranking Civil War officers, Mexico followed closely on the heals of the academy as they cut their teeth in places like Cerro Gordo, Buena Vista and Chapultepec.[6]

Despite the high numbers of West Point officers in the Confederate officer corps, nothing could prevent the large influx of amateur officers into the Confederate service when the war began. As prominent leaders in peace time, many men simply refused to be left out of the 'big fight' and came from every corner of the South, riding

---

[5] Wakelyn (1985) 74–75.
[6] Ibid., 86–89; Waugh (1994) 116–139.

like warriors straight out of *Ivanhoe*, with their baggage trains and slaves following closely behind. Many sought some undefined glory, or saw the war as a way to climb the political ladder at home. One man, the son of a South Carolina planter, clearly saw himself as the reincarnation of Sir Walter Scott's hero. In letters home he thanked Scott for 'teaching me when young, how to rate knightly honor.' Even after suffering a wound at First Manassas he continued to see himself as 'a knight in a beleaguered fortress, & must not pass out with the women & sick, when the castle is to be stormed.' These men also brought with them many of the attributes of Southern chivalry, or gentility, that had governed their lives as civilians. This non-professional breed of officer created almost immediate conflict. Most amateurs lacked any formal military training, and displayed an obvious disdain for the aloofness of the West Pointers, seeing these men as too preoccupied with training and unwilling to get down to the business of fighting. The professionals in turn viewed the amateurs as out-of-place aristocrats, men who started the war and would now do well to get out of the way while the professionals fought.[7]

This conflict between amateur and professional resolved itself in two ways. The West Pointers grudgingly came to admit that some men like John Gordon, Nathan Bedford Forrest and Pat Cleburne could and would be effective leaders without formal officer training. To their credit these non-West Pointers used their intelligence and other natural gifts to learn what they needed to know. Those that could not be effective combat leaders were quickly weeded out after the first year of the war. Although only a few major battles occurred in 1861, the war's first year provided sufficient combat to determine which amateurs had to go. When Robert E. Lee took command in the late spring of 1862, he went directly into battle and then combed through the ranks of the Army of Northern Virginia and tactfully removed or transferred all of those too timid, too stupid or too old to be leading large groups of men in battle. By July 1862, Lee had reorganised his army and found his best commanders. With Stonewall Jackson and James Longstreet leading his two infantry corps, and Jeb Stuart heading his cavalry, Lee went about making modern war as it had never been made before, at least on the North American continent.[8]

---

[7] McPherson (1997) 27. Patterson (1987) 23–26.
[8] Patterson (1994) 34.

Traditionally, chivalry and military training co-existed. One could be both professional and live by the 'code.' However, among the South's professional soldiers, chivalry became identified with an amateur approach to warfare. Part of the perception perhaps lay in a notion prominent among Southern civilians that the war was a great quest. Somehow the righteousness of the cause would alone deliver victory. The professionals knew better. Many had actually seen combat in Mexico and most had friends in the North's officer corps. They understood that bloody work lay ahead. This would not be a war among 'gentlemen.' The stakes were too high. A Southern defeat meant the loss of its way of life, destruction of its institutions, and the exposure of homes and families to the ravages of war.[9]

Some amateurs survived the purge, proved their metal in combat, and shed their amateur label. In the process, these men contributed to the elimination of a prominent feature of Southern chivalry still clinging on within the military ranks. Colonel James B. Griffin of South Carolina served under Joseph Johnston on the Virginia Peninsula in 1862. He had come into the service after helping to recruit a local regiment, a common practice for non-professionals seeking a military command. Griffin lived just below the upper echelon of South Carolina society, and as an officer he would serve at the same station. He had been a leader in his civilian community and many of the men he recruited were among his friends and acquaintances at home. Most soldiers, including Griffin's, initially resisted the rigours of training and military discipline. What they most objected to was being 'ordered' to do anything by men that at home had led by being a 'bit more tactful in their requests.' While Griffin fought their resistance, he at least understood it. The professional officers quickly developed a contempt for this type of attitude among the enlisted ranks. In units where the men continued to elect officers, those that enforced military discipline were exceedingly unpopular, while those that showed their men some deference remained troop favourites. However, both amateur and professional officers alike soon found the enlisted men accepting the demise of 'civilian deference.' The harsh realities of combat led both officers and enlisted men to understand that war left no room for the niceties

---

[9] Robertson (1997) 514–15, 823 n. 80, 822 n. 80.

that characterised their civilian interaction.[10] In battle men acted as one, responded to orders from an officer without hesitation, or they did not survive.[11]

The most obvious deviation from the chivalric ethos by the Confederate officer corps came in the way they conducted war. Ruthlessness, while present in medieval warfare, existed as an aberration to the chivalry ethos, not in concert with it. In an era with small armies, comprised almost exclusively of an elite warrior class, mercy on the battlefield was appropriate, at least as a code of conduct, even if it could not always be practiced. The Civil War brought modern war waged by large armies to the North American continent; armies comprised in large part by men who knew nothing of a chivalric ethos using technologically advanced weapons, most notably the rifled musket, that changed the nature of combat. The common foot soldier could now kill at an effective range of 300–400 yards. The tactical defensive enjoyed a tremendous advantage as attackers continued to assault in mass formations. Most men died from blows inflicted without seeing the face of the man who fired the shot. Battlefield success, even on the defensive, required soldiers to calmly deliver effective fire into an enemy that often charged on the dead run, sometimes screaming, without becoming unnerved. Such discipline required intensive training. Neither soldier nor officer could risk undermining the effectiveness of the unit by suddenly determining that an enemy had placed itself in such an unfavourable position that some level of human decency required a showing of mercy. In fact, some of the war's most terrible slaughters occurred because one side or the other was willing to take full advantage of just such circumstances. At Fredericksburg in December 1862, Longstreet's men stood protected behind a stone wall and mowed down wave after wave of Union infantry. None made it closer than 150 yards of the Confederate position. Longstreet told Lee, 'If you put every man now on the other side of the Potomac on the field to approach me over the same line, and give me plenty of ammunition, I will kill them all.' Likewise, in June 1864, the Confederates at Kennesaw Mountain under Frank Cheatham not only slaughtered General Dan McCook's assaulting troops, but took the life of the

---

[10] MacArthur and Burton (1996) 50–59, 200.
[11] Weitz (1998) 99–125.

general himself. A month later at Petersburg, dazed and confused Union troops trapped in the crater, found the Confederate defenders only too willing to shoot them like 'fish in a barrel.'[12]

The impersonal nature of battle certainly contributed to a 'no quarter' mentality. Combined with the nature of warfare was an officer corps that saw winning as the ultimate goal and realised that to do so one had to kill as many of the enemy as possible by whatever means available. The personal beliefs of Confederate officers varied, but even at its most benevolent the best that could be mustered as a general rule was remorse at having killed so brutally, and not an unwillingness to do so. At Kennesaw Mountain, Cheatham's men were awed by their own handiwork. As the Union troops withdrew, they peered out from behind their defensive position, later dubbed 'Dead Angle,' and could not believe their own eyes. One man from the 9th Tennessee recalled years later, 'A frightful and disgusting scene of death and destruction.' He could not remember ever seeing any ground so completely strewn with dead. Despite his remorse after years of reflection, nothing had prevented he and his comrades from pouring fire down so severely that advancing Union soldiers trampled their own men trying to find refuge from the fire. Some desperate men hid behind narrow saplings or fruitlessly tried to scoop dirt in front of their prone bodies in an effort to create refuge.[13] This collective firepower of the Confederate infantry reflected the mentality of its leaders and demonstrated the proficiency of both officers and men in honing their killing skills.

At the top of the Confederate chain of command stood Robert E. Lee. There are no signs that chivalry in any form influenced the way he waged war. The concept itself is completely absent from any of the biographies on Lee, and while honour played a prominent role in his life, it was 'Southern honour.' Honour drove him to do his duty to home and community, an honour based on reputation and standing among his peers, and not a duty that required deference to a foe. While Lee may have believed in certain absolutes, particularly the desire to do right, his ethical code is best otherwise described as 'situationalist.' Lee possessed an ethical flexibility that allowed him to exercise the harshness or leniency that he felt the

---

[12] Wert (1993) 221; Losson (1989) 159.
[13] Losson (1989) 159–60.

situation demanded. In matters of command Lee believed his active participation in the actual conduct of battle did more harm than good. Once committing his army to battle, he left the conduct of actual combat to his subordinate commanders, commanders with obvious or proven skills who knew what to do in battle. Below Lee was an officer corps that did not embrace chivalry as its code for waging war.[14]

At one end of the military ethos spectrum were two of the Confederacy's most competent and renown officers, Stonewall Jackson and P. G. T. Beauregard. Thomas "Stonewall" Jackson is known even to those who have little, or only a passing interest in the American Civil War. His fame flows from his fighting reputation and his tactical prowess at moving great distances and striking his foe when and where he least expected. Often overlooked in Jackson's legend was his belief in how one should wage war once he was in position to do so. Jackson was one of the few, and perhaps the earliest proponents of the 'black flag' policy.

Three months before the war began in 1861, Jackson had already taken the position that the Confederacy should take no prisoners if war erupted between North and South. Jackson saw the nature of the conflict clearly as 'a dissolution of all bonds of society. It is not alone the destruction of our property, but the prelude to anarchy, infidelity, and the ultimate loss of free responsible government on the continent.' Jackson believed in giving 'no quarter to the violators of our homes and firesides.' By 1862, Jackson recanted such statements, but his willingness to adhere to a policy dictated by his civilian and military superiors did not mean his sentiments ever changed. Jackson merely conceded that the Southern people were not prepared for such warfare, warfare that he had no difficulty reconciling with his own staunch religious beliefs. His duty to God did not preclude him from fulfilling his duty as a soldier. War called upon him to kill and Jackson was not above asking assistance from the almighty in order to do so, nor giving credit to God for his military success.[15]

Evidence that Jackson continued to believe in his own brand of warfare came during his spectacular Shenandoah Valley campaign

---

[14] Thomas (1995) 246, 370–71.
[15] Robertson (1997) 822, n. 80, 514–15; Imboden, (n.d.) I:238; Imboden, (n.d.), II: 293.

in May 1862. As Jackson withdrew down the valley with Union cavalry in hot pursuit, his rear guard stopped and struck a blow. In command was Colonel John M. Patton of the 21st Virginia. Three Union cavalrymen had ridden directly into the regiment and been shot down. In the course of his report to Jackson, Patton lamented at having to shoot the three. Jackson coldly asked, 'why?' Patton replied, 'I should have spared them . . . they were men who had gotten themselves in a desperate situation.' Jackson answered, 'No, Colonel, shoot them all. I don't want them to be brave.'[16]

Jackson was not alone in his beliefs about the way the South should fight, and what was at stake. General P. G. T. Beauregard, one of the heroes of First Manassas, and for a brief time the commander of the Army of Tennessee, shared Jackson's sentiments. In a letter written to Tennessee Governor James T. Porter after the war, Beauregard tried to explain why he and Jackson believed as they did. There was some question whether the North would treat Confederate prisoners as 'prisoners of war,' in light of the Union's position that the South's secession was illegal. Beauregard believed the government should have 'proclaimed a war to the knife, neither asking nor granting quarters. We (he and Jackson) moreover thought the war would thereby come sooner to an end, with less destruction finally of life and property. We thought, also, that such a mode of warfare would strike terror in the armed invaders of our soil.'[17] Beauregard's sentiments were not the thoughts of a man whose mind had changed after years of reflection. His position in 1875 mirrored his stance during the war. In a letter written two weeks after the Battle of First Manassas, Beauregard articulated the nature of the struggle and how the war should be fought:

> We are not fighting for glory or political purpose, but for our homes, firesides & liberties. Should we fail in our undertaking, the sufferings & miseries of the Poles and Hungarians would not be comparable to our own—hence, 'victory or death' should be our motto—& curse be he who shrinks from the task.[18]

For Beauregard it was not only 'war to the knife,' but 'the knife to the hilt.' E. R. Reed, a Vermont Union soldier discovered this men-

---

[16] Robertson (1997) 424.
[17] Beauregard (1875) 41:184–85.
[18] Robertson (1997) 823, n. 80.

tality found its way to the common soldier. Upon taking a Georgia soldier prisoner in early 1862, the Confederate told Reed that they were under orders to 'give no quarter nor receive none, but fight to death.'[19]

While Jackson and Beauregard represented the extreme opinion as to how the war should be fought, they were not the only officers that understood what was at stake and that winning was the only criterion. Perhaps the clearest articulation of this new mode of warfare and the abandonment of any vestige of chivalry, came from Colonel John Singleton Mosby. Mosby's brand of warfare could best be described as guerrilla. However, he was not an irregular, nor fighting without official rank. The Confederate Congress passed the Partisan Ranger Act early in the war authorising President Jefferson Davis to issue military commissions to officers to organise partisan corps. These units stood on the same footing as regular cavalry in terms of rank and pay, but enjoyed the benefits of the law of maritime prize. For the men in such units, military service hearkened back to the days of the mercenary.[20]

In deviating from any notion of chivalry Mosby did not advocate 'no quarter.' His philosophy manifested itself in combat tactics and an emphasis on the element of surprise. In some ways Mosby demonstrates a unique aspect of Southern chivalry, and how little it actually resembled traditional chivalry. Cunning and surprise were entirely consistent with chivalric notions. However, Mosby did not think so; he admitted that 'the charge that I did not fight fair is true. I fought for success and not for display. There was no man in the Confederacy who had less of the spirit of knight-errantry in him, or took a more practical view of war than I did.' He waged war under the theory that the end was to secure peace by destroying the enemy's resources, with as small a loss to his own troops as possible.[21]

Fighting 'fair' was a crucial component of Southern chivalry. Captain B. T. Morris of the 64th North Carolina Infantry, served a portion of the war fighting guerillas in the mountains of North Carolina and Kentucky. His own beliefs show the peculiar feature of Southern chivalry. Morris's chief complaint was that his enemy 'never gave us a fair fight, square up, face-to-face, man-to-man,

---

[19] Reed (1862) I: 111.
[20] Mosby (1887) 80–81.
[21] Ibid.; Thomas (1995) 226.

horse-to-horse.' Stealth and concealment were inconsistent with open
and fair fighting. Mosby's notion that he did not embrace chivalry
also may have come from the nature of his partisan warfare. Even
his adversaries, particularly Union General Philip Sheridan, came to
define Mosby as a 'guerilla,' and Ulysses S. Grant gave permission
to hang any member of Mosby's command captured alive. Mosby
operated almost entirely behind enemy lines within a two-county
area of Virginia for most of the war, yet Union forces had an almost
impossible time finding him. His command often did its work at
night, using the homes and hills of Loudon and Farquier counties
to hide when their work was done. While chivalry allows for tactical prowess, the code would seem to stop short of condoning conduct whereby soldiers hid their identity. When Mosby began to
retaliate by hanging members of the Union cavalry that he captured,
any semblance of chivalry regardless of how it might be defined,
had all but disappeared. If Lee objected to Mosby's methods, he
never said so. Mosby recalled Lee's only criticism being that Mosby
was always getting himself wounded.[22]

The win-at-all-costs ethos did not require guerrilla tactics or exe-
cuting enemy soldiers. Such tactics were the exception rather than
the rule. The prevailing military ethos of the Southern officer corps
was most evident in efforts to professionalise the civilian soldier.
William Hardee never commanded the Army of Tennessee, but he
led its best corps throughout the war. Although little exists to give
insight into Hardee's personal beliefs on warfare, his manual of arms,
the bible for both Union and Confederate drill when the war began,
spoke volumes. Hardee's manual contained six lessons dedicated to
mastery of the rifle, and half related directly to loading and firing.
Hardee reduced the steps of loading and firing from twelve to nine,
and ultimately to four. He emphasised precision and massing firepower.
In conjunction with firing, Hardee placed a new premium on quick-
ness of movement, making rapid deployment possible. All of these
innovations point to a warfare which was designed to optimise killing
effectiveness, and which left no room for hesitation, including any
time to reflect on mercy or compassion for a foe. Hardee's methods not only influenced how the South fought, but were used by
the Union as well.[23]

---

[22] Foote (1974) 805; Inscoe and McKinney (2000) 117; Mosby (n.d.) 148–151;
Grant (1885) II: 110; Mosby (1887) 80–81.
[23] Hughes (1965) 48–49.

Hardee's tactics, and the general mind-set designed to destroy the enemy irrespective of notions of 'fairness' can be seen in his best subordinate. Irish-born Patrick Cleburne served in the British army as an infantryman. He emigrated to the United States and settled in Arkansas where he practiced law before the war. When war clouds loomed in 1860, Cleburne organised and trained one of the Confederacy's first volunteer units, the Yell Rifles, which later became the 15th Arkansas Infantry. As a former infantryman, Cleburne seemed to understand how war would develop. He emphasised weapons training and believed that success in combat would come through constant and effective fire. Cleburne rose to the rank of major-general by 1862 and for most of the war commanded a division. He continued to believe that winning by any method was the only measure of success.[24]

In the wake of the Battle of Shiloh, Cleburne tried to take what lessons he could from the war's first large-scale blood bath. He realised at this early juncture that warfare had lost the orderly column exchanges of fire characteristic of Napoleonic warfare, and had become an organised ambush in the wilderness. Cleburne concluded that sharpshooters, organised on a company level, could turn the tide of battle. He then took the five best marksmen from each of his existing companies and formed special companies of sharpshooting snipers. These long range killers offered not only more tactical flexibility, but demonstrated clearly that Cleburne prized destroying the enemy above all else. Snipers killed silently, and at so great a distance that an enemy never knew what hit him. In 1863 Cleburne's division received five Whitworth rifles from England. With an effective killing range of 500–1000 yards, these weapons and the men Cleburne trained to use them, further depersonalised the business of killing. Cleburne soon had the best sharpshooters in either army, and the presence and effectiveness of these units demonstrated a concept of war far removed from the chivalric ethos. Cleburne's methods spread throughout the army. By 1864, Lee's Army of Northern Virginia used them effectively, as Union General John Sedgwick discovered at Spotsylvania Courthouse, when he lost his life to a sniper he believed was out of range. Sedgwick's last words, addressed to a Union soldier ducking to evade the sniper fire were, 'Why, what are you dodging for? They could not hit an elephant at that distance.' His words

---

[24] Symonds (1997) 52–55, 102–03.

barely cleared his lips when he was struck through the head by a round from a telescopic rifle. Gone was one of the Union's best corps commanders. So much for chivalry—long live modern war.[25]

Snipers proved but one example of a military ethos that rejected chivalry or at least what Southerners believed chivalry stood for. While improved rifles and long range snipers depersonalised killing, the introduction of land mines made it possible to kill without any human presence. Fifty-nine year old Gabriel Rains served as a brigade commander in General Daniel Harvey Hill's division. Although a graduate of the West Point class of 1827, General Rains was more scientist that soldier, and during the Confederate retreat from Williamsburg to Richmond in May 1862, Rains deployed land torpedoes, or mines, along the path of his retreat. The mines delayed the Union pursuit, but General Hill vehemently objected to land mines as not 'a proper or effective method of war.' Rains countered that mines were entirely proper, effective and no different than the long range naval guns then in use by the army to scatter 'death dealing fragments among the innocent and unoffending.' In a compromise move, Rains was reassigned to river defences, where torpedoes were permissible. However, as a testament not only to the changing nature of war, but Robert E. Lee's flexible wartime ethos, the use of land mines, debated in 1862, became common place by 1864. The Confederate capital of Richmond employed the subterranean shells as a welcome part of its defences.[26]

Jeb Stuart, the Confederate figure most often associated with the survival of chivalry on the battlefield, serves as a final reminder that such concepts might have compelled one to fight, and even kept one in the field, but had no place in combat. Stuart often signed personal correspondence 'K.G.S.' The initials stood for 'Knight of the Golden Spurs,' and while Stuart may have dressed like a modern day knight or cavalier, he understood the place chivalry occupied. Consistent with recent historical analysis of the elements of Southern gentility, Stuart believed that chivalry was synonymous with Southern patriotism. It dictated the conduct of a truly gallant Southerner. Chivalry required a man to posses an 'intrepid heart, an invincible spirit and patriotism beyond reproach.' A man carried these virtues

---

[25] Ibid., 126–28; Trudeau (1989) 144–45.
[26] Freeman (1942) 268–69.

into the field with him and it was these attributes that compelled men to go to war. Once at war, these same qualities demanded that each man stay until his duty was done. However, as Mosby testified, Stuart applauded the stealth and strike methods of the cavalry and contrary to the traditional ideal, he saw nothing chivalrous about his methods. Like so many of his fellow officers, when it came to actual fighting, winning was all that mattered.[27]

For some Confederate officers, any notions of chivalry disappeared as the war continued. General William Dorsey Pender, a brigade commander and later a division commander in A. P. Hill's Corps, Army of Northern Virginia, shared Stuart's 'chivalric' sense of duty. Early in the war he wrote his wife from Virginia explaining that 'I sometimes feel that if it were manly and honorable I would be willing to give up all hopes of distinction and military ambition, to live quietly with my wife and children.' However, Pender graduated from West Point and believed that 'anyone with a military education is in honor bound to come forth these times and defend his country.' A year later the full weight of his duty fell on the general. Pender not only found the war harder to bear, but realized that in the course of his service he had strayed far from his Christian beliefs. Pender would not have to endure the rigours of the entire war, he died in 1863 from wounds suffered at Gettysburg.[28]

Richard Ewell, a West Pointer and career army officer understood duty. But for Ewell, that duty flowed from his oath as a soldier and his loyalty to family and community. When he left the U.S. Army to fight for the Confederacy he conceded that it was a question of fighting 'with or against my state. . . . By taking the side of the South I forfeited a handsome position, fine pay and the earnings of twenty years hard service.' Ewell took with him a strong belief in military discipline, an attribute that his units reflected in their fighting skills. Ewell led brigades, divisions and upon Jackson's death in May 1863, he took command of Lee's II Corps. Not only did his men fight well and to the knife, but Ewell openly scoffed at notions of Southern chivalry, particularly those that advocated war as a defense of chivalry. Claims of chivalry flowed freely early in the war. One new recruit denied that the war would last long, claiming 'the scum of the North

---

[27] Yates (1997) 58–60.
[28] Pender (1861–62) 38, 165.

cannot face the chivalric spirit of the South'. Ewell knew better, and by 1862 so did most Confederate soldiers.[29]

Ewell believed the South had to fight and told his cousin Lizinka as the war began, 'I believe we are in the right. . . . Our soil is invaded . . . & there is nothing to be done but what we do.'

But Ewell drew the line at the suggestion that the fight was some-how tied to a romantic notion of chivalry. Writing to Miss Rebecca Ewell in April 1862, he asked, 'Does Lizza still have ideas about chivalry? Here they seem to be pretty generally played out.' Ewell wrote twice more in the summer of 1862 following the Seven Days Campaign that ended July 3, 1862. The fruits of such efficient killing lay all over the fields of eastern Virginia. 'I fully condone with you over the gloomy prospect in regard to the war,' he told his cousin Lizzie, adding:

> Some 100,000 human beings have been massacred in every conceiv-
> able form of horror, with three times that many wounded, all because
> a set of fanatical abolitionists and unprincipled politicians backed by
> women in petticoats and pants and children. The Chivalry that you
> were running after in such a fanatic style in Richmond have played
> themselves out pretty completely, refusing in some instances to get out
> of the state and fight. Such horrors as war brings about are not to be
> stopped when people want to get home. It opens a series of events
> that no one can see to the end.[30]

Ewell would be fighting at the end. As a Jackson subordinate he fought with the same zeal, even if he did not handle well the deci-sion making process presented by a larger command later in the war. By 1862, he had already had enough. The war had all but ended any notions of traditional chivalry, and the aspects of Southern chivalry that drew her men into the war were gone.

Ewell's experiences raise an important aspect of the demise of chivalry. The horrors he recounted did not go unnoticed by those closest to them. The common soldier that the Confederate officer led became fully aware of the fruits of combat, and saw absolutely no honour or chivalry in any aspect of war. Although the Confeder-ate officers abandoned notions of chivalry on their own, they would have had no choice. Given the reality of battle, officers immersed in

---

[29] Pfanz (1998) 120–21, 150–51; McPherson (1997) 17.
[30] Pfanz (1998) 29; Ewell (1862) 109–114.

romantic notions of war would have found the average Confederate soldier impossible to lead.

The writings and reminiscences of the common soldier are part of the rich literary legacy of the war. It would be impossible to provide a taste of all of these common men who in their own eloquent way told the war's story as only they could. However, Hiram Smith Williams, a private in the 40th Alabama Volunteer Infantry provides a representative example of these men's beliefs. His diary entries totally dispel any notion that the Civil War was a chivalrous contest. Williams makes it clear that not only did the officers preach a new kind of warfare, but the men below them embraced it, and were repulsed by its consequences. For Williams and his comrades the Civil War quickly became a struggle merely to survive.[31]

Williams fought in the Army of Tennessee. By 1864 his experiences led him to conclude that 'War is at best horrible . . . but this one (is) so unholy, so bitter, in its progress, so useless as to its results, so absurd as to the establishment of any great and vital principle.' As Sherman invaded Georgia and Joe Johnston retreated south, Williams wrote, 'And still another day of wholesale murder and nothing done to decide the day.' As church bells rang in a nearby town, signalling the Sabbath, Williams lamented, 'I would much rather hear the church bells ringing forth their solemn yet pleasant invitations for us to pass the day like Christians and civilized people than for the engines of war to proclaim in their thunder notes that we pass it amid scenes of carnage and death, like barbarians.' To the common soldier like Williams, the war was contrary to any notion of chivalry. Battle was not honourable, but barbaric. Man did not move closer to God by sacrifice, but rather moved further away because of war's brutality. On August 31, 1864 Williams's unit took part in General John Bell Hood's last ditch effort to save Atlanta. A Confederate frontal assault near Jonesboro met stiff resistance. Williams condemned Hood, and all those responsible for such assaults. 'This horrid useless waste of human life, this wholesale butchery is terrible and should damn the authors for all time.'[32] Chivalry had passed from war, at least from the way men waged war. All that really remained of chivalry lay in the way the Confederate

---

[31] Williams (1864) xii.
[32] Ibid., 33, 85, 110.

military leaders treated civilians, and that too disappeared as the war dragged on.

As brutal as war had become, Confederate officers nevertheless clung to the notion that civilians should be exempt if possible, from the horrors of war. Even Stonewall Jackson felt non-combatants were off limits. Like most of the Confederate army, Jackson found the Union treatment of Southern civilians disgusting. Jackson blamed Union commanders for the conduct of their troops and labeled the burning of homes and wanton destruction of crops and livestock as 'atrocities.'[33] Patrick Cleburne went so far as to pay back the value of goods taken or destroyed, and to return what goods he could that had been looted by anyone from his command. The question that arises is, how much of this was due to some notion of chivalry, and how much could be attributed to the fact that the war was fought in the South and destruction of civilian property would undermine civilian morale and in turn undermine the war effort? In other words, was this nobility or pragmatics? Cleburne's own comments would seem to tip the scale toward pragmatics. In his report to Hardee from Kentucky, Cleburne stated, 'I have paid out of my own pocket for the articles stolen by our men. Confidence is restored, all the houses open, and families returned.'[34] The military necessity of maintaining civilian confidence in the Confederacy appears to have been Cleburne's goal, not some notion of chivalry. Jackson and Cleburne were not alone in advocating that civilians be spared. However, several factors contributed to the Confederate army having to bend, and finally break its rule against involving civilians in the war.

Chivalry, or any martial code that purports to govern war, is difficult to follow when only one side is willing to play by the rules. The South discovered this early in the war in purely military matters when Confederate General Simon Bolivar Buckner prepared to surrender Fort Donelson to Ulysses S. Grant. Buckner inquired about terms and was told, 'No terms except an unconditional and immediate surrender can be accepted. I propose to move immediately upon your works.' Buckner and Grant had been West Point classmates, and Buckner expected more courtesy. In the end he had no choice but to reply, 'the overwhelming forces under your command,

---

[33] Jackson (1895) 226.
[34] Purdue (1973) 96.

compel me, notwithstanding the brilliant success of the Confederate arms yesterday, to accept the ungenerous and unchivalrous terms which you propose.' So much for chivalry among elites. The South and its officers took notice and understood that defeat left one at the mercy of the victor. At Second Manassas in August 1862, some of the men in one of A. P. Hill's brigades exhausted their ammunition and resorted to throwing rocks to defend their position, rather than withdraw or surrender. Those with cartridges remaining fired as their commander Maxey Gregg exhorted them to 'Die here my men, let us die here.' The ultimate expression of a fight to the end mentality came in Lee's statement to the Confederate army at Appomattox, that final surrender had come only after 'The Army of Northern Virginia has been compelled to yield to overwhelming numbers and resources,' and that 'valor and devotion could accomplish nothing that could compensate for the loss.'[35]

With chivalry's demise on the battlefield, the North demonstrated that war, if not 'total,' was going to be harsh on civilians as well as soldiers. While intentional killing and physical abuse of civilians rarely occurred, destruction of civilian property and food supplies became common practice. Early in the war such conduct took the form of unrestrained breaches of discipline, like the looting of stores and shops at Fredericksburg. However, as the war progressed, the destruction became both intentional and calculated. William Sherman destroyed civilian property in Mississippi during the Meridian Campaign in early 1864. That exercise proved to be a test run for his March to the Sea in Georgia during November and December 1864. Philip Sheridan laid waste to the Confederate wheat basket, the Shenandoah Valley, in October 1864. In short, for Confederate officers to follow a code of exempting civilians from the destruction of war proved difficult in the face of Northern tactics.

The second factor that forced the Confederate army to involve civilians in war's hardships was the need for supplies. Throughout the war the Confederate army constantly foraged for food, and since the war took place in the South, this meant taking food from Southern families. Forage operations ranged from small unit excursions, to the deployment of entire divisions, like Longstreet's assignment to the Carolinas in 1863. Longstreet took no part in the Battle

---

[35] Grant (1992) 183–84; Hennessy (1993) 279; Angle and Meirs (1992) 1040.

of Chancellorsville because he and his men were foraging for food and supplies. While the army took what they needed as peacefully as possible, food was in short supply in the South and when the army took for itself, it deprived a needy civilian population of precious provisions.[36]

When the Confederate army finally invaded the North, its civilians faired little better than their Southern counterparts. Destruction or requisition of civilian property varied in intensity. During the Gettysburg Campaign Robert E. Lee issued two orders prohibiting depredations against civilians, but Confederate soldiers nevertheless 'lived well' on their march north. The Army of Northern Virginia emptied barns, rustled cattle and other livestock and cleaned out stores. In a foreshadowing of future conduct, Confederate General Jubal Early had the Caladonia Iron Works, owned by Republican Senator Thaddeus Stevens, burned to the ground. However, the Confederate soldiers heeded the orders of their commander and did not burn private residences and barns.[37]

The restraint of 1863 gave way to a more harsh policy in 1864. During his unsuccessful campaign against Washington D.C. in the summer of 1864, Jubal Early forced ransom from two towns in Maryland, Hagerstown and Frederick, for sums in excess of $200,000. The money was paid to prevent Early from burning the towns. In the course of the campaign the home of Union Postmaster General Montgomery Blair burned to the foundation. Early denied giving such an order, but felt that the destruction of Southern property in the Shenandoah Valley by David Hunter's federal troops justified the burning. In addition to ransom money, Early's men seized large herds of cattle and other provisions. In late July 1864, Early burned Chambersburg, Pennsylvania in retaliation for the destruction of more Southern homes and property in the Shenandoah. Early took full responsibility for the action. Chivalry was no where to be found as modern war had come to the North and civilians could expect no relief.[38]

The Confederate officer corps abandoned any pre-war attributes of chivalry. Modern war required destroying the opposing army and the population's will to endure, leaving little room for mercy towards

---

[36] Wert (1998) 231; Weitz (2000) 108.
[37] Wert (1998) 253.
[38] Early (1994) 385, 388, 394–95, 401–04.

either the enemy or its civilians. However, as chivalry disappeared, something else emerged that brought an element of humanity and compassion to the battlefield. Soldiers on both sides that had begun the war as amateurs, and had survived, shared a new sense of fraternity. This common bond came not from some shared aristocratic status of their leaders, but arose among 'soldiers' from an emerging professional brotherhood of warriors; men that had 'spilled the same blood in the same mud, and felt a compassion for an enemy that shared an identical hardship.

Instances of compassion among soldiers for a wounded or fallen enemy came early in the war. James Wells recalled the story of a wounded Union soldier left on the field at First Manassas. As the man lay bleeding, thirsty and exposed to the hot July sun, a Confederate soldier, himself bleeding from a slight head wound, walked up on the man and said, 'Hello yank, be you wounded, be you much hurt?' The wounded Yankee could muster only enough strength to ask for water, which his enemy courteously replied, 'for suah!' The Confederate soldier tended to the wounded man, made him comfortable and then left as quietly as he had appeared. During the rain swept battle at Chantilly on September 1, 1862, a similar incident occurred when a Union soldier stumbled upon a wounded Confederate. Soaked to the bone, cold, thirsty and in pain, the Confederate soldier asked for water and then thanked his enemy for the generous gift. The Union soldier then took his gum blanket out and covered his fallen foe. In the process both men discovered they belonged to same fraternity, Phi Gamma. The Union soldier also discovered that his fraternity brother was dying. He stayed with him until his last breath, and then wrapped him in that same blanket, dug a shallow grave, and buried him. They were now brothers in a much larger fraternity, that of the soldier, initiation into which had proved much more exacting than either had imagined.[39]

Although not the first evidence of this esprit de guerre, perhaps the most moving incident came in the aftermath of the horrific slaughter at Fredericksburg. The morning following the battle, Sergeant Richard Kirkland of Joe Kershaw's brigade approached Kershaw himself: 'I can't stand this,' he said. The day before, Kirkland played an active part in the deadly work that left so many Union boys

---

[39] Wells (1900) 28:309–11.

strewn on the field before him. 'What's the matter Sergeant,' asked
Kershaw. Kirkland replied, 'All night and all day I have heard those
poor people crying for water. Water! Water! And I can't stand it
any longer. I come to ask permission to go and give them water.'
Kershaw considered the request and then told Kirkland he would
be shot in the head by Union pickets as soon as he stepped out into
the field. Kirkland did not care, saying, 'I am willing to try.' Kershaw
refused to allow Kirkland to show a white handkerchief. Without
the protection of the white flag, Kirkland made his way out into the
wasteland. He could not and would not have spared these men as
they assaulted the day before, but now he moved among them to
ease suffering he had helped inflict. The first man he met had a
shattered leg. Kirkland covered him with his coat, straightened his
broken leg and left him a full canteen of water. For over an hour
Kirkland moved from one sufferer to another with water and com-
fort. Not a shot was fired as he made his rounds. Kirkland fell at
Chickamauga in 1863, but his compassion towards those who shared
the same hardships was never forgotten.[40]

Less subtle instances occurred throughout the war. During the
Battle of the Wilderness in 1864, Private Leroy Edwards and two
comrades pursued retreating federals through the dense undergrowth.
As they crossed a road, Edwards fired, and exclaimed, 'I hit him!'
The small squad pressed on and in a few moments were upon the
Union soldier. Leroy had hit his mark, and upon further discovery
found the man was not as badly hurt as they had thought. Edwards
offered to help the man up and in an almost apologetic tone said,
'I hope your [sic] are not hurt.'[41]

This camaraderie among soldiers did not always occur in battle.
Its most frequent manifestation came in fraternisation among the
rank and file during winter quarters or a hiatus in combat. Soldiers
would meet under a flag of truce to exchange newspapers, tobacco,
coffee and most importantly, stories. Death unfortunately also brought
Confederate and Union soldiers together. Men sometimes met on
burial detail, when only hours before they had been trying to kill
one another. After helping to bury several dead Union soldiers,
Hiram Williams wrote, 'Poor fellows! I would pity the untimely death
of the bitterest foe I have on earth. To think of these men, but a

---

[40] Kershaw (1880) 8:186–188.
[41] Turner (1892) 20:74.

few hours ago in the enjoyment of life and health, now buried by stranger hands.' More enjoyable instances occurred where those that survived had time to meet. During the siege of Port Hudson, one of the last Confederate strongholds on the Mississippi, Union soldiers were actually invited into the Confederate fortifications where they marvelled at the defences and saw the effects of some of their own fire. When the Confederates surrendered, they were treated with the respect accorded fellow soldiers, even though both sides knew prison awaited the vanquished Confederates. Sometimes officers tried to prevent such fraternisation, John Gordon almost sent a Union soldier to prison, but more often than not, officers took part in the camaraderie.[42] However, whether or not officers participated was no longer important. The 'bond' among soldiers had become fellowship, a shared horrific experience of war among men who perhaps never thought of themselves as 'gentlemen.'

This developing sense of a solders' fraternity nevertheless drew strength from the instances where officers took part or initiated conduct that showed some level of compassion for a foe. The most striking example is an overlooked incident in William Hardee's career. During the heated fighting at Tunnell Hill outside Chattanooga, Tennessee in 1863, one of Hardee's brigades took up a position on a hill overlooking an open field. A federal brigade moved out of the woods and into the open field. As the unit formed, Hardee's men poured rifle fire into their columns. The federals retreated back into the woods and then re-emerged. Again their officer reformed them while the Confederates fired into the ranks. Then, after the Union soldiers reformed, their officer had them lie down as he rode up and down the line as if waiting for orders. As the Confederates fired down on the Union soldiers who were now laying on the ground, unable to move or return fire, Hardee rode up and ordered the brigade to stop firing. 'It's murder,' he said.[43]

Hardee's action was clearly out of character, not only for him, but for any member of the Confederate officer corps. One can only speculate as to why he did what he did. Perhaps even this old professional had his limits. What Hardee's conduct did demonstrate

---

[42] Smith and Freret (1886) 14:334–335, 342–43; Unknown (1909) 37:232; Featherston (1906) 36:170–73; Losson (1989) 162–63; Williams (1864) 33; Gordon, (1882) 10:422–23.

[43] Mills (1894) 22:67.

however, is that even the most high ranking Confederate officer shared
more with the lowliest of privates, even the enemy's, than he did
with a civilian of his own rank or class. War was drawing men of all
ranks into a fraternity that no aristocrat, regardless of wealth, standing or political office, could enter, unless he had come through the
rite of passage on the fields of fire. The gentility, that deference and
civility men showed one another in Southern civilian life, was gone.
Respect in war had to be earned, and these Union soldiers apparently earned Hardee's on that day.

Hardee's example was not the only instance of a Confederate
officer showing some compassion for opposing soldiers. When Admiral
David Farragut stormed Mobile Bay, the ironclad *Tecumseh* led the
assault, struck a torpedo and went down. Farragut quickly moved
his flagship, the *Hartford*, to the front and began trying to rescue
drowning survivors. Dick Page commanded the Confederate shore
batteries and he order his men not to fire at boats trying to rescue
the drowning men. After overrunning a Union battery at Reams
Station in 1864, Confederate General McRae and two Captains tried
to save the life on a Union officer that had so courageously manned
the gun. Unfortunately, the man paid for his gallantry and had been
mortally wounded and the Confederates could do nothing for him.[44]

The Confederate surrender in April 1865 did more than end the
American Civil War. It brought an end to the Southern way of life
predicated on slavery. With the demise of gentility went the last bit
of chivalry. However, chivalry as a military code never really existed
during the Civil War. Those aspects of Southern gentility that found
their way into the war quickly fell by the wayside. The struggle that
consumed America over the course of four years brought modern
warfare to America and engulfed both soldier and civilian in a conflict
that offered little, if any, quarter to the combatants and exposed
civilians to the horrors of war as never before in America. The
Confederate military ethos reflected the realities of modern war. It
placed a premium on success above all else, which meant killing as
many of the enemy as possible, using whatever tactics best suited
the situation. The war witnessed the emergence of America's professional soldiers; men who hated war because of its horrors, but as

---

[44] Maury (1894) 22:78; Stedman (1890) 19:116–17.

officers, many had spent their entire lives preparing for just such a thing and were able to conduct it with a brutal efficiency. Perhaps Lee himself said it best as he looked upon the broken federal assaults at Fredericksburg, 'It is well that war is so terrible, we should grow to fond of it.' Yet having said that, he wrote home on Christmas and expressed some remorse that the Union had not pressed harder at Fredericksburg and given him the opportunity to deal them a crushing blow.[45]

In the midst of the brutality a professional ethos emerged among both enlisted men and officers. The American soldier saw war in its full measure and he understood that all soldiers, regardless of side, shared a common bond. This bond occasionally manifest itself in some form of mercy in the midst of battle. More often however, it took the form of compassion in the aftermath of the slaughter, or in the ability of the survivors to put down the passions of the moment and share a smoke, a drink, and a story, luxuries only those that had fought and lived could appreciate.

Bibliography

Primary Sources

Anonymous (1909) "The Battle of Winchester," in *Southern Historical Society Papers. 1876–1959*, 52 vols. (Millswood, New York: 1979) 37:232.
Beauregard, P. G. T. (1875) "Treatment of Prisoners," in *Southern Historical Society Papers. 1876–1959*, 52 vols. (Millswood, New York: 1979) 41:184–85.
Early, J. (1994) *The Memoirs of Jubal Early* (New York: 1994).
Ewell, R. (1935) *The Making of a Soldier: The Letters of General R. S. Ewell*, ed. Percy Gatlin Hamlin (Richmond: 1935).
Featherston, J. (1906) "A Brilliant Page in History of War: Soldiers Fraternize," in *Southern Historical Society Papers. 1876–1959*, 52 vols. (Millswood, New York: 1979) 36: 173.
Gordon, J. (1903) *Reminiscences of the Civil War* (Dayton, Ohio: 1993).
———. (1882) "They Would Mix on the Picket Line," in *Southern Historical Society Papers. 1876–1959*, 52 vols. (Millswood, New York: 1979) 10:422.
Grant, U. S. (1885) *The Personal Memoirs of U. S. Grant* (New York: 1992) 183–84.
———. (1885) "Preparing for the Campaigns of '64," in *Battles and Leaders* (Secacus, New Jersey: 1985) IV, 110.
Hardee, W. (1853) *The Rifle and Light Infantry Tactics* (n.p.: 1853).
Imboden, J. (n.d.) "Incidents of the First Bull Run," in *Battles and Leaders* (Secacus, New Jersey: 1985) I, 238.
———. (n.d.) "Stonewall Jackson in the Shenandoah," in *Battles and Leaders* (Secacus, New Jersey: 1985) II, 288–93.

---

[45] Thomas (1998) 271, 273.

Jackson, M. (1895) *Memoirs of Stonewall Jackson* (Dayton: 1976).

Kershaw, J. (1880) "Richard Kirkland, the Humane Hero of Fredericksburg," in *Southern Historical Society Papers. 1876–1959*, 52 vols. (Millswood, New York: 1979) 8:186–88.

Maury, D. (1894) "How the Confederacy Changed Naval Warfare," in *Southern Historical Society Papers. 1876–1959*, 52 vols. (Millswood, New York: 1979) 22:78.

Mills, R. (1894) "The Bond of Heroism," in *Southern Historical Society Papers. 1876–1959*, 52 vols. (Millswood, New York: 1979) 22:67.

Mosby, J. (1887) *Mosby's War Reminiscences and Stuart's Cavalry Campaigns* (Boston: 1887).

——. (1887) "A Bit of Partisan Service," in *Battles and Leaders* (Secacus, New Jersey: 1985) 148–151.

Pender, W. (1861–63) *The General to His Lady: The Civil War Letters of William Dorsey Pender*, ed. Hassler, W. (Chapel Hill: 1965).

Lee, R. (1865) "Farewell Address," in *Tragic Years: 1860–1865 A Documentary History of the Civil War*. ed. Angle, P. and Meirs, E. (New York: 1992).

Reed, E. R. (1862) *Letters to Vermont From Her Civil War Soldiers Correspondents to the Home Press*, ed. Wickman, D. (Bennington, Vermont: 1988).

Smith, M. and Freret, J. (1886) "Fortification and Siege of Port Hudson," in *Southern Historical Society Papers. 1876–1959*, 52 vols. (Millswood, New York: 1979) 14:334–43.

Stedman, C. (1891) "Battle of Reams' Station," in *Southern Historical Society Papers. 1876–1959*, 52 vols. (Millswood, New York: 1979) 19:116–17.

Turner, J. (1892) "The Battle of Wilderness," in *Southern Historical Society Papers. 1876–1959*, 52 vols. (Millswood, New York: 1979) 20:74.

Wells, J. (1900) "The Phi Gamma in War," in *Southern Historical Society Papers 1876–1959*, 52 vols. (Millswood, New York: 1979) 28:309–311.

Williams, H. (1864) *This War So Horrible: The Civil War Diary of Hiram Smith Williams*, eds. Wynne, L. and Taylor, R. (Tuscaloosa: 1993).

Secondary Sources

Foote, S. (1974) *The Civil War a Narrative: Red River to Appomattox* (New York: 1974) 805.

Freeman, D. S. (1942) *Lee's Lieutenants: A Study in Command, Vol. I* (New York: 1970) 268–69.

Hall, C. (1878) *Military Records of Generals of the Confederate Army 1861–1865* (Austin: 1963).

Hennessey, J. (1993) *Return to Bull Run: The Campaign and Battle of Second Manassas* (New York: 1993).

Hughes, C. (1965) *General William J. Hardee: Old Reliable* (Baton Rouge: 1965).

Inscoe, J. and McKinney, G. (2000) *The Heart of Confederate Appalachia: Western Carolina during the Civil War* (Chapel Hill: 2000).

Losson, C. (1989) *Tennessee's Forgotten Warriors: Frank Cheatham and His Confederate Division* (Knoxville: 1989).

McPherson, J. (1997) *For Cause and Comrades: Why Men Fought in the Civil War* (New York: 1997).

MacArthur, J. and Burton, O. (1996) *A Gentlemen and an Officer: A Military and Social History of James B. Griffin's Civil War* (New York: 1996).

Patterson, G. (1987) *Rebels from West Point* (New York: 1987).

Pfanz, D. (1998) *Richard Ewell: A Soldier's Life* (Chapel Hill: 1998).

Purdue, H. and E. (1973) *Pat Cleburne, Confederate General: A Definitive Biography* (Hillsboro, Texas: 1973).

Robertson, J. (1997) *Stonewall Jackson: The Man, The Soldier, The Legend* (New York: 1997) 424, 514–15, 822–23.

Symonds, C. (1997) *Stonewall of the West: Patrick Cleburne and the Civil War* (Lawrence: 1997).

Thomas, E. (1995) *Robert E. Lee: A Biography* (New York: 1995).

Trudeau, N. (1989) *Bloody Roads South: The Wilderness to Cold Harbor May-June 1864* (Boston: 1989).

Wakelyn, J. (1985) "Civilian Higher Education in the Making of Confederate Army Leaders," in *The Confederate High Command and Related Topics: Themes in Honor of T. Harry Williams* (Shippensburg, Pa.: 1985) 74–75, 86–89.

Waugh, J. (1994) *The Class of 1846* (New York: 1994).

Weitz, M. (1998) "Drill, Training and the Combat Performance of the Civil War Soldier: Dispelling the Myth of Poor, Soldier, Great Fighter," *Journal of Military History* 62 (1998) 99–125.

——. (2000) *A Higher Duty: Desertion Among Georgia Troops during the Civil War* (Lincoln, Neb.: 2000).

Wert, J. (1993) *General James Longstreet* (New York: 1993).

Wyatt Brown, B. (1986) *Honor and Violence in the Old South* (New York: 1986).

Yates, B. (1997) *Jeb Stuart Speaks: An Interview with Lee's Cavalryman* (Shippensburg, Penn.: 1997).

INDEX

HISTORY
OF WARFARE

History of Warfare *presents the latest research on all aspects of military history. Publications in the series will examine technology, strategy, logistics, and economic and social developments related to warfare in Europe, Asia, and the Middle East from ancient times until the early nineteenth century. The series will accept monographs, collections of essays, conference proceedings, and translation of military texts.*

1. HOEVEN, M. VAN DER (ed.). *Exercise of Arms.* Warfare in the Netherlands, 1568-1648. 1997. ISBN 90 04 10727 4

2. RAUDZENS, G. (ed.). *Technology, Disease and Colonial Conquests, Sixteenth to Eighteenth Centuries.* Essays Reappraising the Guns and Germs Theories. 2001. ISBN 90 04 11745 8

3. LENIHAN P. (ed.). *Conquest and Resistance.* War in Seventeenth-Century Ireland. 2001. ISBN 90 04 11743 1

4. NICHOLSON, H. *Love, War and the Grail.* 2001. ISBN 90 04 12014 9

5. BIRKENMEIER, J.W. *The Development of the Komnenian Army: 1081-1180.* 2002. ISBN 90 04 11710 5

6. MURDOCH, S. (ed.). *Scotland and the Thirty Years' War, 1618-1648.* 2001. ISBN 90 04 12086 6

7. TUYLL VAN SEROOSKERKEN, H.P. VAN. *The Netherlands and World War I.* Espionage, Diplomacy and Survival. 2001. ISBN 90 04 12243 5

8. DEVRIES, K. *A Cumulative Bibliography of Medieval Military History and Technology.* 2002. ISBN 90 04 12227 3

9. CUNEO, P. (ed.). *Artful Armies, Beautiful Battles.* Art and Warfare in Early Modern Europe. 2002. ISBN 90 04 11588 9

10. KUNZLE, D. *From Criminal to Courtier.* The Soldier in Netherlandish Art 1550-1672. 2002. ISBN 90 04 12369 5

11. TRIM, D.J.B. (ed.). *The Chivalric Ethos and the Development of Military Professionalism.* 2003. ISBN 90 04 12095 5

12. WILLIAMS, A. *The Knight and the Blast Furnace.* A History of the Metallurgy of Armour in the Middle Ages & the Early Modern Period. 2003. ISBN 90 04 12498 5

13. KAGAY, D.J., VILLALON, L.J.A. (eds.). *Crusaders, Condottieri, and Cannon.* Medieval Warfare in Societies Around the Mediterranean. 2002. ISBN 90 04 12553 1

14. LOHR, E., POE, M. (eds.). *The Military and Society in Russia: 1450-1917.* 2002. ISBN 90 04 12273 7

15. MURDOCH, S. & A. MACKILLOP (eds.). *Fighting for Identity.* Scottish Military Experience c. 1550-1900. 2002. ISBN 90 04 12823 9

ISSN 1385–7827